Horace Gillette Cleveland

A genealogy of Benjamin Cleveland, a great-grandson of Moses Cleveland, of Woburn, Mass., and a native of Canterbury, Windham County

Horace Gillette Cleveland

A genealogy of Benjamin Cleveland, a great-grandson of Moses Cleveland, of Woburn, Mass., and a native of Canterbury, Windham County

ISBN/EAN: 9783337220594

Printed in Europe, USA, Canada, Australia, Japan

Cover: Foto ©ninafisch / pixelio.de

More available books at **www.hansebooks.com**

A GENEALOGY OF BENJAMIN CLEVELAND,

A GREAT-GRANDSON OF

*** CLEVELAND, of Woburn, Mass.,

AND A NATIVE OF

*ERBURY, WINDHAM COUNTY, CONN.

WITH AN APPENDIX.

COMPILED BY HIS GREAT-GRANDSON

*E GILLETTE C****

CHICAGO:
PRINTED FOR THE COMPILER.
1879.

TO

MY VENERATED FATHER,

OREN CLEVELAND,

WHO THIS DAY (MAY 3, 1879,) ENTERS UPON THE NINETY-FIFTH YEAR OF HIS EARTHLY PILGRIMAGE,

AND TO WHOSE EXPRESSED WISH THESE PAGES ARE DUE,

THIS HUMBLE ENDEAVOR, PROMPTED BY FILIAL LOVE AND A DESIRE TO REALIZE THAT WISH, IS MOST REVERENTLY AND AFFECTIONATELY INSCRIBED.

Rand, McNally & Co., Printers, Engravers and Electrotypers, Chicago.

PREFACE.

The inscription on the page opposite must be accepted as the apology, if any is needed, for this publication.

The compiler had his attention directed to the subject as set forth, in the spring of the Centennial year of the Nation, and up to the year 1871, his knowledge of Benjamin and Rachel Cleveland and their decendants, was confined to the posterity of their son Rufus Cleveland, his paternal grandfather. Nor could he have accurately told, if his life had depended upon the telling, who either the brother or the sisters of his grandfather married.

The letter of " Benjamin and Rachel Cleveland," as given on page 10, containing certain references to " Zenas," and " Hovey," and "Hamblin," and " Ephraim Pearson," was all that he had as a foundation to build upon, and the access, of course, to early township or other public records in the New England States. The result of the researches made in leisure hours, while engaged in exacting business pursuits, is now presented. That these records are free from errors it would be folly to pretend, and it is earnestly desired that any found should be pointed out, and made known, so that they may not appear in any future edition. No merit as a literary performance is claimed or deserved, but as evidence of earnest, persevering research, beset and opposed by every discouraging obstacle imaginable, it bears its own testimony, and will at least be appreciated by those who have had any experience in such labor.

The abbreviations used are so few and so apparent in their meaning, as to need no explanation.

The small figures attached to various names, and most likely to puzzle the reader if unused to such publications, are employed to designate the different or successive generations. The starting point is the common ancestor, Moses Cleveland, of Woburn, and he is designated as Moses Cleveland.[1] His children are the *second* generation, and his grandchildren are of the *third* generation, and so on. The Index is elaborate enough to enable the reader to find any particular family readily, and will probably prove sufficient for all practical purposes.

The fact that comparatively few of the descendants of Benjamin and Rachel Cleveland have either sought or acquired public distinction, does not militate against the publication of these records. It will be noted that generally their descendants were devoted to agricultural pursuits, and belonged especially to the *producing classes*—the "bone and sinew" of the country—the honest, frugal and industrious citizens of the commonwealth. All honor to them, then, for such as these the nation can not do without. And, in conclusion, it may be appropriately said of them, as a whole, in the language of the poet Gray—

> "Far from the madding crowd's ignoble strife,
> Their sober wishes never learned to stray;
> Along the cool, sequestered vale of life
> They kept the noiseless tenor of their way."

ANCESTRY OF BENJAMIN CLEVELAND.

MOSES CLEVELAND,[1] of Woburn, Mass., 1641, appears to be the common ancestor of all the "Clevelands" of New England. Family tradition says he emigrated to this country in 1635, from Ipswich, Suffolk, Eng., an indentured apprentice to a housewright or master builder. From the Woburn town records it appears Moses Cleveland was made a freeman in 1643, no doubt upon attaining the age of 21. Sept. 26, 1648, he married Miss Ann Winn, daughter of Edward and Joanna Winn, of Woburn. She was also a native of England. The date and place of her birth not learned, nor does the date of her death appear on the town records, but the death of Moses Cleveland occurred on the 9th Jan., 1701-2. (See Appendix A.)

They had a family of eleven children—seven sons and four daughters, (one child only, the first Joanna, dying in childhood), as follows, all born in Woburn:

1. Moses,[2] b. Sept. 1, 1651; m. Ruth Norton.
2. Hannah,[2] b. Aug. 4, 1653; m. Thomas Henshaw.
3. Aaron,[2] b. Jan. 10, 1655; m. Dorcas Wilson.
4. Samuel,[2] b. June 9, 1657; m. Jane Keyes.
5. Miriam,[2] b. July 10, 1659; m. Thos. Foskett.
6. Joanna,[2] b. Sept. 19, 1661; d. July 2, 1667.
7. Edward,[2] b. May 20, 1663; m. Deliverance Palmer.
8. Josiah,[2] b. Feb. 26, 1666-7; m. Mary Bates.
9. Isaac,[2] b. May 11, 1669; m. Elizabeth Curtice.
10. Joanna,[2] (again), b. April 5, 1670; m. Joseph Keyes.
11. Enoch,[2] b. Aug. 1, 1671; m. Elizabeth Counts, of Charlestown, Mass.

Confining myself for the present to my direct line, I find that—

SAMUEL CLEVELAND,[2] the third son and fourth child of Moses[1] and Ann (Winn) Cleveland, b. in Woburn, June 9,

1657, m. first, in Chelmsford, Mass., May 17, 1680, Jane Keyes, a dau. of Solomon and Frances (Grant) Keyes. She was b. in Newbury, Mass., Oct. 25, 1660, and d. without issue in Chelmsford, Mass., Nov. 4, 1681. He m. second, in Chelmsford, May 23, 1682, Persis Hildreth, dau. of Richard and Elizabeth Hildreth. She was b. in Cambridge, Mass., Feb. 8, 1660; d. in Canterbury, Conn., Feb. 22, 1698. He m. third, wid. Margaret Fish, in Canterbury, Conn., July 25, 1699. He d. in Canterbury, Conn., March 12, 1736. The date and place of death of third wife not learned. (See Appendix B.)

Children, by wife Persis:

1. Persis,[3] b. in Chelmsford, April 21, 1683.
2. Samuel,[3] b. in Chelmsford, Jan. 12, 1685; m. Sarah Boswell.
3. Joseph,[3] b. in Chelmsford, July 18, 1689; m. Abigail Hyde.
4. Elizabeth,[3] b. in Woburn, June 26, 1693; m. John Ensworth.
5. Mary,[3] b. in Canterbury, June 14, 1696; m. Joseph Ensworth.

by wife Margaret:

6. Abigail,[3] b. in Canterbury, April 23, 1700; d. Feb. 23, 1718.
7. Timothy,[3] b. in Canterbury, Aug. 25, 1702; m. Dorothy ——.

And perhaps there were other children not recorded, as the records were evidently very imperfectly kept during these years.

Hinman, in his Catalogue of the Puritan Settlers of Connecticut, gives two more children, Ephraim,[3] and Margaret,[3] to wife Persis. So far as Ephraim[3] is concerned, he may be correct, as there was an Ephraim Cleveland who d. in Canterbury, March 13, 1711. Margaret,[3] he says, m. Gideon Cable in 1717.

Samuel Cleveland[2] was one of the earliest settlers in Plainfield, (or Canterbury), Conn., probably about 1694, and was followed by his brother Josiah,[2] of Chelmsford, Mass., soon after, and subsequently by his brothers Edward,[2] of Kingston, R. I., and Isaac,[2] of Woburn. Canterbury was not incorporated as a town until 1703, and was previously a part of Plainfield.

JOSEPH CLEVELAND,[3] second son and third child of Samuel[2] and Persis (Hildreth) Cleveland, b. in Chelmsford, Mass., July 18, 1689, m. first, in Canterbury, Conn., Feb. 7, 1710-11, Abigail Hyde, dau. of Jonathan and Dorothy (Kidder) Hyde. She was b. in Cambridge, Mass., Aug. 8, 1688, and d. in Canterbury, Conn., Dec. 16, 1724. He m. second, in Canterbury, Conn., (as I interpret the records), March 31, 1725, Sarah Ensworth, a dau. of Tyxhall and Lydia Ensworth. She was b. in Plainfield, Conn., June 12, 1699, and d. in Canterbury, Conn., June 21, 1761. He died in Canterbury, Conn., March 11, 1766. He was called "Sergeant" Joseph, to distinguish him from his cousin "Capt." Joseph,[3] son of Josiah[2] and Mary Cleveland. (See Appendix C.)

Children, by wife Abigail:

1. Ephraim,[4] b. Feb. 3, 1712.
2. Jonathan,[4] b. May 9, 1713; d. March 19, 1734.
3. Benjamin,[4] b. May 20, 1714; m. Rachel ——.
4. Dorothy,[4] b. March 31, 1716.
5. John,[4] b. (probably) in 1718; d. March 5, 1734.
6. Elijah,[4] b. Jan. 5, 1721; m. Alice Lawrence.
7. Persis,[4] bap. April 7, 1723; probably m. Feb. 18, 1745, Henry Bacon, of Pomfret, Conn.

by wife Sarah:

8. Ezra,[4] bap. April 17, 1726; m. Jerusha Newcomb.
9. Samuel,[4] b. June 7, 1730; m. Ruth Darbe.

In regard to the marriage and settlement of some of the children of Joseph Cleveland,[3] the compiler of these records has not been able to determine fully.

There was an Ephraim Cleveland who settled in Dedham, Mass., and m. there, first, Jan. 14, 1734-5, Abigail Curtis, who d. Aug. 30, 1738. He m. second, Nov. 21, 1738, Ruth Nichols, who also d. in Dedham, Oct. 14, 1744. Children were: *Ephraim, Jacob, Sarah, Rebekah* and *Abigail.* There was also an Ephraim Cleveland who m. Hannah Hayward as late as 1747, in Bridgewater, Mass., and they gave their children many of the family names, such as *Joseph, Benjamin, Elijah* and *Persis.* Further investigation may show the identity of one, or possibly both, of them with the Ephraim Cleveland, of Canterbury, Conn. Concerning Dorothy[4] nothing has been ascertained, and it is probable she lived and died a spinster. Elijah[4] is known to have settled in Hillsdale, (formerly Nobletown), Columbia county, N. Y., and is buried there with wife Alice; but Benjamin,[4] Ezra,[4] and Samuel,[4] remained in Canterbury, Conn., where names of children born to them respectively are recorded. A deed of land by Joseph Cleveland, to his "well beloved son, Benjamin Cleveland," bears date "Canterbury, Decem^r ye 23rd, A. D. 1735," with a reservation and proviso which reads as follows:

"Only reserving to my own use and ye use of my family, to get firewood and Timber upon s^d Land during my natural life, & said Land being in full of ye portion my said son shall ever have of my Estate."

Later he seems to have divided his lands between his sons Ezra and Samuel, under date of March 7, 1753, and probably lived near them until his death.

DESCENDANTS OF BENJAMIN CLEVELAND.

BENJAMIN CLEVELAND,[4] a great-grandson of Moses[1] and Ann (Winn) Cleveland, of Woburn, Mass., was born in Canterbury, Windham county, Conn., May 20, 1714. He was the third son and child of Joseph[3] and Abigail (Hyde) Cleveland, and a grandson of Samuel[2] and Persis (Hildreth) Cleveland.

By wife Rachel ———,* whom he married in 1736, he had a family of ten children, as follows:

1. Joseph,[5] b. May 14, 1737; d. Nov. 17, 1749.
2. Benjamin,[5] b. ——— ———, ———; d. Nov. 25, 1749.
3. Dorothy,[5] b. June 10, 1744; d. Nov. 12, 1749.
4. Abigail,[5] b. Aug. 13, 1746; d. June 2, 1832.
5. Zenas,[5] b. Sept. 21, 1748; d. Aug. —, 1821.
6. Rachel,[5] b. May 18, 1750; d. Sept. 27, 1837.
7. Persis,[5] b. Jan. 18, 1752; d. March 30, 1834.
8. Rufus,[5] b. June 14, 1754; d. Feb. 22, 1838.
9. Mary,[5] b. April 14, 1756; d. Jan. 27, 1763.
10. Phebe,[5] b. June 25, 1758; d. Aug. 6, 1838.

Sometime after the marriage of his eldest (surviving) daughter, Abigail, to Samuel Hovey, who had settled in the town of Lyme, Grafton county, N. H., Benjamin Cleveland

---

* The most earnest and persistent endeavors have been made to ascertain the maiden name of this lady, the date and place of her birth, and the names of her parents. Of the six grandchildren living, not one is at all sure of any facts concerning her, save that her given name was *Rachel*. She has been referred to by different correspondents and descendants, as a *Hall*, a *Pearson*, a *Stebbins* and a *Hyde*. Mrs. Lois H. Woodworth, of Concord, N. H., who manifested the liveliest interest in the preparation of this work until her last sickness in 1877, stated that she had always understood her father (Abner Hovey[6]) to say, one of his grandmothers was a *Perkins*, and the other a *Hall*. Certain it is that the mother of Samuel Hovey was Elizabeth *Perkins;* but as yet nothing has been received to determine as certainly the maiden name, etc., of Rachel, wife of Benjamin Cleveland.[4] The compiler will be glad to compensate any one who can furnish the desired information concerning her pedigree.

and his wife also removed to the same town, (in N. H.,) where his wife died in 1792. About this date Samuel Hovey, who became a Baptist preacher, removed from Lyme, N. H., to East Brookfield, Orange county, Vt., and there, greatly enfeebled by old age, Benj. Cleveland died, A. D. 1797.

The following letter, written by Benjamin Cleveland to his son, Rufus Cleveland, (the original of which is in possession of the compiler), is given here to show the unaffected piety and simple-heartedness of the writer, as well as to preserve the document itself from oblivion. It is written in a plain, steady hand, and signed with the *a* in the first syllable of the name, as customarily written by members of the Cleveland family in those days.

"LYME, October 19th, 1786.

"DEAR CHILDREN:

"Our love to you and yours induces us to let you know that through the goodness of God we are in as comfortable states of health as can be expected people of our age will be. But we are not insensible of the decays of nature, for we daily experience those shocks which show that our dissolution draws near. I have a bad cough, but am able to keep about. Your mother is better upon the account of her lameness.

"We have to acquaint you of the sorrowful news of the death of Zenas's two youngest children. Zenas and Rachel have both been sick, but have recovered. Ephraim Pearson and his wife was here about the beginning of September, and were well.

"Mr. Cook, the bearer, is going to Hartford, and he will bring my spectacles when he returns, if they are left at Capt. Chamberlain's, and I hope you will carry them there, and write to us by Mr. Cook.

"Zenas and Hovey and Hamblin and their folks are all well, and remember their love to you and yours.

"From your loving Parents,

"BENJAMIN AND RACHEL CLEAVELAND."

He was in his seventy-third year when he penned the foregoing, and it is to be hoped that the good old gentleman got his spectacles, of which he doubtless stood in great need. (See Appendix D.)

ABIGAIL CLEVELAND,[5] the fourth child of Benjamin[4] and Rachel Cleveland, was b. in Canterbury, Conn., Aug. 13, 1746. She m. in Windham, Conn., Sept. 29, 1763, Samuel

Hovey, son of Samuel and Elizabeth (Perkins) Hovey. He was b. in Windham, Conn., March 7, 1743; d. in East Brookfield, Vt., May 12, 1833. She d. in East Brookfield, Vt., June 2, 1832. She was a woman of a most amiable disposition, and a thrifty housewife. Her love of music was intense, and her voice remarkable for its sweetness, as well as for its power and compass. She was very kind to her aged parents, and watched over and nursed them most tenderly and untiringly in their declining years. Her husband cultivated successfully a farm, and never took anything for his ministerial labors in the way of compensation. They had a family of thirteen children, as follows:

1. Daniel,⁶ b. in Windham, Conn., July 24, 1764.
2. Abner,⁶ b. in Canterbury, Conn., Nov. 5, 1766.
3. Mary,⁶ b. in Canterbury, Conn., May 26, 1768.
4. Rufus Cleveland,⁶ b. in Canterbury, Conn., Aug. 29, 1770.
5. Rebecca,⁶ b. in Canterbury, Conn., Sept. 6, 1772.
6. Samuel,⁶ b. in Lyme, N. H., Oct. 20, 1774.
7. Abiel,⁶ b. in Lyme, N. H., Oct. 30, 1776.
8. Alvan,⁶ b. in Lyme, N. H., March 3, 1779.
9. Abigail,⁶ b. in Lyme, N. H., Dec. 25, 1780.
10. Elizabeth,⁶ b. in Lyme, N. H., April 15, 1783.
11. John Fairfield,⁶ b. in Lyme, N. H., April 11, 1785.
12. Lucy,⁶ b. in Lyme, N. H., March 7, 1787; d.
13. Lucy,⁶ (again), b. in Lyme, N. H., Oct. 15, 1789.

It appears that when Samuel Hovey removed from Windham county, Conn., to Grafton county, N. H., he purchased and settled upon what is known as "Grant's Island" in the Connecticut river, between Lyme, in Grafton county, N. H., and Thetford, in Orange county, Vt. It contains about 30 acres of arable land, free from stone, and the soil very fertile. Here he had early erected a comfortable dwelling house, barn, etc., and here the family dwelt and prospered until after the youngest child was born. In the old records of the Congregational or Presbyterian Society in Lyme, I find the following:

"Lime, Decr 28, 1794, then Abigail Hovey, the wife of Samuel Hovey, by the consent of the Brethren was dismissed from this chh. to join any chh. of Christ which she might choose for her better edification.
Attest: WM. CONANT, Pas."

"Lime, April 13, 1795, then Samuel Hovey, a member of this chh. was recommended to the chh. of Christ in Brookfield."

From the same records it appears that "Samuel Hovey and Abigail Hovey were admitted to the chh. at Lime, June 2, 1782," and on "Nov. 11, 1784, six more ruling elders chosen," among which number is "Samuel Hovey"; showing him to have been an active member in the ecclesiastical organization at "Lime." His connection with the Baptists was after his removal to Brookfield, Vt.

In the burying-ground on "East Hill," Brookfield, Vt., may be found the stones which mark the graves of this worthy pioneer and his wife, bearing the following inscriptions:

"Elder Samuel Hovey, Preacher of the Gospel, died May 12, 1833, aged 90 years and 2 mo."

"Mrs. Abigail Hovey, wife of Elder Samuel Hovey, died June 2, 1832, aged 85 years and 10 mo."

Around them are the graves of many of their kindred and descendants, including children, grandchildren and great-grandchildren, and the living may well learn a lesson from the lives and characters of Samuel Hovey and Abigail Cleveland, his wife.

Daniel Hovey,[6] eldest son and child of Rev. Samuel and Abigail (Cleveland) Hovey, m. in Lyme, N. H., Feb. 18, 1789, Beulah Pingree, dau. of Sylvanus and Mary (Sawyer) Pingree. She was b. in Conn., Feb. 1, 1769; d. in Lyme, N. H., Nov. 26, 1857. He d. in Lyme, N. H., March 1, 1850. Was a surveyor and man of more than ordinary ability, and was greatly respected and beloved by all who knew him.

Children, all b. in Lyme, N. H.:

1. Beulah,[7] b. March 17, 1790; d. May 29, 1817.
2. Daniel,[7] (Dr.), b. March 25, 1792; d. May 6, 1874.
3. Mary,[7] b. June 19, 1794; d. Nov. 27, 1819.
4. Abigail,[7] b. Jan. 31, 1797; d. June 3, 1862.

5. Sarah,⁷ b. June 29, 1799; d. Feb. 20, 1876.
6. Samuel Sylvanus,⁷ b. Sept. 1, 1801; d. Nov. 5, 1819.
7. Elizabeth Perkins,⁷ b. Oct. 22, 1803; d. Aug. 15, 1847.
8. Rhoda Lord,⁷ b. April 14, 1806; res. Hartford, Conn.
9. Josiah Fairfield,⁷ b. May 31, 1808; d. June 2, 1808.
10. Geo. Lewis,⁷ (Rev.), b. Aug. 20, 1810; res. Bricksburg, N. J.

Abner Hovey,⁶ second son and child of Rev. Samuel and Abigail (Cleveland) Hovey, m. in Woodstock, Conn., Feb. 17, 1790, Lois Tucker, dau. of Capt. Stephen and Lois (Lyon) Tucker. She was b. in Woodstock, Conn., Oct. 20, 1769; d. in Lyme, N. H., July 6, 1848. He d. in Lyme, N. H., Jan. 12, 1842. Miller.

Children. all b. in Lyme, N. H.:

1. Lydia,⁷ b. May 15, 1791; d. Nov. 19, 1810.
2. Abigail,⁷ b. March 14, 1793; d. Jan. 1, 1816.
3. Samuel,⁷ b. March 9, 1795; res. Waupaca, Wis.
4. Dudley,⁷ b. Jan. 31, 1797; d. Oct. 28, 1865.
5. Daniel,⁷ b. March 20, 1799; d. March 20, 1799.
6. Esther,⁷ b. March 11, 1800; d. Nov. 27, 1849.
7. Son,⁷) b. March —, 1802; d. March —, 1802.
8. Son,⁷) b. March —, 1802; d. March —, 1802.
9. Rachel,⁷ b. April 5, 1803; d. June 5, 1838.
10. Lois,⁷ b. May 24, 1806; d. Dec. 2, 1877.
11. Abner Bingham,⁷) b. March 12, 1809; d. March 16, 1809.
12. Arba Green,⁷) b. March 12, 1809; d. March 26, 1809.
13. Nancy Bingham,⁷ b. Sept. 22, 1812; d. May 26, 1843.

One son only, of this large family, survives. A daughter of Abigail Hovey,⁷ above mentioned, Mrs. Lydia E. Crawford, resides in Painesville, Ohio. She is the widow of Benjamin Crawford, who resided for many years in East Cleveland, Ohio.

Mary Hovey,⁶ eldest daughter and third child of Rev. Samuel and Abigail (Cleveland) Hovey, m. in Lyme, N. H., Jan. 1, 1788, Joseph Lord, son of John and Ruth (Rogers) Lord. He was b. in Vermont, May 4, 1764, removed to Ohio in 1806, and d. near Jamestown, Green county, Ohio,

Aug. —, 1847. Farmer. She d. in Germantown, Montgomery county, Ohio, April 10, 1859.

Children:

1. Lucinda,⁷ b. ——, 1789; d. ——, 1849.
2. Pamelia,⁷) b. April 21, 1791; d. ——, 1810.
3. Mary.⁷) b. April 21, 1791; d. Aug. 15, 1871.
4. Joseph Tilden,⁷ b. April 14, 1793; d. July 24, 1845.
5. John,⁷) b. Oct. 30, 1795; d. ——, 1829.
6. Alice,⁷) b. Oct. 30, 1795; d. Nov. 12, 1842.
7. Ruth,⁷ b. July 25, 1797; d. Oct. 31, 1874.
8. David,⁷) b. Jan. 5, 1800; d. unm.
9. Jonathan,⁷) b. Jan. 5, 1800; d. ——, 1850.
10. Abiel Hovey,⁷ (Dr.), b. April 26, 1802; res. Bellefontaine, Ohio.
11. Rhoda,⁷ b. ——, 1804; d. ——, 1808.
12. Rebecca,⁷ b. Jan. 10, 1807; d. Sept. 15, 1829.
13. Abigail,⁷ b. April 30, 1811; res. Cincinnati, Ohio.

Dr. Abiel H. Lord,⁷ settled in Bellefontaine, Ohio, where he has practiced medicine since 1823, and where he still resides. His only son, Col. R. S. C. Lord,⁸ graduated at West Point in 1856; served as Brevet Major 1st U. S. Cavalry; during the war of the Rebellion participated in many of the hard-fought battles of the Potomac, was wounded at Gettysburg, Pa., and for gallant and meritorious conduct at the battle of Five Forks, was raised to the rank of Colonel. Was m. to Miss Mary A. Wright, dau. of Dr. Thomas Wright, of Hamilton county, Ohio, in 1863, and d. in Bellefontaine, Ohio, in 1866, leaving a son and daughter, both since dead.

Rufus C. Hovey,⁶ third son and fourth child of Rev. Samuel and Abigail (Cleveland) Hovey, m. in Lyme, N. H., July 17, 1794, Grace Billings, dau. of Benjamin and Amy (Darby) Billings. She was b. in New London, Conn., Nov. 22, 1777; d. in Brookfield, Vt., July 29, 1819. He d. in Brookfield, Vt., July 5, 1817. Farmer.

Children, the eldest b. in Lyme, N. H., the others in Brookfield, Vt.:

1. Rufus Billings,⁷ b. Nov. 17, 1794; d. Jan. 9, 1844.
2. Amy,⁷ b. Dec. 7, 1795; d. May 9, 1818.
3. Orange,⁷ b. Feb. 5, 1797; res. Craftsbury, Vt.
4. Ruth,⁷ b. Nov. 2, 1798; d. May 12, 1812.
5. Silas,⁷ b. March 5, 1801; d. July 29, 1868.
6. Rhoda,⁷ b. April 25, 1803; d. July 6, 1878.
7. Simeon Skinner,⁷ b. April 9, 1805; d. Aug. 28, 1808.
8. Betsey,⁷ b. May 2, 1807; d. Sept. 3, 1808.
9. Simeon Skinner,⁷ (again), b. Nov. 13, 1809; d. Feb. 15, 1842.
10. Asahel King,⁷ b. May 25, 1811; res. Chelsea, Vt.
11. Laura,⁷ b. May 6, 1813; d. Jan. —, 1868.
12. Horace Nelson,⁷ (Rev.), b. Jan. 28, 1815; res. Lowell, Vt.
13. Grace,⁷ b. Jan. 26, 1817; d. Aug. 10, 1819.

Rebecca Hovey,⁶ second daughter and fifth child of Rev. Samuel and Abigail (Cleveland) Hovey, m. in Lyme, N. H., Dec. 25, 1794, James Sanderson, son of James and Sarah (Powers) Sanderson. He was b. in Woodstock, Vt., June 6, 1772; removed to Huron county, Ohio, in 1828; d. in Sherman, (now Weaver's Corners) Ohio, Sept. 2, 1828. She d. in Newton county, Ind., Aug. 14, 1853.

Children:

1. Lola,⁷ b. in Woodstock, Vt., Dec. 21, 1795; d. May 19, 1875.
2. Electa,⁷ b. in Woodstock, Vt., July 16, 1797; d. Oct. 3, 1846.
3. Melissa,⁷ b. in Brookfield, Vt., Feb. 21, 1799; d. July 23, 1844.
4. Rebecca,⁷ b. in Brookfield, Vt., Oct. 11, 1800; res. Weaver's Corners, Huron county, Ohio.
5. Minerva,⁷ b. in Brookfield, Vt., Aug. 4, 1802; res. Fremont, O.
6. James,⁷ b. in Morristown, Vt., April 13, 1804; d. March —, 1841.
7. Sarah,⁷ b. in Morristown, Vt., Feb. 19, 1806; d. unm. in 1828.
8. Asenath,⁷ b. in Morristown, Vt., Aug. 16, 1808; res. Merrimac, Mass.
9. Benjamin,⁷ b. in Morristown, Vt., July 30, 1810; d. June 8, 1851.
10. Joel,⁷ b. in Brookfield, Vt., Dec. 26, 1816; res. Lima, Ind.

Joel Sanderson,⁷ the youngest, is a well-to-do farmer in Lima, Ind.

Samuel Hovey,[6] fourth son and sixth child of Rev. Samuel and Abigail (Cleveland) Hovey, m. first in Brookfield, Vt., Nov. 15, 1798, Amy Billings, dau. of Benjamin and Amy (Darby) Billings. She was b. in New London, Conn., May 5, 1780; d. in Brookfield, Vt., Feb. 13, 1836. He m. second, in Williamstown, Vt., Dec. 7, 1836, Phyletta Kendall, dau. of Timothy and Eunice (Houghton) Kendall. She was b. in Williamstown, Vt., Oct. 7, 1800; d. in Brookfield, Vt., July 22, 1872. He d. July 25, 1856. Farmer.

Children, by wife Amy, all b. in Brookfield:

1. Grace,[7] b. Dec. 3, 1799; d. Sept. 4, 1802.
2. Samuel Wills,[7] b. Sept. 25, 1801; d. March 17, 1866.
3. Abiel,[7] b. Nov. 25, 1803; d. Nov. 25, 1805.
4. Alvan,[7] b. Dec. 4, 1804; res. East Brookfield, Vt.
5. Grace,[7] (again), b. ——, 1807; d. ——, 1807.
6. Permelia,[7] b. Oct. 4, 1809; res. Hartford, Vt.
7. James Harvey,[7] b. July 28, 1811; d. Jan. 3, 1857.
8. Rufus Cleveland,[7] b. Oct. 15, 1816; d. July 12, 1872.
9. Amy Billings,[7] b. Aug. 5, 1821; d. Feb. 16, 1831.

by wife Phyletta:

10. Amy Phyletta,[7] b. July 7, 1838; res. Montpelier, Vt.
11. Althea Loretta,[7] b. Feb. 17, 1840; res. East Brookfield, Vt.

Alvan Hovey,[7] a thrifty farmer and sturdy Democrat, still resides with his good wife in the old Hovey neighborhood, and near the place where his grandfather settled as a pioneer, in 1793.

Abiel Hovey,[6] fifth son and seventh child of Rev. Samuel and Abigail (Cleveland) Hovey, m. in Middlebury, Vt., about the year 1802, Frances Peterson, dau. of John and Frances (———) Peterson. She was b. in Vermont, May 20, 1780(?); d. in Posey county, Ind., Sept. 6, 1836. He d. in Posey county, Ind., July 17, 1823. He came to Indiana in 1818, and was an active and energetic man, of sound judgment and good principles. Farmer.

Children:
1. John,[7] b. Feb. —, 1803; d. April —, 1803.
2. Frances,[7] b. Aug. —, 1806; d. Sept. —, 1830.
3. Eliza,[7] b. Aug. —, 1809; d. Nov. —, 1834.
4. Amanda,[7] b. June 11, 1811; d. Sept. —, 1839.
5. Charlotte,[7] b. Oct. 15, 1813; d. Jan. —, 1856.
6. Charles,[7] b. April 19, 1815; d. Jan. 9, 1862.
7. Minerva,[7] b. Oct. 18, 1819; d. Aug. 16, 1846.
8. Alvin Peterson,[7] (Gen.), b. Sept. 6, 1821; res. Mt. Vernon, Ind.

Gen. Alvin P Hovey,[7] a Judge of the Supreme Court, in the State of Indiana, and late U. S. Minister to Peru, is perhaps the most distinguished of the descendants of Abigail Cleveland.[5] He served with efficiency in the war of the Rebellion, and was esteemed a brave and skillful officer; and in May, 1864, was Brig. General in command of the 1st Div. 23rd Army Corps, in Tennessee. The following note, taken from the "Centennial Historical Sketch of Posey County, Indiana," is here inserted as a brief epitome of his life and public services:

"NOTE.—General Alvin P. Hovey is a native of Posey county, and was a delegate in the convention that framed the new Constitution of the State of Indiana, in 1850. He was Judge of the Circuit Court for the judicial circuit comprising Posey county and ten other counties in the southwestern part of the State, from May, 1851, to May, 1854; and he was Judge of the Supreme Court of Indiana from May, 1854, to 1855. He was United States District Attorney, for the district of Indiana, from 1856 to 1858, when he was decapitated by President Buchanan for supporting Stephen A. Douglas for President, and Daniel W. Voorhees was appointed to fill the vacancy. He was Colonel of the 24th Indiana Volunteers in the late war for the suppression of the Southern rebellion. He was promoted Brigadier General of Volunteers April 13th, 1862, and afterwards, July 9th, 1864, he was promoted Brevet Major General of U. S. Volunteers, "for distinguished and meritorious service during the present war." He commanded at the celebrated battle of Champion Hill, which was the key battle of the Vicksburg campaign, opening the way to the capture of Vicksburg, and General U. S. Grant gave him great credit for running that battle. He was appointed Envoy Extraordinary and Minister Plenipotentiary of the United States to the Government of Peru, South America, Aug. 12, 1865, and resigned in 1870."

He m. in Posey county, Ind., Nov. 24, 1844, Miss Mary Ann James, dau. of Hon. Enoch R. James, of Mount Vernon, Ind. She was b. in Baton Rouge, La., Feb. 22, 1825; d. in Mt.

Vernon, Ind., Nov. 16, 1863. His second wife was the widow of Maj. W. F. Carey, of Cleveland, Ohio, and dau. of Hon. Caleb B. Smith, Secretary of the Interior under President Lincoln. No children by second wife, who died in New York City soon after her last marriage.

By wife Mary Ann he had—

1. Esther,[5] b. Jan. 8, 1846; m. Maj. G. V. Menzies.
2. Enoch James,[5] b. Feb. 7, 1848; d. Aug. 4, 1852.
4. Charles James,[5] b. Jan. 8, 1850; m. Lillie Jaquess.
4. Mary,[5] b. Jan. 13, 1854; d. March 30, 1855.
5. Mary Ann,[5] b. April 1, 1857; d. April 7, 1858.

The General, with his surviving children and grandchildren, resides in Mount Vernon, Posey county, Ind., where all delight to honor the citizen soldier and patriot. Much more might be said in reference to him, but space in the present edition will not permit.

Alvan Hovey,[6] sixth son and eighth child of Rev. Samuel and Abigail (Cleveland) Hovey, m. first, in Brookfield, Vt., April 3, 1803, Nancy Seabury, dau. of Benjamin and Lucretia (Kingsbury) Seabury. She was b. in Conn., Aug. 8, 1780; d. in Brookfield, Vt., Nov. 27, 1856. He m. second, in Brookfield, Vt., Oct. 12, 1857, his cousin, Mrs. Nancy (Hamblin) Bean, dau. of Oliver and Rachel (Cleveland) Hamblin. She was born in Brookfield, Vt., March 8, 1791. He filled the office of a Deacon in the Baptist church for many years. He d. in Brookfield, Vt., Jan. 29, 1864. Farmer. His second wife d. in Enfield, N. H., Aug. 15, 1868.

Children, by wife Nancy Seabury, all b. in East Brookfield, Vt. :

1. Alvan,[7] b. Jan. 12, 1804; d. Jan. 30, 1804.
2. Nancy,[7] b. Feb. 20, 1805; d. Feb. 20, 1805.
3. Benjamin,[7] b. June 15, 1806; d. June 15, 1806.
4. Nancy Seabury,[7] b. Dec. 6, 1807; res. Williamstown, Vt.
5. Alvan Seabury,[7] b. March 27, 1809; d. July 15, 1821.
6. Lucretia Kingsbury,[7] b. Sept. 9, 1813; d. May 7, 1838.
7. Harriet Atwood,[7] b. Nov. 29, 1815; res. Chelsea, Vt.

8. Emily Ann,[7] b. Feb. 12, 1808; res. Chelsea, Vt.
9. Son,[7] (b. June 27, 1822; d. June —, 1822.
10. Son,[7]) b. June 27, 1822; d. June —, 1822.

Abigail Hovey,[6] third daughter and ninth child of Rev. Samuel and Abigail (Cleveland) Hovey, m. in Brookfield, Vt., Jan. 1, 1805, Oliver Hibbard, son of Roger and Sarah (Davison) Hibbard. He was born in Lebanon, N. H., Sept. 27, 1780; d. in East Brookfield, Vt., July 29, 1833. She d. in East Brookfield, Vt., Oct. 11, 1851, surviving her husband eighteen years. He was a farmer.

Children, all b. in Brookfield :

1. Polly,[7] b. Oct. 13, 1805; res. Brookfield, Vt.
2. Amanda,[7] b. Aug. 14, 1807; res. Brookfield, Vt.
3. Oliver Davison,[7] (Rev.), b. Oct. 12, 1809; res. in Michigan.
4. William Lewis,[7] b. Aug. 6, 1816; d. Sept. 20, 1851.
5. Abigail Cleveland,[7] b. Dec. 31, 1818; d. Feb. 16, 1835.
6. Almira,[7] b. Jan. 13, 1821; d. Nov. 24, 1856.
7. Sarah M.,[7] b. Sept. 23, 1826; res. Chelsea, Vt.

Elizabeth Hovey,[6] fourth daughter and tenth child of Rev. Samuel and Abigail (Cleveland) Hovey, m. in Brookfield, Vt., Dec. 25, 1808, Gurdon Hibbard, son of Roger and Sarah (Davison) Hibbard. He was b. in Lebanon, N. H., July 12, 1782; d. in Brookfield, Vt., Sept. 27, 1871. She d. in Brookfield, Vt., March 6, 1864. He was a farmer.

Children, all b. in Brookfield :

1. Mary,[7] b. Oct. 24, 1809; d. May 27, 1859.
2. Gurdon Plummer,[7] b. April 27, 1811; res. Brookfield, Vt.
3. Ruth Hovey,[7] b. Jan. 26, 1813; res. East Brookfield, Vt.
4. Eliza Matilda,[7] b. May 28, 1815; res. Brookfield, Vt.
5. Sarah Davison,[7] b. Oct. 4, 1817; res. Brookfield, Vt.
6. Fanny Burnham,[7] b. Sept. 10, 1819; res. Washington, N. J.
7. Elizabeth Perkins,[7] b. Sept. 5, 1821; res. Methuen, Mass.

John F. Hovey,[6] seventh son and eleventh child of Rev. Samuel and Abigail (Cleveland) Hovey, m. in Milton, Vt., Sept. 16, 1813, Elizabeth Hill, dau. of Benjamin and Elizabeth

(Owen) Hill. She was b. in Milton, Vt., Jan. 25, 1794; d. in Camden, Lorain county, Ohio, April 14, 1864. He d. in Camden, Ohio, Feb. 8, 1870. Farmer.

Children, all b. in Milton, Vt., except the youngest:

1. Samuel Benjamin,⁷ b. Sept. 27, 1814; d. March 20, 1817.
2. Abigail Elizabeth,⁷ b. July 21, 1816; res. McPherson, Kan.
3. Samuel Benjamin,⁷ (again), b. Sept. 21, 1818; res. May, Tuscola county, Mich.
4. John Kean,⁷ b. March 3, 1821; res. Townville, Crawford county, Pa.
5. Alvan Seabury,⁷ b. March 31, 1823; res. Holland, Ohio.
6. Philemon Henry,⁷ b. March 17, 1826; res. Union City, Tenn.
7. Daniel Hill,⁷ b. March 23, 1828; res. McPherson, Kan.
8. Charles Carroll,⁷ b. July 3, 1831; d. April —, 1832.
9. James Prouty,⁷ b. Oct. 29, 1833; res. Clarksfield, Ohio.
10. Rufus Cleveland,⁷ b. Dec. 15, 1836; d. July 1, 1863.

LUCY HOVEY,⁶ sixth daughter and thirteenth child of Rev. Samuel and Abigail (Cleveland) Hovey, m. in Brookfield, Vt., July 7, 1811, Lucius Howes, son of Zachariah and Alice (Bingham) Howes. He was b. in Windham, Conn., May 3, 1790; d. in Lowell, Mass., April 6, 1872. She d. in Chelsea, Vt., Feb. 19, 1827. He was a farmer.

Children:

1. Abner Hovey,⁷ b. Dec. 23, 1811; d. April 3, 1813.
2. Abigail Rosella,⁷ b. Sept. 15, 1814; res. Lowell, Mass.
3. Caroline Matilda,⁷ b. Jan. 26, 1817; res. Lowell, Mass.
4. Nancy Amanda,⁷ b. Nov. 13, 1819; res. Medford, Mass.
5. Lucius Edson,⁷ b. Sept. 30, 1823; res. Maquoketa, Iowa.

(For additional genealogical information as to the Hovey branch, see Appendix E.)

ZENAS CLEVELAND,⁵ the fifth child of Benj. and Rachel Cleveland, was b. in Canterbury, Conn., Sept. 21, 1748. The date and place of his marriage to Eunice Ludington, the names of her parents, or the date and place of her birth, not learned. When he was a lad of perhaps eight or ten years of age, he came in from the hayfield, and while lying down to rest he experienced a sharp pain in one of his legs, so acute as to cause him to scream aloud. In a few days something like a fever sore or ulcer broke out, and when healed he was left a cripple for life. He appears to have learned the trade of a shoemaker. In 1786 he resided in Brookfield, Vt., and buried his two youngest children there in August of that year. All traces of him and his family are lost from the time he left there in 1791, until found in Sullivan county, N. Y., about the year 1811. He was then in poor circumstances, and worked at shoemaking at Bethel, in that county. Shortly after that date he left that place and removed to Litchfield, Bradford county, Pa., where his only son, Zenas Cleveland, Jr., had taken up a wild piece of land. There his wife Eunice died, May 1, 1824, surviving her husband about three years. He d. Aug. 27, 1821, aged nearly 73. They were both buried on the place, a few rods from the house, but no stone marks their resting place now. The farm is now owned and cultivated by Joshua Turk, Esq., who kindly pointed out to me the slight knoll designating the two graves of Zenas Cleveland,[5] and Eunice Ludington, his wife. As nearly as can be ascertained they had a family of six children:

1. Eunice,[6] b. (about) 1773; d. ——
2. Betsey,[6] b. (about) 1776; d. ——
3. Zenas,[6] b. Sept. —, 1778; d. Jan. 13, 1873.
4. Eleanor,[6] b. April 10, 1780; d. Aug. 27, 1869.
5. Anna,[6] b. ——, 1782; d. Aug. 5, 1786.
6. James,[6] b. Oct. 30, 1784; d. Aug. 10, 1786.

An extraordinary effort has been made by the writer to trace this family and descendants, but with the exception of one daughter, Eleanor,[6] with poor success. Either Eunice[6] or Betsey[6] is supposed to have married a man by the name of Wing, who lived at one time near Albany, N. Y., and had a son, Freeman Wing. Every effort so far to trace them has been in vain. (See Appendix F.)

ZENAS CLEVELAND,[5] Jr., son of Zenas and Eunice (Ludington) Cleveland, b. Sept. —, 1778, m. Deborah Kennedy (or

Canada), but the date and place of his marriage, or the dat
and place of her birth, or names of her parents, not learned
They had no children. She died in Litchfield, Bradford
county, Pa., March 22, 1849. Her husband was a burly,
thick set and fearless man, as fond of a rough-and-tumble
fight at militia musters, as the proverbial Irishman at Donny-
brook Fair. He was a very successful farmer, and considered
even wealthy at one time, by his neighbors. He was quite
blind for nearly ten years before his death, and was kindly
cared for in the family of a Mr. Wolcott for many years
previous to that event, which occurred Jan. 13, 1873, in his
95th year.

ELEANOR CLEVELAND,[6] daughter of Zenas and Eunice
(Ludington) Cleveland, b. April 10, 1780, m. first, in
Woodstock, Conn., in 1800, Caleb Burgess, son of Samuel
and Hannah (Sturtevant) Burgess. He was b. in Middleboro',
Mass., about the year 1774, and d. in Ithaca, N. Y., April 14,
1820. He was a shoemaker by occupation. She m. second,
in Ithaca, N. Y., March 9, 1821, Solomon Hallett, son of
William Hallett. He was b. in Dec., 1758, and d. in Afton,
Chenango county, N. Y., June 4, 1841. She d. in same place,
Aug. 27, 1869, in the 90th year of her age. (See Appendix G.)

Children, by first husband, Caleb Burgess:

1. Samuel,[7] b. Aug. 29, 1801; d. Feb. 8, 1870.
2. James,[7] b. April 20, 1803; d. Aug. 27, 1866.
3. Diadama,[7] b. Dec. 9, 1805; d. April 8, 1810.
4. Eunice,[7] b. July 20, 1808.
5. Hannah,[7] b. Aug. 24, 1811.
6. William C.,[7] b. Oct. 14, 1813.
7. Zenas,[7] b. Oct. 20, 1816; drowned March 17, 1830.
8. Eleanor,[7] b. May 29, 1819.

by second husband, Solomon Hallett:

9. Miriam,[7] b. Jan. 31, 1822.
10. Fidelia,[7] b. June 10, 1824; d. Feb. 25, 1826.
11. Sarah Jane,[7] b. July 14, 1828.

Bristol county, Mass., June 30, 82; d. in Morrisville, N. Y., Feb. 15, 1864. She d. in Morrisville, N. Y., Feb. 1, 1857.

Children:
1. Melona,[7] b. March 2, 1809; res. Lebanon, N. Y.
2. Eluna,[7] b. Nov. 17, 1810; d. Dec. 16, 1868.
3. Adaline,[7] b. Aug. 20, 1812; d. Nov. 26, 1865.
4. Hibbard,[7] b. Aug. 17, 1814; res. Morrisville, N. Y.
5. Susan,[7] b. July 11, 1816; res. Peterboro', N. Y.
6. Alexa,[7] b. June 20, 1820; d. July 15, 1845.
7. Savilla,[7] b. Aug. 16, 1830; d. Sept. 5, 1847.

Hibbard Martin,[7] a Deputy Sheriff of the county, resides at Morrisville, N. Y.

Oren Payne,[6] sixth son and eighth child of Edward and Persis (Cleveland) Payne, m. in Wendell, Mass., Feb. 5, 1822, Meorry Taylor Benjamin, dau. of Joel and Sally (Anderson) Benjamin. She was b. in Montague, Mass., Sept. 19, 1790. He d. in Montague, Mass., Sept. 21, 1873. He was a farmer by occupation. . His widow lives at the old homestead, and notwithstanding her great age, continues the management of the place, assisted by her nephews. No children.

John Payne,[6] (M. D.), the seventh son and ninth child of Edward and Persis (Cleveland) Payne, m. in Amherst, Mass., March 13, 1826, Elizabeth Sarah Nelson, dau. of Seth and Sarah (Jones) Nelson. She was b. in Milford, Mass., April 10, 1803. He d. in Janesville, Wis., March 16, 1873. She is living (1878) with her son, Rev. Henry N. Payne, in Lima, Livingston county, N. Y.

Children:
1. Mary Louisa,[7] b. in Morrisville, N. Y., Feb. 17, 1827; d. March 16, 1873.
2. Charles Howard,[7] b. in Morrisville, N. Y., April 15, 1830; res. Janesville, Wis.
3. Sarah Sophia,[7] b. in Morrisville, N. Y., March 21, 1832; res. Footville, Wis.
4. William Henry Harrison,[7] b. in Canastota, N. Y., March 14, 1834; res. Sandwich, Ill.

5. Ann Amelia,[7] b. in Horse Heads, N. Y., Aug. 6, 1838; d. Feb. 15, 1848.
6. Henry Nelson,[7] (Rev.), b. in Horse Heads, N. Y., Nov. 4, 1840; res. Lima, N. Y.

Ira Payne,[6] ninth son and youngest child of Edward and Persis (Cleveland) Payne, m. first, in Montague, Franklin county, Mass., Jan. 1, 1816, Lydia Makepeace, dau. of Seth and Julia (Adams) Makepeace. She was b. in Montague, June 19, 1793; d. in Montague, Aug. 1, 1857. He m. second, in Montague, April 10, 1858, Mrs. Abby (Cummins) Porter, dau. of Reuben and Anna (Joslyn) Cummins. She was b. in Wendell, Mass.; d. in Montague, June 30, 1868. He m. third, in Montague, April 1, 1869, Mrs. Roxiana (Covil) Cross, dau. of Stephen and Roxiana (Clark) Covil. She was b. in Fabius, Onondaga county, N. Y., March 24, 1815. He d. in Montague, Mass., May 8, 1873.

Children, by wife Lydia, all born in Montague:

1. Miranda,[7] b. Nov. 23, 1816; res. Ripton, Vt.
2. Julia Ann,[7] b. Dec. 17, 1818; d. Dec. 9, 1819.
3. William,[7] b. Dec. 1, 1820; res. Monroe, Wis.
4. Calvin,[7] b. April 4, 1823; res. Monroe, Wis.
5. John Adams,[7] b. March 30, 1825; res. Paola, Kan.
6. Susan,[7] b. May 14, 1827; res. North Hadley, Mass.
7. Emeline,[7]) b. Nov. 22, 1831; res. Orange, Mass.
8. Eveline,[7]) b. Nov. 22, 1831; d. Feb. 22, 1832.
9. Julia Ann,[7] (again), b. Sept. 11, 1833; res. Montague, Mass.

(For further genealogical information in regard to the Payne family, see Appendix I.)

Rufus Cleveland,[5] the eighth child of Benjamin and Rachel Cleveland, was b. in Canterbury, Conn., June 14, 1754. He m. first, in Ellington, Conn., Sept. 9, 1779, Mary Chamberlain, eldest daughter of Capt. James and Abigail (Boynton) Chamberlain. She was b. in Coventry, Conn., Aug. 7, 1759; d. in Winsted, Conn., Nov. 13, 1807. He m.

second, in Winsted, Conn., May 1, 1808, Mrs. Alice (Jenkins) Kent, wid. of John Kent, and dau. of Edward and Jerusha (Neal) Jenkins. She was b. in Mass., ——. 1771 ; d. in Winsted, Conn.. Oct. 14, 1833.

Children, by wife Mary :

1. Chester,[6] b. June 30, 1780; drowned Aug. 26, 1795.
2. Clarissa,[6] b. Feb. 6, 1782; d. June 12, 1822.
3. Alexander,[6] b. Oct. 16, 1783; d. Sept. 5, 1860.
4. Oren,[6] b. May 3, 1785; res. Huntsburgh, Geauga county, Ohio.
5. James Chamberlain,[6] b. Jan. 9, 1787; d. Sept. 1, 1875.
6. Horace,[6] b. Feb. 25, 1789; d. Sept. 13, 1864.
7. Mary,[6] b. March 21, 1791; d. Sept. 21, 1791.
8. Nancy,[6] b. Aug. 22, 1792; d. May 20, 1827.
9. Betsey,[6] b. Aug. 31, 1794; d. Oct. 18, 1827.
10. Mary,[6] (again), b. May 23, 1796; d. Oct. 12, 1838.
11. Son,[6] b. June 5, 1798; d. June 5, 1798.
12. Daughter,[6] b. Feb. 17, 1800; d. Feb. 17, 1800.
13. Daughter,[6] b. Sept 14, 1801; d. Sept. 14, 1801.
14. Charles Chester Warner,[6] b. Jan. 20, 1803; res. Catskill, N. Y.

by wife Alice :

15. Alice,[6] b. Oct. 2, 1809; res. Perry, Pike county, Ill.
16. John Kent,[6] b. May 12, 1811; res. Perry, Pike county, Ill.

Rufus Cleveland,[5] was a farmer. He was of medium height, florid complexion, light curly hair, and blue eyes. Was a fine singer, fond of a good story, and industrious and temperate in his habits. He served as a soldier during the Revolutionary war, and paid his marriage fee in one hundred dollars of Continental currency. Being employed by Capt. Chamberlain upon his farm, he conveniently courted and in due time married his first wife, Miss Mollie, eldest daughter of his employer ; and when his father-in-law removed from Ellington, in Tolland county, to Warehouse Point, in East Windsor, Hartford county, Conn., he, with his wife and family, accompanied him. This was in the spring of 1782 or 1783. He remained in East Windsor until the spring of 1787, when he removed to Barkhamstead, Litchfield county, Conn., and purchased a farm of his own on Wallen's Hill. Here his wife died in the autumn of 1807, of a fever contracted from nursing a neighbor's wife, and who also died of the same fever, which at that time prevailed as an epidemic in the neighborhood. Her kindness to the sick, and readiness to watch with and care for them at all times, made her greatly beloved, and her departure from earth was mourned as if a ministering angel had been taken away indeed. In the old burying-ground on the "Hill" may be seen the graves of this worthy couple, and the inscriptions upon the headstones placed there are as follows:

"In memory of Rufus Cleveland, who died Feb. 22, 1838, aged 82 years."

"In memory of Mrs. Mary Cleveland, wife of Rufus Cleveland, and daughter of Capt. James Chamberlain, who died Novem. 13, 1807, in the 49th year of her age."

His second wife, who died of cancer after a distressing and protracted illness, was buried in the village cemetery, in Winsted. The inscription on her tombstone is simply—

"Alice, wife of Rufus Cleveland, died Oct. 14, 1833."

Rufus Cleveland[5] was in his *eighty-fourth* year when he died, and not in his eighty-third, as the inscription indicates. As will be noted, four children are yet living — two by the first and two by the second wife — but very soon the places which know them now, will know them no more forever.

(An account of Capt. James Chamberlain and his descendants will be found in Appendix J.)

CLARISSA CLEVELAND,[6] eldest daughter and second child of Rufus and Mary (Chamberlain) Cleveland, b. in Ellington, Conn., Feb. 6, 1782, m. in Barkhamstead, Conn., July 4, 1799, Daniel White, son of George and Mary (Benton) White. He was b. in Tolland, Conn., Dec. 11, 1774; d. in Winsted, Conn., Dec. 28, 1859. She d. in Barkhamstead, Conn., June 12, 1822. His epitaph is—"*An honest man.*"

Children, all b. in Barkhamstead, Conn.

1. Emily,[7] b. Feb. 9, 1801; d. Dec. 26, 1878.
2. Lavinia,[7] b. Aug. 20, 1803; res. Winchester, Conn.
3. Mary Cleveland,[7] b. Jan. 31, 1805; d. Aug. 27, 1866.

4. Harriet,⁷ b. Jan. 28, 1807; res. Winsted, Conn.
5. Horace Cleveland,⁷ b. Feb. 22, 1809; res. Colebrook. Conn.
6. Urania Clarissa,⁷ b. July 20, 1811; d. Aug. 5, 1839.
7. Philenda Miller,⁷ b. June 11, 1814; d. Nov. 6, 1857.
8. Janette,⁷ b. April 6, 1816; d. July 26, 1816.
9. Daughter,⁷ b. April 6, 1816; d. April 6, 1816.
10. Pembroke,⁷ b. Sept. 18, 1819; res. McGregor, Iowa.

Emily White,⁷ eldest child of Daniel and Clarissa (Cleveland) White, b. in Barkhamstead, Conn., Feb. 9, 1801, m. in Winsted, Conn., Feb. 23, 1825, Hezekiah Goodwin Butler, son of Hezekiah and Hepzibah (Burr) Butler, of Norfolk, Conn. He was b. in New Marlboro', Mass., June 7, 1798; d. in Prompton, Wayne county, Pa., May 27, 1867. She d. in Santa Cruz, Cal., Dec. 26, 1878.

Children:

1. Alphonso Elizur,⁸ b. in New Marlboro', Mass., July 3, 1826; d. Feb. 2, 1851.
2. Samuel Stone,⁸ b. in New Marlboro', Mass., July 12, 1829, m. first, in Elmira, N. Y., May 14, 1853, Sarah Pamela Fields, dau. of Eugene and Sarah (McMahon) Fields. She was b. in Baltimore, Md., Nov. 17, 1824. Divorced in Jan., 1872. He m. second, in Colebrook, Conn., Sept. 24, 1873, Elvira A. Sage, dau. of Hiram and Lucy (Judd) Sage. She was b. in Colebrook, Conn., June 17, 1841. Res. Los Gatos, Cal. Children, by wife Sarah, all b. in San Francisco, Cal.: 1. James Gleason,⁹ b. Feb. 18, 1854. 2. William Alphonso,⁹ b. March 22, 1856. 3. Oresmus Goodwin,⁹ b. Sept. 15, 1859. 4. Eugene Fields,⁹ b. March 31, 1862. 5. Meta Augusta,⁹ b. Sept. 20, 1864; d. Dec. 23, 1870. Children, by wife Elvira: 6. Edward Sage,⁹ b. in Los Gatos, Cal., July 20, 1874.
3. Edward Payson,⁸ b. in Clinton, Pa., May 13, 1834, m. in Princeton, Ill., Aug. 13, 1856, Mary Jane Harvey, dau. of Daniel Harvey, Esq. Children, all b. in Illinois: 1. Ira Goodwin,⁹ b. June 28, 1857; d. Aug. 27, 1858. 2. Edward Payson,⁹ b. Nov. 20, 1858; d. June 12, 1860. Divorced from wife Mary Jane, and resides in Santa Cruz, Cal. Photographer.

4. Mary Elizabeth,⁸ b. in Clinton, Pa., June 5, 1836, m. in Bethany, Pa., Aug. 7, 1852. Seth Lewis Torrey, son of William and Eunice (Lewis) Torrey. He was b. in Dyberry, Pa., Jan. 1, 1820. Children: 1. Martha Elizabeth,⁹ b. in Honesdale, Pa., Nov. 25, 1853, m. in Ottawa, Ill., Oct. 1, 1873, Clinton Macomber, and d. without issue, May 30, 1876. 2. Elsie Lois,⁹ b. in Ottawa, Ill., Aug. 25, 1856. 3. Lewis Butler,⁹ b. in Ottawa, Ill., Sept. 9, 1864.

Lavinia White,⁷ second daughter and child of Daniel and Clarissa (Cleveland) White, b. in Barkhamstead, Conn., Aug. 20, 1803, m. in Winsted, Conn., Oct. 4, 1835, Gideon Hall, son of William and Mary (Smedley) Hall. He was b. in Bethlehem, Conn., June 20, 1775; d. in Winsted, Conn., Feb. 23, 1850. He was an enterprising farmer and quite eccentric, and though very brusque in his manners, was kind and neighborly to the poor and needy. She resides in Winchester, Conn. They had but one child:

1. Jane Catherine,⁸ b. in Winsted, Conn., Oct. 20, 1845, m. in same place, May 9, 1871, Samuel Abel Wetmore, son of Dea. Abel Samuel and Lucy (Hill) Wetmore. He was b. in Winchester, Conn., Sept. 25, 1842. Farmer. Children: 1. Willis LeRoy,⁹ b. Sept. 18, 1872. 2. Arthur Hall,⁹ b. March 27, 1874; d. May 9, 1875. 3. Mary Beecher,⁹ b. March 1, 1876. 4. Charles DeWitt,⁹ b. Sept. 4, 1877.

Mary Cleveland White,⁷ third daughter and child of Daniel and Clarissa (Cleveland) White, b. in Barkhamstead, Conn., Jan. 31, 1805, m. in Winsted, Conn., April 18, 1833, Edward Adams Rugg, son of Seth and Sabrina (Adams) Rugg. He was b. in New Marlboro', Mass., Sept. 20, 1806; d. in Winchester, Conn., April 17, 1862. She d. in Winchester, Conn., Aug. 27, 1866. He was a farmer and much esteemed where he lived.

Children:

1. Son,⁸ b. in Sandisfield, Mass., ——, 1834; d. ——, 1834.
2. Son,⁸ b. in Sandisfield, Mass., ——, 1836; d. ——, 1836.

3. Harlan Page,[8] b. in Sandisfield, Mass., July 16, 1838, m. in Pleasant Valley, Conn., Nov. 29, 1866, Finette Guernsey, dau. of Joseph H. and Elizabeth (Talmadge) Guernsey. She was b. in Waterbury, Conn., Oct. 4, 1842; res. Bridgeport, Conn. They have one child: Arthur Guernsey,[9] b. in New Milford, Conn., Sept. 26, 1869.
4. Urania White,[8] b. in Sandisfield, Mass., Oct. 17, 1839; unm.; res. Winsted, Conn.
5. Mary White,[8] b. in Sandisfield, Mass., June 23, 1841, m. in Winchester, Conn., Dec. 31, 1862, Richard Slocum, son of Richard and Cynthia (Swift) Slocum. He was b. in Colebrook, Conn., Dec. 30, 1838. Farmer; res. Madison, Iowa. Children: 1. Elbert Heman,[9] b. Nov. 1, 1863. 2. Alice Louise,[9] b. June 21, 1867; d. May 30, 1871. 3. Edith May,[9] b. April 16, 1869. 4. Clifford Richard,[9] b. Sept 10, 1872.
6. Edward Payson,[8] b. in Winchester, Conn., Aug. 11, 1843; d. unm. in Meriden, Conn., Nov. 25, 1877.
7. Elizabeth White,[8] b. in Winchester, Conn., Nov. 30, 1845, m. in Winchester, Conn., Dec. 31, 1866, Joseph Thibault, son of John B. and Josephine (Carriveau) Thibault. He was b. in St. Claire, Dorchester, P. Q. (Canada), May 12, 1842. They have one child: Edward Joseph,[9] b. in West Meriden, Conn., Feb. 6, 1868. Res. West Meriden, Conn.
8. Arthur,[8] b. in Winchester, Conn., June 19, 1847; d. in Winchester, Conn., March 24, 1848.

Harriet White,[7] fourth daughter and child of Daniel and Clarissa (Cleveland) White, b. in Barkhamstead, Conn., Jan. 28, 1807, m. first, in Sandisfield, Mass., Dec. 26, 1846, Oren Kellogg, son of Asa and Anna (Webster) Kellogg. He was b. in Sandisfield, Mass., July 20, 1793; d. in Colebrook, Conn., Nov. 4, 1859. She m. second, in Winsted, Conn., July 10, 1863, Anson Harrington, of Northampton, Mass.; separated soon afterwards. He d. Aug. 6, 1878. She is living (1878) in Winsted, Conn. No children by either husband.

Horace Cleveland White,[7] eldest son and fifth child of Daniel and Clarissa (Cleveland) White, b. in Barkhamstead, Conn., Feb. 22, 1809, m. in Sandisfield, Mass., April 10, 1838,

Susan Amelia Wolcott, dau. of Gen. Josiah and Amelia (Bissell) Wolcott. She was b. in Sandisfield, Mass., Jan. 20, 1814. He is a builder and contractor; res. Colebrook, Conn.

Children:

1. Salome Benton,[7] b. in Sandisfield, Mass., April 27, 1839, m. first in Colebrook, Conn., Aug. 1, 1861, Gustavus Archibald Wright, son of Archibald and Marcia (Wadsworth) Wright. She m. second, in Colebrook, Dec. 9, 1874, Horace Aaron Lunn. Children—by first husband: 1. Willie Foster,[8] b. May 13, 1862. By second husband: 2. Horace White,[8] b. Dec. 29, 1875.
2. Mary Bissell,[7] } b. May 11, 1841.
3. Son,[7] } b. May 11, 1841; d. May 13, 1841. She (Mary Bissell White[7]) m. in Sandisfield, Mass., Jan. 1, 1861, Homer Philander Twining, son of Philander and Sarah Amelia (Shepard) Twining. He was b. in Tolland, Mass., Nov. 9, 1839. Children: 1. Clifford Homer,[8] b. Nov. 22, 1866; d. Jan. 27, 1868. 2. Clifford Homer,[8] (again), b. April 22, 1869.
4. Clarissa Amelia,[7] b. in Sandisfield, Mass., Nov. 21, 1843, m. in Colebrook, Conn., April 21, 1867, James Martin. Children: 1. Susan Mary,[8] b. Aug. 4, 1871. 2. Clarissa Augusta,[8] b. June 29, 1874.
5. Susan Adelaide,[7] b. in Sandisfield, Mass., Oct. 31, 1845; d. Feb. 15, 1846.
6. Theresa Lavinia,[7] b. in Sandisfield, Mass., April 25, 1848, m. in Colebrook, Conn., Nov. 23, 1866, Frank Seymour Hale, son of Francis S. and Fanny (Snow) Hale. He was b. in Tolland, Mass., Dec. 13, 1844. Children: 1. Dwight Francis,[8] b. Oct. 21, 1867; d. July 28, 1868. 2. Jennie Leonie,[8] b. Nov. 8, 1872. 3. Homer Twining,[8] b. April 16, 1876.
7. Horace Wolcott,[7] b. in Lee, Mass., July 9, 1853.

Urania Clarissa White,[7] fifth daughter and sixth child of Daniel and Clarissa (Cleveland) White, b. in Barkhamstead, Conn., July 20, 1811; d. at the Mission House in La Pointe, (Lake Superior,) Wis., Aug. 5, 1839, unm. She was imbued with the missionary spirit while a student at Oberlin, Ohio, and volunteered to go as a teacher to the Indians in the Northwest Territory.

Samuel Burgess,[7] m. first, Hannah Loder, of Ithaca, N. Y., by whom he had two daughters, Diana,[8] and Harriet,[8] both dead. His second wife was Elizabeth Dougherty, a native of Philadelphia, Pa., who d. Aug. 7, 1875, without issue. He d. near Belle Vernon, Fayette county, Pa.

James Burgess,[7] d. in Greenwich, Huron county, Ohio, and his three daughters m., and live in Hillsdale county, Mich.

Eunice Burgess,[7] who m. Hiram Hallett, but now a widow, is living at White Pine, Lycoming county, Pa.

Hannah Burgess,[7] now wid. of Moses Draper, is living in Hudson, Ohio. Her first husband was John DeGraw.

William Cleveland Burgess,[7] res. Springfield, Pa.

Eleanor Burgess,[7] wid. of Fredk. Swartwood, res. Mitchell Creek, Tioga county, Pa.

Miriam Hallett,[7] wife of Albert Rounds, and Sarah Jane Hallett,[7] widow of Nelson Cook, reside in Afton, Chenango county, N. Y.

RACHEL CLEVELAND,[5] the sixth child of Benjamin and Rachel Cleveland, was b. in Canterbury, Conn., May 18, 1750. She m. in Tolland, Conn., in 1777, Oliver Hamblin, son of Joel and Polly (Channing) Hamblin. He was b. in Enfield, Conn., Sept. 3, 1751; d. in East Brookfield, Vt., Oct. 28, 1829. She d. in same place, Sept. 27, 1837. Farmer.

They had six children, as follows:

1. Polly,[6] b. ——, 1778; d. Feb. 24, 1808.
2. Betsey,[6] b. May 6, 1780; d. Oct. 13, 1830.
3. Joel,[6] b. Feb. 27, 1783; d. April 18, 1859.
4. Theodotia,[6] b. March 9, 1785; res. North Montpelier, Vt.
5. James,[6] b. May 24, 1788; d. April 2, 1865.
6. Nancy,[6] b. March 8, 1791; d. Aug. 15, 1868.

Rachel Cleveland,[5] was a large and stately woman, of indomitable pluck and courage, and a most industrious worker. At the burning of Royalton, Vt., by the Indians, in 1784, she and her children barely escaped with their lives, and con-

cealed themselves in the forest hard by. She was sep
for more than three weeks from her husband, and each
posed the other killed by the savages. The next child
to them (Theodotia) was marked by the terrible fright to w
the mother had been subjected. They did not return to 1'
alton, but settled in Brookfield, some twelve or fifteen n
further to the northward, and about two miles from the pl
where Samuel Hovey located some six or seven years later.

In the old cemetery not far from the East Brookfield Post
Office are two grave stones, with the following inscriptions
upon them:

"Mr. Oliver Hamblin, died Oct. 28, 1829, in the 79th year of his age."

"Rachel, widow of Oliver Hamblin, died Sept. 27, 1837, in her 88th year."

Polly Hamblin,[6] eldest daughter and child of Oliver and
Rachel (Cleveland) Hamblin, m. in Brookfield, Vt., Sept. 15,
1798, Roswell Shepard, son of Simeon and Rachel (Brooks)
Shepard. He was b. in Alstead, N. H., July 22, 1777; d. in
Brookfield, Vt., Aug. 10, 1864. She d. in Brookfield, Vt.,
Feb. 24, 1808.

Children, all b. in Brookfield, Vt.:

1. Roswell,[7] b. July 9, 1799; d. Sept. 4, 1851.
2. Betsey Hamblin,[7] b. June 1, 1801; res. Hardwick, Mass.
3. Hiram,[7] b. July 4, 1803; res. Barre, Vt.
4. Simeon,[7] b. Oct. 14, 1805; d. Dec. 31, 1873.
5. Joel Hamblin,[7] b. Feb. 16, 1808; res. Williamstown, Vt.

Betsey Hamblin,[6] second daughter and child of Oliver and
Rachel (Cleveland) Hamblin, m. in Brookfield, Vt., July 4,
1806, Samuel Clifford, son of Samuel and Mrs. Sophia (Elliott)
[Bean] Clifford. He was b. in Buscawen, N. H., Dec. 8,
1780; d. in Danbury, N. H., June 4, 1857. She d. in Danbury, N. H., Oct. 13, 1830.

Children, all b. in Danbury, N. H.:

1. Elijah Miner,[7] b. April 24, 1807; d. Sept. 10, 1875.
2. Oliver Hamblin,[7] b. Jan. 18, 1809; res. Medfield, Mass.
3. Polly,[7] b. Oct. 14, 1810; d. Aug. 22, 1830.
4. Sophia,[7] b. Jan. 31, 1813; d. July 11, 1817.

William Plummer,[7] b. Sept. 24, 1814; res. Ware, Mass.
Samuel,[7] b. Feb. 26, 1817; res. Eugene City, Oregon; unm.
7. Sophronia,[7] b. Sept. 30, 1820; d. April 13, 1843.
8. Lorena,[7] b. July 4, 1825; res. Waltham, Mass.

Joel Hamblin,[6] eldest son and third child of Oliver and Rachel (Cleveland) Hamblin, m. in East Brookfield, Vt., Jan. 1833, Mrs. Phila (Maxfield) Dewey, dau. of Stephen and Sarah (Hurd) Maxfield. She was b. in Bradford, N. H., July 24, 1801; d. in Calais, Vt., April 30, 1868. He d. in Hardwick, Vt., April 18, 1859.

Children, both b. in Brookfield, Vt. :

1. Orilla,[7] b. Jan. 6, 1837; res. North Montpelier, Vt.
2. Ellen,[7] b. May 30, 1839; res. Boonsboro', Iowa.

James Hamblin,[6] second son and fifth child of Oliver and Rachel (Cleveland) Hamblin, m. in Brookfield, Vt., Jan. 4, 1816, Lovisa Bigelow, dau. of Josiah and Lucy (Waters) Bigelow. She was b. in Brookfield, Vt., Feb. 22, 1791 ; d. in Brookfield, Vt., July 22, 1866. He d. in Brookfield, Vt., April 2, 1865. Farmer.

Children, all born in Brookfield, Vt. :

1. Nancy,[7] b. Dec. 19, 1816; d. Jan. 9, 1839.
2. Laura,[7] b. Feb. 20, 1818; d. April 4, 1818.
3. Lydia,[7] b. Feb. 8, 1819; d. April 5, 1846.
4. Lucy,[7] b. Sept. 25, 1822; d. Dec. 3, 1843.
5. Philena,[7] b. Nov. 19, 1824; d. Dec. 3, 1840.
6. Rowena,[7] b. May 17, 1827; drowned June 3, 1837.
7. James Monroe,[7] b. April 30, 1829; res. Brookfield, Vt.
8. Lovisa,[7] b. Nov. 17, 1830; d. May 30, 1866.
9. Eliza,[7] b. Feb. 4, 1833; d. Nov. 8, 1857.

James M. Hamblin,[7] the only son and surviving child, resides at the old homestead, in East Brookfield, Vt.

Nancy Hamblin,[6] youngest daughter and child of Oliver and Rachel (Cleveland) Hamblin, m. first, in Brookfield, Vt., March 17, 1814, Folsom Bean, son of John and Polly

(Garvin) Bean. He was b. in Buscawen, N. H., March 2, 1789; d. in Danbury, N. H., Jan. 1, 1851. She m. second, in East Brookfield, Vt., Oct. 1, 1857, her cousin, Alvan Hovey, son of Rev. Samuel and Abigail (Cleveland) Hovey. He was b. in Lyme, N. H., March 3, 1779; d. in Brookfield, Vt., Jan. 29, 1864. She d. in Enfield, N. H., Aug. 15, 1868.

Children, by first husband, Folsom Bean, all b. in Danbury, N. H.:

1. Lovisa,[7] b. Sept. 8, 1815; res. Concord, N. H.
2. Elvira,[7] b. Dec. 22, 1816; d. April 27, 1864.
3. Abigail Hamblin,[7] b. Aug. 24, 1818; res. Enfield, N. H.
4. Joel Hamblin,[7] b. Aug. 11, 1821; res. Hawleysville, Iowa.
5. Lovina Hoyt,[7] b. Aug. 1, 1823; res. Danbury, N. H.
6. Susan Cass,[7] b. April 30, 1829; res. Frankfort, Iowa.
7. Frank Gilbert,[7] b. Feb. 17, 1831; res. Wallace, Iowa.

(For further genealogical information as to the Hamblin branch, see **Appendix H**.)

PERSIS CLEVELAND,[5] the seventh child of Benjamin and Rachel Cleveland, was b. in Canterbury, Conn., Jan. 18, 1752. She m. in Pomfret, Conn., in 1772, Edward Payne, son of Edward and Lois (Kinney) Payne. He was b. in Pomfret, Conn., June 10, 1750; d. in Montague, Mass., June 19, 1845. Farmer. She d. in same place, March 30, 1834.

They had a family of eleven children, as follows:

1. James,[6] b. Dec. 18, 1774; d. April 29, 1834.
2. Edward,[6] b. Oct. 2, 1776; d. Aug. 24, 1866.
3. Lois,[6] b. May 22, 1778; d. Jan. 13, 1809.
4. Lebbeus,[6] b. March 1, 1780; d. Dec. 5, 1782.
5. Alvin,[6] b. Jan. 19, 1782; d. Dec. 11, 1843.
6. Lebbeus,[6] (again), b. Dec. 1, 1783; d. July 28, 1844.
7. Persis,[6] b. Oct. 1, 1785; d. Feb. 1, 1857.
8. Oren,[6] b. June 1, 1787; d. Sept. 21, 1873.
9. John,[6] (Dr.), b. July 1, 1789; d. March 16, 1873.
10. Seril,[6] b. April 28, 1791; d. Oct. 20, 1829, unm.
11. Ira,[6] b. Sept. 29, 1793; d. May 8, 1873.

Persis Cleveland,[5] was of small stature, fair complexion, raven black hair and black eyes. She was very ambitious, with no dower except her beauty, and her marriage into one of the aristocratic families of Connecticut was bitterly opposed by some of her husband's relatives. She was a devoted wife and mother, though somewhat fretful as she grew in years; aided her husband to acquire a handsome property, and reared a large family to habits of energetic industry.

She and her husband were buried in the old cemetery some distance from the village, in the eastern part of the township. The inscriptions upon the marble are as follows:

"Edward Payne, died Jan. 19, 1845, aged 95 years. Erected by Oren Payne."
"Persis, wife of Edward Payne, died March 30, 1834, aged 82 years."

James Payne,[6] eldest son and child of Edward and Persis (Cleveland) Payne, m. in Wendell, Franklin county, Mass., July 4, 1798, Mercy Goddard, dau. of Ebenezer and Hannah (Deth) Goddard. She was b. in Wendell, Mass., Nov. 8, 1778; d. in Richland, Oswego county, N. Y., Oct. 19, 1850. He d. in Richland, N. Y., April 29, 1834. He removed from Montague, Mass., his native place, to Eaton, Madison county, N. Y., in 1809, and eleven years afterwards to Nelson, in the same county, where his youngest child was born. He d. of consumption, after a long illness. Farmer.

Children:
1. Hannah,[7] b. May 1, 1799; res. Fond du Lac, Wis.
2. Brigham,[7] b. Jan. 3, 1801; res. Garnett, Anderson Co., Kan.
3. Sophia,[7] b. July 5, 1804; d. Jan. 31, 1833.
4. Lucinda,[7] b. May 16, 1806; d. June 21, 1861.
5. Samuel Stebbins,[7] b. June 21, 1808; d. April 24, 1834.
6. Persis,[7] b. April 20, 1810; res. Nelson, N. Y.
7. James,[7] b. March 24, 1812; d. May 6, 1855.
8. Lyman,[7] b. April 28, 1814; d. June 10, 1817.
9. Henrietta,[7] b. June 18, 1816; res. Daysville, Oswego Co., N. Y.
10. Selina,[7] b. April 6, 1819; res. Burr Oak, Mich.
11. Lyman,[7] (again), b. May 23, 1822; res. Texas, Oswego Co., N. Y.

Edward Payne,[6] second son and child of Edward and Persis (Cleveland) Payne, m. in Montague, Mass., Oct. 5,

1807, Susan Bancroft, dau. of Kendall and Tabit Bancroft. She was b. in Montague, Mass., May 1 in Montague, Jan. 10, 1856. He d. in Montague, 1866. Farmer.

Children, all b. in Montague:

1. Mary,[7] b. Nov. 9, 1809; res. Montague, Mass.
2. Nathan Cleveland,[7] b. Nov. 5, 1812; d. Aug. 24, 18—.
3. John Fox,[7] b. Aug. 13, 1815; res. Montague, Mass.
4. Edwin,[7] b. Dec. 16, 1816; d. July 19, 1818.

John F. Payne,[7] a prosperous farmer, resides within a mile of the village of Montague.

Alvin Payne,[6] fourth son and fifth child of Edward and Persis (Cleveland) Payne, m. first, in Dana, Mass., Aug. 12, 1806, Betsey Woodward, dau. of Benjamin and Betsey (Hall) Woodward. She was b. in Dana, Mass., May 12, 1784; d. in Montague, Mass., Dec. 17, 1807. He m. second, in Montague, Mass., Fanny Sibley. He d. in Montague, Mass., Dec. 11, 1843.

Child, by wife Betsey:

1. Benjamin,[7] b. June 3, 1807; res. Montague, Mass.

Lebbeus Payne,[6] the fifth son and sixth child of Edward and Persis (Cleveland) Payne, m. in Montague, Mass., Jan. 1, 1816, Martha Locke, dau. of William and Martha Locke. She was b. in Montague, Mass., June 30, 1790; d. in Montague, Mass., Dec. 6, 1820. He d. in Montague, Mass., July 28, 1844. Farmer.

Children:

1. Locke,[7] b. Oct. 20, 1816; res. Montague, Mass.
2. Stephen,[7] b. Sept. 2, 1819; d. Aug. 8, 1840.

Persis Payne,[6] second daughter and seventh child of Edward and Persis (Cleveland) Payne, m. in Leverett, Franklin county, Mass., May 1, 1808, Eluna Martin, son of John and Huldah (Richardson) Martin. He was b. in Attleborough,

Philenda Miller White,[7] sixth daughter and seventh child of Daniel and Clarissa (Cleveland) White, b. in Barkhamstead, Conn., June 11, 1814, m. in Winsted, Conn., Sept. 6, 1835, Elizur Graves Perry, son of Robert and Christiana (Beebe) Perry. He was b. in Oneida, N. Y., Sept. 20, 1809; d. in Fairview, Jones county, Iowa, Oct. 6, 1858. She d. in Ion, Allemakee county, Iowa, Nov. 6, 1857.

Children:

[Janette Martha,[8] a lineal descendant of the 8th generation from Moses,[1] but only an adopted daughter in this family, b. in Winsted, Conn., Feb. 7, 1836, m. first, in Ion, Iowa, June 19, 1858, George Perry, son of Ira and Catherine (Reynolds) Perry. He was b. in Fleming, Cayuga county, N. Y., April 30, 1834; d. June 12, 1861. Child: Ferdinand George,[9] b. Feb. 15, 1859. She m. second, in Winsted, Conn., Dec. 10, 1866, George William Hotchkin, son of Frederic and Nancy (Mattoon) Hotchkin. He was b. Jan. 12, 1836. Children: 1. Walter Raymond,[9] b. July 15, 1872. 2. William Henry,[9] b. Jan. 11, 1874.]

1. Edwin Robert,[8] b. in Winsted, Conn., March 14, 1838; d. in the army, at Annapolis, Md., Nov. 29, 1863, unm.
2. Philo Beebe,[8] b. in Winsted, Conn., April 7, 1840, m. in Anderson, Texas, June 15, 1863, Mary Elizabeth Norton, daughter of William Douglass and Martha (Williams) Norton. She was b. in Bedford, Tenn., April 9, 1844; d. in Navasota, Texas, Jan. 16, 1872. He d. in Navasota, Texas, June 10, 1874. Children: 1. Benjamin Frederic,[9] b. Jan. 27, 1865; d. March 5, 1866. 2. William Douglass,[9] b. Feb. 9, 1867; d. June 13, 1867. 3. Mary Grace,[9] b. Jan. 22, 1871.
3. Lavinia Hall,[8] b. in Winsted, Conn., Oct. 12, 1843; d. May 31, 1844.
4. Frederic Kellogg,[8] b. in Winsted, Conn., Jan. 1, 1847, m. in Springfield, Mass., Oct. 15, 1866, Sarah Maria Lane, dau. of Hosea and Laura (Benjamin) Lane. She was b. in Union Vale, Dutchess county, N. Y., Aug. 2, 1845. He is a printer; res. Springfield, Mass. Children: 1. Leslie Edwin,[9] b. in Hartford, Conn., Aug. 4, 1867. 2. Philo Beebe,[9] b. in Springfield, Mass., Sept. 22, 1877.

5. Lavinia White,* b. in Winsted, Conn., June 11, 1850, m. in Winsted, Conn., May 18, 1871, George William Ball, son of William and Sarah Shattuck (Walker) Ball. He was b. in Townsend, Mass., Oct. 18, 1843. She d. in Winsted, Conn., April 13, 1872. They had one child, Eva,⁹ b. March 5, 1872; d. March 9, 1872.
6. Philenda,⁸ b. Jan. 24, 1852.
7. Martha,⁸ b. May 6, 1854; d. Aug. 31, 1855.

Pembroke White,⁷ youngest daughter and child of Daniel and Clarissa (Cleveland) White, b. in Winsted, Conn., Sept. 18, 1819, m. in Fairview, Jones county, Iowa, July 4, 1860, Caroline Frances Perry, dau. of Ira and Catherine (Reynolds) Perry. She was b. in Fleming, Cayuga county, N. Y., March 11, 1842. He is a sales agent ; res. McGregor, Iowa.

Children, all b. in Iowa :

1. Mary Catherine,⁸ b. Aug. 1, 1861.
2. Jane Caroline,⁸ b. Sept. 9, 1865.
3. Benjamin Lyon,⁸ b. June 8, 1868.
4. Edward Le Grand,⁸ b. Jan. 5, 1874.
5. Bessie Alice,⁸ b. Nov. 3, 1875.

ALEXANDER CLEVELAND,⁶ second son and third child of Rufus and Mary (Chamberlain) Cleveland, b. in East Windsor, Conn., Oct. 16, 1783, m. in Barkhamstead, Conn., Feb. 25, 1805, Mary Kinne, dau. of Rev. Aaron and Anna (Morgan) Kinne. She was b. in Groton, Conn., Aug. 16, 1777; d. in Winsted, Conn., May 13, 1860. He d. in same place, Sept. 5, 1860. They had four children, as follows, all b. in Barkhamstead, Litchfield county, Conn. :

1. Son,⁷ b. Dec. 14, 1806; d. Dec. 14, 1806.
2. Rufus,⁷ b. Dec. 18, 1807.
3. Alexander Pitt,⁷ b. Aug. 1, 1810; d. July 31, 1861.
4. Chester,⁷ b. Jan. 5, 1812; d. Jan. 23, 1812.

Alexander Cleveland,⁶ was a man of small stature, and decided opinions. He represented his town in the Legislature of the State several terms, and was justly esteemed for his sterling integrity. Few men could equal him as a teller of stories and anecdotes, and his fund of them seemed inexhaustible. He was a Whig in politics, and a Calvinist in religion, and ready to defend his views whenever attacked. His death was greatly lamented by his kindred and friends.

RUFUS CLEVELAND,[7] second son of Alexander and Mary (Kinne) Cleveland, b. in Barkhamstead, Conn., Dec. 18, 1807, m. first, in Winchester, Conn., Dec. 9, 1830, Sally Ann Burnham, dau. of Daniel and Clarissa (Carr) Burnham. She was b. in Colebrook, Conn., March 29, 1803, and d. in Barkhamstead, Conn., April 17, 1854. He m. second, in Austerlitz, Columbia county, N. Y., Nov. 2, 1854, his cousin, Mrs. Mary Ann Mallory, dau. of William and Joanna (Church) Kinne. She was b. in Great Barrington, Mass., Dec. 24, 1807; d. in Barkhamstead, Conn., Feb. 28, 1871, without issue.

Children, by first wife:

1. George Brainard,[8] b. Dec. 11, 1831.
2. Rufus Baker,[8] b. Jan. 5, 1834.
3. Daniel Burnham,[8] b. April 5, 1837; d. May 5, 1837.
4. Chester Dwight,[8] b. Oct. 22, 1838.
5. Caroline Elizabeth,[8] b. April 3, 1840.
6. Edwin Fayette,[8] ⎱ b. Sept. 5, 1842; d. Aug. 8, 1851.
7. Ellen Annette,[8] ⎰ b. Sept. 5, 1842; d. Aug. 21, 1861.

Rufus Cleveland,[7] is a farmer by occupation, and resides on "Wallen's Hill," Barkhamstead, (Winsted Society), Conn. He has represented his town in the State Legislature several terms, and filled various offices of trust conferred upon him with strict fidelity. His devoted love and kindness to his second wife, who became entirely blind for several years before her death, only serves to show that under a somewhat rough exterior, he possesses the tenderness of a woman combined with the best characteristics of the true gentleman. Though he has passed the allotted age of man, he is still vigorous and hearty, and content to spend the evening of his days among the hills of Litchfield county, and in sight of his birthplace.

GEORGE B. CLEVELAND,[8] eldest son of Rufus and Sally Ann (Burnham) Cleveland, b. in Barkhamstead, Conn., Dec.

11, 1831, m. in Winsted, Conn., April 16, 1855, Caroline Elizabeth Guernsey, dau. of Joseph H. and Elizabeth (Talmadge) Guernsey. She was b. in Barkhamstead, Conn., Nov. 9, 1837. He served as a member of the State Legislature one or more terms. Farmer ; res. Portland, Conn.
Children :
1. Jane Elizabeth,[9] b. June 17, 1857.
2. Charles Dwight,[9] b. June 18, 1859.
3. Ida May,[9] b. April 12, 1866.
4. Grace Louise,[9] b. Dec. 3, 1873.
5. Rufus George,[9] b. March 11, 1875.

RUFUS B. CLEVELAND,[8] second son of Rufus and Sally Ann (Burnham) Cleveland, b. in Barkhamstead, Conn., Jan. 5, 1834, m. in Winchester, Conn., July 2, 1855, Mary Ann Shores, dau. of William and Mary (Rogers) Shores. She was b. in Sparta, N. J., June 2, 1833. He is a farmer ; res. Winsted, Conn.
Children :
1. Ada Belle,[9] b. May 13, 1857.
2. Anna Cora,[9] b. Sept. 23, 1859.
3. Mary Ellen,[9] b. Feb. 27, 1861; d. May —, 1863.
4. Katie Louise,[9] b. March 28, 1863; d. May 31, 1871.
5. Freddie Baker,[9] b. March 28, 1868.

CHESTER D. CLEVELAND,[8] fourth son of Rufus and Sally Ann (Burnham) Cleveland, b. in Winchester, Conn., Oct. 22, 1838, m. in Oshkosh, Wis., Oct. 20, 1869, Catherine Hughes, dau. of Owen and Sarah (Lloyd) Hughes. She was b. in Cheshire, Eng., Oct. 20, 1842. He is a lawyer ; res. Oshkosh.
Children :
1. Chester Dwight,[9] b. Aug. 24, 1871.
2. Catherine Caroline,[9] b. May 26, 1873.

CAROLINE E. CLEVELAND,[8] eldest daughter of Rufus and Sally Ann (Burnham) Cleveland, b. in Barkhamstead, Conn., April 3, 1840, m. in same place, Oct. 10, 1865, Warren Cady Crane, son of Austin and Eunice Clarinda (Rogers) Crane.

He was b. in Barkhamstead, Conn., July 18, 1841. A retired merchant, formerly of the dry goods house of Harris, Hartley & Co., Broadway, New York; res. Tremont, N. Y.

Children:
1. Frank Warren,⁹ b. Feb. 8, 1867.
2. Ellen Cleveland,⁹ b. Oct. 26, 1869.
3. Harris Hartley,⁹ b. March 11, 1873.
4. Clarence Austin,⁹ b. Oct. 18, 1874.
5. Edith Anna,⁹ b. Nov. 13, 1876.

ALEXANDER P. CLEVELAND,⁷ third son and child of Alexander and Mary (Kinne) Cleveland, b. in Barkhamstead, Conn., Aug. 1, 1810, m. in Winsted, Conn., March 24, 1835, Aurelia Smith, dau. of Dea. Elisha and Sally (Tyler) Smith. She was b. in Winchester, Conn., Aug. 30, 1813. He d. July 31, 1861. She is living at the old homestead on Wallen's Hill. He was a farmer.

Children:
1. Anna Kinne,⁸ b. May 17, 1838; d. March 25, 1859.
2. Henry Elisha,⁸ b. March 16, 1840.
3. Sarah,⁸ b. June 16, 1844.
4. Zebina Smith,⁸ b. Nov. 6, 1845.

Alexander P. Cleveland,⁷ also represented his township in the State Legislature, though less of a politician than his brother Rufus.⁷ He was a plain, unostentatious man of acknowledged piety, combined with the highest moral principles, and a most exemplary Christian life. Of him may be said in the words of the poet Halleck:

> "None knew him but to love him,
> Or named him but to praise."

A plain marble slab marks his grave in Winsted Cemetery, where so many of his kindred are buried.

ANNA K. CLEVELAND,⁸ eldest child of Alexander P. and Aurelia (Smith) Cleveland, b. in Barkhamstead, Conn., May 17, 1838, m. in same place, Sept. 27, 1857, Riley William Smith, son of Lorraine and Polly (Twining) Smith. He was b. in

Tolland, Mass., Jan. 22, 1836. She d. in Winsted, Conn., March 25, 1859, surviving the birth of her infant but a few days.
Child :
1. Son,[9] b. March 7, 1859; d. March 7, 1859.

HENRY E. CLEVELAND,[8] eldest son and second child of Alexander P. and Aurelia (Smith) Cleveland, b. in Barkhamstead, Conn., March 16, 1840, m. in Winchester, Conn., Dec. 29, 1866, Sarah Jane Hine, dau. of Heman Clark and Emeline (Buckley) Hine. She was b. in. Winchester, Conn., Dec. 29, 1845. He is a farmer; res. Barkhamstead, Conn.
Children :
1. Alexander Hine,[9] b. Feb. 8, 1869.
2. Ellen Aurelia,[9] b. Sept. 28, 1873; d. April 11, 1875.

SARAH CLEVELAND,[8] second daughter and third child of Alexander P. and Aurelia (Smith) Cleveland, b. in Barkhamstead, Conn., June 16, 1844, m. in Winsted, Conn., March 20, 1877, Benjamin Chaplin Perkins, son of Augustus Messenger and Ruth Susan (Snow) Perkins. He was b. in Becket, Berkshire county, Mass., March 27, 1845. Farmer ; res. West Winsted, Conn. No children.

ZEBINA S. CLEVELAND,[8] youngest son and child of Alexander P. and Aurelia (Smith) Cleveland, b. in Barkhamstead, Conn., Nov. 6, 1845, m. in same place, Oct. 16, 1872, Frances Rebecca Beecher, dau. of Amos and Phebe (Hart) Beecher. She was b. in Barkhamstead, Conn., Aug. 23, 1845. Farmer; res. Winsted, Conn.
Children :
1. Sarah Russell,[9] b. Sept. 4, 1876.
2. Willie,[9]) b. Feb. 19, 1879.
3. Gracie,[9]) b. Feb. 19, 1879.

[The family register of my father and his descendants follows next in order.]

OREN CLEVELAND,[6] third son and fourth child of Rufus and Mary (Chamberlain) Cleveland, b. in East Windsor,

Conn., May 3, 1785, m. in Enfield, Conn., March 5, 1806, Esther Allen, dau. of Moses and Mary (Adams) Allen. She was b. in Enfield, Conn., Sept. 24, 1785; d. in Huntsburgh, Geauga county, Ohio, May 21, 1869. He is living in Cleveland, Ohio.
Children were eleven in number:

1. Oren Alexander,[7] b. Jan. 1, 1807; d. March 24, 1809.
2. Esther Allen,[7] b. Aug. 24, 1808.
3. Jemima Maria,[7] b. Oct. 18, 1810.
4. James Chamberlain,[7] b. Feb. 26, 1813.
5. Oren Luther,[7] b. March 26, 1815.
6. Mary Clarissa,[7] b. April 8, 1817.
7. William Charles,[7] b. Sept. 8, 1819.
8. Moses Allen,[7] b. Oct. 30, 1822.
9. Son,[7] b. Oct. 31, 1825; d. Oct. 31, 1825.
10. Edward Hooker,[7] b. May 15, 1827.
11. Horace Gillette,[7] b. Jan. 3, 1832.

Oren Cleveland,[6] was brought up by his maternal grandparents at Warehouse Point, East Windsor, Conn. A good student at the academy in the village, he graduated with credit to his preceptors and himself. After his marriage and removal to Litchfield county, Conn., he was much sought for as a school teacher, and taught successfully in various places two summers and fourteen winters. He entered the employ of the firm of Belknap & Hammersly, Booksellers in Hartford, as a canvasser, and traveled over a considerable portion of the New England States. He also sold clocks for Riley Whiting of Winsted, extensively in the New England States and in Eastern New York and Pennsylvania. In 1839 he came to Geauga county, Ohio, to be near his eldest daughter, where he resided up to the death of his wife in 1869. In the fall of that year he took up his residence with his youngest son, a merchant in Cleveland, Ohio. In stature he is about five feet eight inches, and in his prime of life of ruddy complexion, with black hair and dark blue eyes. He was a superior horseman, and was accounted the finest "trooper" in his company. His kindness of heart, combined with a natural politeness of manners and rare conversational powers, not to omit to mention a fund of anecdotes and incidents of travel, made him hosts of friends wherever he went.

Although nearly a century has passed since he first saw the light of day, he still enjoys a fair degree of health, with his mental faculties unimpaired. His memory of persons and past events is certainly very remarkable, to say the least. He has invariably acted with the Whig and Republican parties, though never radical in partisanship. About the year 1814 he united with the Congregational Society in Winsted, Conn., and continued without other ecclesiastical connection until 1872, when, after much reading and reflection, he was confirmed by Rt. Rev. G. T. Bedell, in Grace (Episcopal) Church in Cleveland, Ohio. Contented and happy, in peace and charity with all men, he cheerfully awaits his Master's call from the church militant on earth to the church triumphant in heaven.

His children who grew to adult age were nine in number, and all living.

(For the ancestry of Esther Allen, his wife, see Appendix K.)

ESTHER A. CLEVELAND,[7] eldest daughter and second child of Oren and Esther (Allen) Cleveland, b. in Barkhamstead, Conn., Aug. 24, 1808, m. in New Hartford, Litchfield county, Conn., May 4, 1835, Michael Barnes, son of Michael and Charlotte (Hendricks) Barnes. He was b. in New Hartford, Conn., June 17, 1804; d. in Huntsburgh, Geauga county, Ohio, Dec. 5, 1870. A very successful farmer and prominent man in the county.

Children, all b. in Huntsburgh, Ohio :

1. Son,[a] b. April —, 1836; d. April —, 1836.
2. Oren Michael,[b] b. April 25, 1837, m. in Huntsburgh, Ohio, Jan. 1, 1864, Lucy Ann Kile, eldest dau. of Philander and Sarah Beaman (Clark) Kile. She was b. in Huntsburgh, Ohio, Dec. 16, 1840. He is a farmer; res. Huntsburgh, Ohio. No children, except an adopted daughter, Isabel Alice Smith, b. April 11, 1859.

3. Charlotte Esther,⁵ b. Aug. 13, 1839, m. in Huntsburgh, Ohio, Dec. 1, 1861, Asahel Watson Strong, son of Baxter and Juliana (Strong) Strong. He was b. in Huntsburgh, Ohio, May 16, 1832. Farmer, and for many years a Justice of the Peace; res. Huntsburgh, Ohio. Children, both b. in Huntsburgh: 1. Daughter,⁹ b. May —, 1866; d. May —, 1866. 2. Oren Henry,⁹ b. May 14, 1868; d. Jan. 22, 1869. They afterwards adopted a little boy whom they called Harris Watson, a son of Cassius Marcus and Jennie (Worley) Rose, of Cleveland, Ohio, where he was b. July 16, 1868, and d. in Huntsburgh, June 14, 1877. He was a lad of much promise.

4. Virgil Taylor,⁵ b. Sept. 13, 1842, m. in Claridon, Geauga county, Ohio, June 13, 1866, Ella Louisa Cummings, dau. of Donald McIntosh and Julia Ann (Ball) Cummings. She was b. in Greene, Trumbull county, Ohio, Oct. 20, 1846. He is a farmer and stock-raiser; res. Huntsburgh, on the old homestead of his parents. Children, all b. in Huntsburgh: 1. Wilson Arthur,⁹ b. Sept. 9, 1867. 2. Herbert Virgil,⁹ b. Sept. 18, 1869. 3. Arlington Edward,⁹ b. Jan. 29, 1871, d. Oct. 4, 1873. 4. George Earle,⁹ b. Dec. 29, 1875. 5 and 6. (Twins.) Franklin Michael,⁹ and Frederic Donald,⁹ b. Nov. 26, 1877.

5. Hubert Arthur,⁵ b. Oct. 20, 1844; d. July 7, 1864, from injuries received by a kick of a horse. A young man of unusual promise, his death, so sudden and unexpected, was a terrible blow to the family. He survived but about eighteen hours after being brought in from the meadow where he was fatally hurt by a frightened horse attached to a horse-rake which he was using. His untimely end at the threshold of manhood was an occurrence deeply and universally regretted in the community.

JEMIMA M. CLEVELAND,⁷ second daughter and third child of Oren and Esther (Allen) Cleveland, b. in Barkhamstead, Conn., Oct. 18, 1810, m. first, in New Hartford, Conn., Oct. 11, 1836, Reuel Arnold Watson, son of Harvey and Sally (Wells) Watson. He was b. in New Hartford, Conn., March 11, 1812; d. in Torringford, Conn., Aug. 21, 1851. She m. second, in Avon, Conn., June 12, 1853, Grant Thorburn, son of James and Elizabeth (Fairlie) Thorburn. He was b. in Dalkeith, Scotland, Feb. 18, 1773; d. in New Haven, Conn., Jan. 21, 1863. She m. third, in New Haven, Conn., Sept. 1, 1863, David Curtis Mitchell, son of David and Agnes (Kilpatrick) Mitchell. He was b. in Kilmarnock, Scotland, July 11, 1792; d. in New Haven, Conn., Dec. 10, 1872. No children. She is now living in Winsted, Conn. Her second husband was for many years a resident of New York City, and well known as an author, under the *nom de plume* of "Lawrie Todd."

JAMES C. CLEVELAND,[7] second son and fourth child of Oren and Esther (Allen) Cleveland, b. in Barkhamstead, Conn., Feb. 26, 1813, m. first, in New Hartford, Conn., May 29, 1839, Lucy Watson, dau. of Levi and Lucy (Olmstead) Watson. She was b. in New Hartford, Conn., March 14, 1806; d. in Torringford, Conn., Sept. 29, 1862. He m. second, in Torringford, Conn., Oct. 2, 1864, Mrs. Sarah (Judd) [Roberts] Manchester, dau. of Ezekiel and Avis (Palmer) Judd. She was b. in Canaan, Conn., June 3, 1801; d. in Simsbury, Conn., March 16, 1876. He is living in Newbury, Geauga county, Ohio. Farmer.

Children, by wife Lucy, all born in New Hartford:

1. John Robert McDowell,[8] b. Feb. 20, 1840.
2. Abby Kelley,[9] b. Aug. 18, 1842.
3. Lydia Maria,[9] b. Jan. 6, 1845.
4. James Emanuel,[9] b. Jan. 19, 1851; d. June 16, 1851.

JOHN R. McD. CLEVELAND,[8] eldest son of James C. and Lucy (Watson) Cleveland, b. Feb. 20, 1840; m. in New Hartford, Conn., March 14, 1864, Mrs. Ursuline (Roberts) Perkins, dau. of Pelatiah and Sarah (Judd) Roberts, and sister to Rev. Warren H. Roberts, of Lafayette, Ind. She was b. in Winchester, Conn., May 29, 1836. Divorced. He is a farmer and speculator; res. New Hartford, Conn.

Child:

1. Lucy Charlotte,[9] b. April 21, 1867.

ABBY K. CLEVELAND,[8] eldest daughter of James C. and Lucy (Watson) Cleveland, b. Aug. 18, 1842, m. in Harwinton, Conn., Nov. 25, 1875, Israel Jordan Smith, son of Jeremiah and Eunice (Churchill) Smith. He was b. in Harwinton, Conn., Dec. 11, 1833. No children. Farmer; res. Colebrook, Conn.

LYDIA M. CLEVELAND,[8] second daughter of James C. and Lucy (Watson) Cleveland, b. Jan. 6, 1845, m. in Huntsburgh, Geauga county, Ohio, Feb. 28, 1869, Elijah Hope, son of Edwin and Elizabeth (Bayliss) Hope. He was b. in North Leach, Gloucestershire, Eng., Dec. 31, 1840. Farmer; res. Burton, Geauga county, Ohio.
Children:
1. William Allison,[9] b. in Mentor, Ohio, Dec. 26, 1869.
2. Edward Henry,[9] b. in Kirtland, Ohio, July 5, 1871.
3. Olive Maria,[9] b. in Kirtland, Ohio, Aug. 6, 1873.
4. Calvin Bayliss,[9] b. in Claridon, Ohio, Oct. 27, 1875.

OREN L. CLEVELAND,[7] third son and fifth child of Oren and Esther (Allen) Cleveland, b. in Barkhamstead, Conn., March 26, 1815, m. in New Brunswick, N. J., Sept. 9, 1846, Catherine Elizabeth Nighmaster, dau. of John and Phebe (Smith) Nighmaster. She was b. in Somerset county, N. J., June 28, 1825. He is a collector; res. 330 Union Street, Brooklyn, N. Y.
Children:
1. George Hull,[8] (Rev.), b. in New York City, May 27, 1851.
2. Ada Frances,[8] b. in Brooklyn, Nov. 22, 1854.

REV. GEO. H. CLEVELAND[8] is a minister of the Dutch Reformed Church in Annandale, N. J.

MARY C. CLEVELAND,[7] third daughter and sixth child of Oren and Esther (Allen) Cleveland, b. in Winchester, Conn., April 8, 1817, m. in Huntsburgh, Geauga county, Ohio, April 14, 1864, Edwin Hope, son of William and Elizabeth (Olliffe) Hope. He was b. in Fullbrook, Gloucester, Eng., March 2, 1812. No children. Farmer; res. Burton, Ohio.

WILLIAM C. CLEVELAND,[7] fourth son and seventh child of Oren and Esther (Allen) Cleveland, b. in Barkhamstead, Conn., Sept. 8, 1819. An invalid—never married; resides with his sister, in Burton, Ohio.

MOSES A. CLEVELAND,[7] fifth son and eighth child of Oren and Esther (Allen) Cleveland, b. in Winchester, Conn., Oct. 30, 1822; m. first, in Worcester, Mass., Oct. 10, 1842, Eliza Ann Williams, dau. of Peter Bent and Elizabeth Adams (Moore) Williams. She was b. in Worcester, Mass., Feb. 27, 1824; d. in Worcester, April 5, 1855. He m. second, in Sterling, Mass., Oct. 7, 1857, Mary Emeline Littlefield, dau. of Henry and Tamar D. (Henry) Littlefield. She was b. in Boston, Mass., Aug. 6, 1836. He is a builder; res. Huntsburgh, Ohio. Served under Gen. Banks in the late war.

Children, by wife Eliza Ann:

1. Frances Ann,[8] b. Feb. 28, 1844.
2. Sarah Amarett,[8] b. Sept. 9, 1847.
3. Ellen Maria,[8] b. March 10, 1850.
4. Charles Marvin,[8] b. July 12, 1852.
5. Mary Eliza,[8] b. Feb. 21, 1855.

by wife Mary Emeline:

6. Sumner Allen,[8] b. March 28, 1863.
7. Grant Thorburn,[8] b. July 2, 1873.
8. Oren Henry,[8] b. Nov. 4, 1875.

FRANCES A. CLEVELAND,[8] eldest daughter of Moses A. and Eliza A. (Williams) Cleveland, b. Feb. 28, 1844, m. in Kirtland, Lake county, Ohio, June 6, 1867, Andrew Johnson McWethey, son of Amos and Elizabeth (Johnson) McWethey. He was b. in Kirtland, Ohio, Feb. 10, 1844. Farmer; res. Kirtland, Ohio.

Children, both b. in Kirtland:

1. Mary Elizabeth,[9] b. March 14, 1870.
2. Charles Arthur,[9] b. July 14, 1873; d. March 8, 1874.

SARAH A. CLEVELAND,[8] second daughter of Moses A. and Eliza A. (Williams) Cleveland, b. Sept. 9, 1847, m. in Kirt-

land, Ohio, June 6, 1867, Willard Edgar Tyler, son of Hiram and Sally Ann (Travis) Tyler. He was b. in Chardon, Geauga county, Ohio, April 28, 1847. Farmer; res. Concord, Ohio.
Children:
1. Viola Ann,[9] b. in Concord, Ohio, Jan. 22, 1869.
2. Elva May,[9] b. in Chardon, Ohio, Dec. 21, 1870.
3. Lucien Eugene,[9] b. in Concord, Ohio, March 23, 1873.
4. Mary Estella,[9] b. in Kirtland, Ohio, June 21, 1875; d. Aug. 19, 1877.

ELLEN M. CLEVELAND,[8] third daughter of Moses A. and Eliza A. (Williams) Cleveland, b. March 10, 1850, m. in Holden, Mass., Sept. 11, 1870, Albert Goff, son of Sirbina and Almira (Dunham) Goff. He was b. in Holden, Mass., Nov. 30, 1849. Farmer; res. Holden, Mass.
Children, both b. in Holden:
1. Hattie Mabel,[9] b. April 2, 1871.
2. Albert Walter,[9] b. Sept. 3, 1875.

MARY E. CLEVELAND,[8] fourth daughter and fifth child of Moses A. and Eliza A. (Williams) Cleveland, b. Feb. 21, 1855, m. in Burton, Geauga county, Ohio, Dec. 18, 1873, Marvin Robinson Moss, son of William Chapin and Maria Jane (Robinson) Moss. He was b. in Huntsburgh, Ohio, Aug. 23, 1854. Farmer; res. Huntsburgh, Ohio.
Children, both b. in Huntsburgh:
1. Esther Maria,[9] b. Sept. 11, 1874.
2. Clifton Beardsley,[9] b. Feb. 5, 1876.

EDWARD H. CLEVELAND,[7] seventh son and tenth child of Oren and Esther (Allen) Cleveland, b. in Barkhamstead, Conn., May 15, 1827, m. in Thompson, Geauga county, Ohio, Dec. 14, 1852, Mary Ann Broughton, dau. of Rev. Job and Ann (Mattock) Broughton. She was b. in Canajoharie, N. Y., Oct. 4, 1829. He is a builder; res. Mentor, Lake county, Ohio. He was associated for a short time with the firm of Whelpley & Cleveland, merchants, at Kirtland, Lake county, Ohio.

Children:
1. Mary Lydia,⁸ b. June 24, 1854.
2. George Allen,⁸ b. Sept. 26, 1857.
3. Esther Ann,⁸ b. Dec. 30, 1860.
4. Emma Maria,⁸ b. Dec. 26, 1863.
5. Horace Edward,⁸ b. Dec. 1, 1868.

MARY L. CLEVELAND,⁸ eldest daughter of Edward H. and Mary A. (Broughton) Cleveland, b. June 24, 1854, m. in Kirtland, Lake county, Ohio, Feb. 1, 1873, Charles Samuel Johnson, son of Jonas and Maialena (Jansa) Johnson. He was b. in Sunneby, Sweden, Feb. 16, 1848. Miller; res. Munson, Geauga county, Ohio.
Children:
1. Serena Belle,⁹ b. Aug. 19, 1874.
2. Elsie May,⁹ b. Oct. 31, 1875.

HORACE G. CLEVELAND,⁷ eighth son and youngest child of Oren and Esther (Allen) Cleveland, b. in Winchester, Conn., Jan. 3, 1832, m. in Huntsburgh, Geauga county, Ohio, Jan. 5, 1853, Anna Maria Knapp, dau. of John and Albacinda (Barnum) Knapp. She was b. in Danbury, Conn., Nov. 15, 1831. He is a merchant; compiler of this Genealogy; res. 74 Hamilton Street, Cleveland, Ohio.
Children, all born in Cleveland:
1. Esther Maria,⁸ b. Jan. 19, 1854.
2. Edward Horace,⁸ b. Sept. 24, 1855.
3. Charles Luther,⁸ b. July 5, 1857.

ESTHER M. CLEVELAND,⁸ eldest child of Horace G. and Anna M. (Knapp) Cleveland, b. Jan. 19, 1854, m. in Cleveland, Ohio, July 28, 1874, Prof. Floyd Baker Wilson, son of William Henry and Eveline (Weaver) Wilson. He was b. in Watervleit, Albany county, N. Y., June 23, 1845. Is a graduate of Michigan University, for many years professor of English and Classical literature, and has been a very successful teacher of elocution. Author and Lecturer, and Attorney at Law; res. 33 Winthrop Place, Chicago, Ill.

Children, both b. in Chicago:

1. Ethel Maude,[9] b. Aug. 30, 1875.
2. Coral Eveline,[9] b. May 25, 1878.

JAMES C. CLEVELAND,[6] fourth son and fifth child of Rufus and Mary (Chamberlain) Cleveland, b. in East Windsor, Conn., Jan. 9, 1787, m. first, in Winchester, Conn., Feb. 3, 1813, Philenda Miller, dau. of Lewis and Mary (Allen) Miller. She was b. in Winchester, Conn., Aug. 29, 1793; d. in Philadelphia, Pa., May 19, 1814. He m. second, in Hartland, Conn., Sept. 19, 1816, Sally Taylor, dau. of Prince and Lucy (Adams) Taylor. She was b. in Hartland, Conn., Dec. 8, 1791; d. in Winchester, Conn., Dec. 27, 1819. He m. third, in Salisbury, Conn., Aug. 21, 1820, Lucy Northrup, dau. of Joseph and Mary (Bradley) Northrup. She was b. in Salisbury, Conn., April 20, 1798. He d. in Winsted, Conn., Sept. 1, 1875.

Children, by wife Philenda:

1. Charles Miller,[7] b. May 4, 1814; d. April 3, 1861.

   by wife Lucy:

2. Jane,[7] b. July 21, 1821.
3. Son,[7] b. April 28, 1825; d. April 28, 1825.

James C. Cleveland,[6] was a man of small stature, light hair and blue eyes. Directly after his marriage to his first wife, he removed to Philadelphia, and engaged in business. But the death of his wife within two weeks from the birth of their only son, greatly disheartened him, and he sold out the entire business, stock and fixtures, and returned to his native place where he resided thereafter until his death. He was a representative of his township in the State Legislature in 1834, and filled several offices of trust with ability and scrupulous fidelity. A man of few words but of plain speech when occasion required. He died after a short but severe illness, universally esteemed and respected. His third wife is still living in Winsted, Conn.

CHARLES M. CLEVELAND,[7] only son and child of James C. and Philenda (Miller) Cleveland, b. in Philadelphia, Pa., May 4, 1814, m. in Hartford, Conn., Oct. 7, 1841, Mary Augusta Steele, dau. of John and Lucy (Smith) Steele. She was b. in Hartford, Conn., March 19, 1818. He died in St. Louis, Mo., April 3, 1861. He was a person of considerable literary talent, and the author of several pieces in prose and verse and character "sketches," extensively copied by the Western press. He was the commercial editor of one of the leading St. Louis dailies at the time of his decease. His widow is now living in Winsted, Conn., with her sister-in-law, Mrs. Charles H. Blake, nearly opposite the old homestead.

JANE CLEVELAND,[7] only daughter of James C. and Lucy (Northrup) Cleveland, b. in Winsted, Conn., July 21, 1821, m. in Winsted, Conn., May 11, 1842, Charles Hamlin Blake, son of Dea. Jonathan and Sabra (Bronson) Blake. He was b. in Winchester, Conn., Oct. 17, 1817. Builder; res. in Winsted, Conn. Having been left a handsome fortune by his uncle, Silas Bronson, within a few years, he has retired from active business.

Children, all b. in Winsted:

1. James Cleveland,[8] b. Feb. 9, 1847; d. Jan. 24, 1848.
2. James Cleveland,[8] (again) b. July 12, 1849, m. in Winsted, Conn., Oct. 4, 1870, Anna Beecher, dau. of Rollin L. and Susan Janette (Holmes) Beecher. She was b. in Colebrook, Conn., July 6, 1849. He is a merchant; res. Winona, Minn. Children: 1. Susan Jane,[9] b. April 19, 1872. 2. Mary Cleveland,[9] b. March 22, 1875; d. Aug. 8, 1876.
3. Lorenzo Mitchell,[8] b. April 26, 1851. Teller in Savings Bank, Hartford, Conn.

HORACE CLEVELAND,[6] sixth child of Rufus and Mary (Chamberlain) Cleveland, b. in Barkhamstead, Conn., Feb. 25, 1789, m. in East Windsor, (Warehouse Point) Conn., Aug. 10, 1815, Belinda Baker, dau. of Col. Eliphalet and Clarissa (Cooke) Baker. She was b. in Sandisfield, Mass., Feb. 14, 1795, and d. in Coesse, Whitley county, Ind., Jan. 8, 1866. He d. in Coesse, Sept. 13, 1864. Farmer.

Children:
1. Hannah Cornelia,[7] b. Aug. 15, 1816; d. April 11, 1866.
2. Horace Baker,[7] b. Aug. —, 1818; d. March 12, 1833.
3. Clarissa Belinda,[7] b. Dec. 7, 1819; d. Oct. 24, 1853.
4. Barber Allen,[7] b. April 2, 1822.

Horace Cleveland,[6] was a man of medium stature, enterprising and energetic in his undertakings. He built an extensive distillery in Greene county, N. Y., on the Korteskill river, not far from Catskill, and managed it very successfully for several years. About the year 1835 he abandoned the business and removed to Whitley county, Ind., and pursued the avocation of a farmer until his death. Was President of the County Agricultural Society for many years, and though abrupt in his manners and uncompromising in his opinions, he was highly esteemed in the community where he resided. A Whig and Republican in politics, and a Universalist in his religion.

HANNAH C. CLEVELAND,[7] eldest child of Horace and Belinda (Baker) Cleveland, b. in Enfield, Conn., Aug. 15, 1816, m. first, in Cairo, Greene county, N.Y., April 18, 1834, George Bonestel, son of John and Deborah (Carven) Bonestel. He was b. in New Lebanon, N. Y., Aug. 16, 1812; d. in Cairo, N. Y., Oct. 13, 1837. She m. second, in Whitley county, Ind., Jan. 2, 1847, Miles W. Travis, son of John and Melinda (Wilson) Travis. The place and date of his birth not learned, but he d. in Coesse, Ind., Dec. 21, 1848. She m. third, in Coesse, Ind., Oct. 31, 1855, George Walker, a native of Ireland, and b. in 1802. He d. May 18, 1867. She d. in Coesse, Ind., April 11, 1866.

Children, by first husband, Geo. Bonestel:
1. George Baker,[8] b. Jan. 16, 1835; d. April 7, 1866.
2. Julia,[8] b. Dec. 3, 1836; d. Aug. 16, 1837.

by second husband, Miles W. Travis:
3. Melinda Wilson,[8] b. Jan. 5, 1848; d. Feb. 27, 1867.

Geo. B. Bonestel,[8] only son of George and Hannah C. (Cleveland) Bonestel, b. in Cairo, N. Y., Jan. 16, 1835, m. in

Coesse, Whitley county, Ind., Aug. 23, 1857, Araminta Dormer Kinne, dau. of George Rex and Sylvia S. (Graves) Kinne. She was b. in Allen, Alleghany county, N. Y., May 8, 1838. He d. in Coesse, Ind., April 7, 1866. Farmer. She is living in Oberlin, Ohio.

Children, all b. in Coesse :
1. Eva,[9] b. July 10, 1858; d. March 25, 1874.
2. Charles Chester,[9] b. July 25, 1859.
3. Elmore Ellsworth,[9] b. Feb. 5, 1861; d. May 4, 1866.
4. George Baker,[9] b. Oct. 17, 1866.

Melinda W. Travis,[8] only child of Miles W. and Hannah C. (Cleveland) Travis, b. in Coesse, Whitley county, Ind., Jan. 5, 1848, m. in Coesse, Jan. 29, 1866, John Rollin Douglass, son of Smith and Nancy (Cook) Douglass. He was b. in Lexington, Richland county, Ohio, Nov. 24, 1838. She d. in Coesse, Feb. 27, 1867. No children. He is living in Columbia City, Ind.

CLARISSA B. CLEVELAND,[7] second daughter and third child of Horace and Belinda (Baker) Cleveland, b. in Enfield, Conn., Dec. 7, 1819, m. in Union, Ind., April 13, 1847, James Welsheimer, son of Phillip and Katherine (Daly) Welsheimer. He was b. near Frankfort, Hampshire county, Va., Jan. 22, 1818. She d. in Coesse, Ind., Oct. 24, 1853.

Children :
1. Belinda,[8] b. Jan. 27, 1848; d. March 13, 1848.
2. Phillip Hobart,[8] b. Nov. 8, 1849.
3. Clara Matilda,[8] b. Jan. 3, 1852.

Phillip H. Welsheimer,[8] only son of James and Clarissa B. (Cleveland) Welsheimer, b. in Coesse, Ind., Nov. 8, 1849, m. in Union, Ind., Jan. 18, 1877, Eldora Ruckman, dau. of Isaac and Mary E. (Gunsaullons) Ruckman. She was b. Jan. 5, 1859. Res. Coesse, Ind.

Clara M. Welsheimer,[8] youngest daughter of James and Clarissa B. (Cleveland) Welsheimer, b. in Coesse, Ind., Jan. 3, 1852, m. in Rochester, Fulton county, Ind., June 26, 1869,

William Roudebush, son of Eli and Mary Ann (Reicher) Roudebush. He was b. in or near Massillon, Stark county, Ohio, Jan. 7, 1846. Farmer ; res. Coesse, Ind.
Children, both b. in Union, Ind. :
1. Martha Belinda,⁹ b. Sept. 15, 1871.
2. James Lewis,⁹ b. Dec. 3, 1874.

BARBER A. CLEVELAND,⁷ youngest son of Horace and Belinda (Baker) Cleveland, b. in Catskill, N.Y., April 2, 1822, m. in Coesse, Whitley county, Ind., Jan. 29, 1846, Mary Effie Long, dau. of Jesse and Hannah (Hegler) Long. She was b. in Xenia, Ohio, Feb. 19, 1826. He is a merchant; res. Harper, Iowa. Member of Iowa Legislature, 1875-6.
Children, all b. in Coesse, Ind. :
1. Florence Belle,⁸ b. June 3, 1848; d. April 3, 1852.
2. Emma Jessie,⁸ b. April 20, 1850.
3. Clara Belinda,⁸ b. Jan. 26, 1858.
4. Horace Barber,⁸ b. March 14, 1860.

EMMA J. CLEVELAND,⁸ second daughter of Barber A. and Mary E. (Long) Cleveland, b. April 20, 1850, m. in Harper, Iowa, May 21, 1877, Daniel Rosecrans, son of Daniel and Margaret (Anderson) Rosecrans. He was b. in Lake county, Ind., March 2, 1847. No children. He is Post Master at Harper.

NANCY CLEVELAND,⁶ third daughter and eighth child of Rufus and Mary (Chamberlain) Cleveland, b. in Barkhamstead, Conn., Aug. 22, 1792, m. in same place, Nov. 17, 1813, Alanson Spencer, son of Seth and Jerusha (Pettibone) Spencer. He was b. in New Hartford, Conn., Aug. 7, 1792 ; d. in Hamden, Conn., April 13, 1832. She d. in New Hartford, Conn., May 20, 1827.
Children :
1. Betsey Ellsworth,⁷ b. Sept. 3, 1814; d. Feb. 9, 1816.
2. Frederick Alanson,⁷ b. June 27, 1816.
3. George Cleveland,⁷ b. April 27, 1819.
4. Son,⁷ b. May 20, 1827; d. May 20, 1827.
5. Daughter,⁷ b. May 20, 1827; d. May 21, 1827.

Frederick A. Spencer,[7] eldest son of Alanson and Nancy (Cleveland) Spencer, b. in New Hartford, Conn., June 27, 1816, m. first, in Westfield, Mass., Nov. 25, 1839, Catherine Hastings Bush, dau. of Hezekiah and Marinda (Noble) Bush. She was b. in Pittsfield, Mass., Dec. 3, 1821; d. in Westfield, Mass., June 18, 1843. He m. second, in Easthampton, Mass., May 13, 1846, Julia Ann Ferry, dau. of Solomon and Sophia (Lyman) Ferry. She was b. in Easthampton, Mass., April 12, 1824. Res. Westfield, Mass.

Children, by wife Catherine:

1. Frederic Bush,[8] b. June 4, 1843; d. Sept. 5, 1843.

by wife Julia Ann:

2. Geo. Frederic,[8] b. Oct. 7, 1849; d. March 26, 1873, unm.
3. Nellie Hogarth,[8] b. June 30, 1855.
4. Julia Sophia,[8] b. May 19, 1859.

George C. Spencer,[7] second son and third child of Alanson and Nancy (Cleveland) Spencer, b. in New Hartford, Conn., April 27, 1819, m. first, in Watertown, Conn., Dec. 6, 1839, Eliza Partree, dau. of David and Mary Rhoda (Pitcher) Partree. She was b. in Watertown, Conn., Nov. 24, 1820; d. in Newburgh, N. Y., Sept. 13, 1865.. He m. second, in Watertown, Conn., March 9, 1867, Mrs. Julia Hannah (Castle) Garlock. No children by second wife. Res. Atlanta, Ga.

Children, by first wife Eliza:

1. David Alanson,[8] b. in Watertown, Conn., Sept. 20, 1840, m. in Newburgh, N. Y., Oct. 29, 1868, Ida Jane Raynor, dau. of Nathan Woodhull and Jane Le Count (Palmer) Raynor. She was b. in New York City, Jan. 9, 1848. Children, both b. in Atlanta, Ga.: 1. Raynor Cleveland,[9] b. Dec. 13, 1870; d. July 19, 1871. 2. Mary Eliza,[9] b. Feb. 6, 1873. He is Chief Deputy U. S. Marshall for the Northern District of Georgia. Res. Atlanta, Ga.
2. Sarah Elizabeth,[8] b. in Litchfield, Conn., Aug. 27, 1842; d. in Newburgh, N. Y., Aug. 22, 1863.
3. Mary,[8] b. in Plymouth, Conn., June 16, 1844; d. Sept. 23, 1845.

4. Julia,[8] b. in New Haven, Conn., June 8, 1847; d. in Easthampton, Mass., March 31, 1850.
5. Charles Frederick,[8] b. in Newburgh, N. Y., Feb. 11, 1853; d. May 2, 1855.
6. Ida Jeannette,[8] b. in Newburgh, N. Y., May 3, 1855, m. in Atlanta, Ga., Nov. 19, 1873, Robert Elford Boyd, son of Wallace Wade and Harriet Adaline (Breen) Boyd. He was b. in Marietta, Ga., April 11, 1852. Res. Atlanta, Ga. No children.
7. Clarence Cleveland,[8] b. in Newburgh, N. Y., Sept. 7, 1857; d. Oct. 14, 1859.
8. Harry Huntley,[8] b. in Newburgh, N. Y., Sept. 4, 1860; d. Oct. 22, 1864.

BETSEY CLEVELAND,[6] fourth daughter and ninth child of Rufus and Mary (Chamberlain) Cleveland, b. in Barkhamstead, Conn., Aug. 31, 1794, m. in same town, April 4, 1816, Almon Alcott, son of John Blakeslee and Lois (Gaylord) Alcott. He was b. in Wolcott, Conn., Feb. 22, 1790. She d. in Wolcott, Conn., Oct. 18, 1827. He is a farmer; res. Wolcott, Conn.

Children, all b. in Wolcott:
1. Lois Gaylord,[7] b. March 22, 1817; d. Oct. 5, 1827.
2. Clarissa,[7] b. Sept. 29, 1822; d. June 17, 1847.
3. Sidney Whiting,[7] b. Sept. 6, 1827; d. June 29, 1829.

Clarissa Alcott,[7] second daughter of Almon and Betsey (Cleveland) Alcott, b. in Wolcott, Conn., Sept. 29, 1822, m. in Plymouth, Conn., July 4, 1842, George Mallory Hard, son of Jabez and Sally (Mallory) Hard. He was b. in Goshen, Conn., May 16, 1819. She d. in Bantam Falls, Litchfield county, Conn., June 17, 1847. He res. Bantam Falls, Conn.

Children:
1. Estella Clarissa,[8] b. in Wolcott, New Haven county, Conn., April 27, 1843, m. in Litchfield, Conn., June 18, 1863, Dwight Harry Bunnell, son of Dwight and Estella (Stone) Bunnell. He was b. in Morris, Litchfield county, Conn., July 15, 1840. Res. Bantam Falls, Conn. Children: 1. George Kirby,[9] b. Nov. 9, 1864. 2. Annie Jane,[9] b. Sept. 14, 1870.

2. George Wallace,[7] b. in Wolcott, Conn., Feb. 19, 1845, m. in Litchfield, Conn., Dec. 25, 1872, Anna Eliza Crossman, dau. of Edward and Charlotte (Winslow) Crossman. She was b. in Hudson, N. Y., June 27, 1849. He is a farmer; res. Bantam Falls, Conn. Children: 1. Charlotte Elizabeth,[8] b. June 12, 1874; d. Jan. 20, 1875. 2. Clara Maud,[8] b. Oct. 12, 1875.
3. John Almon,[8] b. in Goshen, Conn., June 4, 1847.

[Don Carlos Littlefield,[7] a lineal descendant of the seventh generation from Moses Cleveland,[1] was early adopted by Almon and Betsey (Cleveland) Alcott, reared as one of their own family, and always esteemed and regarded as "Cousin Carlos" by the grandchildren of Rufus Cleveland.[5] He was b. in Barkhamstead, Conn., Jan. 7, 1818, m. in Berlin, Hartford county, Conn., Oct. 30, 1840, Olive Byington, dau. of Theodore and Olive Byington. She was b. in Southington, Conn., Nov. 14, 1815. He is Superintendent of the Sixth Street Market, San Francisco, Cal.

Children :

1. Theodore Byington,[8] b. in Perry, Ill., Jan. 22, 1845, m. in San Francisco, Jan. 20, 1870, Loleta Green, dau. of Alfred Augustus and Lola (Lagareta) Green. She was b. in San Francisco, Cal., April 3, 1852. He is a contractor; res. San Francisco. Have two children: 1. Perry Alfred,[9] b. Oct. 29, 1870; d. Sept. 4, 1876. 2. Frederic Augustus,[9] b. April 15, 1872.
2. Nellie Aurelia,[8] b. in Peoria, Ill., Sept. 12, 1847.
3. Alice Cleveland,[8] b. in Peoria, Ill., Nov. 22, 1849; d. in San Francisco, Cal., Feb. 10, 1872.]

MARY CLEVELAND,[6] fifth daughter and tenth child of Rufus and Mary (Chamberlain) Cleveland, b. in Barkhamstead, Conn., May 23, 1796, m. in Wolcott, Conn., Dec. 7, 1829, Almon Alcott, son of John B. and Lois (Gaylord) Alcott. He was b. in Wolcott, Conn., Feb. 22, 1790. She d. in Wolcott, Conn., Oct. 12, 1838.

Children, all b. in Wolcott :

1. Sidney Whiting,[7] b. Aug. 1, 1831, m. in Wolcott, Conn., Feb. 19, 1854, Marietta Alcott, dau. of Alvin and Chloe Barnes (Finch) Alcott. She was b. in Wolcott, Conn., March 10, 1834 ; d. in Waterbury, Conn., Oct. 19, 1874. He is a mechanic; res. Waterbury, Conn. Child : 1. Clara Etta,[8] b. in Waterbury, Conn., Sept. 21, 1856.
2. Rufus Cleveland,[7] b. Feb. 28, 1833, m. first, in New Britain, Conn., May 8, 1853, Mary Ballard Pinks, dau. of Jonathan C. and Esther (Flint) Pinks. She was b. in Stafford, Conn., Jan. 16, 1832. Divorced. He m. second, in Oxford, Conn., Sept. 30, 1858, Maria Hitchcock, dau. of George and Ruth Ann (Johnson) Hitchcock. She was b. in Oxford, Conn., July 13, 1838. Res. Seymour, Conn. Children, by wife Mary: 1. Alice Jane Cleveland,[8] b. in New Britain, Conn., June 27, 1854. Teacher in New York City. By wife Maria: 2. Frederic Cleveland,[8] b. in Naugatuck, Conn., April 8, 1860; d. Feb. 4, 1868. 3. Hubert,[8] b. in Naugatuck, Conn., Sept. 24, 1861. 4. George Almon,[8] b. in Naugatuck, Conn., Oct. 22, 1864. 5. William Rufus,[8] b. in Naugatuck, Conn., Feb. 21, 1867. 6. Frank Cleveland,[8] b. in Naugatuck, Conn., April 25, 1869. 7. Antoinette Louisa,[8] b. in West Ansonia, Conn., July 23, 1871. 8. Edith Gertrude,[8] b. in Seymour, Conn., Jan. 15, 1877.
3. Lucien Palmer,[7] b. July 11, 1835, m. in Goshen, Conn., March 22, 1859, Maria Ella Robinson, dau. of Thomas and Rebecca (Perkins) Robinson. She was b. in Goshen, Conn., Nov. 27, 1836. He is a farmer; res. Wolcott, Conn. Children, all b. in Wolcott: 1. Bertha Christine,[8] b. June 7, 1861. 2. Frances Ella,[8] b. May 10, 1864. 3. Lois Betsey,[8] b. Jan. 28, 1866. 4. Eddie Lucien,[8] b. April 20, 1867.
4. Son,[7] b. Oct. 1, 1838; d. Oct. 3, 1838.

CHARLES CHESTER WARNER CLEVELAND,[6] youngest son and child of Rufus and Mary (Chamberlain) Cleveland, b. in Barkhamstead, Conn., Jan. 20, 1803, m. first, in Catskill, N. Y., Feb. 5, 1824, Rachel Halcott, dau. of John and Letitia (Jenkins) Halcott. She was b. in Roxbury, Delaware county, N. Y., Sept. 25, 1804; d. in Catskill, Oct. 8, 1845. He m. second, in New York City, June 18, 1846, Cynthia Bennett, dau. of David and Phebe (Halcott) Bennett. She was b. in Bovina, Delaware county, N.Y., Feb. 25, 1816; d. in Catskill, Greene county, N. Y., June 4, 1877. He is an accountant; res. Catskill, N. Y.

Children, by wife Rachel:

1. Charles Halcott,[7] b. Oct. 22, 1824; d. Sept. 9, 1862.
2. Bolivar,[7] b. Feb. 3, 1826; d. Feb. 4, 1826.
3. Celia,[7] b. Jan. 8, 1827.
4. Elizabeth,[7] b. Jan 12, 1829.
5. Mary,[7] b. Dec. 23, 1830.
6. Belinda,[7] b. July 27, 1833; d. Aug. 9, 1877.
7. Rachel,[7] b. May 22, 1836.
8. Joseph Prentiss,[7] b. Jan. 1, 1839.
9. Martha,[7] b. Sept. 12, 1841; d. Oct. 22, 1847.
10. Phebe Adelaide,[7] b. Aug. 7, 1844; d. Dec. 18, 1873.

by wife Cynthia:

11. Benjamin,[7] b. July 8, 1847; d. Dec. 9, 1870.
12. Julius Austin,[7] b. Feb. 22, 1850.
13. Alexander,[7] b. Aug. 15, 1851.

Charles C. W. Cleveland,[6] is a man of medium height, of fine personal appearance, and a staunch adherent to the Episcopal Church, in which he has been a vestryman and lay reader for many years. In ante-bellum days he was an old line Whig, but latterly has acted politically with the Democratic party. He possesses social qualities of a rare order, and has given much of his time and talents to the promotion of popular education. Since the death of his second wife he has resided a portion of the time with his daughters in Connecticut.

CHARLES H. CLEVELAND,[7] eldest son of Charles C. W. and Rachel (Halcott) Cleveland, b. Oct. 22, 1824, m. in Brooklyn, N. Y., May 17, 1846, Elizabeth Cornish, dau. of Eber and Ruth (Vorce) Cornish. She was b. in Prattsville, Greene county, N. Y., Jan. 22, 1826. He d. in Hartford, Conn., Sept. 9, 1862. Was Editor of the *Catskill Messenger* at one time, and an easy and elegant writer.

Children:
1. Alexander Witter,[7] b. in Williamsburgh, N.Y., March 10, 1847; d. in the Army at Nashville, Tenn., March —, 1863.
2. Ruth,[7] b. in Lexington, Greene county, N. Y., Dec. 22, 1850, m. in Catskill, N. Y., Nov. 3, 1870, Theodore Benjamin Beach, son of George Lewis and Anna (Riley) Beach. He was b. in Catskill, N. Y., March 28, 1847. Children, both b. in Catskill, N. Y.: 1. Arthur Cleveland,[8] b. July 30, 1871. 2. Louis Theodore,[8] b. Sept. 1, 1872.

CELIA CLEVELAND,[7] eldest daughter and third child of Charles C. W. and Rachel (Halcott) Cleveland, b. Jan. 8, 1827, m. in Catskill, N. Y., April 27, 1847, Hervey Vincent Blake, son of Allen and Mabel (Beach) Blake. He was b. in Winchester, Conn., June 29, 1818. Farmer; res. Harwinton, Litchfield county, Conn.

Children:
1. Catherine Cleveland,[8] b. May 21, 1848; d. Feb. 3, 1850.
2. Samuel Allen,[8] b. Aug. 22, 1849; d. Oct. 8, 1849.
3. Charles Lambert,[8] b. Oct. 18, 1850.
4. Allen,[8] b. Feb. 12, 1854; d. March 4, 1854.
5. Celia Elizabeth,[8] b. July 11, 1855.
6. George Halcott,[8] b. Jan. 19, 1858.
7. Mabel Louisa,[8] b. April 22, 1860.
8. Maria Ella,[8] b. Aug. 6, 1864.

Charles L. Blake,[8] son of Hervey V. and Celia (Cleveland) Blake, b. in Winsted, Conn., Oct. 18, 1850, m. in New Haven, Conn., April 6, 1876, Lillian Elizabeth Atwater, dau. of Rev. William Woodruff and Mary Elizabeth (Olmstead) Atwater. She was b. in Hudson, Mich., June 9, 1856.

Celia E. Blake,[8] daughter of Hervey V. and Celia (Cleveland) Blake, b. in Winsted, Conn., July 11, 1855, m. in Essex, Middlesex county, Conn., Oct. 4, 1876, Frederic F. Fuessenich, son of Leonard and Elizabeth Fuessenich. He was b. in Duren, Prussia, May 7, 1848. Druggist; res. Wolcottville, Conn.

ELIZABETH CLEVELAND,[7] second daughter and fourth child of Charles C. W. and Rachel (Halcott) Cleveland, b. Jan. 12, 1829, m. in New York City, Jan. 14, 1847, John Walker Lewis, son of Joseph and Elizabeth (Walker) Lewis. He was b. in Granville county, N. C., Feb. 6, 1814. Merchant; res. Brooklyn, N. Y. He has amassed a fortune by habits of industry and economy, and retired from business altogether a few years ago.

Children:
1. Mary Austin,[8] b. May 8, 1848.
2. Ella Cleveland,[8] b. April 5, 1850.
3. Julius Walker,[8] b. April 5, 1852.
4. Elizabeth French,[8] b. Feb. 14, 1854.
5. Charles Garrett,[8] b. April 11, 1857.

Mary A. Lewis,[8] daughter of John W. and Elizabeth (Cleveland) Lewis, b. in Brooklyn, N. Y., May 8, 1848, m. in Brooklyn, Nov. 6, 1867, Battiste Samuel Phillips, son of Gian Battiste and Catherine (Bennett) Phillipi, of Genoa, Italy. He was b. in Genoa, June 14, 1844. Res. Brooklyn, N. Y. Children:

1. John Lewis,[9] b. Jan. 24, 1869.
2. Elizabeth Cleveland,[9] b. Dec. 31, 1870.

Ella C. Lewis,[8] daughter of John W. and Elizabeth (Cleveland) Lewis, b. in Brooklyn, N. Y., April 5, 1850, m. in Brooklyn, June 1, 1870, Louis Emerson Howard, son of Samuel Emerson and Pamelia (Colman) Howard. He was b. in Brooklyn, N. Y., May 13, 1846. Res. Brooklyn, N. Y.

Children:
1. Emerson Cleveland,[9] b. March 24, 1871.
2. Grace Colman,[9] b. Aug. 31, 1872.

Julius W. Lewis,[8] son of John W. and Elizabeth (Cleveland) Lewis, b. in Brooklyn, N. Y., April 5, 1852, m. in Brooklyn, Dec. 15, 1875, Marie Louise Carhart, dau. of James Dunham and Sarah Virginia (Curd) Carhart. She was b. in

Brooklyn, June 26, 1853. He is a merchant; res. Knoxville, Tenn.

Elizabeth F. Lewis,[8] daughter of John W. and Elizabeth (Cleveland) Lewis. b. in Brooklyn, N. Y., Feb. 14, 1854, m. in Brooklyn, April 27, 1872, Francis Alexander Moran, son of Francis and Mary Frances (McIntyre) Moran. He was b. in Brooklyn, April 20, 1849. Res. Brooklyn, N. Y.
Children:
1. Edith,[9] b. in Weis Baden, Germany, Feb. 22, 1873.
2. Sarah,[9] b. in Brooklyn, N. Y., Feb. 22, 1874.
3. Ethel,[9] b. in Brooklyn, N. Y., June 12, 1875.

MARY CLEVELAND,[7] third daughter and fifth child of Charles C. W. and Rachel (Halcott) Cleveland, b. Dec. 23, 1830, m. in Catskill, N. Y., Oct. 4, 1848, Rev. James Roger Coe, son of Rev. Daniel and Anna (Sweet) [Keyes] Coe. He was b. in Winchester, Conn., March 30, 1818; d. in Oakfield, N. Y., March 16, 1874. She is living in Catskill, N. Y.
Children:
1. Anna Higley,[8] b. Aug. 10, 1849.
2. Sarah Whitman,[8] b. Jan. 13, 1851.
3. George Jarvis,[8] b. May 7, 1853.
4. Charles Cleveland,[8] b. Jan. 13, 1855.
5. Mary Cleveland,[8] b. Dec. 17, 1857; d. Feb. 9, 1860.
6. Frank Lathrop,[8] b. Nov. 21, 1863; d. April 12, 1874.
7. Elizabeth Cleveland,[8] b. Jan. 17, 1865.
8. Robert,[8] b. July 14, 1867.
9. Rachel Halcott,[8] b. Nov. 29, 1870.
10. Margaret Lawrence Sweet,[8] b. April 28, 1873.

Rev. James R. Coe was a clergyman in the Episcopal church, and conducted an academical school for boys at Oakfield, N. Y., very successfully for several years.

Anna H. Coe,[8] daughter of Rev. James R. and Mary (Cleveland) Coe, b. Aug. 10, 1849, m. in Oakfield, N. Y., Dec. 29, 1874, William Henry Van de Carr, son of Henry Shenkel

and Bethia (Hoes) Van de Carr. He was b. in Stockport, Delaware county, N. Y., June 24, 1850.
Child:
1. Harry Shenkel,⁹ b. March 10, 1876.

BELINDA CLEVELAND,⁷ fourth daughter and sixth child of Charles C. W. and Rachel (Halcott) Cleveland, b. July 27, 1833, m. in Catskill, N. Y., June 23, 1856, Charles Kelsey, son of Elisha and Lucinda (Platt) Kelsey. He was b. in Killingworth, Middlesex county, Conn., Nov. 14, 1820. She d. in Centre Brook, Middlesex county, Conn., Aug. 9, 1877.
Children:
1. Rachel Cleveland,⁸ b. March 1, 1858.
2. Charles Elisha,⁸ b. June 29, 1862.
3. Isabella Cleveland,⁸ b. July 25, 1871.

RACHEL CLEVELAND,⁷ fifth daughter and seventh child of Charles C. W. and Rachel (Halcott) Cleveland, b. May 22, 1836, m. in Catskill, N. Y., Oct. 14, 1855, Jonathan Edwards Marsh, son of Elias and Myra (Buss) Marsh. He was b. in Oakham, Mass., June 7, 1827. Res. Elizabeth, N. J.
Child:
1. Frederic Cleveland,⁸ b. Jan. 27, 1857.

JOSEPH P. CLEVELAND,⁷ third son and eighth child of Charles C. W. and Rachel (Halcott) Cleveland, b. Jan. 1, 1839, m. first, in Chippewa Falls, Wis., May 14, 1871, Anna Fernanda Victoria Welles, dau. of Francis and Mary (Lamb) Welles. She was b. in St. Johnsbury, Vt., Nov. 27, 1845; d. in Chippewa Falls, Wis., April 20, 1873. He m. second, in Davenport, Iowa, Sept. 27, 1876, Gretta Fetter Weise, dau. of James H. and Catherine E. (Fetter) Weise. She was b. in Carlisle, Pa., Aug. 26, 1854. Res. Chippewa Falls, Wis.
Child, by wife Anna:
1. Anna,⁸ b. April 17, 1873; d. April 28, 1873.

PHEBE A. CLEVELAND,⁷ seventh daughter and youngest child of Charles C. W. and Rachel (Halcott) Cleveland, b.

Aug. 7, 1844, m. in Catskill, N. Y., Sept. 4, 1867, William Francis Belknap, son of Ebenezer and Mary E. (Nye) Belknap. He was b. in Cooperstown, N. Y., Feb. 10, 1842. She d. in Catskill, N. Y., Dec. 18, 1873. He is a hardware merchant; res. Watertown, N. Y.
Child:
 1. Son, b. Nov. 25, 1873; d. Nov. 25, 1873.

JULIUS A. CLEVELAND,[7] second son and child of Charles C. W. and Cynthia (Bennett) Cleveland, b. Feb. 22, 1850, m. in Cleveland, Ohio, April 22, 1874, Lillian Minerva Fitzpatrick, dau. of Thomas and Minerva (Whittaker) Fitzpatrick. She was b. in Buffalo, N. Y., March 2, 1851. He is a clerk in Cleveland, Ohio.
Children, both b. in Cleveland:
 1. Carrie Adelaide,[8] b. Feb. 1, 1875.
 2. Helen Minerva,[8] b. Oct. 6, 1876.

ALEXANDER CLEVELAND,[7] youngest son and child of Charles C. W. and Cynthia (Bennett) Cleveland, b. Aug 15, 1851, m. in Plymouth, Conn., Dec. 10, 1873, Nora Ryan, dau. of Phillip and Catherine (Day) Ryan. She was b. in Plymouth, Conn., May 13, 1853. He is a mechanic; res. Thomaston, Conn.
Children:
 1. Ruth,[8] b. in Plymouth, Conn., March 1, 1875.
 2. Ella,[8] b. in Thomaston, Conn., Oct. 21, 1876.

ALICE CLEVELAND,[6] eldest child and only daughter of Rufus and Alice (Jenkins) Cleveland, b. in Barkhamstead, Conn., Oct. 2, 1809, m. in Griggsville, Ill., April 26, 1838, Dana Ayres, son of Jason and Betsey (Holman) Ayres. He was b. in Truro, Mass., Dec. 7, 1809. Druggist; res. Perry, Pike county, Ill.
Children:
 1. Delia,[7] b. June 23, 1844.
 2. Charles Dana,[7] b. Sept. 24, 1850.
 3. Horace,[7] b. Aug. 22, 1852; d. Aug. 6, 1853.

Delia Ayres,[7] eldest child of Dana and Alice (Cleveland) Ayres, b. June 23, 1844, m. in Perry, Ill., April 24, 1866, James Burton Carpenter, son of Burton Bradford and Mary (Richards) Carpenter. He was b. in Dixon, Ill., Sept. 10, 1842. Res. Memphis, Tenn.

Children:

1. Charles Dana,[8] b. in Knoxville, Tenn., Aug. 17, 1867.
2. Mary Alice,[8] b. in Knoxville, Tenn., Dec. 12, 1869.
3. Maud,[8] b. in Nashville, Tenn., April 13, 1872.
4. Nellie,[8] b. in Memphis, Tenn., Jan. 17, 1875.
5. Clara Louisa,[8] b. in Memphis, Tenn., May 10, 1877.

John K. Cleveland,[6] only son of Rufus and Alice (Jenkins) Cleveland, b. in Barkhamstead, Conn., May 12, 1811, m. in Humphreysville, Conn., Dec. 25, 1833, Emeline Canfield, dau. of Lewis and Eunice (Steele) Canfield. She was b. in Humphreysville, Conn., Dec. 24, 1812. He is a farmer and merchant; res. Perry, Ill.

Children:

1. Elizabeth,[7] b. Nov. 25, 1834; d. Nov. 25, 1835.
2. Ellen,[7] b. March 8, 1836.
3. Frances,[7] b. March 15, 1838; d. April 16, 1850.
4. Alice,[7] b. Feb. 22, 1841; d. Nov. 10, 1877.
5. Emma,[7] b. April 17, 1843.
6. Eunice Augusta,[7] b. Sept. 25, 1845.
7. Mary,[7] b. June 7, 1849.

John K. Cleveland,[6] is a man of swarthy complexion, black eyes, and tall and muscular frame. He worked in early life at blacksmithing, but after he became forehanded in Illinois, to which State he removed from Wayne county, Pa., in 1837, he engaged in buying and selling live stock, and finally established a store in Perry, Ill. A radical Democrat in politics, a Presbyterian Calvinist in religion, a kind neighbor, and a good citizen.

Ellen Cleveland,[7] second daughter and child of John K. and Emeline (Canfield) Cleveland, b. in Prompton, Wayne county, Pa., March 8, 1836, m. in Perry, Pike county, Ill., July 5, 1853, John White Brown, son of Nelson Reed and Ann Maria (Hughes) Brown. He was b. in Clarksville, Ross county, Ohio, Oct. 14, 1826. Farmer; res. Perry, Ill.

Children:
1. Lulu,[8] b. April 1, 1855.
2. Frank,[8] b. Nov. 3, 1857.
3. Harry,[8] b. Oct. 5, 1859.
4. Nelson,[8] b. Oct. 23, 1861.
5. James,[8] b. Aug. 25, 1864.
6. Ellen,[8] b. June 8, 1868.
7. Eugene,[8] b. June 14, 1872.
8. Alice Maria,[8] b. Dec. 21, 1874.

ALICE CLEVELAND,[7] fourth daughter and child of John K. and Emeline (Canfield) Cleveland, b. in Perry, Pike county, Ill., Feb. 22, 1841, m. in Perry, Ill., Sept. 12, 1858, James A. Eggleston, son of Jabez and Adelia (Foster) Eggleston. He was b. in Glen's Falls, Warren county, N. Y., Aug. 31, 1837. She d. in Aurora, Ill., Nov. 10, 1877. He is a merchant and banker; res. Aurora, Ill.

Child:
1. Frank,[8] b. Aug. 14, 1861.

EMMA CLEVELAND,[7] fifth daughter and child of John K. and Emeline (Canfield) Cleveland, b. in Perry Pike county, Ill., April 17, 1843, m. first, in Perry, Ill., March 20, 1858, George Maxwell Kuhl, son of Leonard Lambert and Mary (Maxwell) Kuhl. He was b. in Raritan, N. J., March 8, 1837; d. in Perry, Ill., April 27, 1866. He was a merchant. She m. second, in Pittsfield, Ill., Aug. 25, 1874, Gilbert Lafayette Seybold, son of James and Olive (Gaskill) Seybold. He was b. in St. Louis, Mo., Oct. 7, 1836. Teacher, etc.; res. Pueblo, Col.

Children, by first husband, G. M. Kuhl:
1. Percy Edward,[8] b. June 4, 1860.
2. Harold George,[8] b. Jan. 20, 1862.
3. Emeline Augusta,[8] b. Aug. 11, 1864.

No children by second husband.

EUNICE A. CLEVELAND,[7] sixth daughter and child of John K. and Emeline (Canfield) Cleveland, b. in Perry, Pike county, Ill., Sept. 25, 1845, m. in Perry, Ill., April 15, 1868, James Harvey Harrison, son of William and Eliza (Looker) Harrison. He was b. in Cincinnati, Ohio, Nov. 9, 1840. Farmer; res. Perry, Ill.

Children:

1. John Henry,[8] b. Dec. 9, 1871.
2. Charles Frederick,[8] b. Feb. 2, 1874.

MARY CLEVELAND,[7] youngest daughter and child of John K. and Emeline (Canfield) Cleveland, b. in Perry, Pike county, Ill., Jan. 7, 1849, m. in Perry, Ill., Sept. 11, 1871, James Higgins, son of Lewis and Mary Ann (Cramer) Higgins. He was b. in Clinton, Hunterdon county, N. J., Oct. 11, 1846. Jeweler; res. Perry, Ill.

Children:

1. Ora,[8] b. Nov. 6, 1872.
2. Arthur,[8] b. Dec. 21, 1874.
3. Alice Ann,[8] b. Dec. 8, 1876.

PHEBE CLEVELAND,[5] youngest daughter and child of Benjamin and Rachel Cleveland, was b. in Canterbury, Conn., June 25, 1758. She m. first, in Ellington, Conn., Feb. 22, 1779, Ephraim Pearson, son of Ephraim and Hannah (Barrett) Pearson. He was b. in East Windsor, Conn., June 18, 1758; d. in Savannah, Ga., about the year 1804. Supposing him lost at sea, she m. in Manchester, Vt., Oct. 13, 1796, Timothy O'Brien, son of Timothy and Margaretta O'Brien. He was b. in Providence, R. I., May 15, 1766; d. in Sherburne, Chenango county, N. Y., Oct. 20, 1827. She d. in same town, Aug. 6, 1838. Her first husband was a trader in Manchester, Vt. In the fall of 1787, he, with others, took a drove of swine to Boston, but failing to dispose of them to their satisfaction, Mr. Pearson chartered a vessel to take his live stock to Halifax. Adverse gales drove the vessel out of her course, and she was captured by a Spanish privateer, and he taken to Algiers, and sold into slavery. Nine years elapsed before he escaped and arrived in Savannah, Ga. His wife, after waiting his return seven years, mourned him as dead, and married again. Learning this fact from his brother, and exacting a sacred pledge that his whereabouts should never be revealed to her during his lifetime, he remained in Savannah, opened a butcher's shop, and prospered for several years, when he died suddenly after a short illness. The pledge given was faithfully observed, and she knew nothing of the matter until after his decease. (For further genealogical information in regard to this branch, see Appendix L.)

Children, by first husband, Ephraim Pearson:

1. Anna,[6] b. Dec. 13, 1779; d. Jan 7, 1829.
2. Mary,[6] b. Jan. 12, 1782; d. Nov. 25, 1857.
3. Eunice,[6] b. Oct. 13, 1784; d. Aug. 22, 1866.
4. Jacob,[6] b. April 28, 1787; d. Dec. 20, 1846.

by second husband, Timothy O'Brien:

5. Joseph,[6] b. July 24, 1797; d. May 2, 1826.
6. Timothy,[6] b. Oct. 25, 1799; living in Poolville, N. Y.
7. Drusilla,[6] b. April 8, 1801; d. Nov. 2, 1838.
8. Sarah,[6] b. Sept. 15, 1803; d. Aug. 7, 1863.

Concerning Phebe Cleveland,[5] her granddaughter, Mrs. Alfred Parsons, of Earlville, N. Y., writes me, May 15, 1878, as follows: "My knowledge of my 'mother's' parents is very limited. Have no recollection of grandfather, nor of any of his peculiar traits of character. Can remember grandmother only as an old lady, seated in her rocking chair, knitting or reading. The last three years of her life her mental faculties were much impaired by a shock of palsy, and I was only ten years old when she was thus mentally benumbed. She was not corpulent, and I remember she had a slim hand and long fingers. The expression of her countenance was that of sternness and sadness — never laughed much." No stone with the proper inscription marks her grave in Sherburne cemetery, though there is said to be one to the memory of her last husband. Who of her descendants will see that this token of respect to her memory is no longer neglected?

Anna Pearson,[6] the eldest daughter and child of Ephraim and Phebe (Cleveland) Pearson, m. in Manchester, Bennington county, Vt., Oct. 11, 1798, Benjamin Sutherland, son of Samuel and Rachel (Purdy) Sutherland. He was b. in Manchester, Vt., Aug. 24, 1775; d. in Manchester, Vt., Oct. 22, 1852. She d. in Manchester, Vt., Jan. 7, 1829. He was a farmer.

Children, all b. in Manchester, Vt:

1. Marcius,[7] b. Nov. 18, 1801; res. Allegan, Mich.
2. Julia,[7] b. June 6, 1803; d. Sept. 24, 1867.
3. Delia,[7] b. Oct. 22, 1804; res. Grafton, Vt.
4. Mary Pearson,[7] b. April 25, 1806; d. Dec. 4, 1865.
5. Ammi,[7] b. Jan. 11, 1808; res. Sharon, Wis.
6. Edgar,[7] b. June 22, 1809; d. Oct. 22, 1877.
7. Seth,[7] b. April 7, 1811; d. unm. Sept. 2, 1842.
8. Samuel,[7] b. Feb. 28, 1813; d. June 2, 1857.
9. Elon Galusha,[7] b. Jan. 23, 1815; res. Panama.
10. Jonah,[7] b. March 10, 1817; res. Waucoma, Iowa.
11. Harriet,[7] b. Dec. 30, 1818; d. Nov. 4, 1826.
12. William,[7] (Dr.), b. Feb. 28, 1820; res. Victoria, Texas.
13. Benjamin,[7] b. Nov. 19, 1821; res. Jerry City, Wood county, O.

Mary Pearson,[6] the second daughter and child of Ephraim and Phebe (Cleveland) Pearson, m. in Manchester, Vt., Jan. 29, 1807, Jonah Sutherland, son of Samuel and Rachel (Purdy) Sutherland. He was b. in Manchester, Bennington county, Vt., Dec. 20, 1779; d. in Edmeston, Otsego county, N. Y., Aug. 5, 1845. Farmer. She d. in Edmeston, Nov. 25, 1857. They came from Manchester, Vt., to Edmeston, N. Y., in the spring of 1816.

Children:

1. Walter,[7] b. Aug. 12, 1807; res. Dunton, Ill.
2. Emeline,[7] b. June 19, 1809; d. unm. Feb. 7, 1842.
3. Anna,[7] b. March 28, 1811; d. unm. June 15, 1835.
4. Benjamin,[7] b. Dec. 1, 1812; d. July 16, 1877.

5. Giles,[7] b. March 25, 1815; d. Oct. 5, 1867.
6. Charles,[7] b. Nov. 4, 1816; res. Sharon, Wis.
7. Mark,[7] b. June 28, 1819; res. Horton, Bremer county, Iowa.
8. Albert,[7] b. Nov. 16, 1821; res. West Edmeston, N. Y.
9. Noyes Palmer,[7] b. April 15, 1824; d. July 22, 1842.
10. Alonzo Wheelock,[7] b. Jan. 12, 1827; res. Edmeston, N. Y.

Eunice Pearson,[6] the third daughter and child of Ephraim and Phebe (Cleveland) Pearson, m. in Manchester, Bennington county, Vt., May 1, 1803, D'Estaing Eaton, son of Nathan and Phebe (Brooks) Eaton. He was b. in Manchester, Vt., June 8, 1782; d. in Brookfield, Madison county, N. Y., Jan. 10, 1847. She d. in New Berlin, Chenango county, N. Y., Aug. 22, 1866. He was a farmer. Removed to the State of New York in 1806.

Children:

1. James,[7] b. in Manchester, Vt., March 24, 1805; d. April 20, 1872.
2. Nancy,[7] b. in Sherburne, N. Y., May 8, 1807; res. Sangerfield, N. Y.
3. Nathan,[7] b. in Brookfield, N. Y., Aug. 30, 1815; d. March 2, 1856.
4. John,[7] b. in Brookfield, N. Y., Feb. 15, 1818; res. Sangerfield, N. Y.
5. Joseph,[7] b. in Brookfield, N. Y., Oct. 12, 1820; res. Pittsfield, Ill.

Jacob Pearson,[6] only son and youngest child of Ephraim and Phebe (Cleveland) Pearson, m. first, in Charleston, S. C., Dec. 25, 1809, Mrs. Eliza Anderson, maiden name not learned, or any particulars of her parentage or family. He brought her to Manchester, where she remained a few months, and then returned South to spend the winter; was taken ill and d. in Charleston, Feb. 3, 1811. He m. second, in Manchester, Vt., June 4, 1812, Rhoda Ewers, dau. of John and Sally (Morley) Ewers. She was b. in Gill, Franklin county, Mass., Dec. 22, 1790; d. in or near Council Bluffs, Iowa, Oct. 30, 1846. He d. in same place, Dec. 20, 1846. It appears that Rhoda, wife of Jacob Pearson,[6] was a very devout though credulous woman in all matters appertaining to religion. She joined the followers of Joseph Smith, the Mormon preacher, but became disenchanted subsequently, perhaps about the time she was taken sick at Council Bluffs, where a portion of the Mormons had encamped after being driven from the States. Her husband was a man of fine appearance, and of indomitable energy. Merchant. He had no children by his first wife.

Children, by wife Rhoda:

1. Phebe Cleveland,[7] b. May 26, 1813; res. Waterville, N. Y.
2. Elizabeth Boyd,[7] b. July 25, 1815; d. Aug. 14, 1871.
3. Josiah Miller,[7] b. April 25, 1817; res. Martinton, Ill.
4. Adaline,[7] b. July 22, 1820; res. Cuyahoga Falls, Ohio.
5. Josephine,[7] b. March 23, 1823; d. unm. Jan. 8, 1850.
6. Ephraim John,[7] b. Oct. 28, 1825; res. Pleasant Grove City, Utah.
7. Elias Frasier,[7] b. July 9, 1827; res. Circleville, Utah.
8. Henry,[7] b. May 24, 1830; d. Nov. 17, 1846.

Mrs. Phebe C. Barnard, and Mrs. Adaline Newman, have each kindly aided the compiler to gather the necessary statistics concerning the family of Jacob Pearson,[6] their father. After he learned of the death of his father, Ephraim Pearson, in Savannah, Ga., he was accustomed to sign his own name as Ephraim J. Pearson.

Joseph O'Brien,[6] eldest son and child of Timothy and Phebe (Cleveland) O'Brien, m. in Sherburne, Chenango county, N. Y., March 18, 1824, Clarissa Stetson, dau. of Benjamin and Mary (Johnson) Stetson. She was b. in Barnard, Windsor county, Vt., Dec. 25, 1794; d. in Sangerfield, Oneida county, N. Y., Oct. 1, 1855. He d. in Sherburne, Chenango county, N. Y., May 2, 1826. She was, unfortunately, deranged for many years previous to her death. No children.

Timothy O'Brien,[6] second son and child of Timothy and Phebe (Cleveland) O'Brien, m. first, in Middlefield, Otsego county, N. Y., Oct. 25, 1822, Mary Chase, dau. of James and

Polly (Utley) Chase. She was b. in Pomfret, Windham county, Conn., Oct. 6, 1799; d. in Poolville, Madison county, N. Y., Sept. 14, 1874. He m. second, in Sherburne, Chenango county, N. Y., Jan. 1, 1875, Minerva Waterhouse, dau. of David and Betsey (Luther) Waterhouse. She was b. in Hanover, York county, Pa., July 26, 1820. He is a farmer; res. Poolville, N. Y.

Children, by wife Mary, both b. in Madison county, N. Y.:

1. James Albert Chase,[7] b. Nov. 11, 1823; d. Sept. 15, 1871.
2. Almira Jane,[7] b. Nov. 29, 1824.

[Mr. Timothy O'Brien, of Poolville, N. Y., is one of the "*six surviving grandchildren*" (1879) of Benjamin and Rachel Cleveland. They may here be recapitulated in the order of their respective ages. Theodotia Hamblin,[6] 94; Oren Cleveland,[6] 94; Timothy O'Brien,[6] 80; Charles C. W. Cleveland,[6] 76; Mrs. Dana Ayres, (Alice Cleveland,[6]) 70; and John K. Cleveland,[6] 68.]

Drusilla O'Brien,[6] eldest daughter and third child of Timothy and Phebe (Cleveland) O'Brien, m. in Sherburne, Chenango county, N. Y., Jan. 8, 1824, Simeon Gilbert Reese, son of Jacob and Anna (Gillett) Reese. He was b. in Sherburne, Chenango county, N. Y., Oct. 6, 1799; d. in Hamilton, Madison county, N. Y., March 5, 1871. She d. in Sherburne, N. Y., Nov. 2, 1838.

Children—eldest b. in Berkshire, Tioga county, N. Y., and the residue in Sherburne, Chenango county, N. Y.:

1. Sarah Caroline Marilla,[7] b. Feb. 24, 1825.
2. Simeon Dewitt Clinton,[7] b. April 23, 1827.
3. Rachel Emeline Clarinda,[7] b. Aug. 31, 1829; d. in 1858.
4. Haskell Galusha Cleveland,[7] b. April 19, 1832.
5. Jacob Gillett,[7] b. Dec. 26, 1833.
6. Martha Ann,[7] b. May 14, 1838; d. Oct. 24, 1838.

Rachel E. C. Reese,[7] became the wife of Geo. Edmund Baker, Esq., of the "Baker Family" Vocalists, and sang with them for several years. She died of spotted fever, in

Waukegan, Lake county, Ill., Aug. 11, 1858. Her musical talent was remarkable, and added much to the fame of these singers.

Sarah O'Brien,[6] youngest daughter and child of Timothy and Phebe (Cleveland) O'Brien, m. in Sherburne, Chenango county, N. Y., May 31, 1827, Ezra Stetson, son of Benjamin and Mary (Johnson) Stetson. He was b. in Barnard, Vt., July 25, 1798; d. in Bouckville, Madison county, N. Y., May 28, 1863. She d. in Sangerfield, Oneida county, N. Y., Aug. 7, 1863.

Children, all b. in Sangerfield, Oneida county, N. Y.:

1. Phebe Louisa,[7] b. April 9, 1828; res. Sangerfield, N. Y.
2. Egbert Joseph,[7] b. Nov. 29, 1833; res. Sangerfield, N. Y.
3. Alvin Cleveland,[7] b. Dec. 17, 1837; d. Dec. 3, 1857.
4. Adelia Drusilla,[7] b. July 3, 1840; res. Marshall, Mich.

This concludes the records for the portion of this genealogy other than the Appendix. In that, extensive additions have been made to all that has preceded, and much more might have been added without exhausting the material on hand and constantly accumulating. Should the compiler ever attempt another edition, many advantageous changes in the general arrangement of the work could doubtless be made. But he indulges the hope that what has been placed before the reader will not appear ambiguous in any sense, or difficult to be comprehended and understood.

It should be stated that a large and complete Genealogy of the Clevelands in this country is in active preparation by James Butler Cleveland,[8] Esq., late of Washington, D. C., but now residing in Oneonta, Otsego county, N. Y. So that this work is in no sense a substitute for the one to be issued at the earliest possible period by him. His assiduity and skill in his researches, so far as the writer can judge, entitle him to rank as one of the best genealogists in the country. Every one who bears the honored name of Cleveland, or is a descendant of any one by that name, near or remote, should put themselves at once into communication with him, and cheerfully, and withal *promptly*, contribute what they know or can obtain about their pedigrees in the Cleveland line. The years are passing rapidly by, and every day the task becomes more difficult as the elder members drop away, and what they alone knew, and could have imparted when living, is thus lost forever. No one can tell how valuable the records of his pedigree may prove to him, or to his descendants. Certain it is that very many will regret that they neglected to perfect and preserve them.

Copy of a letter of inquiry—written by Rev. John Cleveland, of Ipswich, Essex county, Mass., in 1759, to another John Cleveland, Maltster, etc., in England, and the statements in which are, or should be, conclusive as to the pedigree of all New England Clevelands—is here inserted. This Rev. John Cleveland,[4] a son of Josiah[3] and Abigail (Paine) Cleveland, was b. in Canterbury, Conn., April 12, 1722, (O. S.), and could not have been mistaken in such a plain and positive account of his father's grandfather. It is not known that an answer was received from the opulent brewer or maltster, and perhaps the letter of inquiry never reached him. The copy, as originally made by the reverend gentleman himself, is in my possession, and is submitted herewith *verbatim et literatim* :

"SIR :

"Being informed (by the Bearer, one Samuel Bates) of your Name and the Place of your abode, I supposed it highly probable that you are of the same Family that I sprang from. My Great Grandfather's Name was Moses Cleaveland, and came from Ipswich, in Suffolk. He was young when he came to New-England, and was an apprentice to a joyner, and came with His Master. He settled in Woburn, near Boston, married, and had seven Sons, besides Daughters, and his sons all left Children, and all in New-England, of the Name, are his Posterity, and all spell the Name as I do, tho' we are not certain that we spell it exactly as the same Family does in England. Because, as the said Moses was young when he left England, and could not read and write, if I am not misinformed. I have seen the Name spelt as I spell it in Books Printed in England, but most commonly I find it spelt thus, Cleveland, or Clevland, but as you are undoubtedly of ye same Family, if These Lines should come to your Hands I should esteem it a Favour that you would write me, and give me some account of your Family. I am a Minister of yᵉ Gospel and Pastor of a Chh. in Ipswich, in the county of Essex, and Province of The Massachusetts Bay, in New-England.

"Excuse the Boldness and Freedom of your Humble servant and Unknown Friend.

JOHN CLEAVELAND.

" Ipswich, New-England, Dec. 25, 1759."

The superscription, copy of which was also retained, is as follows :

" To Mr. JOHN CLEAVELAND,
Malster in Ipswich, in
County of Suffolk,
Living in Silent St.,
Near St. Clemence Church,
England."

The compiler so far has made no serious attempt to trace the pedigree of Moses Cleveland,[1] in England. To those who have a taste for "the boast of heraldry," the following is given, concerning the family :

" CLEVELAND — (Durham, Eng.)

"*Coat of Arms.*—Per chevron, sable and ermine, a chevron engrailed, counter changed.

"*Crest.*—A demi-old man habited, azure, having on his head a cap, gules, turned up with fur, holding in his dexter hand a spear, proper, having from the blade a golden cord passing behind and coiled in the left hand.

"*Motto.*—Pro Deo, et Patria."

Mr. Hinman, in his "Puritan Settlers," gives the following account of the name: "CLEVELAND, CLEAVELAND.—This family probably derived the name from the town of Cleveland, in the county of Durham, England. The principal branch was seated in the county of York. Early in the 13th century, Sir Guy de Cleveland was present at the siege of Boulogne in France, afterwards at the battle of Poictiers, when he commanded the spearmen. And a branch of this family went into Devonshire, and continued until the male line of the family became extinct." The word itself is a corruption of "Cliff-land," thus certifying beyond question its English origin.

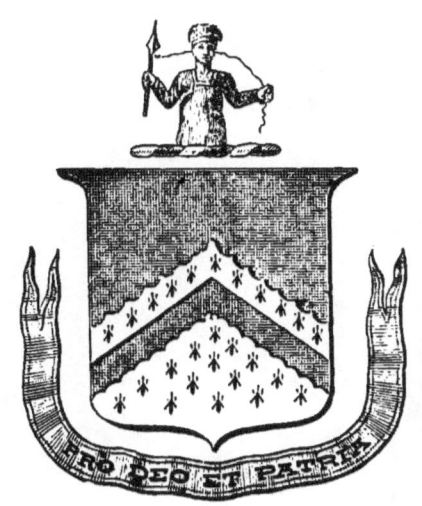

CLEVELAND.

APPENDIX

A.

EDWARD WINN was of Woburn as early as 1641; made a freeman, 1643; and taxed in Woburn in the rate for the country, Sept. 8, 1645. By his wife Joanna he had, Dec. 5, 1641, a son named *Increase*—the first birth entered in the records of Woburn. His daughters *Ann* and *Elizabeth*, and son *Joseph*, probably had their birth in England before. Joanna, wife of Edward Winn, dying March 8, 1649, he m. second, Aug. 10, 1649, Sarah Beal. She also dying March 15, 1680, he m. third, Ann or Hannah, wid. of Nicholas Wood, who survived him, apparently, till 1686. He d. in Woburn, Sept. 5, 1682. In his will, made May 6, 1682, he names his son Increase; his son Joseph's daughter Sarah; the three youngest children of his daughter Ann, wife of Moses Cleveland; and the three youngest children of his daughter Elizabeth, wife of George Polly. His widow likewise made her will, Sept. 9, 1685, which being proved Nov. 1, 1686, is an indication she was then deceased.

Ann Winn m., Sept. 26, 1648, Moses Cleveland,[1] of Woburn. (See page 5, for their children.)

Elizabeth Winn m., May 21, 1649, George Polly, a carpenter by trade; land ordered to be laid out to him in Woburn, Feb. 3, 1649; chosen a surveyor of fences in 1665, and his right to share in the common lands of the town was acknowledged in 1668.

Children:
1. John, b. Dec. 16, 1650.
2. Joseph, b. Dec. 25, 1652.
3. George, b. Jan. 4, 1656.
4. Elizabeth, b. April 14, 1657.
5. Samuel, b. Jan. 24, 1661; d. Feb. —, 1661.
6. Hannah, b. April 6, 1662; d. April 6, 1662.
7. Hannah (again), b. June 28, 1663.

Geo. Polly d. Dec. 22, 1683; and Elizabeth "Polle, widow," d. May 2, 1695.

Joseph Winn m., about 1664, Rebekah Reed, daughter of William and Mabel Reed, and sister of the first George Reed, of Woburn.

Children:
1. Rebekah, b. May 25, 1665; d. April 6, 1679.
2. Sarah, b. Nov. 9, 1666; m. Ebenezer Johnson.
3. Joanna, b. ——, 1668; m. Edward Knight.
4. Abigail, b. June 18, 1670; d. June 25, 1670.
5. Joseph, b. May 15, 1672.
6. Josiah, b. March 15, 1674.

7. Timothy, b. ——, 1676; d. March 22, 1678.
8. Rebekah (again), ⎫ b. Feb. 14, 1679; m. Timothy Spaulding.
9. Hannah,   ⎭ b. Feb. 14, 1679.
10. Anne, b. Nov. 1, 1684; d. Sept. 13, 1686.
11. Timothy (again), b. Feb. 27, 1687; m. Elizabeth Brooks, and had a son Timothy Winn, (Dea.), who became wealthy.

Increase Winn, b. in Woburn, Dec. 5, 1641, m. in Woburn, July 13, 1665, Hannah Sawtell, dau. of Richard Sawtell, and had—

1. Hannah, b. April 11, 1666; m. Samuel Baker.
2. Edward, b. June 15, 1668.
3. Mary, b. May 1, 1670.
4. Sarah, b. Dec. 23, 1672.
5. Abigail, b. Jan. 8, 1678.
6. Rebekah, b. Nov. 5, 1679.
7. Jacob, b. Oct. 4, 1681.
8. Joanna, b. June 24, 1683.
9. Increase, b. Feb. 9, 1685.

"Sergt. Increase Winn" d. Dec. 14, 1690.
"Widow Hannah Winn" d. Feb. 18, 1723.

In reference to the children of Moses[1] and Ann (Winn) Cleveland, the space assigned to this work allows but brief mention. Each will be taken up in the order of birth.

Moses Cleveland,[2] eldest son and child of Moses[1] and Ann (Winn) Cleveland, was b. in Woburn, Mass., Sept. 1, 1651, nearly three years after recorded date of marriage. The compiler is inclined to believe that he was a sea-faring man. He m. Oct. 4, 1676, (according to the Woburn records), Ruth Norton, perhaps a dau. of Francis and Mary Norton, of Charlestown, or, more probably, a dau. of Nicholas and Elizabeth Norton, of Weymouth, Mass. In support of the latter opinion is the fact that Nicholas Norton, Jr., was of Edgartown, (Martha's Vineyard), Mass., in 1669, and that the numerous families of Clevelands on the Island are descendants of Moses[2] and Ruth (Norton) Cleveland. Hence it is reasonable to suppose that near relationship to the Nortons of Martha's Vineyard, brought the descendants of Moses Cleveland[2] to settle there. Mr. Richard J. Pease, of Edgartown, the historian of the Island, confirms this in a letter to Nehemiah Cleveland, Esq., of Brooklyn, N. Y., dated Feb. 19, 1855, in which he says: "You are right in the conjecture formed that our Clevelands come from Moses and Ruth. Ruth Norton was the daughter of Nicholas Norton, the ancestor of all our Nortons. Before his removal to this town he was of 'Weymouth,' where some of his children were born. Nicholas died here in 1690, aged 80 years; his wife Elizabeth soon after him, in the same year."

According to the Woburn records, Moses[2] and Ruth (Norton) Cleveland had but two children in ten years, namely:

1. Anna,[3] b. Nov. 7, 1677; m. —— Bell.
2. Joseph,[3] b. March 31, 1686; probably settled in Nantucket or Martha's Vineyard.

But there was also a son later, perhaps b. in Southold, Long Island, N. Y., whose name was
    3. Ichabod,[3] b. June 25, 1695,

Who m. in Southold, N. Y., Feb. 18, 1716, Anna Moore, who was b. March 5, 1697, and d. May 6, 1785, by whom he had a family of seven children, as follows, all b. in Southold:

    1. Anna,[4] b. Dec. 23, 1717; m. William Case.
    2. Mehetabel,[4] b. Nov. 26, 1724; m. first, Fitzjohn Young, and second, Micah Horton.
    3. Joseph,[4] b. June 27, 1727.
    4. Abigail,[4] b. March 17, 1729; m. Uriah Terry.
    5. Mary,[4] b. June 22, 1731; m. James Hart.
    6. Benjamin,[4] b. June 10, 1736.
    7. Ichabod,[4] b. Feb. 19, 1739.

JOSEPH CLEVELAND,[4] m. Feb. 12, 1750, Mary Horton, dau. of Jonathan and Mary (Tuthill) Horton. She was b. Feb. 8, 1730.
Children, all b. in Southold, N. Y.:

    1. Mary,[5] b. May 29, 1752; m. first, Thomas Hubbard, and second, Elias Grave.
    2. Joseph,[5] b. May 24, 1754; d. March 25, 1756.
    3. Mehetabel,[5] b. Jan. 16, 1757; m. Ezra Griswold.
    4. Joseph,[5] b. Oct. 7, 1759; d. Jan. 30, 1840, unm.
    5. Abigail,[5] b. April 17, 1762; d. Sept. 24, 1805, unm.
    6. Lazarus,[5] b. Dec. 29, 1764; d. March 5, 1847, unm.
    7. Benjamin Norton,[5] b. Aug. 10, 1767.
    8. Anna,[5] b. Sept. 19, 1770; m. Joseph Moore.

BENJAMIN N. CLEVELAND,[5] b. in Southold, Aug. 10, 1767, m. first, in Southold, in 1790, Mary Gardiner, dau. of David and Jerusha (Strong) Gardiner. He was a watch and clock maker, residing in Newark, N. J., where his wife Mary d. May 25, 1795, aged 24.
Children:

    1. Sophronia,[6] b. Feb. 17, 1791.
    2. Mary,[6] b. Nov. 25, 1793.
    3. Joseph,[6] b. Oct. 11, 1794; d. May 11, 1795.

He m. second, Mrs. Sarepta (Skinner) Oliver, dau. of Jonathan Skinner, of Springfield, N. J. She d. in 1862, and is buried at Edenton, N. C.; he d. Dec. 20, 1837, and is buried at Newark, N. J. He was a member of the First Presbyterian Church, Newark. He had by wife Sarepta seven children.

BENJAMIN CLEVELAND,[4] had two wives, names unknown. By his first wife he had a son, Ichabod,[5] b. in Elizabethtown, N. J., in 1765, who m. in 1784, Katurah Baldwin. By his second wife he had a son, Benjamin,[5] b. in same place, Feb. 14, 1781, who m. Elizabeth Gibbs. She was b. in Elizabethtown, N. J., March 25, 1784; d. May 10, 1855. Benjamin Cleveland,[5] d. in Elizabethtown, N. J., March 25, 1857. His descendants are numerous.

ICHABOD CLEVELAND,[4] remained in Southold, N. Y., and m. Mrs. Anna (Corey) Horton, widow of Lazarus Horton. She d. in Southold,

Sept. 25, 1805, aged 73. He d. Oct. 7, 1818, and is buried in the cemetery of the First Church, where a stone marks his grave. They had but one child, a son:

  1. Moses,[5] b. Dec. 6, 1770,

Who m. Jan. 23, 1793, Parnel Conklin, dau. of Jonathan and Parnel (Booth) Conklin. She was b. in Southold, Feb. 16, 1772; d. in same place, Nov. 5, 1857. He d. in Southold, Nov. 14, 1848.

 Children, all b. in Southold:

  1. Moses Conklin,[6] b. July 4, 1795; res. Southold, N. Y.
  2. William Henry,[6] (M. D.), b. Jan. 9, 1797.
  3. Parnel,[6] b. April —, 1799; d. May 19, 1800.
  4. Joseph,[6] b. March 2, 1803; d. March 13, 1852.

MOSES C. CLEVELAND,[6] eldest son of Moses[5] and Parnel (Conklin) Cleveland, was born in Southold, L. I., July 4, 1795. He attended the school of Master Wines Osborn, an instructor of local fame, who taught during many years in "the Brick School House," a building owned by twenty-seven proprietors, of whom Moses Cleveland[5] was one. They sold it, Dec. 30, 1816, to the Trustees of School Dist. No. 5, of the Town of Southold. It stood upon the site now occupied by the Chapel of the Presbyterian Church. The building was taken down in 1844.

In December, 1812, he went to live as an apprenticed cordwainer for three years with Deacon Nathaniel Hubbard, who was doing a large business in tanning and currying, and in the manufacture of boots and shoes, at Mattituck, L. I. He faithfully fulfilled his obligations, won the confidence and esteem of the family in which he lived, and became a skillful workman. Afterwards, in August, 1816, he went to Catskill, N. Y., where he wrought in fine work for a year in the employ of Mr. Gideon Reynolds. He subsequently enlarged his field of observation, and his practice as a skillful workman, in Madison, Hudson City, Goshen, and Newburgh, N. Y.

On the 2nd of June, 1819, he was married by the Rev. Lathrop Thompson, to Sarah, the eldest daughter of Deacon Nathaniel and Sarah (Reeve) Hubbard, in whose family he had lived during his apprenticeship.

About the year 1823 a village began to spring up around the Suffolk County Court House. This village has more recently become known as Riverhead. Mr. Cleveland made this the place of his residence in September, 1824. Judge Miller, in his Centennial History of the Town of Riverhead, speaks of Mr. Cleveland as being, in 1825, one of the active business men of the village. Mrs. Cleveland, after a few days' illness, died there, May 3, 1832, aged 35 years. On the 11th of May, 1833, he was married by the Rev. Abraham Luce to Miss Ency Hubbard, sister of his first wife, who was born at Mattituck, Dec. 16, 1802.

From his earliest years his Christian principles were sound, his moral character was high, and his integrity in business and other relations strict and trustworthy; but it was not until July, 1838, that he made a public confession of his Christian faith and became a full member of the First Church of Southold. Five years later, he was elected to the office of Deacon, and he has fulfilled the duties of the office for thirty-six years. Soon after he became a Deacon, he was chosen to be one of the Trustees of the Church. For a long course of years he has been a Director of the Suffolk County Mutual Insurance Company; and from the origin of Southold Savings Bank, in 1858, his name has been prominent on its Board of Trustees. He has repeatedly filled various offices of public trust to which he has been called by the votes of his fellow townsmen; and his character and usefulness have often been manifest as the guardian of children whose orphanage has caused them to need some wise and faithful man to fill the father's place. He has been especially active in the promotion of temperance throughout the county, and of religion on a far wider field. Perhaps there is no other man living who has attended so many of the meetings of the Suffolk County Temperance Association throughout its whole existence for the last twenty-nine years.

He had but one child,

1. Nathaniel Hubbard,[7] b. June 17, 1834,

Who has given much attention to the genealogy and history of his branch of the Clevelands. Res. Southold, L. I.

WILLIAM HENRY CLEVELAND,[6] second son of Moses[5] and Parnel (Conklin) Cleveland, was born at Southold, L. I., Jan. 9, 1797, where he attended the school of Master Wines Osborn, with his elder brother Moses. In December, 1816, he was examined by the Commissioners of Schools and duly licensed by their certificate as a teacher in the public schools of Southold. He first taught in the village of Oyster Ponds, now known as Orient, L. I. The following spring he entered "Clinton Academy," at East Hampton, L. I., boarding with Rev. Ebenezer Phillips, the principal, who was also pastor of the Presbyterian Church in that place. This academy has the honor of having been one of the first two chartered by the Regents of the University of New York State in 1784. It was named in honor of Gov. George Clinton, by whom it was presented with a bell. During the years 1818 and 1819 Mr. Cleveland was the Preceptor in School Dist. No. 9 of the town of Smithtown, L. I., where, according to the custom of the day, he "boarded around." There he decided to be a physician, and during the time he taught there, was also a student with the resident physician, Dr. C. H. Havens. He m. Feb. 8, 1820, Mary Ann, daughter of Capt. Jonathan and Rebecca (King) Terry, of Oyster Ponds, where she was born June 2, 1798, and where she died precisely ten months after her marriage, Dec. 8, 1820. He then entered Yale College, graduating in 1823. On the twenty-second day of August, 1824, he married Zilpha Thayer, first born of thirteen children of Ebenezer and Phebe (Crowell) Thayer, who was born at Greenfield, Mass., Jan. 22, 1804. He first settled in Enfield, Mass., where he was a successful practitioner for ten years, and then located himself at Shelburne Falls, Mass. After several years, he removed to Springfield, Mass., where he resided until his death, which occurred Feb. 21, 1852. He was the father of eight children, the first five b. in Enfield, Mass., the others in Shelburne Falls, Mass.:

1. William Henry,[7] b. July 23, 1825.
2. Ebenezer Thayer,[7] b. June 1, 1828; d. Sept. 23, 1828.
3. Moses Conklin,[7] b. Nov. 21, 1829; d. Dec. 13, 1829.
4. Parnel Conklin,[7] b. Oct. 9, 1830.
5. George Lyman,[7] b. April 24, 1833; d. May 16, 1835.
6. John Thayer,[7] b. Aug. 16, 1835.
7. Mary Ann Terry,[7] b. Jan. 20, 1838.
8. George Moses,[7] b. Oct. 26, 1840.

Dr. Cleveland was a member of the First Congregational Church in Springfield, of which Rev. Samuel Osgood, D. D., was pastor. His wife Zilpha was also a consistent church member. She d. Sept. 24, 1868.

JOSEPH CLEVELAND,[6] youngest son of Moses[5] and Parnel (Conklin) Cleveland, was born in Southold, March 2, 1803. He early chose to learn the trade at which his father worked, and was apprenticed to a house carpenter at Patchogue, L. I. He became a skillful workman, and afterwards went to Brooklyn, L. I., where, Aug. 5, 1824, he married Jemima Abrams, dau. of Joseph and Martha (Vermilye) Abrams, who was b. in Brooklyn, Jan. 26, 1808. He d. in Southold, March 13, 1852.

Children, all b. in Southold:

1. Moses,[7] b. Feb. 17, 1825.
2. Catharine,[7] b. March 3, 1827.
3. Henry Conklin,[7] b. July 23, 1829.
4. Sarah Hubbard,[7] b. Oct. 21, 1831.
5. Parnel,[7] b. Dec. 10, 1833.
6. Joseph Benjamin,[7] b. Nov. 27, 1838.
7. Mary Zilpha,[7] b. Oct. 26, 1842; d. Oct. 30, 1865.
8. John Demarest,[7] b. Aug. 4, 1845.

HANNAH CLEVELAND,[2] the eldest daughter and second child of Moses[1] and Ann (Winn) Cleveland, b. in Woburn, Mass., Aug. 4, 1653, m. in same place, Sept. 24, 1677, Thomas Henshaw, whose name occurs in the List for the Meetinghouse rate, 1672, but not in the Tax List for 1666, nor among those who had right in the common lands of Woburn, 1668. Of his parentage nothing is learned. He d. Jan. 16, 1700.

Children of Thomas and Hannah[2] (Cleveland) Henshaw were as follows, all b. in Woburn:

1. Elizabeth,[3] b. July 30, 1678; m. John Manser.
2. Thomas,[3] b. Nov. 17, 1680; m. Mary Brooks.
3. Hannah,[3] b. May 21, 1683.
4. William,[3] b. Nov. 25, 1685.
5. Samuel,[3] b. March 13, 1688.
6. Ebenezer,[3] b. March 1, 1691; d. Feb. 28, 1756.
7. Josiah,[3] b. March 1, 1695; d. Jan. 16, 1700.

[The name *Henshaw* but seldom occurs in Woburn records; it is there almost invariably spelled "Henshow," "Hensher," or "Hincher."]

AARON CLEVELAND,[2] second son and third child of Moses[1] and Ann (Winn) Cleveland, b. in Woburn, Mass., Jan. 10, 1655, m. first, in Woburn, Sept. 26, 1675, Dorcas Wilson, probably dau. of John Wilson, who first appears upon the tax lists in Woburn, in the rate for the country, assessed Aug. 26, 1666. His two children, John Wilson, Jr., and Dorcas, must have been born before he came to Woburn, and he d. July 2, 1687. Aaron[2] and Dorcas (Wilson) Cleveland had a family of ten children, as follows:

1. Dorcas,[3] b. Oct. 29, 1676; m. John Knight.
2. Hannah,[3] b. Dec. 18, 1678; d. June 13, 1679.
3. Aaron,[3] b. July 9, 1680; m. Abigail Waters.
4. Hannah,[3] (again), b. June 2, 1687; m. —— Beard.
5. Moses,[3] b. Feb. 24, 1690; m. Mary Johnson.
6. Sarah,[3] b. March 5, 1692; m. Job Richardson.
7. Miriam,[3] b. July 9, 1694.
8. Isabel,[3] b. April 6, 1697; d. Dec. 7, 1714.
9. Ann,[3] b. ——, 1699.
10. Benjamin,[3] b. May 16, 1701; m. Anna Church.

After the death of wife Dorcas, in Cambridge, Mass., Nov. 29, 1714, he m. a second wife, Prudence ——, but had no more children, and d. Sept. 14, 1716, aged, according to gravestone, 62 years.

AARON CLEVELAND,[3] eldest son of Aaron[2] and Dorcas (Wilson) Cleveland, a carpenter by trade, b. in Woburn, Mass., July 9, 1680, m. in Woburn, Jan. 1, 1702, Abigail Waters, a dau. of Samuel and Mary Waters, of Medford, Mass. She was b. Nov. 29, 1683. After the birth of their second child, he appears to have removed to Medford, and thence to Cambridge; after that again to Medford, and subsequently to Charlestown. His mother, Dorcas, d. at his house in Cambridge, in 1714, and his eldest son, Aaron,[4] two years later, and both were buried in Cambridge graveyard. In 1738 he removed to East Haddam, Conn., where he traded extensively in land, and became wealthy. He was commonly known as "Capt." Cleveland. His children were—

1. Aaron,[4] b. in Woburn, Oct. 20, 1702; d. ——, 1716.
2. Samuel,[4] b. in Woburn, May 17, 1704.*
3. Abigail,[4] b. in Medford, May 10, 1706.
4. John,[4] bap. in Cambridge, Oct. 7, 1711; d. young.
5. Josiah,[4] bap. in Cambridge, Nov. 1, 1713; m. Joanna Porter.
6. Aaron,[4] (again), bap. in Cambridge, Oct. 29, 1715; m. Susannah Porter.
7. John,[4] (again), bap. in Cambridge, July 18, 1717.
8. Moses,[4] bap. in Cambridge, July 19, 1719.
9. Mary,[4] bap. in Cambridge, July 7, 1724.

MOSES CLEVELAND,[3] second son and fifth child of Aaron[2] and Dorcas (Wilson) Cleveland, b. in Woburn, Feb. 24, 1690, m. in Canterbury, Conn., Oct. 19, 1717, Mary Johnson, dau. of Obadiah Johnson, of Canterbury, and had, born in Canterbury—

---

* In Vol. XLIII, page 517, Registry of Deeds, [for Suffolk?] under date of May 23, 1743, is a deed from "Samuel Cleveland," of Boston, mariner, in which he calls Aaron Cleveland his father.

1. Miriam,[4] b. Jan. 30, 1718.
2. Dorcas,[4] b. May 9, 1721.
3. Obadiah,[4] b. Sept. 16, 1723.
4. Anna,[4] b. Aug. 15, 1725.
5. Rebecca,[4] b. June 28, 1730.

BENJAMIN CLEVELAND,[3] third son and youngest child of Aaron[2] and Dorcas (Wilson) Cleveland, b. in Woburn, May 16, 1701, m. in Canterbury, Conn., Jan. 1, 1727, Anna Church, by whom he had—

1. Esther,[4] b. in Canterbury, Nov. 5, 1727.
2. Aaron,[4] b. in Canterbury, June 3, 1730.
3. Anna,[4] b. in Canterbury, March 23, 1732.
4. Benjamin,[4] b. in Windham, Aug. 30, 1733; m. Mary Elderkin.
5. Moses,[4] b. in Windham, July 20, 1736; m. Tabitha Spencer.
6. Chloe,[4] b. in Windham, May 30, 1744.

Anna, wife of Benj. Cleveland,[3] d. Oct. 21, 1754.

AARON CLEVELAND,[4] (Rev.), fifth son and sixth child of Aaron[3] and Abigail (Waters) Cleveland, b. in Cambridge, Mass., and bap. there, Oct. 29, 1715, m. in Medford, Mass., Aug. 4, 1739, Susannah Porter, dau. of Rev. Aaron Porter, of Medford. She was b. in Medford, March 1, 1716. Having graduated at Harvard, 1735, he entered the Congregational ministry, and was settled over the Haddam (Conn.) people in 1739. Was dismissed in 1746, and in 1747 was installed over the South Church in Malden, Mass., but dismissed in 1750. He is next heard of at Halifax, Nova Scotia, whence he sailed for England; received holy orders in the Church of England, at London, 1755, and was commissioned, July 1, 1757, by the Society for Propagating the Gospel in Foreign Parts, to take charge of the Episcopal Church in New Castle, Pa., in compliance with the request of that parish. The following is an exact copy of the letter of the Society under whose auspices he was to settle at New Castle. It may be found in the church records at New Castle:

"Charter House, July 1, 1757.
" Good Gentlemen:
"The Society for the propagation of the Gospel in foreign parts, have granted your request, & appointed M[r.] Cleveland their Missionary in your Church; but it is on this express condition, which is now a standing rule in all their missions, that you provide him with a good House and Glebe, & not less than twenty pounds sterling per annum towards his more comfortable support.
"Heartily recommending you & M[r.] Cleveland to God's Blessing,
I am, Sirs,
your very faithful
humble Servant,
PHILIP BEARCROFT.
"To the Church Wardens
& Vestry of the Episcopal
Church of New Castle,
in Pennsylvania."

On his way to Boston to arrange for the conveyance of his family to New Castle, he stopped at the house of his old friend, Dr. Benjamin Franklin, in Philadelphia, was there taken sick and died, Aug. 11, 1757. His remains were buried in Christ Church, Philadelphia. A warm eulogium, written by Dr. Franklin, the editor, appeared in the obituary notice in the *Pennsylvania Gazette*, of Aug. 18, 1757. His widow d. in Salem, Mass., in 1788. His son, Rev. Aaron Cleveland,[5] was the maternal grandfather of Rt. Rev. A. Cleveland Coxe,[7] Bishop of the Diocese of Western New York, and of Hon. Wm. E. Dodge,[7] of New York City. Why it is that none of the numerous and intelligent descendants of this branch of the Clevelands (called the *Aaron* branch) have ever attempted to compile a genealogical record, is unaccountable to the writer. Capt. Stephen Cleveland,[5] an experienced seaman, who received his commission from the first President of the Continental Congress, also Richard Jeffrey Cleveland,[6] author of "Cleveland's Voyages"—a very popular book in its day—were of this branch.

[For account of descendants of SAMUEL CLEVELAND,[2] see pages 5—8, and Appendix B.]

MIRIAM CLEVELAND,[2] the second daughter and fifth child of Moses[1] and Ann (Winn) Cleveland, b. in Woburn, Mass., July 10, 1659, m. in Charlestown, Mass., Dec. 13, 1683, Thomas Foskett, son of John and Elizabeth Foskett. All that is learned of this family would show that John Foskett, of Charleston, 1658, was a householder, 1678. Elizabeth, his wife, was admitted to the Church, April 6, 1673, and two weeks thereafter, April 20th, their children, six in number—John, Thomas, Joshua, Robert, Elizabeth, and Mary—were all baptized; son Jonathan, bap. Nov. 1, 1674, and dau. Abigail, June 6, 1680. The children of Thomas and Miriam[2] (Cleveland) Foskett, as appearing on the Woburn records, are three, namely :

1. Thomas,[3] b. April 26, 1684; d. ——.
2. Elizabeth,[3] b. May 10, 1686.
3. John,[3] b. May 8, 1688; d. July 11, 1689.

The date and place of death of Miriam,[2] or her husband, or anything further concerning the family, has not been ascertained.

EDWARD CLEVELAND,[2] the fourth son and seventh child of Moses[1] and Ann (Winn) Cleveland, b. in Woburn, Mass., May 20, 1663, m. for first wife, as the compiler thinks, (though unable to give place and date, or parentage with certainty), Deliverance Palmer, and at one time lived in Kingston, R. I., though about 1716 he purchased land in Canterbury, Conn. The deed states him to be "late of Kingstown, Rhode Island." While residing in Canterbury his wife died, as the records there show, June 7, 1717, and he m. second, in Canterbury, Jan. 1, 1722, Zeruiah Church, who, so far as appears, bore him no children. It is concluded he returned to Rhode Island and died there, but date not learned.

Children, as far as found, were—

1. Edward,[3] b. (probably) in 1689; m. Rebecca Paine.
2. Isaac,[3] b. (probably) in 1691; m. Susannah Johnson.
3. Samuel,[3] b. (probably) in 1693; m. Mary Darby.
4. Palmer,[3] b. (probably) in 1695; m. Deborah ——.

    5. Mary,[3] b. (probably) in 1697.
    6. Elizabeth,[3] b. (probably) in 1699; m. Jonathan Shepard.

But the order of birth is conjectural, in the absence of records.

EDWARD CLEVELAND,[3] eldest son and child of Edward[2] and Deliverance (Palmer) Cleveland, b. about 1689, m. in Canterbury, Conn., April 17, 1716, Rebecca Paine, dau. of Elisha and Rebecca (Doane) Paine. She was b. about 1690-1. He d. Nov. 3, 1771; his widow d. Feb. —, 1784.

    Children, b. in Canterbury :
1. Joanna,[4] b. July 22, 1717.
2. Rebecca,[4] b. March 16, 1719; m. Daniel Brown.
3. Solomon,[4] b. June 1, 1720; m. Abigail Baker.
4. Palmer,[4] b. Jan. 29, 1722.
5. Deliverance,[4] b. March 10, 1723; m. Isaiah Baker.
6. Silas,[4] b. March 28, 1726; m. Elizabeth Hyde.
7. Experience,[4] b. Sept. 5, 1728.
8. Paine,[4] b. Aug. 30, 1731.

Silas[4] and Elizabeth (Hyde) Cleveland were grandparents to Ex-Gov. Chauncey Fitch Cleveland,[6] of Hampton, Conn.

ISAAC CLEVELAND,[3] son of Edward[2] and Deliverance (Palmer) Cleveland, m. in Canterbury, Conn., Nov. 20, 1721, Susannah Johnson, "daughter of Mary Stevens, formerly Johnson," as stated in the old Church records.

    Children :
1. Johnson,[4] b. Oct. 29, 1722.
2. Lemuel,[4] b. Aug. 13, 1725.
3. Deliverance,[4] b. April 2, 1729.
4. Mary,[4] b. Jan. 10, 1731.
5. Betsey,[4] b. June 11, 1733.
6. Isaac,[4] b. May 13, 1735.

SAMUEL CLEVELAND,[3] son of Edward[2] and Deliverance (Palmer) Cleveland, m. in Canterbury, Conn., Nov. —, 1724, Mary Darby, and he d. in Pomfret, Conn., June 11, 1762.

    Children :
1. Phineas,[4] b. in Canterbury, Oct. 19, 1727.
2. James,[4] b. in Canterbury, July 3, 1730.
3. Curtis,[4] b. in Pomfret, July 5, 1734.
4. Edward,[4] b. in Pomfret, July 4, 1737.
5. Mary,[4] b. in Pomfret, Dec. 4, 1740.
6. Abigail,[4] b. in Pomfret, Aug. 7, 1746.

PALMER CLEVELAND,[3] son of Edward[2] and Deliverance (Palmer) Cleveland, m. in Kingston, R. I., Deborah ——, by whom he had—
1. John,[4] b. July 12, ——.
2. Deborah,[4] b. Aug. 9, ——.
3. Deliverance,[4] b. May —, ——.
4. Mercy,[4] b. June —, ——.
5. Palmer,[4] b. Feb. 22, ——.

The foregoing very unsatisfactory account is all that can be gleaned from the mutilated records of Kingston, R. I., concerning the family of Palmer Cleveland.[3] James Butler Cleveland,[5] of Oneonta, Otsego county, N. Y., is a great-great-grandson of Deliverance,[1] and will no doubt be able in his large work to make it more perfect and intelligible.

JOSIAH CLEVELAND,[2] fifth son and eighth child of Moses[1] and Ann (Winn) Cleveland, b. in Woburn, Mass., Feb. 26, 1667, m. (probably) in 1689, or early in 1690, Mary ——, and settled in the town of Chelmsford, with his brother, Samuel Cleveland.[2] From this fact, and that he followed this brother to Canterbury, Conn., the compiler is disposed to the opinion that he may have married a daughter of Richard and Elizabeth Hildreth, if they had a daughter Mary. There may be no significance in the names given by Samuel[2] and Josiah[2] to the first three children born to each, but it is worth noticing that the second son is Joseph[3] in each case, and possibly named for his uncle Joseph Hildreth, of Chelmsford. Be this as it may, the numerous and intelligent descendants, now living, of Josiah Cleveland,[2] should no longer delay every effort possible to ascertain the maiden name of *Mary*, his wife.

The children, whose names are found on the Chelmsford and Canterbury records, are nine in number, besides a daughter Rachel, who, according to Hinman, m. Jonas Spaulding in 1722:

1. Josiah,[3] b. in Chelmsford, Oct. 7, 1690.
2. Joseph,[3] b. in Chelmsford, June 13, 1692.
3. Mary,[3] b. in Chelmsford, March 17, 1694; m. Richard Adams.
4. John,[3] b. in Chelmsford, June 28, 1696.
5. Jonathan,[3] b. in Chelmsford, March 2, 1698; d. April 5, 1698.
6. Henry,[3] b. in Chelmsford, Dec. 22, 1699.
7. Rachel,[3] b. in ——, (probably) in 1702; m. Jonas Spaulding.
8. Lydia,[3] b. in Canterbury, Dec. 7, 1704.
9. Deliverance,[3] b. in Canterbury, July 13, 1707.
10. Abiel,[3] b. in Canterbury, Oct. 9, 1709.

The last child posthumous, as the father d. in Canterbury, April 26, 1709, aged 42 years.

JOSIAH CLEVELAND,[3] eldest child of Josiah and Mary (——) Cleveland, b. in Chelmsford, Mass., Oct. 7, 1690, m. in Canterbury, Conn., Aug. 7, 1710, Abigail Paine, probably dau. of Elisha and Rebecca (Doane) Paine, and b. Jan. 5, 1688. He d. in Canterbury, Feb. 9, 1750, in the 60th year of his age.

Children, all b. in Canterbury:

1. Keziah,[4] b. Nov. 26, 1711.
2. Josiah,[4] b. April 4, 1713; m. Sarah Lawrence.
3. Abigail,[4] b. June 3, 1715.
4. Elisha,[4] b. Jan. 7, 1717; m. Esther Morse.
5. Lois,[4] b. Dec. 11, 1718.
6. Mary,[4] b. June 29, 1720.
7. John,[4] (Rev.), b. April 12, 1722; m. Mary Dodge.
8. Lydia,[4] b. Feb. 16, 1724; d. March 26, 1745.
9. Ebenezer,[4] (Rev.), b. Dec. 25, 1725; m. Abigail Stevens.
10. Aaron,[4] (Col.), b. Nov. 27, 1727; m. Thankful Paine.
11. Moses,[4] b. April 18, 1730; d. Jan. 1, 1741.

GEN. MOSES CLEVELAND,[5] was the second son of Col. Aaron[4] and Thankful (Paine) Cleveland, and was b. in Canterbury, Jan. 29, 1754;

d. Nov. 16, 1806, aged 52. He was the agent of the Connecticut Land Company, and the city of Cleveland, Ohio, was named in honor of him.

CAPT. JOSEPH CLEVELAND,[3] second child of Josiah[2] and Mary (——) Cleveland, b. in Chelmsford, Mass., June 13, 1692, m. first, in Canterbury, Conn., May 19, 1718, Deborah Butterfield. She d. Nov. 14, 1724, and he m. second, June 24, 1725, Mary Woodward, dau. of John Woodward, and d. May 12, 1752.

Children, by wife Deborah:
1. Jonas,[4] b. Oct. 16, 1718; m. Prudence Phillips.
2. Sybil,[4] b. Jan. 7, 1720; m. —— Cady.
3. John,[4] b. Dec. 31, 1721.

by wife Mary:
4. Deborah,[4] b. Aug. 11, 1726; m. —— Hubbard.
5. Bridget,[4] b. Aug. 12, 1728; m. —— Wedge.
6. Joseph,[4] b. Jan. 19, 1730.
7. Mary,[4] b. April 19, 1731; d. Nov. 8, 1736.
8. Hannah,[4] b. Nov. 2, 1732; d. Nov. 5, 1736.
9. Abijah,[4] b. (probably) in 1734; d. Nov. 3, 1736.
10. Rachel,[4] b. March 3, 1736; d. Nov. 4, 1736.
11. Jonathan,[4] b. Nov. 24, 1737.
12. Jesse,[4] b. Oct. 20, 1739.
13. Mary,[4] b. Aug. 5, 1742; d. Aug. 21, 1742.

It will be noticed the parents buried four children within five days of each other.

REUBEN CLEVELAND,[6] of Chicago, is a grandson of Jesse.[4]

HENRY CLEVELAND,[3] son of Josiah[2] and Mary (——) Cleveland, b. in Chelmsford, Mass., Dec. 22, 1699, m. in Canterbury, Conn., in 1718, Lucy Fitch, dau. of Maj. James Fitch, by whom he had—
1. William,[4] b. July 7, 1719.
2. Nehemiah,[4] b. July 30, 1721.
3. Lucy,[4] b. March 2, 1724.
4. Jabez,[4] b. Nov. 4, 1727; d. Nov. 13, 1736.

With probably other children not recorded, as there was a Jabez[4] (again) b. about 1738.

ISAAC CLEVELAND,[2] sixth son and ninth child of Moses[1] and Ann (Winn) Cleveland, b. in Woburn, Mass., May 11, 1669, m. in Charlestown, Mass., July 17, 1699, Elizabeth Curtice (or Curtis), by whom he had—
1. Curtice,[3] b. Jan. 23, 1701.
2. Anne,[3] b. June 6, 1703; m. Phillip Spaulding.
3. Miriam,[3] b. July 4, 1705; m. Adam Cramer.
4. Keziah,[3] b. Oct. 24, 1709; m. Sylvanus Jones.

CURTICE CLEVELAND,[3] eldest child of Isaac[2] and Elizabeth (Curtice) Cleveland, b. Jan. 23, 1701, m. in Norwich, Conn., Jan. 16, 1734, Remembrance Currier, and had children—
1. Gideon,[4] b. March 5, 1735; d. Jan. 23, 1742.
2. Joanna,[4] b. Oct. 22, 1737.
3. Isaac,[4] b. Aug. 14, 1739; d. Oct. 17, 1739.
4. Isaac,[4] (again), b. Jan. 11, 1741.

5. Gideon,[4] (again), b. July 6, 1743.
6. Anne,[4] b. July 1, 1746.
7. Bela,[4] b. Jan. 15, 1758.

JOANNA CLEVELAND,[2] youngest daughter and tenth child of Moses[1] and Ann (Winn) Cleveland, b. in Woburn, Mass., April 5, 1670, m. in Chelmsford, Mass., May 28, 1690, Joseph Keyes, a brother, probably, of her brother Samuel's first wife.

Children, both born in Chelmsford:
1. Joanna,[3] b. Feb. 10, 1695.
2. Joseph,[3] b. May 1, 1698.

ENOCH CLEVELAND,[2] youngest son and child of Moses[1] and Ann (Winn) Cleveland, b. in Woburn, Mass., Aug 1, 1671, m. first, in Charlestown, Mass., Elizabeth Counts, dau. probably, of Edward and Sarah (Adams) Counts. He was a tailor by occupation; lived successively in Charlestown, Sudbury, Framingham, and Concord, (Mass.), and d. in the latter place, Aug. 1, 1729. His second wife, whom he m. in Marlboro', Mass., July 9, 1719, was Elizabeth Wright, of Concord, Mass.

Children by first wife, born in Sudbury, were—
1. Sarah,[3] b. May 26, 1701.
2. Enoch,[3] b. July 2, 1703.
3. James,[3] b. Oct. 31, 1706.
4. Jonathan,[3] b. March —, 1708.

No births of children born to him are found on records of other towns where he resided.

ENOCH CLEVELAND,[3] son of Enoch[2] and Elizabeth (Counts) Cleveland, b. in Sudbury, Mass., July 2, 1703, by wife Sarah had the following children, born in Berwick:
1. Jonathan,[4] b. June 7, 1726.
2. Enoch,[4] b. May 26, 1728; d. Feb. 28, 1730.
3. Enoch,[4] (again), b. Aug. 31, 1732. Had family by wife Deborah Fassett, in Pomfret and Canterbury, Conn. C. C. Ward, Esq., of Castleton, Vt., is a great-grandson of Enoch.[4]

JONATHAN CLEVELAND,[3] son of Enoch[2] and Elizabeth (Counts) Cleveland, b. in Sudbury, Mass., March —, 1708, m. first, in Concord, Mass., Sept. 29, 1736, Lydia Lamson. After her death in 1743, he m. second, in Acton, Mass., June 16, 1743, Dorothy Shepard. She dying in 1747, he m. third, in Acton, Mass., in 1748, Hannah Hays.

Children, by wife Lydia:
1. Elizabeth,[4] b. June 20, 1740.
2. Lydia,[4] b. Aug. 11, 1742.

by wife Dorothy:
3. Sarah,[4] b. June 9, 1744.
4. Jonathan,[4] b. May 9, 1746.

by wife Hannah:
5. Persis,[4] b. Aug. 5, 1749.

OLIVER CLEVELAND,[4] who m. Azubah Smith, (a sister of James Smith, a distinguished soldier of the Revolutionary war), and settled in Hampton, Washington county, N. Y., is of this branch of Enoch Cleveland,[2] as also Solomon Cleveland,[5] of Fair Haven, Vt., whose wife was Martha Rathbone. But parties interested are referred to the complete Genealogy of the Clevelands, to be issued in due time by James Butler Cleveland, Esq., formerly of Washington, D. C., but now of Oneonta, Otsego county, N. Y.

B.

RICHARD HILDRETH, of Cambridge, Mass., made a freeman, May 10, 1643, had wife Sarah, who d. June 15, 1644. By wife Elizabeth, who d. in Malden, Aug. 3, 1693, aged 68, he had—

1. Elizabeth, b. Sept. 21, 1646.
2. Sarah, b. Aug. 8, 1648.

Removed to Chelmsford, Mass., and there had—

3. Joseph, b. April 16, 1658; m. Abigail Wilson.
4. Persis, b. Feb. 8, 1660; m. Samuel Cleveland.
5. Thomas, b. Feb. 1, 1662.
6. Isaac, b. July —, 1663; m. Elizabeth ——.

Besides Abigail, who m. Moses Parker, of Chelmsford. The father d. in Chelmsford, in 1688, aged 83, according to the gravestone erected to his memory.

Richard Hildreth, the Historian, is a lineal descendant of Richard and Elizabeth Hildreth, of Chelmsford, tracing to Joseph and Abigail (Wilson) Hildreth as above.

The place of the birth of Persis, wife of Samuel Cleveland,[2] is erroneously given on page 6. It is there stated she was a native of Cambridge, Mass. For "Cambridge" read *Chelmsford*.

Nothing concerning Persis,[3] eldest child of Samuel[2] and Persis (Hildreth) Cleveland, has been learned. The Canterbury records are barren of information about her, and she may have died unmarried.

Samuel,[3] son of Samuel[2] and Persis (Hildreth) Cleveland, m. in Canterbury, Conn., Dec. 10, 1719, Sarah Boswell, dau. of Robert Boswell, Esq., of Canterbury. He d. in Canterbury, Oct. 1, 1727. His widow m., Dec. 19, 1731, John Proctor, of Canterbury.

Children, all b. in Canterbury, were—

1. Hannah,[4] bap. May 7, 1721.
2. Eleazer,[4] b. May 26, 1722.
3. David,[4] b. June 1, 1724.
4. Hopestill,[4] b. April 17, 1726.
5. Mehetabel,[4] bap. April 10, 1728; m. Faxon Dean.

Eleazer,⁴ m. in Canterbury, Conn., April 25, 1750, Anne Bradford, and had there—

1. Anne,⁵ b. Nov. 3, 1750.
2. Susannah,⁵ b. July 29, 1752.
3. Squier,⁵ b. July 29, 1754.
4. Mehetabel,⁵ b. July 14, 1756.
5. John,⁵ b. June 29, 1758.
6. Perez,⁵ b. July 17, 1760.
7. Polly,⁵ b. Aug. 19, 1762.
8. Bradford,⁵ b. Sept. 9, 1764.
9. Alice,⁵ b. Dec. 16, 1767.
10. William,⁵ b. Feb. 22, 1771.

David,⁴ m. first, in Canterbury, June 25, 1744, Eunice Backus. She d. Oct. 5, 1749, and he m. second, in Canterbury, Aug. 15, 1750, Rebecca Tracy. She d. Nov. 30, 1754.

Children, by wife Eunice, all b. in Canterbury:

1. Sarah,⁵ b. Sept. 3, 1745.
2. Samuel,⁵ b. Sept. 18, 1747.

by wife Rebecca:

3. Tracy,⁵ b. May 8, 1751.
4. Amy,⁵ b. Jan. 14, 1753.

Tracy,⁵ m. in Canterbury, April 25, 1773, Phebe Hyde, of same place, and had there—

1. Weltha,⁶ b. Feb. 4, 1774.
2. David,⁶ b. Dec. 16, 1775.
3. Azubah,⁶ b. Dec. 25, 1777.
4. Son,⁶ b. Feb. 20, 1779; d. Feb. 24, 1779.
5. Rebecca,⁶ b. July 18, 1780.

He removed to the "Western Reserve" in the State of Ohio, and settled in Kirtland, Ohio, as did perhaps his half-brother, Samuel,⁵ in the neighboring town of Concord.

Hopestill,⁴ m. in Canterbury, May 9, 1754, Patience Benjamin, and had, b. there—

1. Patience,⁵ b. Jan. 12, 1755.
2. David,⁵ b. July 9, 1765.
3. Esther,⁵ b. June 30, 1767.

Elizabeth,³ dau. of Samuel² and Persis Cleveland, m. in Canterbury, Conn., April 2, 1717, John Ensworth, son of Tyxhall Ensworth, of Canterbury.

Children, b. in Canterbury:

1. Tyxhall,⁴ b. Dec. 19, 1717.
2. John,⁴ b. April 5, 1719.
3. Ephraim,⁴ b. April 17, 1723.

Mary,³ dau. of Samuel² and Persis Cleveland, m. in Canterbury, Oct. 5, 1719, Joseph Ensworth, son of Tyxhall Ensworth, of Canterbury. She d. March 11, 1766.

Children, b. in Canterbury:

1. William,[4] b. Feb. 24, 1720; m. Grace Gale.
2. Lydia,[4] b. Aug. 24, 1721; d. young.
3. Jabez,[4] b. April 12, 1723; m. Mehetabel Tracy.
4. Joseph,[4] b. Nov. 28, 1725.
5. Lydia,[4] (again), b. June 16, 1734.

Timothy,[3] son of Samuel[2] and Margaret Cleveland, by wife Dorothy ———, had—

1. Abigail,[4] b. March 27, 1728; m. William Darby.
2. Zipporah,[4] b. Sept. 4, 1729; m. Francis Simonds.
3. Margaret,[4] bap. Dec. 24, 1732; m. Samuel Woodward.
4. Timothy,[4] b. Dec. 29, 1734; m. Esther Fish.
5. Lucretia,[4] b. Feb. 2, 1737; m. Jedediah Darby.
6. Samuel,[4] b. Feb. 23, 1739.
7. Ephraim,[4] b. Aug. 20, 1740; m. Mary Griffin.
8. Cyrus,[4] b. Oct. 2, 1743; d. Feb. 23, 1749.

Dorothy, wife of Timothy Cleveland,[3] d. Aug. 19, 1769.
Timothy Cleveland,[3] d. Jan. 19, 1784.

Timothy,[4] m. in Canterbury, Jan. 30, 1760, Esther Fish, by whom he had—

1. Jacob,[5] b. March 6, 1761.
2. Bethabra,[5] b. Oct. 31, 1763; m. Margaret Pellett.
3. Cyrus,[5] b. May 12, 1766.
4. Jeptha,[5] b. Oct. 7, 1768.
5. Dorothy,[5] b. May 30, 1772.
6. Mary,[5] b. Nov. 6, 1774.
7. Dorothy,[5] (again), b. Oct. 12, 1779.
8. Elkanah,[5] b. June 9, 1782; d. June 21, 1782.

Lieut. Timothy Cleveland,[4] d. Oct. 27, 1804, and his wife Esther, one week later, Nov. 3, 1804, in the 60th year of her age.

Ephraim,[4] m. in Hampton, Windham county, Conn., March 6, 1766, Mary Griffin, dau. of Ebenezer and Hannah (Chandler) Griffin. She was b. in Hampton, Conn., March 16, 1744.

Children:

1. Mary,[5] b. March 30, 1768.
2. Franklin,[5] b. Aug. 13, 1779.

C.

Concerning ELIJAH CLEVELAND,[4] the sixth child of Joseph[3] and Abigail (Hyde) Cleveland, the compiler gives the following brief account, having recently found and traced his descendants. His wife was Alice Lawrence, but of her birth and parentage there is nothing yet ascertained, except that she was born about the year 1730. They were married about the year 1748, and settled in Columbia county, N. Y. A correspondent in Hillsdale furnishes me with a copy of the inscriptions upon their tombtones, in the old burying-ground there, as follows:

"In memory of Mr. Elijah Cleveland, who departed this life Sept. 28, 1794, in the 74th year of his age."

"In memory of Mrs. Alice, wife of Mr. Elijah Cleveland, who died June 12, 1799, in her 69th year."

They had a family of nine children at least, but the order of births can not be given with certainty, as the exact dates of the births of three only have been obtained.

1. Joseph,[5] b. about 1749; m. Elizabeth Fenton.
2. Lucinda,[5] b. about 1751; m. Henry Dibble.
3. Asa,[5] b. about 1753; m. Mary Dibble.
4. John,[5] b. about 1756; m. Elizabeth Scarien.
5. Abigail,[5] b. Feb. 21, 1758; m. first, Thomas Bathrick—second, Peter Smith.
6. Daniel,[5] b. about 1760; m. Amy Dibble.
7. Sarah,[5] b. Jan. 16, 1763; m. Andrew Reynolds.
8. Waitstill,[5] b. Oct. 22, 1764; m. Martha Tabor.
9. Amy,[5] b. about 1767; m. Henry Salisbury.

JOSEPH H. CLEVELAND,[7] of Chicago, is a grandson of Joseph.[5]

EZRA CLEVELAND,[4] son of Joseph[3] and Sarah (Ensworth) Cleveland, m. in 1747, Jerusha Newcomb, dau. of Hezekiah and Jerusha (Bradford) Newcomb. She was b. March 24, 1726. In 1772 they were "late of Tolland, Conn., now of Worthing, Mass." They had b. to them in Canterbury, Conn.:

1. Ezra,[5] b. June 22, 1748; settled in Burlington, Conn.
2. Tyxhall,[5] b. April 26, 1750; settled in Hanover, N. H.
3. Thomas,[5] b. March 25, 1752.
4. Sarah,[5] b. Oct. 29, 1754.
5. Newcomb,[5] b. Nov. 6, 1756; settled in Mass.
6. Jerusha,[5] b. Aug. 31, 1758.
7. Asenath,[5] b. May 16, 1763.
8. Zeruiah,[5] b. March 6, 1765.
9. Dorothy,[5] b. Sept. 14, 1767.

SAMUEL CLEVELAND,[4] son of Joseph[3] and Sarah (Ensworth) Cleveland, m. first, in Canterbury, Conn., May 7, 1751, Ruth Darby. His second wife was Anna Welch.

Children, by wife Ruth:

1. Joseph,[5] b. Feb. 7, 1752; m. ——, and settled in "the West."
2. Mary,[5] b. Feb. 12, 1754; m. Silas Allen.
3. Jedediah,[5] b. May 8, 1756; m. Betsey Cleveland.
4. Abigail,[5] b. Aug. 6, 1758; m. Elder John Hibbard.
5. Zeruiah,[5] b. Feb. 19, 1761; d. Oct. 25, 1766.
6. Samuel,[5] b. Aug. 7, 1763; m. Martha Hibbard.
7. William Darby,[5] b. Feb. 8, 1766; m. Phebe Abbott.
8. Arunah,[5] b. March 21, 1768; d. Aug. 17, 1773.
9. Chester,[5] b. March 28, 1771; m. Mary Hibbard.
10. Sylvester,[5] b. Aug. 22, 1778; m. Relief Converse.

Mrs. Susan Eaton,[6] *nee* Cleveland, daughter to Samuel,[5] can give a very complete account of this branch, several of whom settled in Lower Canada, Province of Quebec. She was b. Nov. 16, 1792; res. East Randolph, Vt.

D.

The compiler regrets his inability to present further information of interest concerning BENJAMIN CLEVELAND,[4] and Rachel his wife, but certainly there has been no lack of zeal in his endeavors to obtain it. He has examined carefully the Probate records in the hope that something might be found to determine the maiden name of the said Rachel. As no will of Joseph Cleveland[3] (son of Samuel[2]) appears on those records, the conclusion is that he died intestate. No grandchild or great-grandchild of Rachel is found bearing her full maiden name, as in the case of *Elizabeth Perkins* Hibbard,[7] youngest child of Elizabeth Hovey,[6] (see page 16), who was named for the mother of Rev. Samuel Hovey. Such partiality in selection of names among the Hoveys may perhaps be excused, but among the Clevelands in the direct line of descent from Benjamin,[4] such neglect to perpetuate an honorable name in our ancestry is utterly indefensible—from a *genealogical* standpoint at least.

It has been intimated to the writer that she was of Welsh extraction, but this seems only a traditionary conjecture. Two excellent though credulous persons, among the multitude of her great-grandchildren, one in New York State and the other in Ohio, and who are wont to consult spiritual *mediums* for answers to vexed questions, confidently advised him, over a year ago, that the mystery concerning her was solved; and, better than all, "the source of the information was unquestionably reliable." But the truth must be told, notwithstanding it may show that the most reliable mediums are liable, like doctors, to disagree. Through one she declared most positively that her name was "Rachel *Norton*," a native of Glasgow, Scotland; and through the other, with equal certainty, that it was "Rachel *Craig*," nativity not given. So the mystery became more mysterious if possible than ever, and "clouds and darkness rest upon it."

On page 60, Vol. VII, of the Canterbury (Conn.) Land Records, may be found the following Deed:

"*To all Christian people to whom these presents shall come—*

"Know ye, that I, Benjamin Cleaveland, of Canterbury, in the County of Windham, in the Colony of Connecticut in New England, for divers good causes and considerations moving, have remised, relieved, and forever quited claim, and by these presents for me and my Heirs doth fully, clearly and absolutely Remise, Release, and forever quit claim unto Jonathan Downing, Senr., of Canterbury, in the County of Windham, and Colony afores^d, in his full and peaceable possession & Teasure and to his heirs and assigns forever, all such right, Title, Interest and Demand whatsoever he the s^d had or ought to have in or to a sartain Brook which runs through the west end of the s^d Cleaveland's Land. To Have and to Hold all the said premises, &c., unto him the said Downing, his heirs and assigns, for the whole term of nine hundred and ninety years. As witness my hand this the Sixteenth Day of August, A. D. 1751.

BENJAMIN CLEAVELAND. [SEAL.]

"Signed, sealed and
delivered in presents of
  SAUMEL STEVENS.
          her
RACHEL ✕ CLEAVELAND.
     mark.

"Received this January the 8th Day, 1751, [1752?], and the same truly recorded.   Attest: STEPHEN FROST."

Whether the wife of Benjamin Cleveland was incapable of writing her signature at all, or whether her agitation in relinquishing her joint right, "in or to a sartain Brook which runs through the west end of the s^d Cleaveland's Land," rendered her unable to do so, is not manifest. Indeed it now matters not. Over a century and a quarter has passed since that Deed was delivered to Jonathan Downing, Sen., and centuries may come and go, till that "whole term of nine hundred and ninety years" expires. What then? "The Brook" will still run its course

"—— to swell the brimming river,"

supplied by the never failing springs of the hills of Windham county— white-clad with the glistening snows of winter, or green-robed with the glorious verdure of each returning summer. Children will play upon its banks and bathe their bare feet in its limpid, sparkling waters, as did of yore the little ones of Benjamin and Rachel Cleveland. Will there be sorrow again like that which filled the hearts and darkened the home of this young couple, when, within a fortnight during that dreary month of November, in the year of grace 1749, three of their five children sickened and died, and were buried side by side in three little graves for violets to grow upon when the spring-tide came—"Joe" and "Bennie" and "Dollie"—leaving only little "Nabby" and baby Zenas—he whose crippled manhood in after years was evidently one continued and heroic struggle with adversity? The father may be pictured to us sad and sedate, with his eyes fixedly gazing out of the window, while the sweeping gusts of early winter rattle the casements, and break and scatter the ice-mailed branches of the trees around the little yard of his "broken home." With Puritan fortitude he endeavors, though vainly, to keep back the tears that silently steal down his cheeks, while he speaks to the sobbing wife and mother,—crushed with their great grief, and worn and weary with watching and vigils by the bedsides of her darlings,— the well remembered words of Holy Writ, "The Lord gave and the Lord hath taken away—blessed be the name of the Lord." There is no answer save a low moan and a fresh outburst of tears. Another Rachel indeed, mourning her first born children and refusing to be comforted. Will this all happen there again? God knows. And, reader, if it so happen, will consolation to the bereaved and sorrowing ones come to their bleeding hearts from words preserved from the flippant utterances of an Ingersoll, or rather from the precious promises to those that mourn, recorded in that Book he now scoffs at and derides?

But the spring time followed, and while the birds were carroling its return, another daughter was born and christened for her mother, Rachel. Within two years more, still another daughter gladdened the household, with the name of her great-grandmother, Persis. Two and a half years later, another son was born, and called Rufus. Was he, or his elder brother Zenas, named for the *father* or *grandfather* of the mother that bore them? Next a daughter Mary, who died in mid-winter, and was laid by the side of her little brothers and sister before attaining her seventh year; and lastly, Phebe, who grew to womanhood, married Ephraim Pearson, and waited and watched in vain for his return from sea, seven long years, with her family of four little ones, in their home in Manchester, Vermont. Was the name of the mother of Rachel, wife of Benj. Cleveland, *Mary*, and grandmother *Phebe?*

Abigail, or "Nabby" Cleveland, was in her sixteenth year when little Mary, her sister, died, and was already engaged to young "Sam" Hovey, the son of a farmer living hard by in the adjoining town of Windham. Her musical talent was the wonder and delight of the neighborhood, and her husband in after years used to say he had often heard her voice, while singing of a clear evening out of doors, a mile and a half away. Perhaps the hearing of the young lover was very acute at that particular period of his life. They were married in the autumn following the death of little Mary, and began the stormy voyage of life together in Windham, Conn., to peacefully close it among the green hills of Orange county, Vermont.

Efforts to obtain the exact date of the death of Benjamin Cleveland and his wife have proved futile. It is stated, however, that "grandma Cleveland" died when Rebecca Hovey[6] was twenty years old, and "grandpa Cleveland" lived five years after her death. So it may be seen, according to this statement, that Rachel, wife of Benj. Cleveland, d. in Lyme, N. H., in 1792, and he d. in East Brookfield, Vt., in 1797. The compiler is sorry to state he can find no stone in the old burying grounds of either town to mark the respective places of burial. Perhaps I ought to say in this connection, that the old burial place, where the dust of the first settlers of Lyme, N. H., reposes, thickly covered (as it was when the writer visited the spot in 1876,) with underbrush and half-grown trees, with here and there a broken headstone, is simply a disgrace to the authorities of the town. Even the Aborigines exhibited more care and respect for the burial place of their dead, than the Anglo-Saxons who are now in possession of the soil.

E.

Dr. Daniel Hovey,[7] eldest son and second child of Daniel and Beulah (Pingree) Hovey, b. in Lyme, N. H., March 25, 1792, m. in Canaan, N. H., Jan. 12, 1817, Hannah Hough Harris, dau. of Joshua and Miriam (Johnson) Harris. She was b. in Canaan, N. H., Feb. 13, 1793; d. in

Brooklyn, N. Y., at the residence of her daughter, Mrs. John K. Hosmer, Aug. 15, 1877. He d. in Greenfield, Mass., May 6, 1874. He was well known as a skillful physician of extensive practice in Franklin county, Mass.

Children:
1. George Harris,[5] b. in Canaan, N. H., Sept. 24, 1817, m. in Bernardston, Mass., Oct. 23, 1855, Nancy Maria Willard, dau. of David and Sarah (Dickman) Willard. She was b. in Greenfield, Mass., June 27, 1830. He is a druggist; res. Greenfield, Mass. No children.
2. Edward Olcott,[8] b. in Canaan, N. H., June 23, 1824; d. July 6, 1824.
3. Luther Sheldon,[8] b. in Canaan, N. H., Aug. 14, 1825; d. Dec. 14, 1875, unm.
4. Maria Luthera,[8] b. in Lyme, N. H., April 6, 1828, m. in Hartford, Conn., April 2, 1850, John Kingsbury Hosmer, son of James D. and Dorothy (Leavens) Hosmer. He was b. in Willimantic, Conn., Nov. 30, 1825. Res. 460 Vanderbilt ave., Brooklyn, N. Y. No children.

Abigail Hovey,[7] third daughter and fourth child of Daniel and Beulah (Pingree) Hovey, b. in Lyme, N. H., Jan. 31, 1797, m. in Lyme, N. H., Jan. 2, 1823, Col. Jesse Carpenter, son of Jesse and Miriam (Fairfield) Carpenter. He was b. in Lyme, N. H., April 5, 1796; d. in Windsor, Conn., July 4, 1876. She d. in Hartford, Conn., June 3, 1862.

Children:
1. Daniel Hovey,[8] b. April 19, 1824, m. in Brookfield, Vt., Nov. 26, 1850, Ruth Estabrook Carleton, dau. of John and Hannah (Estabrook) Carleton. She was b. in Brookfield, Vt., July 15, 1824. He is a farmer; res. Collinsville, Conn. Children: 1. Harriet Abbey,[9] b. in Brooklyn, N. Y., March 9, 1852; authoress and correspondent; res. Geneva, Switzerland. 2. Jesse Fairfield,[9] b. in Chelsea, Vt., Aug. 8, 1853. 3. Samuel Alford,[9] b. in Chelsea, Vt., March 25, 1855; a civil engineer; res. London, Eng. 4. Daniel,[9] b. in Wallingford, Conn., Dec. 21, 1857. 5. John Carleton,[9] b. in Wethersfield, Conn., March 13, 1863; d. Aug. 9, 1863.
2. Elizabeth,[8] b. Oct. 9, 1825, m. in Hartford, Conn., May 6, 1846, Franklin Joshua Forbes, son of Solomon and Betsey (Flint) Forbes. He was b. in East Hartford, Conn., May 6, 1818; merchant tailor; res. Windsor Locks, Conn. Children: 1. Jesse Franklin,[9] b. in Hartford, Conn., Dec. 19, 1847, m. in Cromwell, Conn., Sept. 20, 1877, Jennie Crane Savage, dau. of Charles C. and Maria (Crane) Savage. She was b. in New York City, Nov. 2, 1855. He is a graduate of Amherst College, class of '74, and of Union Theological Seminary, '77; a Congregational Clergyman; res. Warren, Mass. 2. George Fairfield,[9] b. in Hartford, Conn., March 15, 1849, m. in Boston, Mass., June 28, 1877, Lizzie Lemon Prentice Shannon, dau. of Samuel Tibbitts and Martha Ann Prentice (Stevens) Shannon. She was b. in Saco, Me., Jan. 16, 1848. He is a graduate of Amherst College, class of '75. 3. Edwin Horace,[9] b. in New Britain, Conn., Dec. 12, 1850, m. in Thomaston, Conn., Aug. 24, 1875, Mary Jane Potter, dau. of Christopher and Esther (Bradford) Potter. She was b. in Canaan, Conn., Aug. 2, 1846. He is a graduate of Yale College, class of '74; teacher in the High School, Plymouth, Conn. 4. Harriet Elizabeth,[9] b. in Springfield, Mass., Sept. 22, 1852, m. in Cromwell, Conn., Dec. 17, 1872, James Edward Smith, son of Edward and Julia (Stevens) Smith. He was b. in Cromwell, Conn., Nov. 24, 1851. Child: Frederic Stevens,[10] b. March 23, 1874. 5. Ida May,[9] b. in Springfield, Mass., July 31, 1855.

3. Fairfield,[8] b. March 15, 1828; d. May —, 1832.
4. Harriet,[8] b. Dec. 5, 1834, m. in New Britain, Conn., Oct. 1, 1851, Solomon Augustus Holt, son of Dea. Solomon Holt. He was b. in Andover, Mass., Jan. 3, 1832. Res. Brooklyn, N. Y. Children: 1. William Augustus,[9] b. Sept. 15, 1853. 2. Charles Evans,[9] b. May 3, 1858; d. June 1, 1858. 3. Emma Louise,[9] b. Nov. 9, 1861.

Sarah Hovey,[7] fourth daughter and fifth child of Daniel and Beulah (Pingree) Hovey, b. in Lyme, N. H., June 29, 1799, m. first, in Lyme, March 1, 1820, Alpheus Hibbard, son of Roger and Sarah (Davidson) Hibbard. He was b. in Brookfield, Vt., July 12, 1795; d. there, July 14, 1832. She m. second, in Brookfield, April 3, 1837, Daniel Cheeney, son of Jesse and Eleanor (Welch) Cheeney. He was b. in Washington, Vt., Nov. 7, 1815. (Divorced about 1855.) She d. in Rockland, Mass., Feb. 20, 1876.

Children, by first husband, Alpheus Hibbard:

1. Sylvanus Hovey,[8] b. in Brookfield, Vt., Dec. 16, 1820, m. in Chelsea, Vt., April 3, 1844, Philena A. Allen, dau. of Obed and Philena (Bennett) Allen. She was b. in Chelsea, Vt., Jan. 6, 1822. Res. Chelsea, Vt. Children: 1. Josephine Philena,[9] b. in Brookfield, Vt., Jan. 5, 1846. 2. Eveline Alma,[9] b. in Chelsea, Vt., May 24, 1853; d. Jan. 7, 1872, unm.
2. Franklin,[8] b. in Brookfield, Vt., Aug. 20, 1823; d. Oct. 12, 1840.
3. Rhoda Luthera,[8] b. in Brookfield, Vt., Oct. 11, 1829, m. in Chelsea, Vt., July 27, 1853, Charles Mann Burrell, son of Henry and Abigail (Mann) Burrell. He was b. in East Abingdon (now Rockland) Mass., July 15, 1830. Res. Rockland, Mass. Children: 1. Wilbur Forrest,[9] b. Aug. 18, 1856. 2. Sarah Alma,[9] b. Oct. 3, 1861.
4. Alma Elizabeth,[8] b. in Brookfield, Vt., Oct. 20, 1832, m. in same place, Jan. 20, 1850, Joseph Milton Hovey, son of Dudley and Rubie (Allen) Hovey. He was b. in Lyme, N. H., July 8, 1826. Res. Bristol, N. H. Child: Carroll Milton,[9] b. June 11, 1870.

by second husband, Daniel Cheeney:

5. Alpheus Hibbard,[8] b. May 12, 1838, m. in Chelsea, Vt., March 19, 1863, Emma Whitney, dau. of Daniel and Julia (Hall) Whitney. She was b. in Tunbridge, Vt., Dec. 18, 1841. He is a farmer; res. Spencer, Clay county, Iowa. Children: 1. Nellie Alma,[9] b. in Buck Creek township, Bremer county, Iowa, Jan. 2, 1867. 2. Alonzo Daniel,[9] b. in same place, Sept. 12, 1870. 3. Franklin Alpheus,[9] b. in Spencer, Iowa, July 12, 1873; d. Oct. 15, 1873. 4. George Edwin,[9] b. in Spencer, Iowa, Jan. 20, 1875.
6. Ellen Delia,[9] b. Feb. 21, 1841, m. in Rockland, Mass., Jan. 3, 1860, John Burrell (2d), son of Adna and Mary Miller (Crocker) Burrell. He was b. in Rockland, Mass., Dec. 12, 1833. Res. Rockland, Mass. Children, all b. in Rockland: 1. Son,[9] b. Feb. 20, 1861; d. Feb. 20, 1861. 2. Alpheus Merton,[9] b. June 10, 1864. 3. Alice Maud,[9] b. Nov. 17, 1867. 4. Mary Ellen,[9] b. April 26, 1876.

Rhoda L. Hovey,[7] the sixth daughter and eighth child of Daniel and Beulah (Pingree) Hovey, b. in Lyme, N. H., April 14, 1806, m. in Lyme, N. H., June 3, 1832, Philander Allen, son of Ebenezer and Anna (Bennett) Allen. He was b. in Chelsea, Vt., May 19, 1807; d. in Lyme, N. H., Feb. 16, 1851. She is living (1878) with her son at 36 Seymour St., Hartford, Conn.

Children, all born in Lyme, N. H.:
1. Mary Elizabeth,[8] b. Aug. 2, 1834, m. in Lexington, Mass., Oct. 1, 1871, Warren Sherburne, son of Reuben Butterfield and Sarah Rackleife (Staples) Sherburne. He was b. in Charlestown, Mass., April 21, 1833. Is a retired merchant of Boston. No children. Res. Lexington, Mass.
2. George Lewis,[8] b. June 25, 1836, m. in Lawrence, Mass., Dec. 25, 1865, Albina Marble, dau. of Ezra and Ann (Borden) Marble. She was b. in Fall River, Mass., March 30, 1844. He is a farmer; res. Farmington, Conn. Children: 1. Nina Estella,[9] b. in Lawrence, Mass., March 12, 1867. 2. George Edwin,[9] b. in Lawrence, Mass., Dec. 25, 1868. 3. Frank Leyland,[9] b. in Windsor, Conn., Nov. 1, 1870; d. Feb. 27, 1876. 4 and 5. Mary[9] and Florence,[9] (twins), b. in New Britain, Conn., June 4, 1872, and both d. July 28, 1872. 6. Frederic Hovey,[9] b. in New Britain, Conn., June 3, 1873; d. June 27, 1876. 7. Walter Cleveland,[9] b. in Farmington, Conn., Aug. 9, 1877.
3. Edwin Bennett,[8] b. Dec. 28, 1839; was killed in the army at Front Royal, Warren county, Va., May 2, 1862, unm.
4. Sylvanus Frank,[8] b. Aug. 3, 1843, m. in Lawrence, Mass., Oct. 21, 1869, Eliza Leyland, dau. of William and Mary (Hirstwood) Leyland. She was b. in York, Eng., Nov. 10, 1840. He is an Insurance Agent; res. Hartford, Conn. No children.
5. Frederic Hovey,[8] (Rev.), b. Oct. 1, 1845; res. (1877) 143 Chandler St., South Boston, Mass.; unm.

Geo. L. Hovey,[7] (Rev.), the youngest son and child of Daniel and Beulah (Pingree) Hovey, b. in Lyme, N. H., Aug. 20, 1810, m. first, in Lyme, N. H., Dec. 25, 1836, Sarah Gilbert Nelson, dau. of Asa and Sarah (Gilbert) Nelson. She was b. in Lyme, N. H., Sept. 12, 1812; d. in the West Indies (in Kingston, Jamaica), Feb. 22, 1840. No children. He m. second, in Providence, R. I., Feb. 6, 1849, Anna Maria Sibley, dau. of Royal and Lucretia Cargill (Carter) Sibley. She was b. in Uxbridge, Mass., Nov. 3, 1822; d. in Deerfield, Mass., April 2, 1865. No children. He m. third, in Providence, R. I., Aug. 8, 1867, Olivia Capron Marcy, dau. of Augustus and Sally Williams (Carter) Marcy. She was b. in Dudley, Mass., Oct. 18, 1839. Res. Bricksburg, N. J.

Child, by wife Olivia:
1. Daughter,[8] b. April 27, 1872; d. April 27, 1872.

[The following letter from Rev. Geo. L. Hovey, concerning the family of Daniel,[5] the eldest child of Rev. Samuel and Abigail (Cleveland) Hovey, can not prove uninteresting, and is inserted entire:]

"Bricksburg, July 25, 1877.

"H. G. Cleveland, Esq.:

"We think as you have done so much you ought to be helped as much as is in our power to do, though that is little. As to my father's children all I can do for you is as follows—(I will not repeat dates of births and deaths, as you have them already):
1. Beulah, died unmarried, aged 27.
2. Daniel. I can only urge George or Maria to write for you the account of his marriage and the births and deaths of his three children. There are no grandchildren, and Luther died unmarried.
3. Mary, died unmarried, in Lyme, N. H.
4. Abigail. I will write to Harriet or Elizabeth for the account of this family,

5. Sarah. Have sent to her daughters to write you.
6. Samuel Sylvanus, died in Lyme, while preparing for college, unmarried.
7. Elizabeth P., died unmarried. Was a very successful teacher for many years, in Mansfield, Ohio, and Middletown, Conn., and in the Blind Asylum at South Boston.
8. Rhoda Lord. You have this account.
9. Josiah Fairfield, died in infancy.
10. George Lewis, born Aug. 20, 1810 (not 1809).

"It seemed foreordained that I should stay at home and take care of my parents, my only surviving brother having commenced the study of medicine the year that I was born. In 1831, I joined the Congregational Church in Lyme, N.H., and in 1832 the claims of the West began to press upon the Eastern churches, calling for their young people to go there as teachers and preachers. I had already felt a desire to become a minister, and had commenced study at Thetford Academy, Vt. In 1833, the Rev. J. J. Shipherd came from the West, and unfolded his plan for a colony and a college at Oberlin, Ohio. Many of the best members of our churches went thither as colonists, and I decided to go there to pursue my studies, leaving my sister Rhoda to bring home her husband, a young farmer, to take my place in caring for my parents. Reaching Oberlin in the autumn of 1833, I found it a small settlement composed of a dozen log houses and one frame building, in a dense forest, some six miles from any town. In 1836, I was married to the friend of my childhood, Miss Sarah G. Nelson, who had removed with her friends to that place, and to whom I had been several years engaged. In 1837, while a member of the Theological class, I was licensed to preach, by the Loraine County Association; and in 1838, ordained by the same body as a missionary. In Nov., 1839, in company with several others, myself and wife went as missionaries to the emancipated negroes in the island of Jamaica, W. I. We were not sent by any society, but looked for our support to the people to whom we ministered. On the 1st of Feb. following my wife died, and in July, 1842, I returned to this country, worn out with my labors in that climate, but hoping, after a season of rest, to be able to resume my work among that people to whom I had become greatly attached. But for the next four years, I was able to do but little except occasionally to present the case of those people to the churches and to individuals. In 1846, I received an appointment from the Am. Miss. Association to raise $6,000 for the Jamaica Mission. In the autumn of 1847, I became an Agent of the Foreign Evangelical Society in connection with Drs. Baird, Kirk and others, having my office in Boston. In 1849, Feb. 6, I married Miss Anna M. Sibley, of Providence, R. I., who died April 2nd, 1865. In May, 1850, the Foreign Evangelical Society united with the American Protestant Society and the Christian Alliance, under the name of the American and Foreign Christian Union. From that time till the autumn of 1871, I remained with the Society as its Agent or District Secretary for New England, though in 1851 I spent six months in Europe, and at two different times made extensive tours through the South in the interests of the Society. Since the autumn of 1871, when I came to Bricksburg, N. J., my health has prevented me from occupying continuously any post of arduous labor, but I have for a time acted as Agent for Lincoln University, and am at present Financial Agent of Am. and For. Christian Union, with special reference to raising money for its Evangelical work in France. In 1867, Aug. 8, I married Miss Olivia C. Marcy, of Providence, R. I., who acts as my confidential clerk or private secretary, else you could have got nothing out of me except by word of mouth, for I do not even write out my sermons, much less a letter the length of this, as my head has always been too troublesome to allow of it.

"You ask for a sketch of my father. I can only say I could easier write his biography than a sketch that would do him justice. Near the close of the Revolutionary war his father was drafted into the army, and he though but seventeen years of age was accepted as his substitute. While acting as a scout he was taken prisoner near Lake Champlain, and carried to Quebec, Canada. Being in prison with an Englishman of education, who took pleasure in teaching him arithmetic and surveying, a thirst for learning more was awakened, and on his return home, at the close of the war, he commenced studying with Rev. Dr. Burton, Thetford, Vt., with a view to entering Dartmouth College. This was prevented by the failure of his health, and he was employed by Government in surveying the new townships of Northern Vermont. Another benefit of his soldier life and what appeared the misfortune of imprisonment, was his receipt of a pension for life, which was continued to his widow after him. He was passionately fond of the business of surveying, and his apology for not writing me on his 80th birthday was that *he was out surveying*. His sight, which had failed for years, had become strong again, and his hair retained its color, and though three miles from church, he often preferred walking to riding, for the sake of the exercise. Though settled upon a farm, he was engaged in teaching during the winter for twenty-five years, till most of his children had received their common school education. He usually held one or more town offices, and often assisted in the settlement of the estates of his neighbors and friends. Though too doubtful of his own religious state to join the church till late in life, he was eminently a religious man, always maintaining prayers in his family and in his school. He was the first Sunday School Superintendent I ever knew, and among the first in New Hampshire; and continued his connection with the S. S. either as Supt. or teacher as long as he lived. His love for children increased with his years, and he was greatly beloved by them in return. Though a moderate drinker, as to the use of ardent spirits so universal in his day, he was one of the first to place himself under the banner of total abstinence, giving up for the sake of others what he conceived to be the real advantages of a restricted use of such stimulants. In fine, he was a good man, and a just, and his memory is precious. He was the most honest, unselfish man I ever knew. If he erred at all, it was in loving his neighbor *better* than himself—(a characteristic which has descended to some of his children. Mrs. H.)

"I fear you find it hard work to get the matter you want for your book, but hope others have been more satisfactory people to inquire of than you have found me. If my nieces do not respond, I will try again, but I have directed them to write to your address as the shortest and most direct way for you to get the information you wish for.

"As to my maternal ancestors, I never was acquainted with them and could n't say much in regard to them. I only remember going to my grandfather's funeral when I was four years old, and that when reproved by my sister for not crying, I said, "I can't, because I have n't any pocket handkerchief." My grandmother lived to a great age. Most of their descendants went to the West, and are unknown to fame and me.

"This is all I can do at this time.

"With kind regards, yours,
"GEORGE LEWIS HOVEY."
(By Mrs. Hovey.)

Another sketch of Daniel Hovey,[6] from the pen of his niece, Mrs. Ruth Hovey Sprague,[7] is here inserted, and will be no less interesting than the preceding one by his son.

"Daniel, eldest son of elder Samuel and Abigail (Cleveland) Hovey, was born in Canterbury, Conn., July 24th, 1764. In his childhood or early youth his parents removed to the town of Lyme, N. H.

"On the 16th of October, 1781, he, with four others, were sent on a scout from a fort in Corinth and were fired upon in the town of Jericho by a party of sixteen tories, some of whom were acquainted with, and had partaken of the hospitality of the family. One member of the scouting party was mortally wounded and died the next day. The scouts jumped into some high brakes and thick bushes, and hid themselves. Four of them were soon discovered, and three being asked in turn how many there were, answered "four"; when the fourth one was asked, being a very honest fellow, he answered "five." Thereupon search was made for the fifth, and Daniel was discovered. On being ordered he at once gave up his arms, but he told me that for awhile he trembled excessively. He said, "One said on hearing my account 'I would not have given up my gun'; another, 'I would not have come from my cover'; but none of them know what they would have done." The leader of the tories shook him by the hand, inquired after the health of his father, and said if he had him there he would treat him. It appeared this tory was supposed to be a patriot, and had been told of the contemplated expedition of the scouts.

"The four scouts were taken to Quebec and imprisoned; Daniel being confined in the same cell with an elderly prisoner of good education, who had been for some years a teacher. They sold a part of their allowance of food, and bought paper and a few books, and *at this seminary* the ready scholar acquired a considerable part of his education. They were permitted to exercise occasionally in making pickets under a guard, outside the prison walls. A charitable lady occasionally sent them a welcome present of some nice little dish as an addition to their prison fare. After a captivity of eleven months, his father received intelligence that an exchange of prisoners had been made, and that the son was liberated. He went a day's journey to meet his footsore son, lent him the horse, and walked home by his side.

"After the close of the war our scout married Beulah Pingree, a highly accomplished and very beautiful young lady, and settled on the banks of the Connecticut, in the town of Lyme, Grant's island being a part of his farm. In addition to his farming business, he taught in the district schools of the town more than twenty winters; filled nearly all offices of honor and trust; was active in establishing a circulating library; was often chosen to settle differences among his neighbors and townsmen; never had a lawsuit, and was "Uncle Daniel" to all, young or old, of his acquaintance.

"Having for many years received from a grateful Government a pension for the patriotic services of his youth, and having lived to a good old age and seen his six children useful, beloved and respected, the dear old saint departed to that rest that remaineth to the people of God.

"In stature he was short, had dark brown hair and blue eyes; was very unassuming in his appearance, and in his countenance and manner of speaking resembled his mother more than any other of his children I ever knew. In his will he bequeathed a Bible to each of his grandchildren and one to his grandnephew, D. H. Sprague, my younger son. (Deceased.)

"His elder son, Daniel, became a practicing physician in Lyme for many years, having been educated at Dartmouth College.

"The younger son, his youngest child, became a minister of the gospel, and at one time was a missionary in the West Indies, subsequently laboring in the southern New England States.

"His four daughters were highly intelligent, accomplished and beautiful women, one of whom, Elizabeth, was, I think, the most engaging lady whose acquaintance and friendship I ever enjoyed. She devoted several years of her life to teaching in New Hampshire; in Vermont, where I had the good fortune to be favored by her instruction; and in Ohio, where she passed five years in teaching in several schools and academies.

"But excepting the youngest son and daughter they are all 'Beyond the river.' Peace to their ashes. I loved them well."

It is said that Daniel Hovey[6] left among his papers a full and carefully prepared account of his ancestry (*Hoveys* and *Clevelands*), but strangely enough no one now seems to know what became of the document after his decease. The following inscription upon his monument in the cemetery at Lyme, N. H., was prepared in accordance with his wish :

"Daniel Hovey, born in Windham, Conn., July 24, 1764, married Beulah Pingree, of Hanover, Feb. 18, 1789—by whom he had four sons and six daughters. Died March 2, 1850, aged 86."

Abigail Hovey,[7] the second daughter and child of Abner and Lois (Tucker) Hovey, b. in Lyme, N. H., March 14, 1793, m. in Wentworth, N. H., Dec. 10, 1811, Joshua Rouen, son of Jacob and Sarah (Copp) Rouen. He was b. in Rouen, France, Jan. 23, 1790; d. in Wentworth, N. H., from injury, by falling of a tree, Oct. 16, 1816. She d. in Wentworth, Jan. 1, 1816.

Children, b. in Lyme, N. H.:

1. Lydia Elmina,[8] b. June 14, 1813, m. first, in Solon, Cuyahoga county, Ohio, Nov. 28, 1838, Thomas Carmel Clough, son of Leavitt and Abigail (Morrill) Clough. He was b. in Canterbury, Merrimac county, N. H., Feb. 16, 1812; d. in Solon, Ohio, Oct. 14, 1839. Farmer. She m. second, in East Cleveland, Ohio, April 3, 1842, Benjamin Crawford, son of Luther and Elizabeth (Wilbur) Crawford. He was b. in Tolland, Conn., April 24, 1794; d. in East Cleveland, Ohio, July 29, 1863. Farmer and lumberman. She resides in Painesville, Lake county, Ohio, with the widow of her eldest son. Children, by first husband, Thomas C. Clough: 1. Thomas Carmel,[9] b. in Solon, Ohio, March 4, 1840, m. in East Cleveland, Ohio, June 8, 1863, Margaret Dorsch, dau. of John M. and Margaret (Hochreiter) Dorsch. She was b. in Bavaria, Germany, Nov. 4, 1838. He d. in East Cleveland, Ohio, Dec. 28, 1865. Farmer. Child: Henrietta,[10] b. in East Cleveland, Ohio, Aug. 11, 1864. By second husband, Benj. Crawford: 2. Hannah Elizabeth,[9] b. in East Cleveland, Ohio, Jan. 8, 1843; d. Feb. 11, 1843. 3. Clay,[9] b. in East Cleveland, Ohio, Dec. 13, 1844, m. in same place, March 18, 1874, Sarah G. Isom, dau. of Thomas and Mary (Elphick) Isom. She was b. in Skaneateles, N. Y., Feb. 28, 1848; res. Caseville, Mich. No children.
2. Sarah Abigail,[8] b. April 21, 1815, m. first, in Charlotte, Vt., April 1, 1835, Moses Atwood, son of Ethan and Caroline Atwood. He was b. in Charlotte, Vt., April 4, 1814; d. in Harbor Creek, Erie county, Pa., Sept. 14, 1848. She m. second, in Erie county, Pa., May, 1849, Charles Taylor, a son of John Taylor, from whom she was divorced within a year after marriage. She m. third, in Cleveland, Ohio, Dec. 5, 1853, Sidney Huntley, who was b. in 1810, and d. March 29, 1868. She d. in Cleveland, Ohio, April 14, 1874. No children by second or third husband. Children, by first husband, Moses Atwood: 1. Son,[9] b. in Charlotte, Vt., Feb., 1836; d. Feb., 1836. 2. Mary Eliza,[9] b. in Harbor Creek, Pa., Nov. 4, 1845, m. in Cleveland, Ohio, Jan. 13, 1858, (at the age of 12 years and two months) William Henry Aldrich, son of Thomas M. and Sarah M. (Ellis) Aldrich. He was b. in Providence, R. I., March 14, 1834. Railroad engineer; res. Cleveland, O. Children: 1. Eliza Mary,[10] b. in Cleveland, Ohio, Sept. 19, 1860; d. Sept. 6, 1861. 2. Sarah Emma,[10] b. in Cleveland, Ohio, Aug. 4, 1862. 3. Charles Thomas,[10] b. in Columbus, Ohio, Sept. 30, 1867. 4. Cora May,[10] b. in Cleveland, Ohio, Dec. 19, 1874; d. July 1, 1875.

Samuel Hovey,[7] eldest son and third child of Abner and Lois (Tucker) Hovey, b. in Lyme, N. H., March 9, 1795, m. in same place, May 10, 1816, Lucy Walker Bishop, dau. of John and Sarah (Kimball) Bishop. She was b. in Lyme, N. H., May 24, 1798; d. in Lyme, April 24, 1852. He d. in Waupaca, Wis., July 9, 1878.

Children, all b. in Lyme, N. H.:

1. John Dudley,[8] b. June 5, 1817; d. June 10, 1817.
2. Samuel Lewis,[8] b. Oct. 11, 1818; drowned July 3, 1831.

3. John Bishop,[8] b. Aug. 12, 1820, m. in Newbury, Vt., Nov. 24, 1842, Melissa Mack Hall, dau. of John and Polly (Moses) Hall. She was b. in Newbury, Vt., April 10, 1823. Res. Stoneham, Mass. Children: 1. Melissa Ann,[9] b. in Lyme, N. H., Nov. 28, 1843, m. in Stoneham, Mass., March 15, 1872, Phillip Leon King, son of Leander and Emily (Story) King. He was b. in Philadelphia, Pa., July 16, 1837. They have children, born in Stoneham, Mass.: 1, Hubert Leon,[10] b. Jan. 16, 1873. 2. Frank Warren,[10] b. Sept. 4, 1874. 2. John Lewis,[9] b. in Springfield, N. H., March 31, 1847; d. in Stoneham, Mass., June 11, 1865. 3. Ida Josephine,[9] b. in Stoneham, Mass., Sept. 22, 1855, m. in same place, June 24, 1875, Warren Nathan James, son of Abiel and Sarah Anna (Smith) James. He was b. in Eastport, Washington county, Me., Sept. 14, 1849. Children, b. in Stoneham, Mass: 1. Charles Warren,[10] b. Jan. 12, 1876; d. Feb. 21, 1876. 2. Josephine Hovey,[10] b. Sept. 10, 1877.

4. Sylvanus Sumner,[8] b. July 12, 1822, m. first, in Medford, Mass., March 31, 1853, Lydia Tyler, dau. of Kimball and Charlotte (Noyes) Tyler. She was b. in North Haverhill, N. H., July 18, 1838; d. in Lynn, Mass., Feb. 15, 1866. He m. second, in Lynn, Mass., Oct. 22, 1868, Mary Jane Tyler, a sister of his first wife. She was b. in Warren, N. H., June 25, 1835; d. in Lynn, Mass., March 27, 1874. He d. in Lynn, Mass., April 28, 1877. Children, by wife Lydia: 1. Albini Sumner,[9] b. in Stoneham, Mass., Jan. 12, 1854, m. in Lynn, Mass., Dec. 23, 1874, Henrietta Janette Quimby, dau. of Enoch Russell and Mary Jane (Bubier) Quimby. She was b. in Freeport, Iowa, Oct. 31, 1856. Child: Arthur Sumner,[10] b. May 13, 1877. 2. Ellie Blanche,[9] b. in North Haverhill, N. H., March 12, 1858, m. in Lynn, Mass., Nov. 8, 1876, George William Ingalls, son of William Harrison and Annette (Stickney) Ingalls. He was b. in Medford, Mass., Nov. 8, 1856. Express agent; res. Lynn, Mass.

5. Abner Bingham,[8] b. Nov. 12, 1825, m. in Stoneham, Mass., March 4, 1849, Malvina Lydia Bryant, dau. of Ebenezer and Sophia (Bryant) Bryant. She was b. in South Reading, Mass , Aug. 11, 1832. Res. Stoneham, Mass. Children, all born in Stoneham: 1. Louise Sophia,[9] b. Sept. 20, 1851, m. in same place, Jan. 4, 1873, Gustavus Bryant, son of James and Rebecca (Stubbs) Bryant. He was b. in Portland, Me., March 28, 1848. Res. Stoneham, Mass. Children: 1. Malvina Lydia,[10] b. Nov. 9, 1873. 2. Frank,[10] b. Dec. 21, 1876. 2. Frank Abner,[9] b. Dec. 31, 1857. 3. Charles Sumner Alphonso,[9] b. Sept. 29, 1865.

6. Lucy Louise,[8] b. May 9, 1828; d. Jan. 6, 1847.
7. Son,[8] b. April 5, 1831; d. April 26, 1831.
8. Son,[8] b. April 1, 1834; d. April 1, 1834.
9. Sarah Lorinda,[8] b. in Lyme, N. H., March 12, 1835, m. in Elba, Wis., May 10, 1853, Charles Johnson, son of James and Fanny (Blunt) Johnson. He was b. in Bulwick, Northamptonshire, Eng., in 1802. Farmer; res. Waupaca, Wis. Children: 1. Silas Samuel,[9] b. Oct. 18, 1854. 2. Lucy Ann,[9] b. April 10, 1856, m. in Waupaca, Aug. 6, 18.6, Taylor Looker, son of Stephen and Margaret (House) Looker. He was b. near Utica, N. Y., Jan. 26, 1850. Child: Grace Belle,[10] b. Sept. 8, 1878.
10. Rhoda Lucinda,[8] b. in Lyme, N. H., April 3, 1841, m. in Elba, Wis., Jan. 26, 1862, John Frederic Wiedman, son of John and Ertmunda (Kuen) Wiedman. He was b. in Posen (near Eam), Prussia, June 21, 1835. Farmer; res. Waupaca, Wis. Children: 1. Hattie Amelia,[9] b. March 21, 1863. 2. Frederic Albert,[9] b. Oct. 31, 1872. 3. Mary Alice,[9] b. Dec. 25, 1875.

Dudley Hovey,[7] second son and fourth child of Abner and Lois (Tucker) Hovey, b. in Lyme, N. H., Jan. 31, 1797, m. in Lyme, April

17, 1820, Rubie Allen, dau. of Pelatiah and Letitia (Knapp) Allen. She was b. in Lyme, N. H., Jan. 25, 1799; d. in Haverhill, N. H., Dec. 15, 1869. He d. in Haverhill, Oct. 28, 1865. Farmer. It may be noticed as a remarkable fact, that the three eldest children of this worthy couple met with tragical and untimely deaths.

Children:

1. Simeon Allen,[8] (Rev.), b. in Lyme, N. H., Jan. 2, 1821, m. in Jackson county, Tenn., Dec. 15, 1842, Melissa Scanlon, dau. of Robert and Sarah (Wright) Scanlon. She was b. in Jackson county, Tenn., Nov. 19, 1827, and is now (1877) living in Nashville, Tenn. He became a Disciple preacher, and during the late war served as a chaplain in the Confederate army. In January, 1870, he was in Memphis, Tenn., on business, since which date all trace of him has been lost by his family and friends. It is conjectured he was killed shortly after at Johnsonville, Tenn., but whatever may have happened, his fate is shrouded in mystery. He was a man of fine appearance and of ability. Children: 1. Sarah Louann,[9] b. in Franklin county, Ill., Aug. 8, 1844, m. in Linden, Perry county, Tenn., Dec. 22, 1857, Granville Bowman Turner, son of David and Elizabeth (Cruise) Turner. He was b. in Monroe county, Ky., Jan. 14, 1841. Farmer; res. Gamaliel, Ky. They have: 1. Simeon Allen,[10] b. Feb. 16, 1866. 2. Virginia,[10] b. Jan. 15, 1869. 3. Bettie Scanlon,[10] b. Sept. 10, 1871. 4. Mary Isabella,[10] b. Dec. 21, 1874. 5. Ruth Ellen,[10] b. July 1, 1876. 2. Isabella,[9] b. in Franklin county, Ill., Sept. 3, 1847, m. first, in Linden, Tenn., Dec. 25, 1869, Benjamin Franklin Dillehay, son of Green H. and Susan (Allen) Dillehay. He was b. in Murray county, Tenn., Nov. 28, 1848, and d. from a railway accident near Nashville, Tenn., Nov. 10, 1873. She m. second, in Nashville, Davidson county, Tenn., July 10, 1876, John Calvin West, son of Levi and Susan Caroline (Holden) West. He was b. in Lauderdale county, Ala., Nov. 27, 1853. Children, by first husband, B. F. Dillehay: 1. Edward Franklin,[10] b. Aug. 8, 1869. 2. Allen,[10] b. Aug. 15, 1872; d. Oct. 30, 1874. By second husband, John C. West: 3. Herbert,[10] b. April 25, 1877. 3. Mary Louise,[9] b. in Clinton county, Tenn., Feb. 13, 1849, m. in Perry county, Tenn., March 5, 1867, George Washington Boyce, son of William H. and Mary L. (Mayfield) Boyce. He was b. in Palestine, Lewis county, Tenn., March 27, 1846. Farmer; res. Farmer's Valley, Tenn. Children: 1. Son,[10] b. ——, 1868; d. ——, 1868. 2. William Henry,[10] b. Nov. 7, 1871. 3. John Granville,[10] b. May 10, 1874. 4. Ellen Rubie,[9] b. in Gainesborough, Tenn., Jan. 20, 1851, m. in Linden, Perry county, Tenn., Sept. 29, 1867, Marshall Andrew Dodson, son of Marshall and Emily (Brown) Dodson. He was b. in Williamson county, Tenn., Jan. 8, 1849. She d. in Linden, Perry county, Tenn., Feb. 13, 1868. No children. 5. Melissa Allen,[9] b. in Gainesborough, Tenn., Oct. 8, 1864; d. in Gainesborough, Tenn., March 20, 1865.

2. Eber Davis,[8] b. in Lyme, N. H., Nov. 23, 1822; was a sea captain. He m. in Bradford, Vt., Oct. 16, 1848, Amanda B. Preston, dau. of Washington and Abigail (Lane) Preston. She was b. in Concord, N. H., July 24, 1824. They had but one child, a son,[9] b. March, 1851; d. April, 1851. Capt. Hovey sailed in 1852, as mate of the steamship "Independence" which was wrecked off Montigordia Bay. While heroically endeavoring to save a lady passenger that had been washed overboard, he was unfortunately drowned in the attempt, March 26, 1852. His widow is living (1877), in Charlestown, Mass.

Appendix.

3. Alvan Seabury,[8] b. in Lyme, N. H., June 5, 1824. On attaining his majority, in the year 1845, he went to the State of Maine and engaged in a very successful land speculation. After closing up his affairs, and with a considerable amount of money, drafts, etc., upon his person, he started on his return home, but was never heard of afterwards. His fate may be imagined, but like that of his eldest brother, a shroud of mystery covers it.
4. Joseph Milton,[8] b. in Lyme, N. H., July 3, 1826, m. in Brookfield, Vt., Jan. 20, 1850, Alma Elizabeth Hibbard, dau. of Alpheus and Sarah (Hovey) Hibbard. She was b. in Brookfield, Vt., Oct. 20, 1832. Res. Bristol, N. H. They have one child: Carroll Milton,[9] b. in Jesup, Iowa, June 11, 1870.
5. Mary Lucinda,[8] b. in Lyme, N. H., May 29, 1828, m. in East Abingdon, Mass., Sept. 9, 1857, Hiram Frederic Herbert, son of Joseph and Susan (Mitchell) Herbert. He was b. in Haverhill, N. H., Nov. 4, 1823; d. in Waco, Texas, June 25, 1869. She is living (1877) in Haverhill, N. H. He was a daguerrean artist. No children.
6. John Nelson,[8] b. in Newbury, Vt., June 5, 1830, m. in Haverhill, N. H., Nov. 30, 1856, Sophia Sarepta Johnson, dau. of John and Betsey (Erwin) Johnson. She was b. in Haverhill, Jan. 13, 1832. He is a farmer; res. Otterville, Iowa. No children.
7. Samuel Lewis,[8] b. in Newbury, Vt., Sept. 21, 1831, m. in Chelsea, Vt., May 3, 1853, Julia Frances Hatch, dau. of Amos S. and Lucy (Piper) Hatch. She was b. in Chelsea, Vt., May 20, 1834. He is a farmer; res. Jesup, Iowa. Children: 1. Charles Eber,[9] b. Aug. 27, 1855; d. May 17, 1875. 2. Mary Belle,[9] b. March 16, 1862. 3. Nellie Marcia,[9] b. Feb. 11, 1864. 4. Lucy Rubie,[9] b. April 4, 1869.
8. George Ide,[8] b. in Bradford, Vt., Feb. 21, 1834; d. April 19, 1834.
9. Isabella Barron,[8] b. in Bradford, Vt., Aug. 1, 1836, m. in Bradford, Dec. 21, 1856, Nathan Hammond Batchelder, son of David and Sally T. (Willard) Batchelder. He was b. in Bridgewater, N. H., April 20, 1823. Carriage maker; res. Haverhill, N. H. Children: 1. Frederic Perkins,[9] b. Dec. 17, 1864. 2. Mary Allen,[9] b. Sept. 13, 1869; d. Oct. 26, 1869.
10. William Barron,[8] b. in Bradford, Vt., July 4, 1844, m. in Haverhill, N. H., July 31, 1867, Luella Ann Page, dau. of James and Elmira (Greenleaf) Page. She was b. in Haverhill, N. H., Dec. 20, 1844. He is a florist; res. Norwich, Conn. They have only one child: Helen Allen,[9] b. Nov. 11, 1869.

Esther Hovey,[7] third daughter and sixth child of Abner and Lois (Tucker) Hovey, b. in Lyme, N. H., March 11, 1800, m. in Lyme, N. H., Jan. 22, 1828, John Clyde, son of Daniel and Margaret (McAdams) Clyde. He was b. in Windham, Rockingham county, N. H., Nov. 6, 1791; d. in Lyme, N. H., Oct. 9, 1858. She d. in Lyme, Nov. 27, 1849. Children, all b. in Lyme:

1. John Downer,[8] b. Jan. 2, 1829, m. in Fremont, Minn., Dec. 1, 1862, Sarah Amelia Hendershott, dau. of Charles and Caroline (Robinson) Hendershott. She was b. in Hornersville, Steuben county, N. Y., April 20, 1844. He is a farmer; res. Argo, Minn. Children, all born in Fremont, Minn.: 1. John,[9] b. Sept. 1, 1863. 2. Hannah Louise,[9] b. June 29, 1867. 3. Katie,[9] b. June 22, 1869. 4. Imogene,[9] b. May 26, 1872. 5. Charles Eugene,[9] b Feb. 18, 1875; d. April 25, 1875. 6. Annabel,[9] b. April 10, 1876.
2. Samuel Sylvester,[8] b. March 11, 1830; d. March 9, 1833.
3. Abner Hovey,[8] b. Oct. 8, 1831; drowned near Cairo, Ill., by sinking of the steamer "Odd Fellow," Aug. 1, 1871. He was unmarried.

4. Moses Sylvester,[8] b. Nov. 18, 1833, m. in 1862, Ellen E. Taylor, of whom nothing further is known by his relatives, and he d. shortly afterward in California. The exact date, etc., not ascertained, though many letters have passed through the mails on the subject. It is understood his widow married again, and is residing in the West somewhere.
5. Hannah Louisa,[8] b. Jan. 18, 1836, m. in Troy, Orleans county, Vt., March 4, 1861, Samuel Willard Colburn, son of William and Anna (Clyde) Colburn. He was b. in Lyme, N. H., June 29, 1827. Builder and contractor; res. Saratoga, Minn. Children, all b. in Troy, Vt.: 1. Edgar Willard,[9] b. Dec. 20, 1861. 2. Sylvester Murray, b. May 17, 1863. 3. Arthur Clyde,[9] b. Dec. 11, 1864.

Rachel Hovey,[7] fourth daughter and ninth child of Abner and Lois (Tucker) Hovey, b. in Lyme, N. H., April 5, 1803, m. in Enosburgh, Vt., Nov. 20, 1835, Josiah Burroughs, son of William and Rachel (Searls) Burroughs. He was b. in Nottingham, N. H., Dec. 28, 1809, and is living (1877) in Belvidere, Lamoille county, Vt. She d. in Belvidere, Vt., June 5, 1838.
Children:
1. Son,[8] b. Sept. 20, 1836; d. Sept. 20, 1836.
2. Son,[8] b. June 2, 1838; d. June 2, 1838.

Lois Hovey,[7] fifth daughter and tenth child of Abner and Lois (Tucker) Hovey, b. in Lyme, N. H., May 24, 1806, m. in Canaan, N. H., Aug. 14, 1825, George Woodworth, son of Sylvanus and Tamasin (Nevins) Woodworth. He was b. in Dorchester, N. H., Oct. 5, 1793; d. in Hebron, N. H., April 18, 1864. She d. in Concord, Mass., Dec. 2, 1877, of a heart disease, after many weeks of acute suffering, borne with much fortitude.
Children were twelve in number, and all born in Grafton county, N. H.:
1. Leigh Richmond,[8] b. Aug. 7, 1826, m. in Springfield, Ill., June 18, 1862, Hannah Mather Lamb, dau. of James and Susan Hill (Cranmer) Lamb. She was b. in Springfield, Ill., July 6, 1838. He d. in Springfield, Ill., May 28, 1865. They had one child: Julia Lamb,[9] b. in Springfield, Ill., June 18, 1863; d. July 8, 1863.
2. William Henry,[8] b. Jan. 14, 1828, m. in Lunenburgh, N. H., Dec. 8, 1849, Caroline Matilda Balch, dau. of Adin and Martha (Gee) Balch. She was b. in Lunenburgh, N. H., April 21, 1824. He is Probate Judge; res. Ionia, Mich. Children: 1. Henry Dodge,[9] b. in Salmon Falls, N. H., March 10, 1851, m. in Pewamo, Mich., Nov. 27, 1873, Maggie H. Rosecrans, dau. of Almon and Caroline (Brown) Rosecrans. She was b. in Lyons, Mich., March 5, 1866. Child: Bertha,[10] b. Nov. 6, 1874. 2. Son,[9] b. in Salmon Falls, N. H., Nov. 9, 1853; d. Nov. 9, 1853. 3. Son,[9] b. in Pewamo, Mich., Dec. 5, 1868; d. Dec. 5, 1868.
3. Esther Tamasin,[8] b. Dec. 14, 1829, m. in Peoria, Ill., Sept. 17, 1860, Benj. Franklin Ellis, son of Joseph and Elizabeth (Atwood) Ellis. He was b. in Middletown Point, N. J., Jan. 21, 1826. Res. Peoria, Ill. Children, all b. in Peoria: 1. Edward Murdock,[9] b. Aug. 17, 1861; d. Aug. 30, 1861. 2. Edith Antoinette,[9] b. Sept. 6, 1862; d. June 28, 1863. 3. Elizabeth Tisdale,[9] b. Dec. 27, 1863. 4. Benjamin Franklin,[9] b. June 19, 1865. 5. and 6. (twins). Esther Tamasin,[9] b. May 31, 1869; d. June 4, 1869. Louise Woodworth,[9] b. May 31, 1869.

4. John Ball,* b. Jan. 25, 1832; d. in Hebron, Grafton county, N. H., Jan. 23, 1853.
5. George Thornton,* b. Aug. 2, 1834, m. in Concord, N. H., Oct. 31, 1859, Frances Cecilia Wallace, dau. of Samuel and Theodosia (Littlefield) Wallace. She was b. in Homer, Cortland county, N. Y., Feb. 28, 1837. Child: Louise Ellis,[9] b. in Greenville, Mich., July 24, 1860; d. in Pewamo, Mich., Feb. 22, 1861.
6. Sarah Frances,* b. June 21, 1836; res. Concord, Mass., unm.
7. Elizabeth Kimball,[8] b. April 2, 1839, m. in Concord, N. H., March 19, 1862, Peter Whittemore, son of Caleb and Dorcas (Taylor) Whittemore. He was b. in Bridgewater, N. H., May 28, 1821. Children: 1. Amy Florence,[9] b. Nov. 12, 1863. 2. George Kimball,[9] b. June 6, 1864; d. Sept. 6, 1867. 3. Lucia Elizabeth,[9] b. Nov. 26, 1868. 4. Luther Leigh,[9] b. July 8, 1875.
8. Artemas Brooks,[8] b. April 15, 1841, m. in Lowell, Mass., Dec. 25, 1865, Lucia Mahala Brooks, dau. of Artemas Lysias and Sarah (Phelps) Brooks. She was b. in Lowell, Mass., July 5, 1840. Res. Lowell, Mass., where children as follows were all born: 1. Artemas Brooks,[9] b. Oct. 6, 1866. 2. Henry Phelps,[9] b. Dec. 12, 1867. 3. Lucia Brooks,[9] b. Sept. 9, 1869; d. July 23, 1870. 4. Sarah Elizabeth,[9] b. Jan. 19, 1872; d. Feb. 27, 1872.
9. Albert Bingham,* b. April 7, 1843, m. in Lisbon, N. H., Sept. 30, 1873, Mary Angeline Parker, dau. of Charles and Amelia Emily (Bennett) Parker. She was b. in Lisbon, N. H., May 15, 1849. He is a merchant; res. Concord, N. H. Child: Edward Knowlton,[9] b. Aug. 25, 1865.
10. Grace Lowella,[8] b. June 14, 1845, m. in Hebron, N. H., Jan. 22, 1870, Daniel Quincy Clement, son of Moses Williams and Tamar (Little) Clement. He was b. in Warren, N. H. Children: 1. Edward Woodworth,[9] b. March 26, 1871. 2. Louise Tamar,[9] b. Feb. 20, 1873. 3. Frederic Putnam,[9] b. Nov. 15, 1875. 4. Albert Daniel,[9] b. Oct. 30, 1877.
11. Edward Baker,[8] b. March 27, 1847, m. in Franklin, Conn., Sept. 9, 1875, Helen Whiton, dau. of John Milton and Fidelia (Wilson) Whiton. She was b. in Stoddard, N. H., May 3, 1849. Res. Concord, N. H. No children.
12. Louisa Maria,[8] b. May 17, 1850, m. in Lisbon, N. H., May 13, 1872, Lucius Alfred Young, son of James Riley and Amelia Emily (Harris) Young. He was b. in Lisbon, N. H., July 10, 1850. Children: 1. Sarah Frances,[9] b. in Concord, N. H., July 30, 1875. 2. James Riley,[9] b. in Bristol, N. H., Jan. 23, 1877; d. in same place, Sept. 23, 1877.

Nancy B. Hovey,[7] sixth daughter and thirteenth child of Abner and Lois (Tucker) Hovey, b. in Lyme, N. H., Sept. 22, 1812, m. in Lyme, June 5, 1834, (Rev.) Moses Flint, a Baptist minister, and a son of (Capt.) Moses and Elizabeth (Spaulding) Flint. He was b. in Lyme, Jan. 17, 1811, and d. there, April 5, 1842. She d. there (of pneumonia) May 26, 1843. She was a woman of great personal beauty and loveliness of character, and her death was greatly lamented.

Children, all b. in Lyme:

1. Elizabeth Spaulding,* b. March 17, 1835, m. in Dunbarton, N. H., Sept. 1, 1859, Johnson Colby McIntyre, son of Timothy and Martha (Colby) McIntyre. He was b. in Dunbarton, N. H., Aug. 4, 1827. Res. Goffstown, N. H. Child: Lois Elizabeth,[9] b. in Dunbarton, Nov. 28, 1860.

2. Moses Atwood,⁷ b. Jan. 31, 1837, m. in Manchester, N. H., March 19, 1861, Hannah Sophronia Balch, dau. of Theodore and Sally (Lovejoy) Balch. She was b. in Lyme, N. H., June 25, 1843. He is a farmer; res. Deep River, Iowa. Children: 1. Edwin Atwood,⁹ b. in Manchester, N. H., Dec. 3, 1862. 2. Theodore Balch,⁹ b. in Monroe, Iowa, Nov. 28, 1865. 3. Sarah Elizabeth,⁹ b. in Indianapolis, Ind., April 27, 1868. 4. Levi Carroll,⁹ b. in Keokuk, Iowa, Dec. 28, 1871; d. May 5, 1876. 5. Moses Delos,⁹ b. in Deep River, Iowa, Sept. 30, 1873. 6. Emma Frances,⁹ b. April 27, 1877.

Lucinda Lord,⁷ eldest daughter and child of Joseph and Mary (Hovey) Lord, b. in Windsor, Vt., ———, 1789, m. in Green county, Ohio, in 1839, William Fraser, a native of Scotland, but nothing is learned further about his parentage or nativity. He d. in Germantown, Montgomery county, Ohio, date unknown. She also d. in Germantown, about 1849. They had no children.

Pamelia Lord,⁷ second daughter and child of Joseph and Mary (Hovey) Lord, b. in Windsor, Vt., April 21, 1791, m. in Green county, Ohio, about the year 1808, John Crary, of whom nothing has been learned except that he was a native of Vermont. They had a daughter,

    1. Phebe,⁸ b. in 1809 or 1810, who d. young.

The mother d. in 1810.

Mary Lord,⁷ third daughter and child of Joseph and Mary (Hovey) Lord, b. in Windsor, Vt., April 21, 1791, m. in Warren county, Ohio, in 1809, Josiah Bradbury, son of David and Susannah (Craig) Bradbury. He was b. near Elizabethtown, in Essex county, N. J., Dec. 9, 1785; d. in Wabash county, Ind., June 20, 1872. She d. in same place, Aug. 15, 1871. Children :

1. Susannah,⁸ b. Oct. 11, 1809; d. Aug. 16, 1855, unm.
2. Joseph,⁸ b. Dec. 3, 1810; d. June 5, 1811.
3. John Lord,⁸ (Rev.) b. Sept. 29, 1812, was a local methodist preacher, m. ———. He d. Oct. 8, 1866, leaving a family of three daughters, namely, Isabella,⁹ Matilda,⁹ and Virginia,⁹ the latter, Mrs. Virginia Boxell, said to be living in Marion, Grant county, Ind.
4. James,⁸ b. Dec. 9, 1814, m. ———. He d. March 13, 1848, leaving one child, Leona.⁹
5. Lucinda Araminta,⁸ b. Aug. 26, 1816, m. Rev. Hugh Fulton, and said to reside near Somerset, Ind.
6. Mary,⁸ b. Jan. 11, 1819, m. Edward Kelley. She d. Dec. 27, 1875, leaving two daughters, Ida Jane,⁹ and Martha Araminta,⁹ who are now (1879) attending the Normal School in Valparaiso, Ind.
7. David,⁸ b. March 10, 1821, m. first, ——— Crabtree, who d. of cholera within a fortnight afterwards. Supposed to be living with second wife, name unlearned, or his place of residence, or anything about him or his family.
8. Sarah Jane,⁸ b. Feb. 17, 1825, m. in Dora, Wabash county, Ind., April 26, 1857, Peter Edwin Duzan, son of William and Sarah (Williams) Duzan. His mother was the daughter of a famous scout of Gen. Washington, in old Revolutionary days. He was b. in Greenup county, Ky., March 20, 1823. [The first wife of Peter E. Duzan was the youngest daughter of John Lord.⁷] He is a farmer. Res. Dora, Ind. Child: Emma Frances,⁹ b. in Lockport, Ind., May 26, 1858; d. in Dora, Ind., Oct. 24, 1876.

9. Rebecca Ann,[8] b. Sept. 29, 1827, unm ; res. Dora, Ind.
10. Abner Marsh,[8] b. Jan. 8, 1830; res. Riverton, Mich.
11. Prosper Nichols,[8] b. June 22, 1832, m. in Dora, Ind., ———, by whom he has two children, Albert Rudolph,[9] and Blanche,[9] dates of births not given.
12. Samuel Harrison,[8] b. March 20, 1834; d. Sept. 22, 1849.
13. Abiel Hovey Lord.[8] b, Feb. 19, 1837; d. March 26, 1862.

The compiler regrets the incompleteness of the records of this (Josiah Bradbury's) branch and descendants, and has repeatedly urged the answers in full to his inquiries but without avail.

Joseph T. Lord,[7] eldest son and fourth child of Joseph and Mary (Hovey) Lord, b. in Windsor, Vt., April 14, 1793, m. in Urbana, Champaign county, Ohio, April 16, 1811, Maria Ross, dau. of William and Winnifred (Rector) Ross. She was b. in Kentucky, Jan. 13, 1793; d. in Cooper, Sangamon county, Ill., Oct. 17, 1852. He d. in same place, July 24, 1845.

Children:

1. Mary Ann,[8] b. Jan. 12, 1813, m. first. in Springfield, Ohio, Feb. 9, 1837, William McElroy, son of Robert McElroy. He was b. in Huntingdon county, Pa., in 1813; d. in Springfield, Ill., Feb. 1, 1844. She m. second, in Springfield, Ill., Nov. 28, 1844, John Francis Hondorf, son of Caspar and Leena Hondorf. He was b. in Amsterdam, Holland, Oct. 1, 1802; d. in Champaign, Ill., Sept. 28, 1876. Occupation, tailor. She is living (1877) in Champaign, Ill. Children by husband, Wm. McElroy: 1. Joseph Robert,[9] b. ———, 1836. 2. Eliza Jane,[9] b. April 10, 1839. 3. William Henry,[9] b. ———, 1842. 4. Ann Maria,[9] b. ———, 1844. By husband, John F. Hondorf: 5. Ann Sophia,[9] b. Sept. 4, 1845. 6. Mary Elizabeth,[9] b. Aug. 14, 1848. 7. Sabilla Jane,[9] b. June 17, 1852. 8. John Francis,[9] b. Oct. 13, 1857. 9. Charles Newton,[9] b. March 29, 1860.
2. Minerva Maria,[8] b. Oct. 27, 1818, m. in Sangamon county, Ill., May 21, 1840, Henry Fiery, son of Joseph and Catherine Fiery. He was b. in Washington county, Md., March 25, 1815. Farmer; res. Edinburgh, Ill. Children: 1. Mary Elizabeth,[9] b. March 16, 1841. 2. Sarah Catherine,[9] b. Aug. 4, 1843. 3. Ann Maria,[9] b. March 6, 1846. 4. Joseph Francis,[9] b. Dec. 27, 1848. 5. Alice Jane,[9] b. July 4, 1851. 6. Lewis Edwin,[9] b. July 12, 1854. 7. Eliza Medora,[9] b. March 2, 1857. 8. John Henry,[9] b. Nov. 13, 1859
3. William Nelson,[8] b. Feb. 13, 1821, m. in Sangamon county, Ill., in 1851, Sarah Jane Neer, dau. of Hiram and Anna Neer. She was b. in Clark county, Ohio, Sept. 15, 1835. Children: 1. Mary Ann,[9] b. Jan. 10, 1852. 2. James Edwin,[9] b. Oct. 13, 1853. 3. William Harvey,[9] b. March 6, 1856. 4. Emma Frances,[9] b. Nov. 12, 1857. 5. Sarah Annette,[9] b. Dec. 28, 1861. 6. Ida May,[9] b. July 18, 1863. 7. Charles Henry,[9] b. July 6, 1865. 8. Nellie Grant,[9] b. March 1, 1869. 9. Nora Elizabeth,[9] b. Nov. 16, 1870. 10. Minnie Florence,[9] b. June 16, 1875.
4. Edwin Harvey,[8] b. Sept. 4, 1822, m. in Yam Hill county, Oregon, Aug. 6, 1861, Mrs. Mary Elizabeth (Brown) Ransdale, dau. of Thomas Hinton and Sophia Western (Hussey) Brown. She was b. in Sangamon county, Ill., Nov. 15, 1836. He is a stock-raiser; res. Heppner, Umatilla county, Oregon. Children, all b. in Oregon: 1. Annette Sophia,[9] b. July 18, 1862. 2. Charles Edwin,[9] b. May 29, 1864. 3. Richard Hinton,[9] b. April 6, 1866. 4. Ionia,[9] b. Feb. 25, 1868. 5. Roswell Tilden,[9] b. April 1, 1870. 6. Elnora Edith,[9] b. June 26, 1873. 7. Alena Agnes,[9] b. Dec. 4, 1875.

5. Elizabeth Winnifred,[8] b. Sept. 7, 1825, m. in Sangamon county, Ill., Andrew Jackson Ross; res. Rochester, Ill. He is a blacksmith by occupation, and has a family of five children. She d. Dec. —, 1865.
6. Philander Augustus,[8] b. Oct. 3, 1819, m. in Mechanicsburgh, Ill., Nov. 28, 1850, Margaret Ann Oliver, dau. of Burrell and Maria (Barcalow) Oliver. She was b. in Mechanicsburgh, Ill., March 1, 1833. He is a farmer; res. Mount Pulaski, Ill. Children: 1. Joseph Edwin,[9] b. May 10, 1852; d. Jan. 28, 1869. 2. William Alanson,[9] b. June 8, 1857. 3. John Henry,[9] b. May 27, 1860. 4. Lundy Augustus,[9] b. Oct. 5, 1862; d. Feb. 6, 1865. 5. Alice Florence,[9] b. July 13, 1865; d. Nov. 6, 1865.
7. Joseph Edwin,[8] b. Feb. 27, 1831, m. in Fort Scott, Kansas, March 2, 1862, Mrs. Elizabeth Ellen (Harris) Miller, dau. of William H. and Louisa (Sheets) Harris. She was b. near Parkersburgh, Wood county, Va., Aug. 18, 1833. He was killed by a fall in a mill, at Wyandotte, Kansas, Jan. 27, 1865. She is living (1878) with third husband, Wm. Stitt, in Del Norte, Colorado. Children: 1. Joseph Edwin,[9] b. in Twin Springs, Linn county, Kansas, Nov. 27, 1862; d. in Kansas City, Mo., July 5, 1863. 2. Louisa Alice,[9] b. in Niantic, Macon county, Ill., May 21, 1864, and is living (1879) in Del Norte, Rio Grande county, Col.
8. James Newton,[8] b. March 22, 1837, m. in ——, Elizabeth Rhinehart, and supposed to reside in Oregon. Occupation, stock-raising.
9. Permelia Alice,[8] b. May 1, 1840, m. in ——, William McFarland; have two children. She d. March —, 1866. Res. Taylorville, Ill.; occupation not learned.

John Lord,[7] (or John *Paine* Lord,[7]) second son and fifth child of Joseph and Mary (Hovey) Lord, b. in Windsor, Vt., Oct. 30, 1795, m. first, in ——, Ohio, Nov. 9, 1819, Mary Bogart, dau. of Oliver and Jane Bogart. Date and place of her birth not learned. She d. in Cincinnati, Ohio, in the year 1828. He m. second, in Danville, Ill., about the year 1832, Verlinda Otwell, dau. of Richard and Cynthia Ann Otwell. Date and place of her birth or death not ascertained. He d. in Ottawa, La Salle county, Ill., Oct. 20, 1860.

Children, by wife Mary:

1. Joseph Oliver,[8] b. in Cincinnati, Ohio, Nov. 5, 1820; said to have been drowned in the Ohio river off the steamer Roselle, in 1837.
2. Jane Elizabeth,[8] b. in Cincinnati, Ohio, Nov. 5, 1822, m. in Ottawa, Ill., July 10, 1837, Jacob Franklin Reeder, son of David and Sarah (Whittaker) Reeder. He was b. in Montgomery, Ohio, March 11, 1815. Farmer; res. Streator, La Salle county, Ill. Children: 1. Joseph Oliver,[9] b. Dec. 15, 1838, m. Feb. 13, 1862, Julia Cochran; have two children. 2. Juliette,[9] b. Jan. 3, 1840, m. Feb. 25, 1858, Benjamin Shaeffer; have four children. 3. Cynthia Ann,[9] b. Nov. 14, 1841, m. Oct. 10, 1864, John Lornberger; have five children. 4. Oscar,[9] b. Oct. 9, 1843, m. in Seneca, Ill., April 16, 1873, Sophia Weidman; no children. 5. William C.,[9] b. April 30, 1846, m. Feb. 16, 1871, Dorcas McFadden; have two children. 6. Mary A.,[9] b. May 23, 1848, m. April 22, 1870, George Quaife; have four children. 7. Nathaniel M., b. July 3, 1850, m. Jan. 1, 1879, Jennie M. Knox. 8. Adella,[9] b. Dec. 6, 1857. 9. Charles,[9] b. March 30, 1865.

3. Mary Ann,[s] b. in Cincinnati, Ohio, May 12, 1825, m. in Lockport, Ind., Dec. 25, 1842, Peter Edwin Duzan, son of William and Sarah (Williams) Duzan. He was b. in Greenup county, Ky., March 20, 1823. Farmer; res. Dora, Wabash county, Ind. She d. in Lockport, Ind., Aug. 22, 1856. Children: 1. John William,[9] b. in Vermillion, Ind., Dec. 15, 1843; was a soldier in the Union army; m. in Indiana, March 14, 1866, Mary Ellen Dick. Birth and parentage not given. She d. Nov. 28, 1875. He d. Jan. 28, 187.). Children: 1. Edwin Jerome,[10] b. Oct. 16, 1867; d. Oct. 23, 1870. 2. Lulu Belle,[10] b. Dec. 19, 1869. 3. Charles Merritt,[10] b. May 8, 1874. 2. Sarah Jane,[9] b. in Lockport, Ind., Dec. 4, 1845. 3. Mary Catharine,[s] b. in Lockport, Ind., Feb. 4, 1848. 4. Henry Sandham,[9] b. in Lockport, Ind., Oct. 27, 1850; d. Sept. 6, 1852. 5. Oliver Edwin,[s] b. in Lockport, Ind., Dec. 22, 1852. 6. Elizabeth Ellen,[s] b. in Lockport, Ind., March 22, 1856; d. Dec. 8, 1859.

by wife Verlinda:

4. Cynthia Ann,[s] b. in Danville, Ill., about 1834; died young.
5. Jonathan,[s] b. in Danville, Ill., about 1836; d. in Lockport, Ind., Aug. —, 1856.
6. Richard,[s] b. in Danville, Ill., about 1839; d. in Lockport, Ind., in 1851.
7. Ellen,[s] b. in Springfield, Ind., about 1841, m. in 1856, Isaac Frazee, and two years after removed to Bates county, Mo. He was reported to have died in the army during the late war. Nothing further of the family is known.
8. ———,[s] b. in Springfield, Ind., about 1843; d. in Lockport, Ind., in 1846.

Alice Lord,[7] fourth daughter and sixth child of Joseph and Mary (Hovey) Lord, b. in Windsor, Vt., Oct. 30, 1795, m. first, in ———, Ohio, in 1815, James Berryman, parentage and place of nativity unknown. He d. in the city of Cincinnati, about the year 1819. She m. second, in Cincinnati, Oct. 19, 1822, Samuel Harrison, son of Adonijah and Abigail (Havens) Harrison. He was b. in Newark, N. J., July 20, 1794, and is living (1877) in Elenor, Clermont county, Ohio. She d. in Cincinnati, Ohio, Nov. 11, 1842.

Children, by husband, James Berryman:

1. Louisa Amanda,[s] b. Oct. 17, 1816, m. first, Oct. 18, 1834, Dolby Merritt, b. 1812 and d. July 28, 1849. She m. second, Dennis Donoway, who was b. in Montreal, Canada, July 9, 1824. No children by either husband. Res. La Fayette, Ind.
2. William Edmund,[s] b. Sept. 3, 1818, m. in Cincinnati, Ohio, Nov. 30, 1840, Sarah Jane Leslie, dau. of John E. and Mary Ann (Haynor) Leslie. She was b. in Albany, N. Y., Dec. 20, 1826. Res. (1877) No. 2808 N. 12th St., St. Louis, Mo. Children: 1. Mary Louisa,[9] b. Oct. 6, 1846, m. in Cincinnati, Aug. 16, 1866, William C. Fithian; res. Emporia, Kan.; have a family of four children. 2. Katherine Cook,[9] b. June 29, 1848, m. in Cincinnati, Ohio, Dec. 30, 1869, Samuel Horace Glenny, son of Samuel and Anna (Hilt) Glenny. He was b. in Lebanon, Warren county, Ohio, May 6, 1845; res. St. Louis. They have: 1. Alice Belle,[10] b. Dec. 19, 1870. 2. Arthur Horace,[10] b. Dec. 11, 1873. 3. Ada Gertrude,[9] b. July 19, 1852, m. in Cincinnati, Ohio, June 4, 1871, Crawford C. Adams. Res. Washington, D. C. They have three children. 4. Hattie Fithian,[9] b. Oct. 16, 1865.

by husband, Samuel Harrison:

3. Margaret,* b. July 30, 1823, m. in Cincinnati, Ohio, Dec. 26, 1840, Charles George. Every effort to obtain further information has been fruitless.
4. Lucinda Alice,* b. March 5, 1825, m. first, in Cincinnati, Ohio, Oct. 14, 1841, Henry Ingraham, who d. there, July 20, 1848. She m. second, James Ritter, and resides at No. 445 Ninth St., in Cincinnati, Ohio. Whether she has a family or not it is impossible to say.
5. Oliver Kelley,[8] b. May 27, 1827; d. Nov. 13, 1856, unm.

Ruth Lord,[7] fifth daughter and seventh child of Joseph and Mary (Hovey) Lord, b. in Windsor, Vt., July 25, 1797, m. first, in ——, Ohio, in 1815, Aaron Bennett, son of William and Mary Bennett. He was b. near Richmond, Va., in 1793, and d. in St. Louis, Mo., Nov., 1817. She m. second, in Cincinnati, Ohio, in 1819, John Lewis, a native of Scotland, who d. in New Orleans, La., in 1821. She m. third, Rev. William Fraser, the former husband of her sister Lucinda. After the death of Fraser, she m. fourth, Rev. John Kemp; and subsequently m. fifth, John Stout. All efforts to obtain some account of the birth and parentage of these successive husbands of Ruth Lord,[7] have signally failed. The compiler understands that John Stout, the last matrimonial venture of this lady, was also a preacher of some note in that part of the State. She d. in Evansport, Ohio, Oct. 31, 1873.

Children, by husband, Aaron Bennett:

1. Aaron,[8] b. in Cincinnati, Ohio, Dec. 14, 1815, m. in Springfield, Ohio, July 2, 1841, Rebecca Schaefer, dau. of John Cramer and Mary (Winters) Schaefer. She was b. in Germantown, Ohio, May 28, 1819. He is a dealer in staves, etc.; res. Evansport, Ohio. Children: 1. William Thomas,[9] b. May 13, 1842, m. in Defiance, Ohio, Jan 1, 1864, Mary Spangler, dau. of John and Elizabeth Spangler, a native of Switzerland, b. ——. No children. 2. Orlando,[9] b. May 13, 1845, m. in Bryan, Ohio, Sept. 21, 1869, Margaret Ann Buck, dau. of John and Catherine Buck. She was b. near Bucyrus, Crawford county, Ohio, Jan. 30, 1849. Res. Evansport, Ohio. Children: 1. Minnie Belle,[10] b. Sept. 10, 1870. 2. Van Orla,[10] b. April 9, 1872; d. May 4, 1876. 3. Valentine,[9] b. Dec. 14, 1846; d July 14, 1867. 4. Mary Alice,[9] b. Sept. 14, 1849, m. in Defiance, Ohio, Oct. 4, 1868. Thomas Harbaugh Kinthigh, son of John and Hannah Rebecca (Evans) Kinthigh. He was b. in Evansport, Ohio, June 6, 1841. Teacher; res. Evansport. Children: 1. John Edward,[10] b. Feb. 14, 1872. 2. Jessie Belle,[10] b. April 21, 1873. 3. James Bennett,[10] b. April 12, 1874. 4. Mary Idessa,[10] b. April 2, 1875. 5. Fannie Ethel,[10] b. July 2, 1877. 5. Susan May,* b. May 17, 1851. 6. Caroline,[9] b. Feb, 28, 1853, m. in Defiance, Ohio, July 6, 1872, Harrison Taylor Kinthigh, son of John and Hannah Rebecca (Evans) Kinthigh. He was b. in Springfield, Ohio, May 30, 1851. Cooper; res. Hicksville, Ohio. Children: 1. Maggie Belle,[10] b. June 20, 1873. 2. Forrist,[10] b. Sept. 8, 1874. 3. Mary Willnetta,[10] b. May 25, 1877. 7. Addaline,[9] b. Feb. 25, 1855; d. Aug. —, 1861. 8. Fanny,[9] b. May 1, 1856; d. April 26, 1857. 9. Louisa Adele,[9] b. Feb. 15, 1858. 10. Clara Belle,[9] b. Dec. 10, 1860.

by husband, John Lewis:

2. Mary Jane,* b. in Cincinnati, Ohio, May 28, 1820, m. in Germantown, Ohio, Feb. 10, 1834, Frederic George Replogle, son of Phillip and Elizabeth (Gossard) Replogle. He was b. in Hagerstown, Md., Nov. 19, 1811, and is living (1877) in Evansport, Ohio. She d. in Evansport, Sept. 4, 1858. Children: 1. Louisa Editha,[9] b. April 13, 1835, m. in Germantown, Ohio, in 1853, Jeremiah Swartzel, son of John Charles and Mary Elizabeth (Crist) Swartzel. He was b. in Germantown, Sept. 19, 1827. Children: 1. John Coleman,[10] b. May 28, 1854 2. Emma Jane,[10] b. Oct. 4, 1856. 3. Charles Daniel,[10] b. April 10, 1858. 4. Mary Louisa,[10] b. Nov. 2, 1860. 5. William James,[10] b. Dec. 10, 1863. 6. Frank Lewis,[10] b. Feb. 25, 1865. 7. Oliver Jeremiah,[10] b. Oct. 8, 1866. 8. Andrew Patrick,[10] b. March 17, 1868. 9. Peter Robert,[10] b. Feb. 22, 1870. 10. Edward Lord,[10] b. May 12, 1874. 2. Charles Demeters,[9] b. July 14, 1837, m. in Springfield, Ohio, Oct. 27, 1861, Alice Maria Sprague, dau. of William B. and Harriet M. (Carter) Sprague. She was b. in Springfield, Ohio, Aug. 22, 1843. Res. Evansport, Ohio. Children: 1. Mary Alice,[10] b. March 15, 1863. 2. Charles Elmer,[10] b. June 4, 1865. 3. John Stout,[10] b. April 3, 1867. 4. George Horace,[10] b. Nov. 2, 1870. 5. Bertha Harriet,[10] b. June 18, 1873. 6. Grace Edna,[10] b. Nov. 24, 1876. 3. Caroline Cordelia,[9] b. Dec. 16, 1839, m. Zedekiah Dawson. Res. Marysville, Ind. 4. William Malcolm,[9] b. Oct. 28, 1841, m. Lucy Austin. Res. Evansport, Ohio. 5. Rebecca Alice,[9] b. Feb. 29, 1843, m. in Evansport, Ohio, Oct. 16, 1866, John Freeman Evans, son of Isaac and Catherine (Eicher) Evans. He was b. in Evansport, Ohio, Jan. 3, 1840. No children. Res. Bryan, Ohio. 6. Aaron Bennett,[9] b. June 5, 1846, m. in Williams Center, Ohio, May 12, 1872, Mary Ellen Caulkins, dau. of Dr. Daniel and Lydia Ann (Russell) Caulkins. She was b. in Greenville, Knox county, Ohio, Feb. 10, 1854. He is a painter; res. Bryan, Ohio. Children: 1. Leona,[10] b. in Hicksville, Ohio, July 2, 1873. 2. Wilbert Clyde,[10] b. in Bryan, Ohio, Oct. 26, 1875. 7. Edward,[9] b. Aug. 29, 1848; d. young. 8. Mary Jane,[9] b. Aug. 28, 1849; d. young. 9. Moses,[9] b. Sept. 7, 1851. 10. Emma Jane,[9] b. Nov. 7, 1855. 11. Flora Fredonia,[9] b. Aug. 7, 1857, m. in Evansport, Ohio, Julian J. Butts. Res. Saginaw, Mich.

Jonathan Lord,[7] fourth son and ninth child of Joseph and Mary (Hovey) Lord, b. in Windsor, Vermont, Jan. 5, 1800, m. first, in Newtown, Hamilton county, Ohio, Jan. 22, 1824, Sarah Stewart, dau. of Alexander and Sarah (McKibbin) Stewart. Date and place of her birth not learned, but she d. in Newtown, Ohio, about 1833. He m. second, Dec. 25, 1834, Mrs. Margaret (Hatfield) Jones, dau. of William and Nancy (Craig) Hatfield. She was b. in Virginia, Nov. 13, 1802; d. in Newtown, Ohio, Aug. 26, 1862. He d. in same place, in 1850.

Children, by wife Sarah:

1. David Alexander,* b. Oct. 24, 1824; d. Aug. 28, 1825.
2. Mary Jane,* b. Jan. 5, 1826; d. at the South, unm.
3. Sarah Ann,[8] b. April 6, 1828, m. John Webster, and had a family, but separated from her husband. She is now living in Ross county, Ohio, at Harper's Station.
4. Nancy,[8] b. Dec. 14, 1830; d. ——, 1832.
5. Julia Ann,*) b. Feb. 8, 1832; d. ——, 1832.
6. Eliza,[8]) b. Feb. 8, 1832; d. of cholera in 1847, in Batavia, Clermont county, Ohio, aged 15.

by wife Margaret:

7. Emeline,[s] b. Sept. 25, 1835, m. in Tobasco, Ohio, Nov. 29, 1860, Nathaniel Fraser, son of William and Jemima (Kitchel) Fraser. He was b. near Madisonville, Hamilton county, Ohio, Oct. 25, 1823. Joiner; res. Tobasco, Ohio. Children: 1. Cora,[9] b. March 8, 1862. 2. Benton,[9] b. March 18, 1864; d. Dec. 26, 1864. 3. Emma,[9] b. July 9, 1866. 4. William,[9] b. July 28, 1868.

8. Julia Ann,[s] b. Jan. 23, 1838, m. in Cincinnati, Ohio, July 28, 1853, William Witham, son of Gideon and Esther (Dutton) Witham. He was b. in Withamsville, Hamilton county, Ohio, Dec. 16, 1830. Blacksmith; res. Tobasco, Ohio. Children: 1. Lewis Gideon,[9] b. Aug. 11, 1854. 2. Nathaniel Fremont,[9] b. July 4, 1856, m. in Withamsville, Ohio, Dec. 25, 1877, Mary Elizabeth Archer, dau. of William and Martha (Bennett) Archer. She was b. in Highland county, Ohio, Dec. 13, 1856. 3. Owen Allen,[9] b. May 8, 1866.

9. Almira Jane,[s] b. July 11, 1844, m. in Newtown, Ohio, June 5, 1872, James Hanks, son of William and Elizabeth (Kanatzar) Hanks. He was b. in Decatur county, Ind., (near Greensburg), Aug. 28, 1842. No children; have an adopted son, called Arthur Hanks, b. in Pleasant Ridge township, Hamilton county, Ohio, Sept. 21, 1873.

Dr. Abiel H. Lord,[7] fifth son and tenth child of Joseph and Mary (Hovey) Lord, b. in Windsor, Vt., April 26, 1802, m. in Bellefontaine, Ohio, May 27, 1824, Letitia McCloud, dau. of William and Elizabeth (Boswell) McCloud. She was b. in Green county, Ohio, Feb. 14, 1805; d. in Bellefontaine, Ohio, Aug. 22, 1875. [Her mother was a native of Philadelphia, and married Wm. McCloud in that city.] The Dr. is still living in the place where he located after a proper course of medical study, May 8, 1823. He was three times elected Treasurer of Logan county, Ohio.

Children, all b. in Bellefontaine:

1. Maria Eliza,[8] b. April 23, 1825, m. in Bellefontaine, Ohio, May 18, 1841, Lorenzo Gavit More, son of Robert and Sallie (Gavit) More. He was b. in Licking county, Ohio, March 13, 1818. Farmer; res. Bellefontaine, Ohio. Children: 1. Robert Abiel,[9] b. March 17, 1842. 2. Caroline Lord,[9] b. May 23, 1844, m. Feb. 18, 1874, William Andrew Parish, son of Robert and Sarah (Turner) Parish. He was b. in Logan county, Ohio, Feb. 13, 1849. 3. Joseph Lord,[9] b. June 11, 1847. Printer; res. DeGraff, Logan county, Ohio. 4. Letitia McCloud,[9] b. Aug. 10, 1849. 5. Sally Gavit,[9] b. Dec. 4, 1851; d. Dec. 18, 1876. 6. Richard Lord,[9] b. May 4, 1854. 7. Minnie Melvina,[9] b. Nov. 4, 1865.

2. Lucinda,[8] b. July 2, 1828, m. in Bellefontaine, Ohio, March 31, 1846, Thomas Lee Wright, M. D., son of Dr. Thomas and Sophia (Huntington) Wright. He was b. in Ohio, Aug. 13, 1825. Res. Bellefontaine, Ohio. Children: 1. Abiel Lord,[9] b. April 3, 1847, m. in Bellefontaine, Ohio, March 4, 1869, Clara Gregg, dau. of Israel and Roxiana (Olds) Gregg. She was b. in Lithopolis, Fairfield county, Ohio, Aug. 27, 1849. He is a physician; res. Bellefontaine, Ohio. Child: Thomas Huntington,[10] b. Nov. 30, 1869. 2. Thomas Huntington,[9] b. April 30, 1849. Attorney-at-Law.

3. Minerva,[s] b. April 15, 1830, m. in Bellefontaine, Ohio, Aug. 6, 1862, her cousin, George Martin Hackenger, son of Protus and Abigail (Lord) Hackenger. He was b. in Cincinnati, Ohio, June 20, 1835. She d. in Bellefontaine, Ohio, Oct. 3, 1876. He is a farmer. Children: 1. Richard Lord,[9] b. March 29, 1864. 2. James Clarence,[9] b. April 12, 1869.

4. Richard Sprigg Canby,* (Col.), b. Oct. 26, 1832, m. in Hamilton county, Ohio, July 4, 1863, Mary Angelina Wright, dau. of Dr. Thomas and Sophia (Huntington) Wright. She was b. in Carthage, Ohio, July 12, 1834. He d. of pneumonia, in Bellefontaine, Ohio, Oct. 15, 1866. [His widow is now wife of James K. Goodwin, Esq., of Peoria Ill.] Children: 1. Richard Stanton,⁹ b. in Hamilton county, Ohio, April 9, 1864; d. May 26, 1867. 2. Edith Sheridan,⁹ b. May 24, 1865; d. Sept. 8, 1865.

A short sketch of Col. Lord is given on page 14, but the following obituary notice at the time of his death is here inserted, as a just tribute to a brave and Christian soldier of the nation:

"[Communicated.]

"THE LATE MAJOR RICHARD S. LORD."

"EDS. COM.—Major Richard S. Lord, who died in Bellefontaine, Ohio, on the 15th inst., deserves more than a passing notice. He was one of those working soldiers, who, having no 'friend at court,' had to depend upon his own resources, and stand upon his own merits in his conflict with the world, and he did it well.

"Graduating at West Point creditably, he soon entered the cavalry arm of the service, for which he had a decided preference. Stationed for several years in New Mexico and Arizona, he was still in the far West when the civil war broke out. His record as a soldier is most honorable; he participated in the following, amongst other conflicts, and in all those enumerated he was in command of his regiment—the 1st United States Cavalry: Val Verde, New Mexico, February 21, 1862; Apache Ranche, March 8, 1862; Stoneman's raid against Richmond, April and May, 1863; Beverly Ford, Virginia, June 9, 1863; Aldie, June 18, 1863; Middleburgh, June 19, 1863; Upperville, June 21, 1863; Gettysburg, July 1 to 3, 1863; Williamsport, Virginia, July 6, 1863; Boonsborough, July 7 and 8, 1863; Funktown, July 9, 1863; Dinwiddie Court House, March 30 and 31, 1865; Five Forks, April 1, 1865; Sutherland Station, April 2, 1865; Bevil's Bridge, April 3, 1865; Deaconsville, the same day.

"In all of these engagements Major Lord shone as a brave and skillful officer. He was painfully wounded at the battle of Funktown, and his conduct at the battle of Five Forks was the theme of the public commendation in all the newspapers of the land, at the period when it was fought, and called out the special and personal approval of Major General Sheridan, and was the occasion of his receiving brevet promotion.

"After the surrender of General Lee, the First Cavalry was detailed as the escort of General Sheridan, Major Lord commanding. Upon this duty he continued until ordered to California with his regiment, last winter.

"Major Lord was high minded and most honorable in all his instincts. Knowing that 'thrift follows fawning,' he refused to humiliate himself to attain position. He was always of the opinion that the high honor which only can give self-respect, is the brightest gem that adorns the escutcheon of a soldier. Like all brave men he was tender hearted and abhorred cruelty; and he never forgot while in the line of his duty as a soldier, what was due to humanity.

"His last illness was lingering and painful in the extreme; but he bore the bodily and mental anguish of consumption with calm courage and patient resignation. He was yet young, and had many ties that it was hard to sever. But throughout all, his voice was the most cheerful of any in his room: and long after he knew the moorings of life were irrecoverably lost, and he was drifting out from sight and from sound, thus feeling and thus speaking, he entered, unappalled, the impenetrable mist.

"He died a Christian. Leaving behind him his companions in arms, with many a longing, lingering look, he enlisted in a better and higher service, and became, as he himself expressed it, a soldier of the Cross.

"Surely such a man deserves well of his country, and the tear of gratitude and affection, and the poor compliment of a public notice of his deeds and memory, but illy repay a life of toil and devotion to the interests of his country.

W."

Rebecca Lord,[7] seventh daughter and twelfth child of Joseph and Mary (Hovey) Lord, b. in Hamilton county, Ohio, Jan. 10, 1807, m. in Cincinnati, Ohio, Sept. 20, 1827, John Hoskinson, son of Rev. Josiah Hoskinson, of Portsmouth, Ohio. Date of his birth or death not ascertained. She d. in Portsmouth, Ohio, Sept. 15, 1829. They had a child:

1. Daughter,[8] b. Sept. 15, 1829; d. soon.

Abigail Lord,[7] youngest daughter and child of Joseph and Mary (Hovey) Lord, b. in Hamilton county, Ohio, April 30, 1811, m. in Cincinnati, Ohio, Jan. 16, 1828, Protus Hackenger, son of Joseph and Clara (Wyman) Hackenger. He was b. in Baden, Germany, June 9, 1806. Farmer; res. Sedamsville, near Cincinnati, Ohio.

Children, all b. in or near Cincinnati, Ohio, and baptized into the Roman Catholic Church:

1. Mary Alice,[8] b. Oct. 16, 1830, m. in Cincinnati, Ohio, Sept. 12, 1850, Phillip Hoffman, son of Phillip and Mary Wyatt (Golder) Hoffman. He was b. in Cincinnati, Ohio, March 4, 1827. Children: 1. Phillip,[9] b. in Cincinnati, Ohio, Aug. 27, 1850; d. Nov. 4, 1850. 2. Charles,[9] b. in Cincinnati, Ohio, Sept. 9, 1851. 3. Phillip,[9] (again), b. in Cincinnati, Ohio, Jan. 14, 1854; d. Sept. 11, 1875. 4. Francis,[9] b. in Jackson, Ohio, Feb. 24, 1856; d. March 17, 1860. 5. Alice,[9] b. in Jackson, Ohio, Jan. 16, 1858. 6. William,[9] b. in Jackson, Ohio, Feb. 5, 1860. 7. Laura,[9] b. in Newport, Ky., March 15, 1862. 8. Agnes,[9] b. in Miami, Ohio, Feb. 1, 1865. 9. John,[9] b. in Aberdeen, Ohio, Aug. 3, 1867.
2. Josephine,[8] b. March 16, 1833; d. May 2, 1851.
3. George Morton,[8] b. June 20, 1835, m. first, in Bellefontaine, Ohio, August 6, 1862, his cousin, Minerva Lord,[8] dau. of Dr. Abiel Hovey and Letitia (McCloud) Lord. She was b. in Bellefontaine, Ohio, April 15, 1830; d. in same place, Oct. 3, 1876. He m. second, in Bellefontaine, Ohio, Dec. 20, 1877, Ada Eva Stierwalt, dau. of Andrew and Martha (McFadden) Stierwalt. She was b. in Bellefontaine, Ohio, May 4, 1858. Children, by wife Minerva: 1. Richard Lord,[9] b. March 9, 1864. 2. James Clarence,[9] b. April 12, 1869.
4. William Henry,[8] b. Nov. 18, 1838; d. July 14, 1841.
5. Agnes,[8] b. Jan. 6, 1840, m. in Cincinnati, Ohio, May 1, 1860, Francis Garritt Frommeyer, son of John Frederic and Mary Elizabeth (Strawcamp) Frommeyer. He was b. in Cincinnati, Ohio, April 17, 1839; d. in Sedamsville, Ohio, Jan. 30, 1876, where she still resides, about half a mile from the residence of her parents. Children: 1. Mary Frances,[9] b. Sept. 1, 1862. 2. Agnes Philomena,[9] b. May 18, 1864. 3. Josephine,[9] b. April 2, 1866; d. Oct. 12, 1867. 4. John Francis Edward,[9] b. Oct. 2, 1868. 5. Albert Eugene,[9] b. May 30, 1870. 6. Vincent Frederic,[9] b. Feb. 22, 1873; d. Nov. 2, 1873. 7. Arthur Ferdinaud,[9] b. March 29, 1875.
6. Mary Magdalene,[8] b. March 17, 1843, m. in Cincinnati, Ohio, Sept. 26, 1865, Joseph Ernst, son of Francis and Anna Maria (Wilmer) Ernst. He was b. in Westphalia, Prussia, Dec. 10, 1836. Res. St. Genevieve, Mo. Children: 1. Francis Joseph Adam,[9] b. in St. Peters, Ind., Sept. 23, 1866. 2. John Edward,[9] b. in New Offenburgh, Mo., Nov. 5, 1868. 3. William Anthony,[9] b. in New Offenburgh, Mo., Nov. 26, 1870; d. there, June 12, 1871. 4. Mary Alice,[9] b. in New Offenburgh, Mo., May 3, 1872. 5. Florence,[9] b. in St. Genevieve, Mo., Nov. 6, 1874. 6. Henry,[9] b. in St. Genevieve, Mo., Jan. 13, 1877.

7. William Henry,[8] b. March 17, 1845, m. in Cincinnati, Ohio, Jan. 24, 1868, Elizabeth Christina Cook, dau. of William and Christina (Felwich) Cook. She was b. in Delphi, Ohio, Jan. 22, 1849. He is a farmer; res. Sedamsville, Ohio. Children: 1. Louisa May,[9] b. Oct. 17, 1868. 2. William Henry,[9] b. June 30, 1872; d. Aug. 31, 1872. 3. James Ritter,[9] b. Jan. 10, 1874. 4. John Cook,[9] b. Dec. 4, 1875.
8. James Ritter,[8] b. Aug. 20, 1846. Res. Cincinnati, Ohio. Clerk at Hunt's Hotel; unm.
9. Joseph Lord,[8] b. Nov. 15, 1849; res. Cincinnati, Ohio; unm.
10. Charles Francis,[8] b. July 20, 1853; res. Cincinnati, Ohio; unm.
11. Sarah Jane,[8] b. July 3, 1856; resides with her parents in Sedamsville, Ohio.

Rufus B. Hovey,[7] eldest son and child of Rufus C. and Grace (Billings) Hovey, b. in Lyme, N. H., Nov. 17, 1794, m. in Williamstown, Vt., Jan. 14, 1819, Polly Kendall, dau. of Timothy and Eunice (Houghton) Kendall. She was b. in Williamstown, Vt., July 7, 1797. He d. in Albany, Vt., Jan. 9, 1844. She is living (1878) in Albany, Vt. He was a man widely known and eminently esteemed for his devotion to every good work, and the conscientious performance of every known duty.

Children, first five b. in Brookfield, Vt., and the others in Albany, Vermont:

1. George,[8] b. November 6, 1819, m. in Albany, Vt., March 24, 1842, Maryetta Reed, daughter of Barzillai H. and Betsey (Sweetland) Reed. She was b. in Vernon, Vt., Oct. 30, 1819. He is a farmer; res. Independence, Iowa. Children: 1. Nelson King,[9] b. Dec. 19, 1842, m. Nov. 17, 1870, Nancy Melrose, dau. of Charles and Hester (Price) Melrose. She was b. in Perry, Iowa, March 29, 1850. He is a farmer; res. Vermillion, Dakotah. Children, all b. in Jesup, Buchanan county, Iowa: 1. Willie Richmond,[10] b. Sept. 18, 1871. 2. Fannie May,[10] b. Sept. 6, 1873. 3. Effie,[10] b. Feb. 20, 1875. 4. Jennie,[10] b. May 12, 1877. 2. Betsey Maria,[9] b. Oct. 2, 1844, m. March 7, 1863, William S. Richmond, son of Ichabod and Almira (Gifford) Richmond. He was b. in ———, C. W., in 1841. Farmer; res. Jesup, Iowa. Children: 1. Alice Almira,[10] b. June 12, 1864. 2. Adelaide,[10] b. May 10, 1866. 3. Albert,[10] b. Aug. —, 1868. 3. George Billings,[9] b. Dec. 6, 1846, m. in Coral, McHenry county, Ill., July 3, 1872, Emily Jane Ross, dau. of William Samuel and Harriet Adelia Ross. She was b. in Sherman, N. Y., June 24, 1851. Children: 1. Edmund Lee,[10] b. June 7, 1873. 2. Mary Adelia,[10] b. Aug. 10, 1875. 4. Dana Wellington,[9] b. Nov. 20, 1849. Merchant; res. Winthrop, Iowa. 5. Barzillai Reed,[9] b. Sept. 12, 1851, m. in Buchanan county, Iowa, Feb. 4, 1874, Susan Strickland Baldwin, dau. of Charles Cotesworth Pinkney, and Sarah Ann (Woodward) Baldwin. She was b. in Bradford, Vt., April 21, 1852. Child: 1. Jay Baldwin,[10] b. in Jesup, Iowa, Oct. 15, 1876. 6. Frank Washington,[9] b. May 24, 1854, m. in Coral, McHenry county, Ill., Dec. 5, 1877, Helen Maria Freeman, dau. of John Henry and Hannah Maria (Ross) Freeman. She was b. in Waterloo, Iowa, Sept. 24, 1857.
2. Son,[8] b. Aug. 2, 1821; d. Aug. 2, 1821.
3. Daughter,[8] b. July 23, 1822; d. July 23, 1822.

4. Elias Seabury,[x] b. Oct. 4, 1823, m. in Brookfield, Vt., Jan. 26, 1847, Martha Maria Fisk, dau. of Artemas and Catherine (Colt) Fisk. She was b. in Brookfield, Vt., Dec. 30, 1827. He is a farmer; res. Swanton, Iowa. Children: 1. Almira Martha,[9] b. in Albany, Vt., Dec. 11, 1849, m. in Independence, Iowa, in 1869, Charles Henry Little, son of Moses and Sarah (Cook) Little. Date and place of birth not learned. Children: 1. Sarah Climena,[10] b. Aug. 17, 1870. 2. Charles Herbert,[10] b. Dec. 9, 1873. 3. Martha Alice,[10] b. Jan. 20, 1879. 2. Rufus Billings,[9] b. Feb. 13, 1852; d. Sept. —, 1855. 3. Catherine,[9] b. Nov. 21, 1858; d. Feb. 17, 1859. 4. Horace Nelson,[9] b. Feb. 1, 1860. 5. Caroline Allen,[9] b. Sept. 18, 1862.

5. John Billings,[8] b. Nov. 27, 1825, m. in Albany, Vt., May 26, 1853, Ellen Chamberlin, dau. of Eli and Achsah (Delano) Chamberlin. She was b. in Albany, Vt., Nov. 4, 1824. He is a farmer; res. Albany, Vt. Children, all b. in Albany, Vt.: 1. Wallace Henry,[9] b. Oct. 13, 1854. 2. Lillie Ellen,[9] b. Aug. 17, 1858; d. Aug. 25, 1869. 3. Selma Violet,[9] b. Feb. 1, 1861.

6. Alvin,[x] b. Aug. 7, 1827, m. first, in Albany, Vt., Jan. 18, 1853, Lydia Abby Smith, dau. of Silas and Lucy (White) Smith. She was b. in Vershire, Vt., Feb. 4, 1827; d. in Albany, Vt., April 20, 1870. He m. second, in Coral, Ill., March 14, 1871, Susan Eliza Clemons, dau. of Wesley and Lucretia (Smith) Clemons. She was b. in Wells, Vt., Feb. 23, 1836. He is a photographer; res. Burr Oak, Jewell county, Kansas. Four children, by wife Lydia, two sons and two daughters, died in infancy; by wife Susan: 1. Daughter,[9] b. Oct. 8, 1872; d. Oct. 8, 1872. 2. William Alvin,[9] b. Feb. 8, 1874, in Evanston, Ill.

7. Son,[x] b. July 9, 1829; d. July 9, 1829.

8. Lewis,[8] b. Jan. 3, 1831, m. in Linn county, Iowa, June 15, 1855, Marcia A. Ufford, dau. of Thomas J. and Sophia H. (Cutler) Ufford. She was b. in Glover, Vt., June 28, 1832. He d. in Swanton, Iowa, April 5, 1877. She is living (1879) in Swanton, Iowa. Children: 1. Clara Sophia,[9] b. July 5, 1862; d. March 15, 1867. 2. Julia Idella,[9] b. Oct. 3, 1864. 3. Hattie Ellsworth,[9] b. Oct. 19, 1866; d. Sept. 9, 1870. 4. Emma Polly,[9] b. Oct. 17, 1868.

9. Elijah Adams,[x] b. Feb. 13, 1833, m. in Albany, Vt., July 4, 1857, Rhoda Lyman. She was b. in Glover, Vt. Date not learned. He is in the drive-well business; res. Tampico, Whiteside county, Ill. Children: 1. Adele,[9] b. about 1859; d. Dec. 25, 1869. 2. Silas,[9] b. about 1861. 3. Maurice,[9] b. about 1864.

10. Timothy Kendall,[x] b. Oct. 20, 1835, m. in Littleton, Iowa, Dec. 15, 1860, Electa B. Little, dau. of Moses and Sarah (Cook) Little. She was b. in LaSalle county, Ill., Jan. 20, 1844. He is a miller; res. Littleton, Iowa. Children, four in number: 1. Alice,[9] b. April 18, 1862; d. Sept. 6, 1863. 2. Nellie,[9] b. Feb. 9, 1864. 3. Susie,[9] b. March 14, 1871. 4. Edmund,[9] b. July 30, 1873.

11. Mary Ann,[x] b. Aug. 30, 1837, m. in Albany, Vt., Dec. 27, 1858, Madison Cowles, son of Charles and Anna (Metcalf) Cowles. He was b. in Irasburgh, Vt., April 7, 1833. Farmer and carpenter; res. Albany, Vt. Children: 1. Daughter,[9] b. Dec. 30, 1862; d. same day. 2. Almira Howard,[9] b. March 21, 1864. 3. Son,[9] b. Dec. 2, 1865; d. same day. 4. Archie Billings,[9] b. Jan. 5, 1870; d. Sept. 11, 1870. 5. Roscoe Madison,[9] b. March 4, 1871. 6. Clarence Porter,[9] b. Aug. 30, 1875. 7. Herbert Hayes,[9] b. Aug. 10, 1877.

12. Emily Darling,[x] b. July 4, 1839, m. in Independence, Iowa, Jan. 10, 1871, Jesse Rogers Beede, son of Nathan and Mary A. (Rogers) Beede. He was b. in Albany, Vt., Aug. 28, 1837. Farmer; res. Vermillion, Dakotah Territory. Child: 1. Addie Electa,[9] b. Sept. 1, 1875.

13. Susan Livingston,⁸ b. Jan. 14, 1842, m. in Albany, Vt., Aug. 10, 1862 Jesse Rogers Beede, son of Nathan and Mary A. (Rogers) Beede. He was b. in Albany, Vt., Aug. 28, 1837. Res. Vermillion, Dakotah. She d. Sept. 8, 1870. Child: Willie Hovey,⁹ b. July 30, 1867.

Amy Hovey,[7] the eldest daughter and second child of Rufus C. and Grace (Billings) Hovey, b. in Brookfield, Vt., Dec. 7, 1795, m. in Brookfield, Vt., Nov. 29, 1816, David Burroughs, son of Timothy Burroughs, from Alstead, N. H. He was b. in Alstead, N. H., in 1793; d. in Brookfield, Vt., Jan. 17, 1845. She d. in Brookfield, Vt., May 9, 1818. No children.

Orange Hovey,[7] second son and third child of Rufus C. and Grace (Billings) Hovey, b. in Brookfield, Vt., Feb. 5, 1797, m. first, in Chelsea, Vt., Feb. 5, 1818, Clarissa Williams, dau. of Charles and Ann (Perry) Williams. She was b. in Chelsea, Vt., April 15, 1799; d. in Albany, Vt., June 4, 1855. He m. second, in Craftsbury, Vt., Dec. 12, 1855, Mrs. Louisa Maria (Wood) Hidden, widow of Oliver Hidden, and dau. of Dexter and Mary (Lines) Wood. She was b. in Craftsbury, Vt., Jan. 20, 1800. He is a farmer; res. Craftsbury, Vt.

Children:

1. Orange,⁸ b. in Brookfield, Vt., Oct. 9, 1818, m. in Belgrade, Kennebec county, Me., March 2, 1845, Matilda Abbey Penney, dau. of George Hamilton and Jane (Bickford) Penney. She was b. in Belgrade, Me., Dec. 4, 1825. He is a scythe polisher by occupation; res. West Waterville, Me. Children: 1. Son,⁹ b. Sept. 22, 1846; d. Sept. 22, 1846. 2. Son,⁹ b. Oct. 31, 1849; d. Oct. 31, 1849. 3. George Lorin,⁹ b. in North Wayne, Kennebec county, Me., Nov. 7, 1855. He is an Express messenger on the Somerset R. R.; res. W. Waterville, Me.; unm.
2. Clarissa Ann,⁸ b. in Brookfield, Vt., Sept. 8, 1820, m. in Albany, Vt., Feb. 12, 1851, Jonathan Hartwell Wheeler, son of Jonathan and Polly (McClure) Wheeler. He was b. in Amherst, N. H., Nov. 5, 1821. Sash and blind manufacturer; res. Oshkosh, Wis. Children: 1. George Hartwell,⁹ b. in Nashua, N. H., March 23, 1852; unm. An accountant; res. Milwaukee, Wis. 2. Frank Hovey,⁹ b. in Merrimac, N. H., March 20, 1859. An accountant also; res. Milwaukee, Wis.
3. Abiel,⁸ b. in Brookfield, Vt., Jan. 23, 1822; d. in Northfield, Vt., Sept. 8, 1826.
4. Oliver Perry,⁸ b. in Northfield, Vt., July 22, 1825, m. a Mexican lady, name unknown and d. in Santa Fe, New Mexico, Aug. 9, 1862, leaving, it is said, a handsome property.
5. Lucinda,⁸ b. in Northfield, Vt., Sept. 4, 1828, m. in Albany, Vt., Aug. 30, 1846, Josiah D. Hood, son of Amos and Sally (Smith) Hood. He was b. in Chelsea, Vt., June 9, 1817; d. in Chelsea, Vt., Jan. 6, 1878. She is living (1878) in Chelsea, Vt. Children: 1. Oliver Perry,⁹ b. in Albany, Vt., March 11, 1849, m. in Chelsea, Vt., Feb. 19, 1873, Abbie Louisa Tucker. 2. Clara Amanda,⁹ b. in Albany, Vt., Jan. 3, 1851; d. in Chelsea, Vt., June 4, 1863. 3. Alice May,⁹ b. in Chelsea, Vt., June 11, 1858; d. there, May 29, 1863. 4. Emma Minnie,⁹ b. in Washington, Vt., Oct. 8, 1867.
6. William Palmer,⁸ b. in Northfield, Vt., Oct. 8, 1831. Res. (in 1871) Downieville, Cal.

7. Amanda Malvina,[8] b. in Northfield, Vt., Jan. 10, 1837, m. in Albany, Vt., March 3, 1862, George Stephen Fogg, son of Stephen and Dorothy (Smith) Fogg. He was b. in Chelsea, Vt., June 30, 1838; res. North Tunbridge, Vt. She d. in Albany, Vt., Aug. 10, 1875. Child: 1. Daughter,[9] b. Aug. 31, 1872; d. Aug. 31, 1872.

Silas Hovey,[7] third son and fifth child of Rufus C. and Grace (Billings) Hovey, b. in Brookfield, Vt., March 5, 1801, m. in Chelsea, Vt., in April, 1823, Polly Annis, dau. of Solomon and Susan (Bosworth) Annis. She was b. in Chelsea, Vt., March 8, 1801; d. in Albany, Orleans county, Vt., Aug. 21, 1859. He d. in Albany, Vt., July 29, 1868. Farmer.

Children:

1. William,[8] b. in Brookfield, Vt., May 23, 1824, m. in Albany, Vt., Aug. 30, 1847, Philena Allen, dau. of Wells and Martha (Paine) Allen. She was b. in Albany, Vt., March 5, 1826, and is now living (1878) in Oberlin, Ohio. He d. in Oberlin, Ohio, July 25, 1868. Merchant. Children: 1. Frank,[9] b. April 28, 1853, m. in Oberlin, Ohio, Sept 25, 1874, Mary Etta Harvett, dau. of Amasa Warner and Catherine (Beeman) Harvett. She was b. in LaGrange, Ohio, May 25, 1856. Res. Oberlin, Ohio. Child: 1. Lena Carlotta,[10] b. Oct. 24, 1875. 2. Willie,[9] b. Dec. 3, 1863.
2. Mary,[8] b. in Albany, Vt., July 26, 1826; d. March 9, 1832.
3. Ariel Burnham,[8] (Dr.), b. in Albany, Vt., Feb. 9, 1829, m. in Sandusky, Ohio, June 20, 1849, Susan Boyce, dau. of William and Anna (Johnson) Boyce. She was b. in Danville, Canada West, April 11, 1827. He is a surgeon and physician; res. Tiffin, Seneca county, Ohio. Children: 1. Zenobia Irene,[9] b. in Oberlin, Ohio, May 16, 1851; d. in Tiffin, Ohio, Nov. 17, 1854. 2. Lola Irene,[9] b. in Tiffin, Ohio, Sept. 17, 1854, m. in Tiffin, Ohio, Sept. 17, 1873, Charles Van Tyne,[9] of Sandusky, Ohio. Children: 1. Orvilla,[10] b. ——, 1875. 2. Charles Hovey,[10] b. ——, 1877. 3. and 4. (twins). Orvilla Ariel,[9] and Orvilla Susan,[9] b. in Tiffin, Ohio, March 11, 1860; d. respectively, Aug. 1 and 2, 1860. 5. Earl Burnham,[9] b. in Tiffin, Ohio, Dec. 22, 1861; d. Oct. 16, 1875.
4. Laura,[8] b. in Albany, Vt., Feb. 21, 1831; d. April 14, 1831.
5. Silas,[8] b. in Albany, Vt., Feb. 2, 1833; d. Aug. 15, 1841.
6. Mary,[8] b. in Albany, Vt., July 17, 1835; d. Aug. 16, 1841.
7. Ziba,[8] b. in Albany, Vt., May 26, 1838; d. July 13, 1844.
8. Lauretta P.,[8] b. in Albany, Vt., Nov. 14, 1840, m. in Albany, Vt., Aug. 27, 1859, Henry Lathrop Kendall, son of Austin and Maria (Harrington) Kendall. He was b. in Cavendish, Vt., Sept. 17, 1836. Jeweler; res. Tiffin, Ohio. Children: 1. Willie,[9] b. in Albany, Vt., Oct. 24, 1861; d. March 1, 1864. 2. George Woodward,[9] b. in Albany, Vt., Dec. 21, 1865; d. March 29, 1866. 3. Ella May,[9] b. in Tiffin, Ohio, May 7, 1871.

Rhoda Hovey,[7] third daughter and sixth child of Rufus C. and Grace (Billings) Hovey, b. in Brookfield, Vt., April 25, 1803, m. in Brookfield, Vt., Nov. 27, 1823, Moses Ordway, son of Moses and Nancy (Bean) Ordway. He was b. in Tunbridge, Vt., July 7, 1798; d. in Williamstown, Vt., Nov. 26, 1866. She d. in Chelsea, Vt., June 22, 1878. He was a farmer.

Children:

1. Charlotte Elizabeth,[8] b. Aug. 31, 1824, m. in Williamstown, Vt., March 18, 1868, John Haskell Edson, son of Dr. John and Susannah (Haskell) Edson. He was b. in West Randolph, Vt., Sept. 12, 1827; d. in Northfield, Vt., Sept. 13, 1872. Foundryman. She is living (1879) in Northfield. They had no children.
2. Franklin,[8] b. Jan. 19, 1826, m. in Williamstown, Vt., Nov. 14, 1850, Maria Hatch, adopted dau. of Asa Hatch, Williamstown, Vt. She was b. in Williamstown, Vt., Oct. 25, 1832. He d. in Chelsea, Vt., June 26, 1865. [She is now wife of Elisha G. Longee, North Tunbridge, Vt.] Children: 1. George Wallace,[9] b. in Brookfield, Vt., Sept. 20, 1851; d. in Chelsea, Vt., June 8, 1855. 2. Walter Melvin,[9] b. in Chelsea, Vt., Aug. 24, 1854, m. in Chelsea, Vt., May 5, 1877, Lucy Humphrey, dau. of Lyman Humphrey. Child: 1. Edward,[10] b. in Chelsea, Jan. 31, 1879. 3. Harriet Jane,[9] b. in Chelsea, May 12, 1857.
3. Martin Frederic,[8] b. Dec. 11, 1827, m. in Brookfield, Vt., June 7, 1852, Diana Burnham, dau. of Ariel and Sally (Paine) Burnham. She was b. in ——, Aug. 18, 1833. He is a farmer; res. Chelsea, Vt. Children: 1. ——,[9] b. April 19, 1853; d. April 20, 1853. 2. Ella Diana,[9] b. Jan. 28, 1856. 3. Addie Sallie,[9] b. Oct. 13, 1858. 4. Frederic,[9] b. Aug. 5, 1863. 5. Grace,[9] b. Aug. 4, 1874.

Simeon S. Hovey,[7] fifth son and ninth child of Rufus C. and Grace (Billings) Hovey, b. in Brookfield, Vt., Nov. 13, 1809, m. first, in Albany, Vt., Nov. 26, 1833, Emeline Chamberlain, dau. of Eli and Sally (Stanley) Chamberlain. She was b. in Albany, Vt., Nov. 10, 1812; d. in Albany, Vt., without issue, July 5, 1834. He m. second, in Brownington, Vt., Nov. 28, 1835, Ann Bliss Gross, dau. of Col. Gilbert and Esther Burgess (Hilliard) Gross. She was b. in Brownington, Vt., April 3, 1818; d. in Newbury, Vt., March 17, 1865. He d. in Albany, Vt., Feb. 15, 1842. Merchant. Member of State Legislature in 1841, and much esteemed by all who knew him for his amiable character.

Children, by wife Ann:

1. Henry La Fayette,[8] b. Jan. 25, 1838; d. Feb. 25, 1841.
2. Helen Mar,[8] b. Oct. 29, 1840, m. in Derby Line, Vt., July 7, 1862, William Jondro, son of Joseph D. and Charlotte (Mitchell) Jondro. He was b. in Derby Line, Vt., July 18, 1837. Res. Derby Line, Vt. No children.
3. Harriet Almira,[8] b. May 17, 1842, m. in Chicopee, Mass., May 12, 1864, Joseph Addison Carter, son of Horatio Nelson and Marcia Salome (Brown) Carter. He was b. in Plymouth, Vt., Sept. 12, 1835. She d. in Chicopee, Mass., May 16, 1878. Res. Chicopee, Mass. Children, all b. in Chicopee: 1. Mary Ella,[9] b. March 9, 1866. 2. Belle,[9] b. Jan. 29, 1868. 3. Addison Hovey,[9] b. March 13, 1869; d. Sept. 8, 1869. 4. Edith Hovey,[9] b. Aug. 13, 1870. 5. Helen Gertrude,[9] b. Feb. 25, 1872. 6. Nelson Brown,[9] b. June 1, 1876. 7. George William,[9] b. April 26, 1878.

Asahel K. Hovey,[7] sixth son and tenth child of Rufus C. and Grace (Billings) Hovey, b. in Brookfield, Vt., May 25, 1811, m. first, in Williamstown, Vt., March 17, 1836, Martha Downing, dau. of Rufus and Mary (Wells) Downing. She was b. in Brookfield, Vt., June 1, 1813; d. in Albany, Vt., Oct. 4, 1839. He m. second, in Chelsea, Vt., April 9, 1845, Rocina Chastina Martin, dau. of Daniel and Betsey (Moseley) Martin. She was b. in Williamstown, Vt., April 13, 1813. He is a farmer; res. Chelsea, Vt. No children.

Laura Hovey,[7] fifth daughter and eleventh child of Rufus C. and Grace (Billings) Hovey, b. in Brookfield, Vt., May 6, 1813, m. in Albany, Vt., Dec. 13, 1831, Seth Phelps, son of Joshua and Hannah (Fowler) Phelps. He was b. in Pembroke, N. H., April 6, 1804. She d. in Albany, Vt., Jan. 12, 1868. He is a farmer; res. Albany, Vt.
Children:
1. Simonds Fowler,[8] b. March 17, 1834, m. in Newport, Vt., Dec. 15, 1860, Susan Jane Critchett, dau. of Aaron and Mahala (Noyes) Critchett. She was b. in Epsom, N. H., March 11, 1839. He is a farmer; res. Lowell, Vt. Children: 1. George Hovey,[9] b. in Lowell, Vt., July 17, 1862. 2. Ida Belle,[9] b. in Albany, Vt., June 16, 1866.
2. George Hovey,[8] b. Feb. 13, 1838; d. Jan. 2, 1862, unm.
3. Betsey Grant,[8] b. March 31, 1843 ; unm.

Horace N. Hovey,[7] (Rev.), seventh son and twelfth child of Rufus C. and Grace (Billings) Hovey, b. in Brookfield, Vt., Jan. 28, 1815, m. first, in Irasburgh, Vt., May 26, 1836, Fanny Caroline Kellum, dau. of John and Deborah (Haines) Kellum. She was b. in Irasburgh, Vt., Oct. 29, 1814; d. in Lowell, Vt., Feb. 12, 1873, and was buried in the cemetery in West Albany, Vt. He m. second, in Bethel, Vt., Dec. 23, 1873, Myrtilla Eglantine Hitchcock, dau. of Newton and Submit (Perkins) Hitchcock. She was b. in Westfield, Vt., Sept. 29, 1837. He is living in Lowell, Vt. A Baptist preacher, of force and talent.
Children, by wife, Fanny Caroline:
1. Charles Kellum,[8] b. in Albany, Vt., July 14, 1837; res. Lowell, Vt.; unm.
2. Arthur Judson,[8] (Rev.), b. in Albany, Vt., April 3, 1842, m. in Providence, R. I., June 27, 1872, Ella Experience Mason, dau. of Nathan and Emeline (Armington) Mason. She was b. in Providence, R. I., Jan. 4, 1840. He is pastor of the Baptist Church in Stoneham, Mass. Children: 1. Daughter,[9] b. April 15, 1873; d. June 19, 1873. 2. Horace Mason,[9] b. April 6, 1877.
3. Laura Elizabeth,[8] b. in Albany, Vt., March 12, 1847. She is a teacher in Dorchester High School, Boston, Mass.
4. Annie Catharine,[8]) b. in Albany, Vt., Aug. 6, 1852; res. Lowell, Vt.
5. Fannie Caroline,[8]) b. in Albany, Vt., Aug. 6, 1852, m. in Stoneham, Mass., May 5, 1874, Dr. Anson Joseph Golden, son of Warden and Eliza Elizabeth (Moffet) Golden. He was b. in Sutton, P. Q., May 15, 1848. Physician and surgeon; res. Maiden Rock, Wis. Children: 1. Verna Jennie,[9] b. in River Falls, Wis., April 30, 1876. 2. Laura Elizabeth,[9] b. in Maiden Rock, Wis., Nov. 3, 1878.
6. Albert Silas,[8] b. in Albany, Vt., Sept. 28, 1856. Clerk in a grocery store, Stoneham, Mass.

Under date of June 4, 1879, Rev. Horace N. Hovey closes a letter addressed to the compiler of this work, as follows:

"As to myself I hardly know what to write, or what I wrote in my former letter. For some eight years after marriage I was a farmer in the town of Albany, Vt. Commenced in the ministry in 1842. In the spring of 1843 left the farm and removed to the village, in Albany, and entered upon the work of the ministry, and had the charge of the church most of the time until the fall of 1866. In that time I had the pastoral charge of the church in Newport for eight years—in Irasburgh for three years—preaching at these places one-half the time and at Albany the other half. In July, 1876, I removed my family to Lowell, Vt., my present residence, having had the charge of the small Baptist Church here for nearly three years. Since July, 1876, my labors have continued here unbroken, except the time for rest on a journey to visit friends in Illinois, and some three months in the summer of 1874, to visit my daughter in River Falls, Wis.

"I shall be highly gratified to receive any sheets of your forthcoming volume, and as highly pleased to render any service you may wish in my power. Mail time has come, and I close in haste.

Your cousin truly,
HORACE NELSON HOVEY."

Mrs. Ruth Hovey Sprague, of East Brookfield, Vt., furnishes the following sketch of this family:

"Rufus Cleveland Hovey, fourth child of Elder Samuel and Abigail (Cleveland) Hovey, was born A. D. 1770, and married Grace Billings, with whom he resided in the town of Brookfield, Vt., where he died at the age of 46, leaving a widow with nine children, the youngest being an infant daughter. His eldest son, Billings, assumed the care of the family, honoring his father by his affectionate care of his mother, brothers and sisters. To see Billings bring his infant sister to the Sabbath services, and place her tenderly in the mother's arms, was pleasant; and a gratified smile, chased by a tear, would pass round the circle, seated on those same long benches.

"But two years after the death of the father, both mother and infant fell victims to the same fever that was fatal to the husband and father. Billings in the meantime had married a worthy lady, Miss Polly Kendall, and brought her into the family. She remarked, after the death of the mother, that if she was ever to marry Billings she married him at the right time, for she had learned how to manage the family.

"In the family were two young men, Orange and Silas; besides Rhoda, Simeon, Asahel, Laura and Horace; these five having for guardians their uncles, Samuel and Alvan, who resided within a quarter of a mile on either side. This large family, in addition to their own children, Billings and Polly cared for and educated to the satisfaction of both guardians and wards.

"At this time Billings was not a professor of religion, but his wife was a pious lady. There being great interest felt in the community on the subject of religion, evening meetings were frequently held, and 'Polly,' being very anxious for her husband, had arranged with a younger member of the family to stay at home and care for the children, that Billings might accompany her on this evening to a meeting at Uncle Samuel's. This, Billings declined, and she went without him, praying as she went. After she had gone, Billings concluded to go privately, as it was now dark. He and Uncle Samuel's son, Willis, who had also absented himself from the meetings, crept silently into an adjoining room to listen to the exercises. Now, there were among the praying brethren, two, viz., Uncle Samuel, and Deacon Edward Sprague, who were especially gifted in prayer —(an eccentric person said, 'When they pray, how the blessings shell down,')— and on this evening their petitions seemed more solemn and weighty than usual. Before their prayers were finished, behold! the door opened; Billings and Willis walked into the room, fell on their knees, acknowledged their sins, begged for and obtained pardon. Billings retired for the night, and I have heard him say he heard a sound like a heavy stone falling and rolling across the room; and these words, 'Whoso falleth on this stone shall be broken, but on whomsoever it shall fall, it shall grind him to powder.' To all human appearance, perhaps few have lived a more Christian life.

"His brothers and sisters coming to maturity, he sold the farm which had been his father's, divided to each child his patrimony, removed fifty miles north to the town of Albany, where land was cheap, and made himself a new home. To this place his brothers and one sister gathered, and with his own sons made a new 'Hovey neighborhood.' There, his death occurred many years after, and the news passed in Brookfield, 'Good brother Billings has gone.' His aged widow still resides among her children in Albany.

"Of Uncle Rufus I can say little. All I remember of him is attending his funeral. My mother was much attached to him, and often spoke of him very affectionately. His youngest son has been a minister of the Gospel, and has preached in Lowell, Vt., many years.

"Another item or two of Uncle Daniel: His grandson, Sylvanus Hibbard, tells me that when he was surveying the towns in the eastern part of the State, he lost his knife, and, having his pen to mend, he mended it with his hatchet. At one time he walked from his home in Lyme to Brookfield, to visit his father's family, on the frozen snow crust, in company with another man. It could not have been less than twenty-eight or thirty miles—a good day's work.

"I know scarcely anything of Uncle Abner. Probably you have received his history from Mrs. Woodworth. R. H. SPRAGUE."

Lola Sanderson,[7] eldest daughter and child of James and Rebecca (Hovey) Sanderson, b. in Woodstock, Vt., Dec. 21, 1795, m. in Chelsea, Vt., Jan. 1, 1815, Gurdon Lincoln, son of Samuel and Prudence Lincoln. He was b. in Windham, Vt., Jan. 25, 1787, and d. in Madison, Ohio, July 5, 1864. She d. in Osakis, Douglas county, Minn., May 19, 1875.

Children :

1. Oliver Gurdon,[8] b. in Chelsea, Vt., Oct. 31, 1816, m. in Chelsea, Vt., May 13, 1875, Mary Augusta Hood, dau. of Elihu and Eliza (Stevens) Hood. She was b. in Chelsea, Vt., Feb. 28, 1836. He is a farmer; res. Chelsea, Vt. No children.
2. Samuel,[8] b. in Chelsea, Vt., April 25, 1818, m. first, in Glover, Vt., July 3, 1851, Mary Patterson Vance, dau. of John M. G. and Laura (Patterson) Vance. She was b. in Glover, Vt., May 13, 1822; d. in Albany, Vt., July 10, 1860. He m. second, in Newport, Vt., July 10, 1861, Violetta Rebecca Jones, dau. of Ebenezer and Rebecca (Adams) Jones. She was b. in Newport, Vt., June 27, 1832. He is a farmer; res. Newport, Vt. No children by wife Violetta. Children, by wife Mary: 1. Alice Marietta,[9] b. March 6, 1855. 2. Samuel,[9] b. Sept. 22, 1857; d. Sept. 24, 1857. 3. Daughter," b. July 2, 1860; d. July 2, 1860.
3. Roswell,[8] b. in Chelsea, Vt., Nov. 9, 1819, m. in same town, Nov. 10, 1841, Lucy D. Hood, dau. of Amos and Sally (Smith) Hood. She was b. in Chelsea, Vt., June 19, 1823, and is living (1878) at 12 Stark street, Manchester, N. H. He d. in Chelsea, Vt., Dec. 24, 1874. Child: 1. Marcella,[9] b. in Albany, Vt., June 19, 1844.
4. Almira Lola,[8] b. in Walden, Vt., Aug. 14, 1822, m. in Albany, Vt., Dec. 22, 1847, Samuel Bickford, son of Samuel B. and Abigail (Critchet) Bickford. He was b. in Epsom, N. H., Dec. 5, 1826; d. in Washington, D. C., July 25, 1863. Widow living (1878) in Chelsea, Vt. Children, all b. in Albany, Vt.: 1. Cordelia Elizabeth,[9] b. Dec. 5, 1848, m. in Chelsea, Vt., Aug. 18, 1866, Albert Dennison. Res. Chelsea, Vt. No children. 2. Mary Abby,[9] b. Jan. 11, 1851, m. in Chelsea, Vt., March 27, 1867, Benj. Franklin Smith, of Chelsea, where they reside. Children: 1. Eva May,[10] b. April 18, 1868. 2. William Henry,[10] b. May 26, 1870. 3. Arthur Monroe,[10] b. April 21, 1872. 4. Roswell James,[10] b. Nov. 21, 1875. 5. Nellie Elizabeth,[10] b. April 27, 1878. 3. John William,[9] b. April 4, 1853, m. in Osakis, Minn., Nov. 28, 1875, Jane Curtis. Res. Osakis, Minn. Children: 1. Nolan Earl,[10] b. April 28, 1877. 2. Ernest Melvin,[10] b. Oct. 15, 1878. 4. Julia Theresa,[9] b. Sept. 30, 1856, m. in Brookfield, Vt., March 31, 1875, Adna B. Downs. Res. Williamstown, Vt. Child: 1. Frankie Adna,[10] b. Aug. 8, 1877. 5. Oliver Gurdon,[9] b. March 22, 1861. Res. Chelsea, Vt.

Appendix.

5. James Sanderson,[8] b. in Walden, Vt., July 14, 1824, m. in Roxbury, Vt., Jan. 1, 1845, Elizabeth Hugh Baker, dau. of Dean and Hannah (Parmenter) Baker. She was b. in Holden, Mass., Oct. 2, 1825. He d. in Berryville, Va., Aug. 11, 1864, having enlisted on the 2nd of May, 1864, in the Union Army, 144th Regt. O. V. M., Company K. On the very day of his death his youngest child was born, and his widow bravely sustained her family of ten children (the eldest only eighteen at the time of the father's death), educated them, and is now living (1878) in Whitehouse, Lucas county, Ohio, with her second husband, William Hoile. Children: 1. Sarah Elizabeth,[9] b. in Albany, Vt., March 9, 1846, m. in Adrian, Mich., July 14, 1874, Allison T. Hale, parentage and place and date of birth not learned. Res. Greenwich, Ohio. Two children: Clyde,[10] and Rose.[10] 2. James Oscar,[9] b. in Lowell, Vt., Dec. 8, 1847, m. in Waterville, Lucas county, Ohio, April 30, 1874, Alice P. Creplever, parentage and place and date of birth not learned. Res. Waterville, Ohio. Children: 1. Florence Mabel,[10] b. May 3, 1875. 2. John Asher,[10] b. Nov. 30, 1877. 3. Cynthia Eliza,[9] b. in Brookfield, Vt., July 31, 1849; d. in Montgomery, Wood county, Ohio, Aug. 11, 1866. 4. Clara Amelia,[9] b. in Lowell, Vt., July 30, 1851, m. in Bowling Green, Wood county, Ohio, Oct. 24, 1870, Peter Keiser. Res. Holgate, Henry county, Ohio. Children: 1. Willie,[10] b. Oct. 28, 1871; d. April 8, 1872. 2. Oscar,[10] b. Feb. 28, 1873. 3. Susannah,[10] b. April 4, 1875. 4. Lucy,[10] b. Sept. 13, 1878. 5. Harriet Emma,[9] b. in Ballville, Sandusky county, Ohio, March 26, 1854, m. in Monroeville, Ohio, March 10, 1874, John Reeves. Res. Monroeville. No children. 6. Martha Elvira,[9] b. in Fremont, Ohio, Feb. 1, 1856, m. May 20, 1875, William H. Weaver. Res. Holgate, Ohio. No children. 7. Mary Rosanna,[9] b. in Madison, Ohio, Jan. 11, 1858, m. in Adrian, Mich., Oct. 2, 1877, Oscar Sisson. Res. Greenwich, Ohio. No children. 8. Rubie Ella,[9] b. in Montgomery, Wood Co., Ohio, Oct. 17, 1859. 9. Lucy Edna,[9] b. in Montgomery, Ohio, June 29, 1861. 10. Nellie Caroline,[9] b. in Montgomery, Ohio, Aug. 11, 1864.

6. Levina,[8] b. in Walden, Vt., Dec. 17, 1825, m. first, in Northfield, Vt., May 17, 1846, Eri Wood Wilder, son of Daniel and Elizabeth (Blake) Wilder. He was b. in Stark, Coos county, N. H., Oct. 14, 1818. She was divorced, and m. second, in Elmore, Ottawa county, Ohio, Thomas Blake, a son of John Blake. He was b. in Canada, July 25, 1818, and resides in Genoa, Ottawa county, Ohio. She is supposed to be living in or near Cleveland, Ohio, having separated from her second husband. She had no children by either husband. Her first husband, Eri W. Wilder, d. in Farmer, Defiance county, Ohio, 18—.

7. Alvin Hovey,[8] b. in Danville, Vt., June 19, 1828, m. in Osakis, Minn., Oct. 1, 1874, Catharine L. Graham, parentage and place and date of birth unknown. They reside in Wadena, Minn., and have one or two children.

8. Prudence,[8] b. in Walden, Vt., Feb. 11, 1831, m. in Albany, Vt., June 28, 1853, Hiram Mason Works, son of Hiram Mason and Nancy (Gates) Works. He was b. in Craftsbury, Vt., May 7, 1832. Res. Mountain Lake, Minn. Children: 1. Francis Adelbert,[9] b. Sept. 1, 1858. 2. Charles Hiram,[9] b. Aug. 14, 1860.

9. Rebecca,[8] b. in Walden, Vt., April 14, 1833; d. April 10, 1851.

10. Emily,[8] b. in Chelsea, Vt., June 29, 1836, m. in Madison, Ohio, Dec. 7, 1865, Martin Van Buren McCrillis,[8] her cousin, son of Brigham and Rebecca (Sanderson) McCrillis. He was b. in Dresden, N. Y., March 10, 1838. Farmer; res. Mountain Lake, Minn. Children: 1. Ida May,[9] b. Sept. 25, 1866. 2. Jessie Myrtle,[9] b. April 11, 1868. 3. and 4. (twins). Lovell Milan,[9] and Milo Lowell,[9] b. Dec. 24, 1870.

Electa Sanderson,[7] second daughter and child of James and Rebecca (Hovey) Sanderson, b. in Woodstock, Vt., July 16, 1797, m. in Williamstown, Vt., Dec. 26, 1822, Joshua Luce, son of Daniel and Edith (Bakeman) Luce. He was b. in Williamstown, Vt., Dec. 7, 1796; d. in Lower Sandusky (now Fremont), Ohio, Feb. 10, 1842. Farmer. She d. in same place, Oct. 3, 1846. Children:

1. Edith,[8] b. in Williamstown, Vt., Feb. 21, 1824, m. in Fremont, Ohio, May 27, 1843, her cousin, Ephraim Flynt, son of Leonard and Anna (Luce) Flynt. He was b. in Williamstown, Vt., date unknown. She d. in Williamstown, Oct. 2, 1846, without issue.
2. Simon,[8] b. in Williamstown, Vt., July 19, 1825, m. in Mattole Valley, Cal., Feb. 21, 1860, Mary Ann Fleener, parentage and place and date of birth not learned. Res. Petrolia, Cal. Children: 1. William,[9] b. March 4, 1861. 2. Amelia,[9] b. May 13, 1863. 3. Hettie,[9] b. May 6, 1865; d. March 24, 1867. 4. Ida,[9] b. Dec. 18, 1869. 5. Lillie,[9] b. Feb. 21, 1874. 6. Rose,[9] b. Dec. 24, 1877.
3. Daniel,[8] b. in Williamstown, Vt., May 25, 1827, m. in Kentucky, Jan. 15, 1854, Elizabeth Lovina Cull. She was b. in Washington county, Ky., April 26, 1836. Names of her parents not ascertained. Res. Haywood, Cal. Children: 1. Lucinda Frances,[9] b. Dec. 23, 1854. 2. Eliza Lovina,[9] b. Aug. 20, 1856; d. Jan. 15, 1857. 3. George Pierce,[9] b. Jan. 17, 1861. 4. Alice Crowell,[9] b. Dec. 7, 1866. 5. Mary Amelia,[9] b. Sept. 9, 1868.
4. Amelia,[8] b. in Oxford, Erie county, Ohio, March 31, 1829, m. in Tiffin, Seneca county, Ohio, May 2, 1847, Phillip Vroman, son of John and Nancy (Becker) Vroman. He was b. in South Worcester, Otsego county, N. Y., Aug. 20, 1823. Farmer, etc.; res. Put-in Bay, Ohio. Children: 1. Daniel Phillip,[9] b. in Sandusky City, Ohio, April 21, 1848, m. in Cincinnati, Ohio, Nov. 1, 1871, Alice Bertrand, dau. of William and Mary E. (Pettit) Bertrand. She was b. in Ironton, Lawrence county, Ohio, March 6, 1850. Res. Put-in Bay, Ohio. Children: 1. Blanche Amelia,[10] b. Sept. 9, 1872. 2. Mary Elizabeth,[10] b. July 23, 1874. 3. Myrtle,[10] b. Jan. 6, 1878. 2. Frank,[9] b. in Groton Centre, Ohio, July 5, 1854; d. in Put-in Bay, Ohio, June 23, 1866. 3. George Henry,[9] b. in Put-in Bay, Ohio, Feb. 29, 1860. 4. Salmon Weldon,[9] b. in Put-in Bay, Ohio, Dec. 30, 1870.
5. George,[8] b. in Oxford, Erie county, Ohio, Nov. 11, 1830; d. in Fremont, Ohio, May 10, 1850.
6. Joshua,[8] b. in Townsend, Ohio, April 18, 1836, m. in Put-in Bay, Ohio, Nov. 4, 1867, Lucinda Longnecker, dau. of Benjamin and Matilda (Gillett) Longnecker. She was born in ——. Res. Haywood, Cal. Children: 1. Oliver,[9] b. Sept. 18, 1868; d. Dec. 30, 1875. 2. Frank,[9] b. Dec. 12, 1869. 3. Annie Pauline,[9] b. Aug. 12, 1871. 4. Ida May,[9] b. May 27, 1874.

Melissa Sanderson,[7] third daughter and child of James and Rebecca (Hovey) Sanderson, b. in Brookfield, Vt., Feb. 21, 1799; d. in Waterville, Lucas county, Ohio, July 23, 1854, unm., aged 55 years.

Rebecca Sanderson,[7] fourth daughter and child of James and Rebecca (Hovey) Sanderson, b. in Brookfield, Vt., Oct. 11, 1800, m. in Brookfield, Vt., Nov. 1, 1818, Brigham McCrillis, son of Robert and Rachel (Lovell) McCrillis. He was b. in Corinth, Orange county, Vt., April 18, 1796; d. in Sherman, Huron county, Ohio, June 17, 1864. Farmer. His widow is living (1878) in Weaver's Corners, Huron county, Ohio. Children:

1. Son,[s] b. in Corinth, Vt., Dec. 3, 1819; d. Dec. 14, 1819.
2. Harriet,[s] b. in Corinth, Vt., May 7, 1821, m. first, in Norwalk, Ohio, Sept. 25, 1840, John Hinkle, son of David and Eva Hinkle. Date and place of his birth not learned. He d. in New London, Ohio, Jan. 31, 1845. She m. second, in Richland county, Ohio, Aug. —, 1847, David Crowl, of whom nothing is now known except his death, Aug. 18, 1850. She d. in Richland county, Ohio Jan. 12, 1850. Children, by first husband, John Hinkle: 1. James,[9] b. March 2, 1842; d. Sept. 2, 1843. 2. John Calvin,[9] b. Sept. 18, 1843; d May 10, 1844. 3. Harriet Jane.[9] b. May 30, 1845; d. Oct. 17, 1858. By second husband, David Crowl: 4. Anna Rebecca,[9] b. June —, 1848; d. Jan. 30, 1850.
3. Lovell,[s] b. in Williamstown, Vt., Oct. 26, 1823, m. in Norwalk, Ohio, Sept. 25, 1845, Electa Bond, dau. of Thomas and Lydia (Farley) Bond. She was b. in Arcadia, Wayne county, N. Y., July 26, 1827. He is a farmer; res. Weaver's Corners, Ohio. Children: 1. Alice,[9] b. Nov. 13, 1846; d. March 4, 1849. 2. Austin,[9] b. Oct. 29, 1848; d. Feb. 16, 1864. 3. Celia,[9] b. Nov. 13, 1851, m. in Sherman, Ohio, March 31, 1875, Frank Bloomer, son of George and Sally Ann (Johnson) Bloomer. He was b. in Sherman, Ohio, Dec. 9, 1847. Res. Sherman. No children. 4. Frank,[9] b. Nov. 25, 1854; d. March 19, 1860. 5. Willie,[9] b. March 15, 1857; d. March 15, 1860. 6. Allie,[9] b Dec. 11, 1859.
4. Daniel Hovey,[s] b. in Williamstown, Vt., Feb. 9, 1826, m. in Fredonia, Washington county, Wis., Nov. 19, 1847, Laura Jane Bunce, dau. of William and Sarah (Hamilton) Bunce. She was b. in Villanova, Chautauqua county, N. Y., Sept. 2, 1831. Farmer; res. Tryonville, Crawford county, Pa. Children (first three b. in Fredonia, Wis., the others in Steuben, Crawford county, Pa.): 1. Adelia Minerva,[9] b. Feb. 19, 1849; d. July 26, 1849. 2. Emma Jane,[9] b. Oct. 28, 1850. 3. and 4. (twins.) Etta Anna,[9] and Eda Amma,[9] b. Aug. 3, 1852; the latter d. Aug. 5, 1852. 5. William Daniel,[9] b. Nov. 6, 1858. 6. Frank Devillo,[9] b. Sept. 30, 1861. 7. Addie Eliza,[9] b. Jan. 11, 1865. 8. Charles Eugene,[9] b. June 14, 1868. 9. Ralph Edmund,[9] b. July 19, 1874; d. Jan. 31, 1875.
5. Samuel Hovey,[s] b. in Dresden, Yates county, N. Y., Aug. 22, 1827, m. in Steuben, Pa., April 3, 1859, Lovisa Bunce, dau. of Jacob and Mary Ann (Fields) Bunce. She was b. in Broome county, N. Y., Oct. 24, 1840. He is a farmer; res. Monroeville, Ohio. Children: 1. Francis,[9] b. Feb. 23, 1860. 2. Ina Rebecca,[9] b. March 8, 1862; d. March 12, 1865. 3. Selden,[9] b. Nov. 12, 1864. 4. Orvie,[9] b. March 16, 1867. 5. Cora Ann,[9] b. March 14, 1869. 6. Florence,[9] b. Feb. 26, 1871. 7. Burton,[9] b. Aug. 4, 1873. 8. Joel Sanderson,[9] b. March 13, 1876. 9. Myrta May,[9] b. Apr. 3, 1879.
6. Son,[s] b. in Dresden, N. Y., Feb. 22, 1829; d. Feb. 22, 1829.
7. Daughter,[s] b. in Dresden, N. Y., May 10, 1831; d. May 10, 1831.
8. Martin Van Buren,[s] b. in Dresden, N. Y., March 10, 1833, m. in Madison, Ohio, Dec. 7, 1865, Emily Lincoln,[s] his cousin, and dau. of Gurdon and Lola (Sanderson) Lincoln. She was b. in Chelsea, Vt., June 29, 1836. He is a farmer; res. Mountain Lake, Minn. Children: 1. Ida May,[9] b. Sept. 25, 1866. 2. Jessie Myrtle,[9] b. April 11, 1868. 3. and 4. (twins). Lovell Milan,[9] and Milo Lowell,[9] b. Dec. 24, 1870.
9. Joseph Warren,[s] b. in Sherman, Ohio, July 2, 1840, m. in Norwalk, Ohio, Dec. 28, 1869, Catherine Anna Ruth Fairchild, dau. of John and Catherine Jane (McKelney) Fairchild. She was b. in Cedar Village, Mich., June 1, 1851. Res. Occident, Sonoma county, Cal. Children: 1. Clarence Warren,[9] b. Nov. 8, 1871; d. Sept. 4, 1877. 2. Dora Luella,[9] b. March 23, 1873. 3. Lulu Louisa,[9] b. Nov. 20, 1874. 4. Frederic,[9] b. Oct. 10, 1875.

10. Milo,* b. in Sherman, Ohio, Oct. 2, 1842, m. in Clyde, Ohio, Oct. 2, 1867, Frances Lucinda Hollis, dau. of Manly and Lucinda H. (Booth) Hollis. She was b. in Sherman, Ohio, Sept. 2, 1846. He is a Justice of the Peace, and Post Master at Weaver's Corners, Ohio. Children: 1. Bertha,⁹ b. Oct. 2, 1869. 2. Willie Manly,⁹ b. Nov. 15, 1873.

Minerva Sanderson,⁷ fifth daughter and child of James and Rebecca (Hovey) Sanderson, b. in Brookfield, Vt., Aug. 4, 1802, m. in Williamstown, Vt., Aug. 4, 1826, Jeremiah Arling, son of Israel and Hannah (Brown) Arling. He was b. in Portsmouth, N. H., April 15, 1805; d. in Columbia City, Whitley county, Ind., Sept. 1, 1878. She is living (1878) in Columbia City, Ind. Children:

1. Charles Wesley,⁸ b. in Williamstown, Vt., May 24, 1827, m. in Fremont, Ohio, July 19, 1849, Sarah Metz. Parentage and date and place of birth unknown. She d. in Fremont, Ohio, Aug. 17, 1856. He is living (1878) in Fremont, Ohio. Children: 1. William Henry,⁹ b. May 6, 1850, m. ——, and resides in Clyde, Ohio. 2. Charles Franklin,⁹ b. Jan. 5, 1853; d. Feb. 25, 1853.
2. Son,⁸ b. in Williamstown, Vt., July 19, 1831; d. July 19, 1831.
3. Asenath,⁸ b. in Oxford, Seneca county, Ohio, Oct. 17, 1832, m. in Columbia City, Ind., May —, 1848, Lewis D. Miller. Parentage and date and place of birth not learned. Occupation, cooper. He d. July 7, 1856, and she d. April 8, 1864. They had only two children: 1. John Wesley,⁹ b. Feb. 9, 1849. Res. somewhere in the State of Michigan. 2. George Franklin,⁹ b. March 21, 1851. Res. somewhere in the State of New York.
4. Son,⁸ b. in Oxford, Ohio, June 16, 1834; d. July 7, 1834.
5. Minerva,⁸ b. in Oxford, Ohio, July 27, 1835, m. in Columbia City, Ind., March —, 1853, Christopher Columbus Miner, son of Samuel and Betsey (Hamilton) Miner. Date and place of birth not ascertained. Drayman; res. Columbia City, Ind. Children: 1. Minerva Lucetta,⁹ b. Oct. —, 1854; d. Sept. —, 1855. 2. Laura Ann Elizabeth,⁹ b. July 15, 1856. 3. Lillie Lovina,⁹ b. Jan. 24, 1858, m Henry Sylvester Menaugh, and has two children. 4. John Joseph,⁹ b. Dec. 25, 1860. 5. Leander Jeremiah,⁹ b. Nov. 25, 1871; d. Aug. 19, 1872.
6. Hannah,⁸ b. in Oxford, Ohio, March 21, 1838, m. in Columbia City, Ind., Charles Henry Heaton, son of George and Anna (Mosier) Heaton. Date and place of birth not learned. He is a carpenter; res. Columbia City, Ind. Have had five children, four are living. Names and dates of births, etc., not given.
7. Harvey Hollister,⁸) b. in Read, Seneca county, Ohio, March 26, 1840.
8. Hiram Atwood,⁸ ʃ b. in Read, Seneca county, Ohio, March 26, 1840. Harvey Hollister,⁸ m. first, in Sandusky, Ohio, Sept. 3, 1861, Lovisa Lucilla Woodford. Parentage not ascertained. She was b. in Sandusky, Ohio, April 3, 1842, and d. in Sandusky, Ohio, March 6, 1867. He m. second, in Fremont, Ohio, Sept. 6, 1869, Eliza Cornelia Collins, dau. of Jedediah and Barbara Ann (Sterner) Collins. She was b. in Avon, Mich., April 22, 1842. He is a book agent; res. Fremont, Ohio. Children, by wife Lovisa: 1. Alfred Henry,⁹ b. July 27, 1862. 2. Ellen May,⁹ b. Dec. 15, 1865. By wife Eliza: 3. Grace Eliza,⁹ b. Jan. 4, 1871. 4. Minnie Minerva,⁹ b. Oct. 4, 1872. 5. Reginald Collins,⁹ b. Jan. 29, 1875. 6. Harvey Hollister,⁹ b. June 30, 1878.
Hiram Atwood,⁸ m. Maria Foutz, by whom he has had six children, four now living. Her parentage and place and date of birth unknown, also names, dates of births, etc., of the children. Res. in or near Columbia City, Ind.

9. Melissa,[8] b. in Sampson, Ohio, July 5, 1842, m. in Columbia City, Ind., Jan. 29, 1863, Simon Perkins Miner, son of Samuel and Betsey (Hamilton) Miner. He was b. in Akron, Ohio, but date not learned; d. in Columbia City, Ind., Oct. 7, 1875.

10. William Henry,[8] b. in Sampson, Ohio, Dec. 27, 1845, m. in Fremont, Ohio, Castilla Skinner, (parentage and date and place of birth not given), by whom he has four children. Res. Fremont, Ohio.

James Sanderson,[7] eldest son and sixth child of James and Rebecca (Hovey) Sanderson, b. in Morristown, Vt., April 13, 1804, m. first, in Berlin, Huron county, Ohio, Sept. 28, 1830, Sally Ann Miller, dau. of Thomas and Sally (Worthington) Miller. She was b. in Michigan, Oct. 16, 1808; d. in Huron county (Hunt's Corners), Ohio, April 29, 1841. He m. second, in Lyme, Huron county, Ohio, July 4, 1841, Almira Pattee, dau. of Richard and Lucinda (Spaulding) Pattee. She was b. in Derby, Vt., Jan. 21, 1814. He is a farmer; res. Pilot Grove, Newton county, Ind. No children by second wife.

Children, by first wife, Sally Ann, all b. in Huron county, Ohio:

1. Eliza Alvina,[8] b. June 18, 1831; d. in Port Mitchell, Noble county, Ind., Aug. 13, 1845.
2. George Washington,[8] b. Dec. 30, 1832; d. in Norwalk, Ohio, Dec. 20, 1836.
3. Elizabeth Jane,[8] b. Feb. 3, 1834, m. in Morocco, Newton county, Ind., April 15, 1855, Isaac Brock Wiltse, son of Martin and Hester (Coleman) Wiltse. He was b. in Farmersville, Canada, Aug. 30, 1830, where his parents are now living. Res. Belle Park, Ill. Children: 1. Ida,[9] b. in Farmersville, Canada, July 11, 1856. 2. Albert Ernest,[9] b. in Newton county, Ind., May 7, 1858. 3. William Erwin,[9] b. in Kankakee county, Ill., April 19, 1860. 4. Carrie May,[9] b. Sept. 11, 1866. 5. Royal Russell,[9] b. Oct. 18, 1870. 6. Anna Elizabeth,[9] b. Feb. 13, 1879.
4. Andrew Jackson,[8] b. June 19, 1837, m. in Newton county, Ind., April 10, 1860, Mary Catherine Brunton, dau. of Daniel and Margaret Brunton. Date and place of her birth and present place of residence not learned. He d. in the army, Dec. —, 1863, leaving one child: 1. Emma Frances,[9] b. Nov. 24, 1862.
5. Thomas Miller,[8] (Rev.), b. Feb. 12, 1841, m. in Jackson, Ind., Jan. 1, 1860, Mary Jane Carr, dau. of John D. and Mary Carr. She was b. in Kosciusco county, Ind., Oct. 6, 1842. He is a Free Will Baptist minister; res. Pilot Grove, Ind. Children: 1. Alice Elvira,[9] b. June 29, 1861. 2. Algernon Phillip,[9] b. Oct. 25, 1864. 3. Charles William,[9] b. June 11, 1868. 4. Henry Wilbur,[9] b. March 25, 1873; d. Jan. 9, 1874. 5. Arthur Erwin,[9] b. Aug. 1, 1877.

Asenath Sanderson,[7] seventh daughter and eighth child of James and Rebecca (Hovey) Sanderson, b. in Morristown, Orleans (now Lamoille) county, Vt., Aug. 15, 1808, m. first, in Vermillion, Huron county, Ohio, May 24, 1829, Capt. Harvey Horton Hollister, son of Jesse and Annie (Horton) Hollister. He was b. in Vermont, March 17, 1806; a shoemaker by trade, but followed the Lakes during the season of navigation, and at one time commanded the "Louisa Jenkins." His parents came to Ohio in 1815. He d. of cholera at his home in Vermillion, Ohio, Aug. 20, 1834, after an illness of ten hours. She m. second, in Oxford,

Ohio, July 5, 1835, Rev. Oliver Atwood, son of James and Elizabeth (McAllister) Atwood. He was b. in Vermont, ——, 1808; a Methodist minister, whose missionary zeal prompted him to remove, in July, 1837, to the territory of Iowa, to make a home for his family and act as local preacher in that portion of the far West. In the latter part of the month of August, 1838, he left home with the expectation of being absent about four weeks, his objective point being some forty miles distant. Not returning at the expiration of the time specified, his wife and friends became alarmed about him, and, on making inquiries, found that he had been at the Indian village (now Iowa City) some ten days before on his way home, and had purchased at the store there articles for the use of his family. Upon this intelligence, the neighbors turned out *en masse*, to search for him, the place where he was last seen alive being about ten miles only from his residence. His body was discovered, bearing the evident marks of tomahawk and scalping knife, and torn and mangled by beasts of prey. No doubt existed that he had fallen a harmless and unoffending victim to savage barbarity, and it was thought he had been killed to atone for the death of a prominent brave of the tribe, at the hands of a man by the name of Ross, who had been arrested for the deed, broke jail, and escaped out of the country. But Indian vengeance must be satisfied, and one pale face is as good as another to the red man of the forest, to wipe out his real or fancied wrongs. The date of Rev. Oliver Atwood's sad death was Sept. 20, 1838. His widow returned to her friends in Ohio, and m. third, in Sherman, Huron county, Ohio, Aug. 21, 1839, Hiram Atwood, a brother of her late husband, and a tailor by trade. He was b. in New Hampshire, Jan. 30, 1816, and d. of cancer of the stomach, in Bradford, Mass., April 20, 1873. She is living with one of her sons, in Portland, Me.; res. 125 Franklin street.

Children, by first husband, Harvey H. Hollister:

1. Polly,[8] b. in Berlin, Huron county, Ohio, Oct. 10, 1832; d. Oct. 14, 1832.
2. Annie Rebecca,[8] b. in Vermillion, Huron county, Ohio, July 10, 1834, m. first, in East Bethel, Vt., Jan. 7, 1856, Henry Atwood, son of James and Elizabeth (McAllister) Atwood. He was b. in Rochester, Vt., ——, 1818; d. in Lincoln, Vt.,——, 1858. She m. second, in Lincoln, Vt., Jan. 1, 1859, Ira Gove, parentage and date and place of birth not given. Farmer. He enlisted in the beginning of the war of the Rebellion, in the 6th Vt. Regt., and after serving two years re-enlisted as a veteran; was wounded in the left shoulder by a sharp-shooter, and d. June 19, 1863. Children, all b. in Randolph, Vt., by first husband, Henry Atwood: 1. Elroy Adelbert,[9] b. Nov. 5, 1856. 2. Arthur,[9] b. ——, 1858; d. ——, 1863. 3. Eva,[9] b. ——, 1860; d. ——, 1867. By second husband, Ira Gove: 4. Emma Asenath,[9] b. in Lincoln, Vt., Oct. 15, 1859. 5. Mary Louisa,[9] b. June 8, 1861.

by second husband, Rev. Oliver Atwood:

3. Son,[8] b. in Muscash, Ohio, May 27, 1836; d. May 27, 1836.
4. Oliver Harvey,[8] b. in Iowa, July 27, 1838; d. in Sherman, Ohio, Nov. 16, 1838.

by third husband, Hiram Atwood:

5. Washington Irving,[9] b. in Lodi, Seneca county, Ohio, Feb. 9, 1841, m. in Auburn, Androscoggin county, Me., Oct. 2, 1862, Abbie Frances Hartwell, dau. of Alexander and Emily Hartwell. She was b. in Auburn, Me., date unknown. He is a hardware merchant and silver plater; res. Merrimac, Mass. Children: 1. Inez Blanche,[9] b. in Lyndon, Vt., March 2, 1864. 2. Irving Henry,[9] b. in Merrimac, Mass., Sept. 28, 1874.
6. Arthur Hiram,[8] b in Lewisville, Huron county, Ohio, June 23, 1843, m. in Auburn, Me., May 2, 1863, Elizabeth Hartwell, dau. of Alexander and Emily Hartwell. She was b. in Auburn, Me., date not given. His occupation, silver plater; res. Portland, Me., at 125 Franklin street.
7. Alfred Eugene,[8] b. in Ballville, Sandusky county, Ohio, Sept. 6, 1845, enlisted in the Union Army, Aug. 28, 1862, with his father, in the 17th Maine Regt.; d. in camp on the Rappahannock, of typhoid pneumonia, Jan. 11, 1863.
8. Emma Isabel,[8] b. in Fremont, Ohio, July 12, 1848; d. in Lincoln, Vt., Sept. 28, 1850.

Benjamin Sanderson,[7] second son and ninth child of James and Rebecca (Hovey) Sanderson, b. in Morristown, Vt., July 30, 1810, m. in Vermillion, Erie county, Ohio, Aug. 30, 1835, Mary Rose Clay, dau. of Thomas and Rebecca (Rose) Clay. She was b. in Sparta, Sussex county, N. J., Dec. 19, 1816, removed with her parents to Ohio in 1834, and is living (1878) in Vermillion, Ohio, with her second husband, John Bassett. He (Benjamin Sanderson[7]) d. in Camden, Lorain county, Ohio, of typhoid fever, June 8, 1851.
Children:

1. Rebecca Rose,[8] b. in Oxford, Seneca county, Ohio, June 11, 1836; d. Sept. 27, 1840.
2. Harvey Hollister,[8] b. in Oxford, Ohio, Aug. 9, 1837, was a soldier in Company II, 41st O. V. M., and d. in Corinth, Miss., June 20, 1862. He m. Nov. 1, 1858, Mary Bradley (parentage and place and date of birth not given), by whom he had: 1. Sheldon,[9] b. Sept. 25, 1859. 2. Harvey,[9] b. April 15, 1861. His widow m. again to Mr. John Cross, and removed to the West.
3. Sarah,[8] b. in Camden, Lorain county, Ohio, Dec. 22, 1840, m. in Camden, Ohio, Jan. 7, 1863, John Leake, and has six children: 1. Herbert,[9] b. Feb. 5, 1864. 2. Irving,[9] b. March 13, 1866. 3. Fannie,[9] b. Sept. 24, 1868. 4. Ella,[9] b. Dec. 7, 1870. 5. Lewis,[9] b. March 24, 1876. 6. Hattie,[9] b. Feb. 3, 1878. He is a plow manufacturer; res. North Amherst, Ohio.
4. Henry Clay,[8] b. in Thompson, Seneca county, Ohio, May 5, 1844, was a soldier in the same regiment with his brother, and d. in Camden, Lorain county, Ohio, Feb. 21, 1863, unm.
5. Martha D.,[8] b. in Camden, Ohio, March 9, 1847, m. Dec. 25, 1866, Theodore Hulbert, of Elyria, Ohio, where they reside. He is a machinist. Children: 1. Albert,[9] b. in Elyria, Ohio, Oct. 29, 1868. 2. Arthur,[9] b. in Elyria, Ohio, May 8, 1870. 3. Mary,[9] b. in North Amherst, Ohio, Jan 11, 1872. 4. Frances,[9] b. in North Amherst, Ohio, Jan. 26, 1874. 5. Grace,[9] b. in North Amherst, Ohio, Aug. 16, 1876. 6. Julia,[9] b. in North Amherst, Ohio, Aug. 11, 1878.
6. Elizabeth,[8] b. in Camden, Lorain county, Ohio, May 19, 1849, m. in Vermillion, Ohio, March 9, 1874, John Miller, a farmer; res. Vermillion, Ohio. Children: 1. Julia,[9] b. in Vermillion, Ohio, Sept. 16, 1875. 2. Viola,[9] b. in Vermillion, Ohio, May 11, 1877; d. May 29, 1877.

7. Benjamina,* b. in Camden, Lorain county, Ohio, June 30, 1851, m. Dec. 24, 1870, William E. Bassett, and reside in North Amherst, Ohio. He is an engineer. Children: 1. Mary,⁹ b. in Vermillion, Ohio, June 10, 1871. 2. Julia,⁹ b. in Brownhelm, Ohio, Oct. 30, 1872; d. March 30, 1873. 3. John,⁹ b. in Berlin, Ohio, July 12, 1874. 4. Charles,⁹ b. in Berlin, Ohio, Jan. 20, 1877.

Joel Sanderson,⁷ youngest son and child of James and Rebecca (Hovey) Sanderson, b. in Brookfield, Vt., Dec. 26, 1816, m. in Sherman, Huron county, Ohio, Aug. 7, 1842, Mary Ann Legg, dau. of Thomas and Ann (Purchas) Legg. She was b. in Somersetshire, Eng., Aug. 11, 1816. He is a farmer; res. Lima, LaGrange county, Ind.
Children:
1. George Washington,⁸ b. in Sherman, Ohio, April 28, 1843, m. in Van Buren, Ind., Dec. 25, 1866, Calista Maria Rice, dau. of Erastus and Frances Maria (Bean) Rice. She was b. in Bristol, Ohio, Dec. 25, 1839. He is a farmer; res. Quincy, Branch county, Mich. Children, all b. in Quincy: 1. Estella Calista,⁹ b. Nov. 30, 1868. 2. Joel Erastus,⁹ b. July 6, 1870. 3. and 4. (twins). Marion Washington,⁹ and May Maria,⁹ b. Feb. 22, 1873. 5. Myrta Eliza,⁹ b. Sept. 1, 1877.
2. James,⁸ b. in Fawn River, Mich., Oct. 30, 1845, m. in Lima, Ind., March 6, 1879, Mary Elizabeth Keplinger, dau. of Elias and Emily Ann (Haverstock) Keplinger. She was b. in Dover, Tuscarawas county, Ohio, Jan. 1, 1854. He is a farmer; res. Lima, Ind.
3. Wilbur Fisk,⁸ b. in Fawn River, Mich., Feb. 3, 1847, m. in Sturgis, Mich., April 13, 1873, Harriet Rudesil, dau. of Jacob and Margaret (Tennant) Rudesil. She was b. in Fort Wayne, Ind., Aug. 14, 1847. He is a farmer; res. Lima, Ind. Children: 1. Clara May,⁹ b. March 8, 1874. 2. Gracie,⁹ b. April 3, 1876.
4. Sarah Ann,⁸ b. in Greenfield, Hancock county, Ind., Oct. 9, 1848, m. in Lima, Ind., June 7, 1877, Wm. John F. Mott, son of Wm. B. and Annie M. (Shaffer) Mott. He was b. in Philadelphia, Pa., Oct. 31, 1847. Cigar maker; res. Kalamazoo, Mich.
5. Rebecca,⁸ b. in Greenfield, Ind., March 23, 1850, m. in Lima, Ind., Feb. 3, 1870, Ammi Kalahan Parham, son of Richard and Mary Ann (Walker) Parham. He was b. in Greenfield, Ind., May 24, 1844. Farmer; res. Bronson, Branch county, Mich. Children: 1. Frank Elliott,⁹ b. Jan. 30, 1871. 2. Wilbur Wood,⁹ b. Dec. 11, 1872; d. June 1, 1873. 3. Mary Rosetta,⁹ b. Feb. 9, 1875. 4. Effie Maud,⁹ b. Aug. 30, 1878.
6. Eva,⁸ b. in Greenfield, Ind., Sept. 14, 1853, m. in Sturgis, Mich., April 8, 1873, Aaron Wood Parham, son of Richard and Mary Ann (Walker) Parham. He was b. in Greenfield, Ind., May 8, 1842. Farmer; res. Fawn River, Mich. Children: 1. Marshall Elburtus,⁹ b. March 8, 1874. 2. Lillian Irene,⁹ b. Oct. 24, 1876.
7. Asenath,⁸ b. in Greenfield, Ind., Aug. 22, 1855, m. in Coldwater, Mich., April 3, 1873, Loren Elliott Parham, son of Richard and Mary Ann (Walker) Parham. He was b. in Fawn River, Mich., Dec. 10, 1848. Farmer; res. Fawn River, Mich. Children: 1. Frederic Newton,⁹ b. July 4, 1874. 2. Allen Eugene,⁹ b. July 23, 1876. 3. Gertrude,⁹ b. Jan. 6, 1879.
8. Charlotte Estella,⁸ b. in Greenfield, Ind., Nov. 15, 1857, m. in Lima, Ind., Dec. 25, 1877, George Washington Monroe, son of Jesse and Hannah (Merritt) Monroe. He was b. in Mattison, Branch county, Mich., July 19, 1855. Farmer; res. Mattison, Mich. Child: 1. Clarence Elroy,⁹ b. Feb. 7, 1879.

Appendix.

Samuel W. Hovey,[1] eldest son and second child of Samuel and Amy (Billings) Hovey, b. in Brookfield, Vt., Sept. 25, 1801, m. in Williamstown, Vt., Dec. 5, 1822, Betsey Kendall, dau. of Timothy and Eunice (Houghton) Kendall. She was b. in Alstead, N. H., July 2, 1795; d. in Merrimack, Sauk county, Wis., April 24, 1865. He d. in same place, March 17, 1866. Farmer.
Children:

1. Samuel Kendall,[8] b. in Brookfield, Vt., Nov. 30, 1823, m. first, in Merrimack, Wis., Jan. 28, 1851, Melvina Sutton, dau. of David and Maria (Hunt) Sutton. She was b. in Sparta, Livingston county, N. Y., Aug. 1, 1831; d. in Merrimack, Wis., March 31, 1855. He m. second, in Merrimack, Wis., Nov. 25, 1855, Rebecca Ann Bostwick, dau. of Charles and Mary (Delargee) Bostwick. She was b. in Norfolk, St. Lawrence county, N. Y., May 11, 1834. He is a farmer; res. Westside, Noble county, Minn. Children, by wife Melvina: 1. David Willis,[9] b. Jan. 21, 1852. 2. Melvaine,[9] b. March 3, 1855, m. in Austin, Mower county, Minn., April 11, 1877, Emma Ralph. By wife Rebecca: 3. Mary Melvina,[9] b. July 24, 1859. 4. Amy Jane,[9] b. Sept. 30, 1861. 5. Caroline Ella,[9] b. April 26, 1865. 6. Betsey Ann,[9] b. April 2, 1868.
2. Eunice Permelia,[8] b. in Albany, Orleans county, Vt., April 20, 1832, m. in Merrimack, Wis., Feb. 5, 1854, Isaac Emerson, son of Matthew and Sarah (Willis) Emerson. He was b. in Lincolnshire, Eng., Dec. 7, 1827. Farmer; res. Westside, Noble county, Minn. Children, all b. in Merrimack, Wis.: 1. Matthew James,[9] b. May 25, 1854. 2. Betsey Lovina,[9] b. Nov. 26, 1860, m. in Westside, Minn., April 5, 1877, Dr. Henry Paine Bunce, son of Dr. John Bunce. He was b. in Janesville, Wis., May 22, 1847. Res. Luverne, Rock county, Minn. 3. Sarah Amelia,[9] b. Sept. 10, 1864.

Alvan Hovey,[7] third son and fourth child of Samuel and Amy (Billings) Hovey, b. in Brookfield, Vt., Dec. 4, 1804, m. in Hartland, Vt., Feb. 26, 1827, Mary Dodge Trask, dau. of Ebenezer and Abigail (Dodge) Trask. She was b. in Beverly, Mass., June 10, 1805. He is a farmer; res. East Brookfield, Vt.
Children, all b. in Brookfield:

1. Abigail Libby,[8] b. May 18, 1828; d. May 29, 1828.
2. Mary Ann Nancy,[8] b. June 15, 1829, m. in East Brookfield, Vt., April 22, 1849, Urban Lathrop Bixby, son of Nathan and Lydia (Lathrop) Bixby. He was b. in Chelsea, Vt., Dec. 18, 1824. Farmer; res. East Brookfield, Vt. Children, all born in East Brookfield: 1. Ida Alelia,[9] b. June 23, 1851, m. in Randolph, Vt., March 14, 1869, Everett Clifton Newell, son of Joseph and Sarah Davison (Hibbard) Newell. He was b. in Oxford, Vt., May 13, 1847. Farmer; res. Chelsea, Vt. Children: 1. Daughter,[10] b. Dec. 13, 1872; d. Dec. 13, 1872. 2. Florence Emeline,[10] b. Jan. 8, 1874; d. March 28, 1875. 3. Bertha Eudora,[10] b. Dec. 14, 1877; d. March 21, 1878. 4. Eulela May,[10] b. March 3, 1879. 2. Mary Eva,[9] b. June 20, 1853. 3. Alvan Hovey,[9] b. Jan. 28, 1859. 4. Charles Hunter,[9] b. Aug. 4, 1862. 5. Urban Willis,[9] b. Dec. 26, 1865.
3. Ebenezer Trask,[8] b. May 24, 1832, m. in Williamstown, Vt., Dec. 6, 1855, Emily Downing, dau. of Jessie W. and Julia (Libby) Downing. She was b. in Chelsea, Vt., Jan. 30, 1839. He d. in East Brookfield, Vt., Sept. 23, 1862. No children.

4. Emeline,[8] b. Aug. 27, 1834, m. in East Brookfield, Vt., Jan. 1, 1855, Hiram Wells Chafey, son of Hiram and Asenath (Kendall) Chafey. He was b. in Brookfield, Vt., Oct. 22, 1830. She d. in Brookfield, Aug. 13, 1856. Child: 1. Flora Emeline,[9] b. Dec. 5, 1855; d. Aug. 20, 1856.

Permelia Hovey,[7] third daughter and sixth child of Samuel and Amy (Billings) Hovey, b. in Brookfield, Vt., Oct. 4, 1809, m. in Brookfield, Vt., March 17, 1833, Bela Downing, son of Rufus and Mary (Wells) Downing. He was b. in Chelsea, Vt., Dec. 12, 1804. Mechanic; res. Hartford, Windsor county, Vt.
Children, all b. in Brookfield, Vt.:

1. Mary Hovey,[8] b. Nov. 20, 1833, m. in Chelsea, Vt., March 5, 1857, Dennison Goodrich Crain, son of Elijah and Nancy (Clifford) Crain. He was b. in Brookfield, Vt., March 27, 1827. Trader; res. Fort Atkinson, Wis. Child: 1. Charles Chester,[9] b. April 28, 1861.
2. Samuel Hovey,[8] b. Oct. 27, 1835; d. March 17, 1836.
3. Alvan Hovey,[8] b. June 27, 1837, m. in Vermont, March 4, 1861, Lizzie Phyletta Case, dau. of Hubbard and Phyletta (Page) Case. She was b. in Barnard, Vt., July 13, 1839. He is a mechanic; res. Fort Atkinson, Wis. Children: 1. Daughter,[9] b. ——, 1862; d. ——, 1862. 2. Eddie Ernest,[9] b. Nov. 23, 1863. 3. Alice May,[9] b. May 9, 1866. 4. Georgie Glenn,[9] b. Aug. 9, 1875.
4. Martha Minerva,[8] b. Feb. 16, 1840; d. April 16, 1856.
5. Luna Estella,[8] b. Sept. 7, 1842, m. in Sharon, Vt., March 22, 1865, Hazen Moses West, son of Hazen Moses and Mary Ann (Cloud) West. He was b. in Norwich, Vt., April 13, 1842. Farmer; res. Hartford, Vt. Child: 1. Jossie Dean,[9] b. July 19, 1867; d. July 30, 1868.
6. Lydia Permelia,[8] b. Feb. 12, 1844, m. in Hartford, Vt., Jan. 15, 1870, Nelson Walter White, son of Ethan and Rosetta (Cummings) White. He was b. in Dorchester, N. H., Feb. 21, 1838. Mechanic; res. Hartford, Vt. No children.
7. Edward Blake,[8] b. Feb. 9, 1846, m. in Hillsdale, Mich., Oct. 29, 1875, Hortense Olney, dau. of Leonard and Matilda Olney. She was b. in Hillsdale, Mich., April ——, 1848. He is a merchant; res. Grand Rapids, Mich. Child: 1. Leonard Bela,[9] b. in Grand Rapids, Mich., March 2, 1877.
8. Eliza Maria,[8] b. July 1, 1848, m. in Norwich, Vt., Sept. 2, 1873, Alonzo Chapin Martin, son of Allan and Hannah (May) Martin. He was b. in Barnston, P. Q., (Canada), March 23, 1843. Merchant; res. Hartford, Vt. Child: 1. Millie May,[9] b. June 23, 1875.

James H. Hovey,[7] fourth son and seventh child of Samuel and Amy (Billings) Hovey, b. in Brookfield, Vt., July 28, 1811, m. in Brookfield, Dec. 5, 1832, Rachel Downing, dau. of Rufus and Polly (Wills) Downing. She was b. in Chelsea, Vt., May 2, 1811, and is living (1878) in Hartford, Vt. He d. in Brookfield, Jan. 3, 1857.
Children :

1. Lewis William,[8] b. June 6, 1835, m. in Williamstown, Vt., Feb. 2, 1864, Matilda Frances Hixon, dau. of Albert and Rachel (Goodrich) Hixon. She was b. in Brookfield, Vt., June 30, 1844. Res. Boston, Mass. Child: 1. Albert Harvey,[9] b. May 14, 1867.
2. Cordelia,[8] b. Oct. 10, 1840; d. April 20, 1842.
3. Charles Wilber,[8] b. May 7, 1843; d. while a soldier in the army, in winter of 1863, unm.

Rufus C. Hovey,[1] fifth son and eighth child of Samuel and Amy (Billings) Hovey, b. in Brookfield, Vt., Oct. 15, 1816, m. in Hartford, Vt., March 6, 1844, Caroline Mary Clark, dau. of Hyde and Caroline (Brooks) Clark. She was b. in Hartford, Vt., May 24, 1810, and is living (1878) in East Brookfield, Vt. He d. in East Brookfield, Vt., July 12, 1872. Farmer.

Children :
1. Sarah Emily,[8] b. in Brookfield, Vt., Aug. 6, 1845; d. March 11, 1863.
2. Caroline Ella,[8] b. in Chelsea, Vt., Sept. 7, 1849; d. March 19, 1863.

Amy P. Hovey,[7] eldest daughter and child of Samuel and Phyletta (Kendall) Hovey, b. in Brookfield, Vt., July 7, 1838, m. in same place, Aug. 4, 1864, Edwin Smiley Hibbard, son of Gordon P. and Isabella (Hemenway) Hibbard. He was b. in East Brookfield, Vt., Oct. 13, 1839; d. in Montpelier, Vt., Nov. 22, 1876. Builder. A man of earnest and active Christian character, and a deacon in the Baptist Church. They had no children.

Althea L. Hovey,[7] youngest daughter and child of Samuel and Phyletta (Kendall) Hovey, b. in Brookfield, Vt., Feb. 17, 1840, m. in same place, March 27, 1861, James Alexander Trask, son of James Gray and Eliza Melvina (Alexander) Trask. He was b. in Brookfield, Vt., March 1, 1836. Farmer; res. East Brookfield, Vt.

Child :
1. James Edgar,[8] b. in East Brookfield, Vt., March 9, 1865.

Mrs. Ruth Hovey Sprague sends, by request, the following sketch of her Uncle Samuel :

"Samuel Hovey, the sixth child of Elder Samuel and Abigail C. Hovey, was born Oct. 20, 1774, and married Amy Billings, a sister of Grace, who was wife to his brother Rufus. He was a man of middling stature, had, like the other members of the family, blue eyes and brown hair, was of a social, friendly nature, and was very much respected by the community and beloved by his family. He was honored by the Legislature of the State with the appointment to the office of Justice of the Peace. It fell to his lot to care for his aged parents during many years of their age and infirmities, which duty he fulfilled to the entire satisfaction of the family. He was a kind husband, a tender parent, and a dutiful son.

"He was for many years a prominent member of the Baptist Church, which his influence and example helped to sustain.

"He was twice married, his second choice being a maiden lady, Phyletta Kendall, a sister of that Polly who was wife of his nephew, Billings. At his death he left two sons and a daughter by his first wife, and two daughters, the children of his widow.

R. H. SPRAGUE."

Frances Hovey,[7] the eldest daughter and second child of Abiel and Frances (Peterson) Hovey, b. in Rutland, Vt., Aug. —, 1806, m. in Mount Vernon, Posey county, Ind., May 17, 1831, John Mitinger, parentage and place and date of birth not ascertained, and who died, as also his wife, in Sept. —, 1836. No children.

Eliza Hovey,[7] second daughter and third child of Abiel and Frances (Peterson) Hovey, b. in Rutland, Vt., Aug. —, 1809, m. in Mount Vernon, Ind., June 17, 1829, Andrew Suter Gamble, son of Joseph and Martha (Crabtree) Gamble. He was b. in Christian county, Ky., March 10, 1808, and d. in Mount Vernon, Ind., June 20, 1838. She d. in same place, Nov. —, 1834.

Children:
1. Daughter,[8] b. April 16, 1830; d. April 16, 1830.
2. Joseph Hovey,[8] b. April 16, 1832, and was killed in a political quarrel, Aug. 8, 1864; unm.

Amanda Hovey,[7] third daughter and fourth child of Abiel and Frances (Peterson) Hovey, b. in Rutland, Vt., June 11, 1811; d. in Mount Vernon, Ind., Sept. —, 1839. She never married. Gen. Alvin P. Hovey,[7] her brother, puts the date of her death as occurring in 1837.

Charlotte Hovey,[7] fourth daughter and fifth child of Abiel and Frances (Peterson) Hovey, b. in Montpelier, Vt., Oct. 15, 1813, m. first, in Mount Vernon, Ind., July 13, 1829, George La Farry, who d. the year following, leaving no children. Nothing known of his parentage or place and date of birth. She m. second, in Mount Vernon, Ind., Aug. 18, 1831, Thomas Stone Veatch, parentage not learned. He was b. in Hagerstown, Md., Jan. 5, 1810. She obtained a divorce from her second husband (who went to California about 1842), and m. third, in Mount Vernon, Ind., Oct. 12, 1837, Aaron Culbertson Moore. His parentage, birth, etc., not communicated. She m. fourth, in Mount Vernon, Ind., Feb. 24, 1851, Jacob Fisher, son of Jacob and —— (Haines) Fisher. He was b. in Philadelphia, Pa., Jan. 5, 1806; d. in Mount Vernon, Ind., Aug. 16, 1877. He was a farmer. She d. in Mount Vernon, Ind., Jan. —, 1858.

Children, by second husband, Thomas S. Veatch:
1. Virgil Stone,[8] b. in Mount Vernon, July 23, 1832, m. in ——, June 23, 1858, Margaret Abigail Oatman, dau. of Jesse and Abigail Oatman. She was b. in Floyd county, Ind., June 28, 1840. Res. Evansville, Ind. Children: 1. Henry Abbott,[9] b. July 4, 1861. 2. Jessie,[9] b. Feb. 28, 1865. 3. and 4. (twins.) John Oatman,[9] and Joseph Ross,[9] b. June 16, 1867. 5. Phillip Claudius,[9] b. July 1, 1874.
2. Charles,[8] b. about 1834.

by third husband, Albert C. Moore:
3. Mary,[8] b. about 1839, m. in ——, about 1860, Seth Spanton, parentage and place and date of birth not learned. She d. in Paterson, N. J., ——, 1876. No answers vouchsafed to repeated letters for the family records.
4. Alvin,[8] b. about 1843, m. in ——, a widow Bradley, of whose birth and parentage nothing is learned; and said to reside in Terre Haute, Ind. No attention paid to the letters sent him by the compiler; so the record remains thus meagre and imperfect.
5. Lucy,[8] b. about 1845; unm.; she is said to reside in Paterson, N. J.

by fourth husband, Jacob Fisher:
6. Esther,[8] b. Oct. 7, 1856, m. Dec. 13, 1877, Charles H. Barter, son of John H. and Mary (Ashworth) Barter. He was b. in Mount Vernon, Ind., June 28, 1854. She d. in Mount Vernon, Nov. 8, 1878. Child: 1. Clarence,[9] b. Nov. 7, 1878.

Charles Hovey,[7] second son and fifth child of Abiel and Frances (Peterson) Hovey, b. in Middlebury, Vt., April 19, 1815, m. in Mount Vernon, Ind., Oct. 9, 1836, Lucinda Nesler, dau. of Christopher and Sarah (Dunn) Nesler. She was b. in Mount Vernon, Ind., July 25, 1822. He d. in Mount Vernon, Jan. 9, 1862. She is living (1878) in Mount Vernon, Ind.

Children, all b. in Mount Vernon:

1. Alvina,[8] b. Sept. 26, 1837; d. April 5, 1838.
2. Lizzie,[8] b. May 28, 1839, m. in Black township, Ind., ——, 1859, Isaac Baker, son of John and America (Montgomery) Baker. He was b. in Mount Vernon, Ind., Jan. 8, 1838. Children: 1. Charles,[9] b. June 10, 1860; d. July 5, 1860. 2. Edward,[9] b. Dec. 21, 1861; d. Oct. 9, 1862. 3. Frank,[9] b. March 28, 1863. 4. Nellie,[9] b. April 18, 1865. 5. Jesse,[9] b. June 17, 1867. 6. Isa,[9] b. Feb. 8, 1869; d. Oct. 19, 1869.
3. Henry,[8] b. April 20, 1841; d. June 4, 1841.
4. Jerome,[8] b. June 1, 1842; d. June 19, 1858.
5. Fannie,[8] b. Aug. 1, 1845, m. in Mount Vernon, Ind., March 27, 1865, Robert Fulton Dunn, son of James and Mary (Hintchell) Dunn. She d. in Mount Vernon, Ind., July 9, 1872. He is a pilot. Date and place of his birth not learned. Children: 1. Lulie,[9] b. Jan. 1, 1866; d. Sept. 18, 1869. 2. Mary,[9] b. Nov. 28, 1868. 3. Robert,[9] b. April 4, 1869; d. April 20, 1870.
6. Charles,[8] b. Dec. 29, 1847, m. in New Haven, Ill., Sept. 5, 1870, Louisa Bailey, dau. of Wyndar and Amanda (McKenzie) Bailey. She was b. in Shawneetown, Ill., March 11, 1850. He is a blacksmith. Child: 1. Lillie,[9] b. Oct. 7, 1872.
7. Helen,[8] b. March 4, 1850, m. in Mount Vernon, Ind., Oct. 29, 1868, Thomas Jefferson Gardom, son of Samuel and Lucilla (Herald) Gardom. He was b. in Illinois, April 27, 1847. Blacksmith by occupation. She d. in Mount Vernon, July 12, 1873. Children: 1. Samuel,[9] b. March 4, 1869; d. Aug. 1, 1873. 2. Eva,[9] b. April 7, 1871. 3. Helen,[9] b. Dec. 21, 1872; d. Jan. —, 1874.
8. Alvin,[8] b. Sept. 5, 1852; d. July 11, 1873.
9. Grace,[8] b. July 4, 1854, m. in Mount Vernon, Ind., Nov. 19, 1870, William Craw, parentage and place and date of birth not learned; d. in Morley, Scott county, Mo., March 7, 1871. She d. in Mount Vernon, Ind., July 22, 1873.
10. Eva,[8] b. June 15, 1856; d. July 22, 1873.
11. Mary,[8] b. March 26, 1858; d. Jan. 5, 1866.
12. Josephine,[8] b. Aug. 26, 1859.
13. Lucy,[8] b. July 2, 1862; d. Sept. 23, 1863.

Minerva Hovey,[7] fifth daughter and seventh child of Abiel and Frances (Peterson) Hovey, b. in Mount Vernon, Ind., Oct. 18, 1819, m. first, in same place, March 10, 1836, Andrew Suter Gamble, son of Joseph and Martha (Crabtree) Gamble. He was b. in Christian county, Ky., March 10, 1808; d. in Mount Vernon, Ind., June 20, 1838. She m. second, in Mount Vernon, Ind., ——, 1842, Edmund Bacon, son of Charles Bacon, who was b. Feb. 25, 1812. She d. near Mount Vernon, Ind., Aug. 16, 1846. The date of his death not learned.

Children, by first husband, A. S. Gamble:

1. Martha,[8] b. Jan. 19, 1837; d. Oct. 20, 1838.

2. Andrew Suter,⁵ b. Feb. 10, 1839, m. in Mount Vernon, Ind., Oct. 25, 1866, Celia Lichtenberger, dau. of Aaron and Elizabeth (Noel) Lichtenberger. She was b. in New Harmony, Ind., Nov. 6, 1845. He is a commission merchant; res. Evansville, Ind. Children: 1. Belle,⁹ b. in Mount Vernon, Ind., Aug. 16, 1867; d. in Evansville, Ind., Nov. 31, 1869. 2. Andrew Suter,⁹ b. in Evansville, Jan. 5, 1870. 3. Aaron Lichtenberger,⁹ b. in Evansville, Oct. 21, 1871.

by second husband, Edmund Bacon:

3. Charles,⁸ b. Nov. 2, 1844; d. in Hindman, Ky., Nov. 10, 1862.
4. Daughter,⁸ b. Aug. 16, 1846; d. Aug. 30, 1846.

Gen. Alvin Peterson Hovey,⁷ the youngest son and child of Abiel and Frances (Peterson) Hovey, b. in Mount Vernon, Ind., Sept. 6, 1821, m. first, in Mount Vernon, Nov. 24, 1844, Mary Ann James, dau. of Hon. Enoch Randolph and Esther (Lowry) James. She was b. in Baton Rouge, La., Feb. 22, 1825; d. in Mount Vernon, Ind., Nov. 16, 1863. He m. second, in Grace Church, New York City (?) (date unknown), Mrs. Rosa Alice (Smith) Carey, dau. of Hon. Caleb Blood Smith, of Indiana, and widow of Maj. Wm. F. Carey, of Cleveland, Ohio. She was b. in Indiana. Date not given. A short sketch of Gen. Hovey's life and public services will be found on page 17. His res. is Mount Vernon, Ind.

Children, all b. in Mount Vernon:

1. Esther,⁸ b. Jan. 8, 1846, m. in New York City, Nov. 11, 1869, Maj. Gustavus Varsa Menzies, son of Samuel Garber and Sally Ann (Winston) Menzies. He was b. in Boone county, Ky., Dec. 25, 1844, and at the time of his marriage was Lieut. Commander in the U. S. Navy. Now practicing law in partnership with his father-in-law, under the style of Hovey & Menzies. Children: 1. Daughter,⁹ b. Aug. 26, 1870; d. Aug. 26, 1870. 2. Mary,⁹ b. Oct. 5, 1872. 3. Juliette,⁹ b. April 22, 1874. 4. Winston,⁹ b. Nov. 22, 1875.
2. Enoch James,⁸ b. Feb. 7, 1848; d. Aug. 4, 1852.
3. Charles James,⁸ b. Jan. 8, 1850, m. in Evansville, Ind., March 16, 1871, Lillie Jaquess, dau. of Jonathan and Parna (Whittlesey) Jaquess, Esq. She was b. in Poseyville, Ind., May 6, 1850. He is a merchant; res. Mt. Vernon, Ind. Children: 1. Alvin Jaquess,⁹ b. Dec. 27, 1871. 2. Mabel,⁹ b. Sept. 1, 1873. 3. Mary,⁹ b. Aug. 17, 1875. 4. Randolph Jaquess,⁹ b. March 26, 1879.
4. Mary,⁸ b. Jan. 13, 1854; d. March 30, 1855.
5. Mary Ann,⁸ b. April 1, 1857; d. April 7, 1858.

The following letter, written by Gen. Hovey to a cousin in Chelsea, Vt., during the late war, is here given:

"HEADQUARTERS, GEN. HOVEY'S DIVISION,
CHARLESTOWN, TENN., May 2, 1864.

"DEAR COUSIN:

"I have just received your letter dated March 27th. I am the son and only surviving child of your uncle Abiel Hovey, who left Vermont in 1818 or 1819, and settled in Indiana. One letter written to me by my uncle Alvin is all that I have ever received from the family until the arrival of yours.

"My father died in 1823, leaving my mother with seven children—Fanny, Eliza, Amanda, Charlotte, Charles, Minerva and myself, then less than three years of age. My mother died in 1836, and my sisters are all dead; and all but Fanny and Amanda leaving families. My only brother Charles was killed last January, a year ago, by a cannon. He also leaves a family. Our residences are at Mount Vernon, Indiana.

"My wife died last October, leaving me two children—a daughter Essie, now finishing her education at Madam Hoffman's School in the city of New York, and my son Charlie who is at school in Evansville, Indiana.

"I am now at Charlestown, Tenn., in command of the 1st Division of the 23rd Army Corps, which will move in the morning in the direction of Dalton, where we soon expect to have a severe battle. My history is known in the West, and if you should have any curiosity in regard to it, I trust you will find that our common name has never suffered by any conduct of mine.

"I truly thank you for the information that you have so kindly furnished me in regard to our family. I trust that I shall some day be able to visit my father's family and see my relatives. I have never yet met even a cousin of my father's family. My regards to all my kindred who may feel an interest in my welfare.
Yours truly,
ALVIN P. HOVEY."

Nancy S. Hovey,[7] second daughter and fourth child of Alvan and Nancy (Seabury) Hovey, b. Dec. 6, 1807, m. in Brookfield, Vt., April 3, 1827, Andrew Burnham, son of Enoch and Eunice (Martin) Burnham. He was b. in Williamstown. Vt., Jan, 10, 1799. Farmer; res. Washington, Vt.

Children:

1. Nancy,[8] b. Nov. 28, 1827; d. Nov. 29, 1827.
2. Nancy Luthera,[8] b. March 29, 1829; d. April 23, 1829.
3. James,[8] b. June 23, 1831, m. in Barre, Vt., Nov. 5, 1854, Abbie Thompson, dau. of John and Abigail (Abbott) Thompson. She was b. in Barre, Vt., May 1, 1837. He is a farmer; res. Washington, Vt. Children: 1. Fred. Leslie,[9] b. Dec. 14, 1855; d. Dec. 30, 1859. 2. Hattie May,[9] b. Dec. 19, 1859. 3. Elton Hovey,[9] b. May 30, 1864.
4. Alvin Hovey,[8] b. Dec. 15, 1833; d. March 17, 1841.
5. Harriet Hovey,[8] b. June 29, 1835, m. in Williamsburgh, Vt., Sept. 8, 1861, Asa Herbert Pepper, son of Willard and Rachel (Taylor) Pepper. He was b. in Washington, Vt., Dec. 28, 1835. Farmer; res. Washington, Vt. Children: 1. Willard Andrew,[9] b. June 29, 1863. 2. Carrol Leslie,[9] b. Jan. 20, 1869; d. April 18, 1869. 3. Lillian May,[9] b. May 6, 1873.
6. Fanny Flavilla,[8] b. May 8, 1837, m. in Barre, Vt., Feb. 17, 1856, John Ryland Seaver, son of Alvan and Amanda (Farnham) Seaver. He was b. in Williamstown, Vt., Feb. 17, 1831. She d. Feb. 27, 1862. He is a farmer; res. Montpelier, Vt. Child: 1. Harry Wendell," b. May 24, 1859.
7. Andrew,[8] b. Oct. 19, 1838, m. in Chelsea, Vt., June 14, 1860, Mary Elizabeth Cabot, dau. of Hyde and Mary (Wiggin) Cabot. She was b. in Chelsea, Vt., May —, 1842; d. May 1, 1871. He is a farmer; res. Braintree, Vt. Children: 1. Herbert Fayette,[9] b. June 10, 1862. 2. Charles Cabot,[9] b. July 2, 1865.
8. Lucretia Elizabeth,[8] b. Dec. 7, 1840, m. in Williamstown, Vt., May 5, 1869, Thomas Warren Goodrich, son of Joseph and Sarah (Glidden) Goodrich. He was b. in Brookfield, Vt., March 19, 1838. Farmer; res. Williamstown, Vt. Child: 1. Joseph Carroll,[9] b. Feb. 27, 1870.
9. Luther,[8] b. Sept. 7, 1842, entered the Union Army, Sept. 1, 1862, and participated in numerous engagements; was wounded, June, 1864, and sent to the Hospital in August, where he remained till December of that year; was afterwards captured by Mosby, but escaped at great peril; was at the surrender of Gen. Lee; and discharged July 3, 1865. Res. Washington, Vt.
10. William Pride,[8] b. May 11, 1844; d. April 10, 1845.
11. Walter,[8] b. Dec. 9, 1846.

12. Emily Frances,[8] b. May 24, 1850, m. in Williamstown, Vt., Jan. 22, 1876, Charles Albert Rich, son of Eli and Mary (Wright) Rich. He was b. in Williamstown, Vt., April 22, 1849. Farmer; res. Washington, Vt. Children: 1. Adis Frank,[9] b. May 6, 1877. 2. Fred. Walter,[9] b. Feb. 13, 1879.

Lucretia K. Hovey,[7] third daughter and sixth child of Alvan and Nancy (Seabury) Hovey, b. in Brookfield, Vt., Sept. 9, 1813, m. in same place, April 4, 1834, Joseph Perkins, son of David and Sarah (Douglas) Perkins. He was b. in Chelsea, Vt., May 17, 1806. Farmer; res. Barre Village, Vt. She d. in Barre, Vt., May 7, 1838.
Child:
1. Joseph L.,[8] b. in East Brookfield, Vt., Feb. 9, 1835, m. in Barre, Vt., Nov. 6, 1862, Abbie Jane Peck, dau. of Jonathan J. and Maria Jane (Tucker) Peck. She was b. in Groton, Vt., Feb. 12, 1838. He is a dentist; res. St. Johnsbury, Vt. Children: 1. Abbie Josephine,[9] b. May 4, 1865; d. Aug. 12, 1865. 2. Isabel,[9] b. June 23, 1867. 3. Carl Douglas,[9] b. Sept. 20, 1870.

Harriet A. Hovey,[7] fourth daughter and seventh child of Alvan and Nancy (Seabury) Hovey, b. in Brookfield, Vt., Nov. 29, 1818, m. in Brookfield, Vt., June 27, 1838, George Dunham Bacon, son of Ebenezer and Elizabeth (Austin) Bacon. He was b. in Washington, Vt., April 4, 1807. Farmer; res. Chelsea, Vt.
Children, all b. in Chelsea:

1. Lucina Victoria,[8] b. May 10, 1839; d. Sept. 12, 1856.
2. George Hovey,[8] b. Sept. 16, 1840, m. in Chelsea, Vt., March 22, 1866, Sarah Eudora Cram, dau. of Daniel and Hannah (Hackett) Cram. She was b. in Chelsea, Vt., March 22, 1846. He is a farmer; res. Chelsea, Vt. Children: 1. Mabel Eudora,[9] b. Jan. 29, 1867. 2. Elizabeth Maria,[9] b. Aug. 16, 1870. 3. Daniel George,[9] b. Jan. 26, 1872; d. May —, 1876. 4. Benjamin,[9] b. Sept. 9, 1878.
3. Julia Elizabeth,[8] b. March 17, 1842, m. in Chelsea, Vt., March 17, 1860, John Hibbard Sprague,[8] son of John and Ruth Hovey (Hibbard) Sprague. He was b. in East Brookfield, Vt., Nov. 5, 1838. Farmer; res. Brookfield, Vt. Children: 1. John Vandever,[9] b. in Chelsea, Vt., Dec. 22, 1860. 2. George Edward,[9] b. in Chelsea, Vt., Feb. 23, 1865. 3. William Hibbard,[9] b. in Chelsea, Vt., Jan. 1, 1867. 4. Ruth Hibbard,[9] b. in Brookfield, Vt., Feb. 21, 1874.
4. Erdix Newton,[8] b. April 20, 1844, m. in Chelsea, Vt., June 14, 1870, Mary Mehitabel Goodwin, dau. of David Joseph Farnham and Adaline Electa (Wells) Goodwin. She was b. in Chelsea, Vt., Nov. 3, 1847. He is a farmer, living in Chelsea, Vt. Children: 1. Alice May,[9] b. Aug. 3, 1873; d. Sept. 27, 1877. 2. Richard Wells,[9] b. Feb. 22, 1877.
5. Nancy Maria,[8] b. June 29, 1853, m. in Williamstown, Vt., April 19, 1874, Oliver Dutton Metcalf, son of Jackson Dickerson and Hannah Elizabeth (Dutton) Metcalf. He was b. in Chelsea, Vt., Oct. 20, 1848. Farmer; res. Brookfield, Vt. No children.

Emily A. Hovey,[7] youngest daughter and eighth child of Alvan and Nancy (Seabury) Hovey, b. in Brookfield, Vt., Feb. 12, 1818, m. in Brookfield, Vt., Jan. 26, 1842, David Emery, son of Jonathan and Nancy (Eaton) Emery. He was b. in Grantham, N. H., Dec. 5, 1817. Farmer; res. Chelsea, Vt.
Children, all b. in East Brookfield, Vt.:

1. Frederic Wilbur,⁵ (Dr.), b. Aug. 15, 1843, m. in Chelsea, Vt., Dec. 31, 1869, Sarah Maria Bagley, dau. of Dr. George King and Susan Maria (Worthley) Bagley, of Ware, Mass. She was b. in Topsham, Vt., Dec. 21, 1851. Res. Chelsea, Vt. Children: 1. Lillian Ella,⁹ b. in Chelsea, Vt., May 19, 1871. 2. Georgiana,⁹ b. in Chelsea, Vt., Sept. 22, 1878.
2. Walter Hovey,⁵ b. Oct. 14, 1847.
3. Rosette Emily,⁵ b. April 9, 1852.
4. Albert Bigelow,⁵ b. May 6, 1859.

Mrs. Sprague contributes the following sketch of the family:

"Alvan Hovey, eighth child of Elder Samuel and Abigail C. Hovey, was born March 3, 1779.

"Some of his childish sayings have been preserved by tradition in the family. When a very little fellow, his father, being absent in the patriot army during the Revolutionary war, wrote to his mother; and she, while reading the letter, shed tears over it. Little Alvan looked up, full of sympathy, saying: "What 'oar (roar) for, mammy? Daddy home." When, a few years older, he had been guilty of some childish fault, his vexed father approached him rather hastily, Alvan looked on all sides and petitioned, 'Please, sir, don't knock me over that stump!' When, older still, being at school, the teacher at different times gave leave to the scholar at the foot of the class to pronounce a word for the class to spell, and whoever could spell it was to stand at the head of the class, Alvan, being at the foot, had leave to name a word to the class. 'Spell cotton.' Commencing at the head, the word went through the class, and, according to Alvan, was missed by each in turn. The teacher says: "Alvan, you must spell it yourself." 'W-o-r-s-t-e-d; oh! it is worsted.' And Alvan marched to the head of his class without further invitation.

"He married Nancy Seabury, a lady of a very respectable family, by whom he had four daughters and one son. The son died of fever at the age of eleven years. Subsequently he lost a pair of male infants, which caused the sorrowing father to exclaim, 'A living son is too great a blessing for me.' He received into his family, at different times, several sons of other people, whom he educated and clothed, and received their labor on his farm till their majority. He was for many years a deacon in the Baptist Church and a highly respectable member of the community. He was the inventor of a horse rake, for which the Government granted him a patent.

"His wife having died, he married the widow Bean, who was a daughter of Oliver and Rachel (Cleveland) Hamblin, being his own cousin. After his death she received an annuity from his estate during the remainder of her life. His daughters were eminently beautiful and accomplished ladies, three of whom are still living. He was an uncommonly handsome man, with a sedate smile on his face and his long white hair curling over his shoulders. He, as well as his mother, brothers and sisters, were very sweet singers, as were nearly all of the Hovey name; but that agreeable accomplishment was entirely denied to the venerable elder, as well as to myself.

R. H. SPRAGUE."

[To correct the list of children born to Oliver and Abigail (Hovey) Hibbard,⁶ (see page 19), the following more accurate record is presented:

1. Polly,⁷ b. Oct. 13, 1805; d. Jan. —, 1869.
2. Amanda,⁷ b. Aug. 14, 1807; res. Brookfield, Vt.
3. Oliver Davison,⁷ (Rev.), b. Oct. 12, 1809; res. Wyandotte, Mich.
4. Lewis,⁷ b. Sept. 10, 1811; d. ——, 1811.
5. Son,⁷ b. Jan. 12, 1813; d. ——, 1813.

6. Son,[7] b. May 20, 1814; d. ——, 1814.
7. William Lewis,[7] b. Aug. 6, 1816; d. Sept. 20, 1851.
8. Abigail Cleveland,[7] b. Dec. 31, 1818 ; d. Feb. 16, 1835.
9. Almira,[7] b. Jan. 13, 1821; d. Nov. 24, 1856.
10. Sarah Marinda,[7] b. Sept. 23, 1826; res. Chelsea, Vt.]

Polly Hibbard,[7] eldest daughter and child of Oliver and Abigail (Hovey) Hibbard, b. in Brookfield, Vt., Oct. 13, 1805, m. in Brookfield, Vt., Nov. 7, 1826, William Caldwell Clark, adopted son of Edmund and Martha (Kelley) Clark. He was b. in Barre, Mass., ——, 1803; d. in Manchester, N. H., Nov. —, 1859. She d. in Philadelphia, Pa., at the residence of her son, Daniel W. Clark,[8] Jan. —, 1869.
Children:
1. Edmund Bertrand,[8] b. in Chelsea, Vt., Aug. 20, 1829, m. in Manchester, N. H., Aug. 15, 1857, Frances Ann Osgood, dau. of Nathan Bailey and Clarissa (Dow) Osgood. She was b. in Suncook, Merrimack county, N. H., June 29, 1835. He resided sometime in Havre de Grace, Md. He is a sign and ornamental painter; res. Dixon, Lee county, Ill. No children.
2. Oliver Hibbard,[8] b. in Chelsea, Vt., Nov. 2, 1833, enlisted in the Union Army, Oct. 7, 1861, served through the war of the Rebellion, and was honorably discharged Oct. 2, 1864, by reason of the amputation of his left leg at the knee. He obtained a pension from the Government. Res. 336 Dickinson street, Philadelphia, Pa. He m. in Mount Carmel, Pa, Sept. 8, 1875, Matilda Fisher, dau. of James P. and Eliza Fisher. She was b. in Shamokin, Pa., date not learned. Children : 1. Gertrude May,[9] b. in Shamokin, Pa., June 23, 1876. 2. Eliza Mabel,[9] b. in Philadelphia, Pa., Dec. 3, 1877.
3. Daniel Wellington,[8] b. in Eden, Lamoille county, Vt., Jan. 3, 1835, m. in Philadelphia, Pa., Feb. 9, 1858, Mary Amanda Howett, dau. of Hon. Joseph and Elizabeth Wilson (Matthews) Howett. She was b. in Lancaster, Pa., July 4, 1837. He is a merchant, now doing business at 328 Chestnut street, Philadelphia ; res. 1227 same street. Children : 1. Jefferson Howett,[9] b. in Lancaster, Pa., Nov. 26, 1858. 2. Mary Minerva,[9] b. in Philadelphia, Jan. 6, 1861. 3. Henry Wentz,[9] b. in Philadelphia, April 5, 1863. 4. William Lewis,[9] b. in Philadelphia, Dec. 3, 1864. 5. Charles Howett,[9] b. in Harrisburgh, Pa., Feb. 13, 1873.
4. William Lewis Hibbard,[8] b. in Eden, Lamoille county, Vt., Jan. 13, 1837, m. Aug. 12, 1871, Anna E. Bare, dau. of Elias and Mary Bare. Place and date of birth not given. Res. Philadelphia, Pa. No children.
5. Martha,[8] b. in Eden, Lamoille county, Vt., Nov. 10, 1838, m. in Francistown, Hillsborough county, N. H., June 29, 1857, John Wellington Martin, son of John and Catherine (Connor) Martin. He was b. in Burlington, Vt., May 12, 1834. He is a farmer ; res. Dixon, Lee county, Ill. Children: 1. George Frederic,[9] b. in Havre de Grace, Md., April 1, 1867. 2. John Lewis Herbert,[9] b. in State Line, Warren county, Ind., July 17, 1872. 3. Bertrand Benwood,[9] b. in Dixon, Ill., May 17, 1877.

Amanda Hibbard,[7] second daughter and child of Oliver and Abigail (Hovey) Hibbard, b. in Brookfield, Vt., Aug. 14, 1807, m. in Brookfield, Vt., Jan. 28, 1828, John Alden Wright, son of Jesse and Elizabeth (Wills) Wright. He was b. in Chelsea, Vt., Aug. 14, 1804. Farmer; res. East Brookfield, Vt.

Children, all b. in Brookfield:
1. Eliza Jane,[8] b. Sept. 24, 1829; d. Feb. 28, 1856, unm.
2. Oliver Lewis,[8] b. Sept. 17, 1833, m. in Royalton, Vt., Dec. 12, 1867, Esther Grant, dau. of Edward and Anna (Durkee) Grant. She was b. in East Brookfield, Vt., ——, 1846. Child: 1. Nellie Jane,[9] b. Sept. 2, 1871.
3. Ellen Amanda,[8] b. May 21, 1838, m. in East Randolph, Vt., Sept. 18, 1856, Alonzo Roberts, son of Daniel G. and Hannah (Green) Roberts. He was b. in Tunbridge, Vt., Sept. 18, 1827. Farmer. Children: 1. Emma Eliza,[9] b. Oct. 12, 1857. 2. Mary Frances,[9] b. July 1, 1861.

Oliver D. Hibbard,[7] (Rev.), eldest son and third child of Oliver and Abigail (Hovey) Hibbard, b. in Brookfield, Vt., Oct. 12, 1809, m. first, in Evans, Erie county, N. Y., Nov. 27, 1837, Maria Cornelia Curtiss, dau. of Caleb and Polly (Bradley) Curtiss. She was b. in Evans, N. Y., May 1, 1819; d. in Evans, N. Y., Feb. 23, 1840. He m. second, in Sugar Grove, Warren county, Pa., Mrs. Catherine (Barr) Jolls, widow of Jeremiah Platt Jolls, and daughter of John and Sarah (McFall) Barr. She was b. near Belfast, Ireland, April 25, 1810. He is a Presbyterian clergyman; res. Wyandotte, Mich.

Children, by wife Maria:
1. Julia Maria,[8] b. in Collins, Erie county, N. Y., Oct. 13, 1839; d. in Evans, Erie county, N. Y., Oct. 10, 1841.

by wife Catherine:
2. Frederic Miles,[8] b. in Carrol, N. Y., June 29, 1843, m. in Wyandotte, Wayne county, Mich., March 9, 1873, Emma Zeller, dau. of Henry Harrison and Lucinda (Sarver) Zeller. She was b. in Marion, Grant county, Ind., Dec. 1, 1849. He is a salesman ; res. Muncie, Ind. Children: 1. Rose Parepa,[9] b. in Wyandotte, Mich., Dec. 11, 1873. 2. Mary Cowles,[9] b. in Wyandotte, Mich., Oct. 10, 1875. 3. Don Frederic,[9] b. in La Fontaine, Ind., May 6, 1878.

William L. Hibbard,[7] fifth son and seventh child of Oliver and Abigail (Hovey) Hibbard, b. in Brookfield, Vt., Aug. 6, 1816, m. in same place, Sept. 23, 1836, Harriet Atwood Sprague, daughter of Edward and Asenath (Corliss) Sprague. She was b. in Randolph, Vt., Jan. 24, 1818; d. in North Stratford, N. H., Feb. 16, 1861. He d. in Montpelier, Vt., Sept. 20, 1851. Teacher.

Children:
1. Edward Sprague,[8] b. in Brookfield, Vt., Aug. 5, 1837, m. in same place, June 16, 1862, Abby Folsom, dau. of Smith Folsom. Place and date of her birth not learned. Divorced. He d. in Stanwood, Iowa, Jan. 9, 1872. Children: 1. Coralin,[9] b. May 15, 1862; d. Dec. —, 1865. 2. Clarence,[9] b. May 1, 1864.
2. Oliver Davison,[8] b. in Brookfield, Vt., Jan. 14, 1840, m. first, in Bloomfield, Vt., Jan. 16, 1861, Octavia Fuller, dau. of William Fuller. She was b. in Bloomfield, Vt., March 15, 1838; d. in Mechanicsville, Iowa, Dec. 29, 1865. He m. second, in Mechanicsville, Feb. 5, 1867, Ella A. Grace, dau. of John and Hannah P. (Palmer) Grace. She was b. in Colburn, Ontario, Aug. 5, 1839. No children by second wife. By wife Octavia he had a family of four children, all of whom died in infancy. He is a farmer; res. Stanwood, Iowa.

3. Coralin Adelia,[8] b. in Washington, Vt., Oct. 14, 1844, m. in Brunswick, Vt., Oct. 14, 1861, Frank Rolfe, son of William Rolfe, and a native of North Stratford, N. H., but date of birth not learned. She d. in Brunswick, Vt., Feb. 27, 1863. Child: 1. Daughter,[9] b. Aug. 16, 1862; d. Jan. —, 1863.

Almira Hibbard,[7] fourth daughter and ninth child of Oliver and Abigail (Hovey) Hibbard, b. in Brookfield, Vt., Jan. 13, 1821, m. in Brookfield, Vt., March 7, 1843, Amos Emery, son of Jonathan and Nancy A. (Eaton) Emery. He was b. in Chester, Rockingham county, N. H., March 27, 1820. Farmer; res. Chelsea, Vt. She d. in Brookfield, Vt., Nov. 24, 1856.
Children, both b. in Brookfield:

1. Amos George,[8] b. Oct. 6, 1844, m. in Chelsea, Vt., March 20, 1867, Climena Allen, dau. of Sereno and Lydia (Gustin) Allen. She was b. in Chelsea, Vt., March 26, 1843. He is a manufacturer of hulled corn; res. 19 Gilman street, East Somerville, Mass. Child: 1. Allen Amos,[9] b. in Chelsea, Vt., Dec. 26, 1867.
2. Albert Eugene,[8] b. Aug. 11, 1848, m. first, in Chelsea, Vt., Feb. 9, 1868, Laura Luella Corliss, dau. of Stephen and Mary (Wilcox) Corliss. She was b. in Hooksett, Merrimack county, N. H., Nov. 26, 1850; d. in Chelsea, Vt., Sept. 2, 1873. He m. second, in Brookfield, Vt., Aug. 8, 1877, Hattie Maria Durkee, dau. of Ezra and Caroline Maria (White) Durkee. She was b. in Brookfield, Vt., Sept. 29, 1858. Res. Chelsea, Vt. No children.

Sarah M. Hibbard,[7] youngest daughter and child of Oliver and Abigail (Hovey) Hibbard, b. in Brookfield, Vt., Sept. 23, 1826, m. in Brookfield, Vt., Oct. 9, 1859, Amos Emery, son of Jonathan and Nancy A. (Eaton) Emery. He was b. in Chester, N. H., March 27, 1820. Farmer; res. Chelsea, Vt. Children, both b. in Brookfield, Vt.:

1. Curtis Stanton,[8] b. Nov. 6, 1861.
2. Wilson Seward,[8] b. Nov. 9, 1863.

Rev. Oliver D. Hibbard,[7] of Wyandotte, Mich., writes, in answer to inquiries, the following, which is given entire:

"Your double favor, bearing date the 17th inst., has just come to hand. Contents being noted, I snatch the fugitive moments as I can to say that in October, 1833, I left my old New England home, and pushed westward, leaving mountains and valleys, rocks and rivers, and childhood's friends behind. Slowly the images photographed on the inner tablet of my soul faded, and present scenes and engrossments commanded all the view. For awhile letters came and went, but the intervals grew longer and longer. New scenes sprung up around me, and new friends knocked at my door. New songs fell on my ear—new sights—new forms of beauty looked at me on every hand, and challenged and transfixed my gaze. Once—just once—I wended my way back to the storm-beaten cliffs of my native North, to see my mother, my only brother, my three sisters—two of whom were in the house where they were born, and one two miles only distant—to see my uncles, and aunts, and cousins, and my father's and grandparents' graves. It had been fourteen years from the time of my leaving. I preached every Sabbath, and the graves preached also.

"Soon after my return to my pastorate in Western New York, my mother and my brother died of bilious typhus fever, within twenty days of each other.

"By and bye the muttering thunders began to rumble, the pulse of the nation to beat faster and faster, and anon the whole land rocked in the fearful storm. You know the dreadful story. Perhaps you went to the front. My first commission was dated May 8, 1861, Chaplain of the 64th N. Y. Regt., and on September 16th following I was ordered to report immediately for duty at Elmira, N. Y. I was with my regiment through thick and thin until about the middle of October, 1864, when I applied for a discharge and was mustered out. In December following, I came to Wyandotte, and—here I am.

"Believe that I remain as ever, yours,   O. D. HIBBARD.

"P. S.—I wish, before I close, to bear my humble testimony to the excellences of my venerated grandmother Hovey, formerly Abigail Cleveland. She was remarkable for truthfulness, patience and piety—in fact, for every domestic and Christian virtue. In all the sweet and gentle graces of perfect womanhood, she stood in her humble walks and ways as a grand exemplification. My mother, named for her, inherited many of her attributes, with a splash of her father's fire and irritability. I think my grandmother had a brother Zenas—what do you know of him? She had a sister, wife of Oliver Hamblin, of Brookfield, Vt. Have you traced that branch?   O. D. H."

Another of Mrs. Sprague's admirable sketches is added:

"Abigail Hovey, ninth child of Elder Samuel and Abigail C. Hovey, was born Dec. 25, 1780. She was married in Brookfield, Vt., to Oliver Hibbard, whose parents were emigrants from Connecticut. She and her husband resided on a small farm in the vicinity of their respective parents, suffering the hardships and enjoying the pleasures incident to the dwellers in a new settlement. They were frequent attendants at Sabbath worship in the school house, with the long benches, and many are the times they have ridden to the meetings—about a mile—on one horse, with each a child in arms. As their family increased in numbers, the parents and children rode together in a common farm-cart, drawn by a yoke of oxen; for pleasure carriages were then unknown in the community, or were few in number. She always seemed to feel the presence of poverty very sensibly, endeavoring to compel limited means to make a respectable appearance. Although an excellent cook, she was accustomed to disparage the fare set before her friends and family. Her pious husband's answer usually was: 'It is good enough for saints; too good for sinners.' She was large in form—would probably weigh 180 or more; was extremely quick and sensitive in her feelings, and resembled her father in features and mental character, more than her mother. She was quick, active and diligent in household occupations—a very neat housekeeper.

"Of her ten children, seven lived to maturity, and many are the hours under the paternal roof that their voices have made sweet music together. About the year 1833, her husband died of dropsy, bequeathing to her their pleasant home and whatever property he possessed. She died of fever, at more than seventy years of age. Both her sons were excellent teachers; the oldest, Oliver Davison, afterwards became a minister of the Gospel, and settled in the West; Wm. Lewis, the younger son, devoted the last years of his life to commercial pursuits, and died at Montpelier, of a fever, leaving three children, the younger son, Oliver, being the only one now living. Two daughters, out of those ten children, are still living.

    R. H. SPRAGUE."

Mary Hibbard,[7] eldest daughter and child of Gurdon and Elizabeth (Hovey) Hibbard, b. in Brookfield, Vt., Oct. 24, 1809, m. in same place, Dec. 23, 1828, Ezra Wills, son of Joel and Lois (Perigo) Wills. He was b. in Tunbridge, Vt., Oct. 1, 1808, and is still living there. She d. in Tunbridge, Vt., May 27, 1859.

Children:

1. William Wallace,[8] b. in Chelsea, Vt., June 18, 1829, m. in South Royalton, Vt., July 4, 1852, Mary Lavinia Thurston, dau. of William and Clarissa (Church) Thurston. She was b. in Rochester, Vt., Jan. 24, 1835. He is a machinist; res. Janesville, Wis. Children: 1. Ellen Lavinia,[9] b. in Lebanon, N. H., Oct. 16, 1854. 2. George Mills,[9] b. in Palatine, Ill., Sept. 8, 1856, m. in Janesville, Wis., Feb. 14, 1877, Ethelinda Wright, dau. of Orville and Clarissa (Thurston) Wright. She was b. in Emerald Grove, Wis., July 19, 1857. Child: 1. Zula Ethel,[10] b. in Janesville, Wis., Oct. 4, 1877.
2. Lucinda Isadore,[8] b. in Brookfield, Vt., July 19, 1833; d. April 6, 1835.
3. George Washington,[8] b. in Brookfield, Vt., June 8, 1835, m. first, April 10, 1861, Gertrude Louisa Walker, parentage and place and date of birth not given. She d. after they came West, and he m. second, a lady whose name, etc., has not been communicated. He is a railroad engineer, and resides in Belle Plaine, Iowa. Child, by wife Gertrude: 1. George Wallace,[9] b. in Haverhill, Mass., Sept. —, 1861; d. Feb. —, 1866.
4. Eliza Lucretia,[8] b. in East Randolph, Vt., April 16, 1838, m. in ——, Vt., Oct. 22, 1859, Aaron Alvah Currier, son of David D. and Eliza (Putney) Currier. He was b. in Wentworth, N. H., July 19, 1837. Res. Lawrence, Mass. Children, all b. in Lawrence: 1. Alice Cora,[9] b. Oct. 9, 1860; d. July 9, 1862. 2. Addie Alma,[9] b. March 29, 1862. 3. Carrie Lucretia,[9] b. June 18, 1864. 4. Ella Cora,[9] b. May 4, 1870. 5. John Alvah,[9] b. July 7, 1876. 6. Albert,[9] b. April 15, 1878.
5. Benjamin Porter,[8] b. in East Randolph, Vt., Jan. 6, 1840, m. first, in Woodstock, Ill., Dec. 12, 1867, Helen Maria Wright, dau. of Benjamin Franklin and Lucinda (Runlett) Wright. She was b. Oct. 28, 1843, and divorced July 11, 1873. He m. second, Feb. —, 1874, Annie ——, parentage and place and date of birth not learned; she is supposed to be living in Milwaukee, Wis. He is a railroad engineer by occupation, but is now (1879) in the mines of Colorado. Children, by wife Helen: 1. Franklin Porter,[9] b. in Chicago, July 12, 1869; d. in Milwaukee, Oct. 22, 1870. 2. William Everett,[9] b. in Milwaukee, Feb. 26, 1871; d. March 22, 1871. By wife Annie: 3. Mary,[9] b. Nov. —, 1874.
6. Mary Lucina,[8] b. in East Randolph, Vt., April 19, 1841, m. in ——, Vt., Sept. 26, 1864, Lieut. George Greenleaf Hutchins, son of Ephraim and Amy (Dearborn) Hutchins. He was b. in Ashburnham, Mass., Feb. 5, 1833. Res. North Sherburne, Vt. Children: 1. Florence Corinne,[9] b. May 17, 1866. 2. Glen Burwell,[9] b. Dec. 13, 1868. 3. Harry Howard,[9] b. Feb. 22, 1876.
7. Thomas Perigo,[8] b. in East Randolph, Vt., June 18, 1843, m. in Lawrence, Mass., July 4, 1866, Josephine Ayer, dau. of Peleg Ayer, of Lawrence, Mass., where she was b. in 1849. Divorced. He is a carpenter; res. Lawrence, Mass. No children.
8. Ezra Herman,[8] b. in East Randolph, Vt., July 16, 1848. Railroad engineer; res. Toledo, Iowa.
9. Caroline Estella,[8] b. in South Royalton, Vt., May 23, 1853, m. in ——, Vt., Oct. 5, 1873, William Halliday, son of William and Jane (Lawrence) Halliday. He was b. in Andover, Mass., June 17, 1853. Res. not learned. No children.

Gurdon P. Hibbard,[7] only son and second child of Gurdon and Elizabeth (Hovey) Hibbard, b. in Brookfield, Vt., April 27, 1811, m. in Chelsea, Vt., Jan. 1, 1839, Isabella Hemenway, dau. of Jonathan Wilder and Sylvia (Hastings) Hemenway. She was b. in Chelsea, Vt., Aug. 21, 1814. He is a farmer; res. East Brookfield, Vt.

Children, all b. in Brookfield:

1. Edwin Smiley,[8] b. Oct. 3, 1839, m. in Brookfield, Vt., Aug. 4, 1864, Amy Phyletta Hovey,[7] dau. of Samuel and Phyletta (Kendall) Hovey. She was b. in Brookfield, Vt., July 7, 1838. He d. in Montpelier, Vt., Nov. 22, 1876, much lamented. They had no children.
2. Franklin Plummer,[8] b. Jan. 3, 1843, enlisted in the Union Army, and d. near Coal Harbor, Va., June 10, 1864.
3. Arthur Edgar,[8] b. June 20, 1847, m. in Brookfield, Vt., Jan. 1, 1875, Caroline Sargent, dau. of Thomas Irving and Mary Ann (Elliott) Sargent. She was b. in Brookfield, Vt., Oct. 2, 1851. He is a farmer; res. East Brookfield, Vt. Child: 1. Edwin Irving,[9] b. Sept. 21, 1878.
4. Isabella Luella,[8] b. March 27, 1849, m. in Chelsea, Vt., Sept. —, 1870, Andrew Norton Woodruff, son of Harrison and Janette (Winn) Woodruff. He was b. in West Windsor, Vt., Jan. 28, 1845. Farmer. Child: 1. Harrison Gurdon,[9] b. June 1, 1872.
5. Alpheus Gurdon,[8] b. Oct. 5, 1850, m. in Brookfield, Vt., Aug. 29, 1875, Clara Martha Buck, dau. of William Leland and Lois Dickinson (Gaylord) Buck. She was b. in Northfield, Vt., Aug. 29, 1857. No children. Res. not given.

Ruth H. Hibbard,[7] second daughter and third child of Gurdon and Elizabeth (Hovey) Hibbard, b. in Brookfield, Vt., Jan. 26, 1813, m. in Brookfield, Vt., Nov. 5, 1837, John Sprague, son of Edward and Asenath (Corliss) Sprague. He was b. in Randolph, Vt., April 6, 1815. Farmer; res. East Brookfield, Vt.

Children, both b. in Brookfield, Vt.:

1. John Hibbard,[8] b. Nov. 5, 1838, m. in Chelsea, Vt., March 17, 1860, Julia Elizabeth Bacon, dau. of George Dunham and Harriet Atwood (Hovey) Bacon. She was b. in Chelsea, Vt., March 17, 1842. He is a farmer; res. East Brookfield, Vt. Children: 1. John Vandever,[9] b. in Chelsea, Vt., Dec. 22, 1860. 2. George Edward,[9] b. in Chelsea, Vt., Feb. 23, 1865. 3. William Hibbard,[9] b. in Chelsea, Vt., Jan. 1, 1867. 4. Ruth Hibbard,[9] b. in Brookfield, Vt., Feb. 21, 1874.
2. Daniel Hovey,[8] b. May 12, 1843; d. in Chelsea, Vt., July 21, 1855.

Sarah D. Hibbard,[7] fourth daughter and fifth child of Gurdon and Elizabeth (Hovey) Hibbard, b. in Brookfield, Vt., Oct. 4, 1817, m. in Brookfield, Vt., Feb. 11, 1841, Joseph Newell, son of Joseph and Weltha (Strong) Newell. He was b. in Oxford, N. H., Aug. 9, 1811. Farmer; res. Brookfield, Vt.

Children:

1. Franklin Hibbard,[8] b. in Oxford, Vt., Dec. 8, 1842, m. in Williamstown, Vt., Jan. 1, 1865, Alma Maria Brewer, dau. of Alanson and Sarah (Dutton) Brewer. She was b. in Tunbridge, Vt., Nov. 7, 1845. He is a farmer; res. Brookfield, Vt. Children: 1. Eliza Maria,[9] b. Jan. 13, 1867. 2. Frederic Elton,[9] b. Nov. 13, 1868.
2. Joseph Gurdon,[8] b. in Oxford, Vt., May 30, 1845, m. in Chelsea, Vt., Jan. 28, 1879, Louisa Celia Vincent, dau. of Stephen and Phebe (Hale) Vincent. She was b. in Chelsea, Vt., June 11, 1843. Trader; res. Somerville, Mass.

3. Everett Clifton,[8] b. in Oxford, Vt., May 13, 1847, m. in Randolph, Vt., March 14, 1869, Ida Alelia Bixby, dau. of Urbane and Mary Ann (Hovey) Bixby.* She was b. in East Brookfield, Vt., June 23, 1851. He is a farmer; res. Chelsea, Vt. Children: 1. Daughter,[9] b. Dec. 13, 1872; d. Dec. 13, 1872. 2. Florence Emeline,[9] b. Jan. 8, 1874; d. March 28, 1875. 3. Bertha Eudora,[9] b. Dec. 14, 1877; d. March 21, 1878. 4 Eulela May,[9] b. March 3, 1879.
4. George Flint,[8] b. in Oxford, Vt., March 14, 1849. He is an engineer; res. Deer Island, Boston Harbor, Mass.; unm.
5. Silas Davis,[8] b. in Brookfield, Vt., Jan. 14, 1851, m. in Randolph, Vt., Aug. 9, 1873, Mary Kirth Wheatley, dau. of Jesse C. and Sarah Ann (Sprague) Wheatley. She was b. in Brookfield, Vt., July 13, 1855. He is a farmer; res. Brookfield, Vt. Child: 1. Eva Wheatley,[9] b. June 26, 1874.
6. Sarah Elizabeth,[8] b. in Brookfield, Vt., June 26, 1856.
7. Herbert Llewellyn,[8] b. in Brookfield, Vt., Nov. 11, 1861.

Fanny B. Hibbard,[7] fifth daughter and sixth child of Gurdon and Elizabeth (Hovey) Hibbard, b. in Brookfield, Vt., Sept. 10, 1819, m. in East Brookfield, Vt., Sept. 10, 1844, Nathan Davis, son of Nathan and Lydia (Wentworth) Davis. He was b. in Boston, Mass., Nov. 23, 1819. She d. in Washington, N. J., May 23, 1872.

Children:
1. Caroline Adaline,[8] b. in Norwich, Vt., June 26, 1845; d. Feb. 5, 1856.
2. Frank Igo,[8] b. in Norwich, Vt., Jan. 27, 1847, m. in South Stanhope, Morris county, N. J., May 19, 1870, Mulvina Heaton, dau of Francis Joseph and Sarah (Slack) Heaton. She was b. in Drakeville, Morris county, N. J., June 26, 1847. He is employed on the M. & E. R. R.; res. Port Morris, N. J. Child: 1. Fannie Heaton,[9] b. in Irvington, Essex county, N. J., June 15, 1872.
3. Josephine,[8] b. in Ludlow, Vt., July 12, 1849. Res. Washington, N. J.
4. Frederic Napoleon Nathan,[8] b in Middle Granville, N. Y., Sept. 1, 1851, m. in Suckasunny, Morris county, N. J., Oct. 29, 1871, Charlotte Ann Brown, dau. of Rankins and Sarah (Youngs) Brown. She was b. in Port Morris, N. J., Sept. 20, 1851. He is a machinist; res. Port Morris, N. J. Child: 1. Charles Frederic,[9] b May 16, 1873.
5. Fannie,[8] b. in Washington, N. J. ——, 1858; lived only three days.

Elizabeth P. Hibbard,[7] youngest daughter and child of Gurdon and Elizabeth (Hovey) Hibbard, b. in Brookfield, Vt., Sept. 5, 1821, m. in same place, April 25, 1847, Solomon Stoddard, son of Solomon and Mary (Buckland) Stoddard. He was b. in Washington, Vt., Dec. 27, 1801; d. in Methuen, Mass., Aug. 13, 1874. She is living (1878) in Methuen, Mass.

Children, all b. in Brookfield, Vt.:
1. Emma Flavilla,[8] b. Feb. 17, 1842, m. in Methuen, Mass., Oct. 1, 1865, Enoch Holt, son of Enoch and Rachel (Packer) Holt. He was b. in Methuen, Mass., Nov. 9, 1809. Children, all b. in Methuen, Mass.: 1. Ina Estella,[9] b. July 20, 1866; d. March 22, 1878. 2. Rachel Cora,[9] b. Jan. 31, 1870. 3. Bertie,[9] b. May 13, 1872; d. May 21, 1872. 4. Emma Elizabeth,[9] b. Aug. 11, 1874; d. March 22, 1875. 5. Enoch Christiansen,[9] b. Dec. 26, 1875. 6. Alfred May,[9] b. May 1, 1877; d. March 15, 1878.

2. King Solomon,[8] b. Feb. 12, 1849, m. in Washington, Vt., April 1, 1871, Cordelia Mindwell Colby, dau. of Allison and Albina (Moody) Colby. She was b. in Corinth (or Vershire), Vt., Oct. 10, 1854. Res. Miller's Falls, Mass. Child: 1. Zilpha Viola,[9] b. June —, 1873.
3. Ariel Burnham,[8] b. Dec. 24, 1855.

Concerning her own parents Mrs. Sprague contributes the following interesting account:

"Elizabeth Perkins Hovey, tenth child of Elder Samuel and Abigail C. Hovey, was born on Grant's Island, in Connecticut river, containing sixty acres of excellent land. A slight bluff near the centre of the island was adorned by a house and barn, to one of which a canoe was fastened during times of high water—all of the remaining land being submerged. At the time of her birth, April 15, 1783, the ice of the river being deeply covered with water, and rapidly thawing, the company invited on the occasion were carried across on men's shoulders. The family remained in this island home till her ninth year, and the little fishes were among her earliest playthings. She delighted to feed them with crumbs of bread and bits of meat, and her brothers, designing to terrify her, caught her and tossed her into the water, but instead of being terrified, she was delighted.

"From the island, the family removed to Norwich, Vt., and at the age of twelve, they again removed to Brookfield. Here she became a pupil in a little log school house, which was afterwards burned. Her health during three years was very delicate, and she was believed by her family to be in a confirmed consumption; but at the age of eighteen it greatly improved, and a journey on horseback, with a change of air and diet, confirmed it.

"At the age of nineteen she formed a contract of marriage with Gurdon Hibbard, a brother of Oliver, he being one year her senior; but constant labor as a journeyman carpenter destroyed his health, and he was pronounced by his physicians, after a year of medical treatment, to be in a hopeless consumption. But he was not hopeless. He performed a journey on horseback to Saratoga Springs, in the State of New York, in opposition to the strenuous advice of his family, they never expecting to see him come back alive. After drinking the water a few weeks, his racking cough abated, and his violent night sweats disappeared. After his recovery, he bought fifty acres of land near his father, built himself a barn, set out an orchard, and was finally married, on Dec. 25, 1809, after an engagement of seven years; her father officiating at the ceremony, and presenting her a Bible as a wedding gift. The next day she rode behind her husband on horseback to his father's, about three-fourths of a mile, in a part of whose house they made a temporary home while he should build himself a house.

"Her furniture consisted of two tables, two chests of drawers, six kitchen chairs and a rocking chair, two bedsteads, a large wheel, a linen wheel, a quill wheel, reel and swifts manufactured by her father, a looking glass, and some necessary crockery. She had devoted some years to sewing, making men's clothing, which was as lucrative as any employment for young women, at that time; she was therefore able to furnish beds with bedding, sheets and pillow cases, also very beautiful table cloths and towels of her own manufacture.

"Her wedding cloak was of scarlet broadcloth, reaching nearly to her feet, the body, armholes, cape and standing collar trimmed with silk velvet ribbon, nearly three inches wide; her bonnet, black velvet, with very little trimming; and, no doubt she was thought to make a very respectable appearance on a pillion. She had very deep blue eyes—they passed for black in the evening—dark brown hair, a very full forehead, and a fair skin. She was taller than any of her sisters, and weighed at her marriage (as did her husband), just one hundred and sixty pounds.

"She was a splendid singer, the best of the family, equal to her mother. She sang, in her girlhood, more than sixty songs, and I have heard that while singing 'The Exile of Erin,' tears would fall fast from the eyes of the company of auditors, excited by the music and the pathos of the song. Her children were indifferent singers, but her husband had a very fine cultivated voice; her grandchildren and great-grandchildren are some of them excelled only by her. There was music indeed when the husband and wife, by their own fireside, their children for auditors, sung the old fugue tunes which were then passing out of use among the people, but have sometimes returned, and been popular with musical choirs.

"By close economy they were enabled to make at different times additions to the farm, till it numbered between two and three hundred acres; to build two additional barns and a very convenient farm house. Her husband, a few years after marriage, introduced the first Spanish merinoes into the town, having bought a pair of lambs for one hundred dollars of Wm. Jarvis, late Consul from the United States to Spain. Two spinners were hired two or three months in the summer, and, some years as many as two hundred pounds of wool were manufactured into cloth, she doing the weaving; the cloth, when dressed, compared favorably with imported broadcloth, and commanded one dollar and a half to two dollars per yard. These spinners worked in the room where she and her little daughters were performing the household work for the family. While the work went on, beautiful hymns were sung, and there was much happiness under a very humble roof.

"After fourteen years of married life, their son and six daughters having been taught, began to take the places of hired laborers, and in the succeeding years mother and daughters performed music on wheels and loom, which, if not equal to the piano, yet had a very cheerful sound, and besides helped to render the family comparatively independent. The long evenings of winter were passed with a table in the centre of the room, the mother and daughters employed in knitting or sewing, at the same time listening to the vocal reading of the father, who was extremely fond of books.

"The oldest daughter married at the age of nineteen, the third went to reside in New Hampshire with a cousin, and the second was about to follow to New Hampshire as a teacher; the mother's heart began to feel bereaved. Her cry was, 'Joseph is not, Simeon is not, and ye will take Benjamin also.' But swiftly passed the fleeting years. All the children departed to other homes, excepting the third daughter, who returned to the paternal roof, and relieved the mother of her burden of labor while moving down the vale of years. Finally, at the age of eighty-one, after one day's illness, she folded her tired hands, gently closed her eyes and breathed her latest breath, and slept that sleep which seemed more like translation than death.

"Her daughters, with loving hands, robed the sacred remains for burial, and she rests in hope of a glorious immortality. Her husband survived her eight years, a most disconsolate mourner. He said to his daughter, 'There has been no day that I have not thought of her.' During all the years of their married life she had been the chief company he sought, had been consulted in all business affairs, and although a feeble woman in health, had borne her full share of the family burdens. I never knew a more conscientious person. She was worthy of all the confidence and affection she received from him and her children.

"Like all her sisters whom I have seen she resembled her father in features, but, more than any, she resembled her mother in the qualities of her mind. In all her work she was extremely nice, 'so exquisite with her needle.' Six of her children survived her; and in hope of meeting her in a world where is no death, we laid her in that cemetery where her parents and daughter, and many other relatives are laid, and where, eight years after, we laid her husband by the side of her who was the choice of his youth.
RUTH H. SPRAGUE."

Abigail E. Hovey,[1] eldest daughter and second child of John F. and Elizabeth (Hill) Hovey, b. in Milton, Vt., July 21, 1816, m. in Camden, Lorain county, Ohio, Jan. 1, 1837, Daniel Waugh, son of Daniel and

Irene,(Smedley) Waugh. He was b. in Camden, Oneida county, N. Y., Aug. 21, 1801; d. in McPherson, Kansas, Oct. 2, 1878. Farmer. She is living (1879) in McPherson, McPherson county, Kansas.
Children:

1. Albert Freeman,[8] b. Oct. 17, 1837, m. in Onion River, Sheboygan county, Wis., June 3, 1868, Lena Beeler, dau. of John and Elizabeth (Reoser) Beeler. She was b. in Volksberg, Unter Alsasz, Germany, Feb. 2, 1844. He is a farmer; res. Jackson, McPherson county, Kansas. Children: 1. Frank Albert,[9] b. in Sheboygan Falls, Wis., July 8, 1869. 2. Fannie Elizabeth,[9] b. in Sheboygan Falls, Wis., July 1, 1871. 3. Mary Lena,[9] b. in McPherson, Kansas, Feb. 13, 1879.
2. Clarissa Elizabeth,[8] b. March 24, 1840; d. Sept. 3, 1842, in Camden, Ohio.
3. Sydney Horace,[8] b. Dec. 21, 1841; d. Aug. 22, 1860, in Sheboygan Falls, Wis.
4. Emma Letitia,[8] b. Sept. 6, 1843, m. in Sheboygan Falls, Wis., Feb. 11, 1864, Alvin Birney Bliss, son of David and Jane (Lay) Bliss. He was b. in Lorain, Jefferson county, N. Y., April 15, 1839. Farmer; res. McPherson, Kansas. Children: 1. Eva Jane,[9] b. in Plymouth, Wis., Nov. 26, 1864. 2. Mary Elizabeth,[9] b. in Sheboygan Falls, Wis., May 28, 1867. 3. Carrie Grace,[9] b. in McPherson, Kan., Nov. 2, 1873. 4. Zina Lay,[9] b. June 1, 1876; d. Feb. —, 1878.
5. Lurena Elizabeth,[8] b. June 4, 1847; d. Oct. 21, 1861, in Sheboygan Falls, Wis.
6. Frances Emily,[8] b. Sept. 9, 1850; d. Oct. 13, 1861, in Sheboygan Falls, Wis.

Samuel B. Hovey,[7] second son and third child of John F. and Elizabeth (Hill) Hovey, b. in Milton, Vt., Sept. 21, 1818, m. in Eden, Delaware county, Ohio, Oct. 28, 1843, Dorinda Pierce, dau. of Milton and Fanny (Evans) Pierce. She was b. in Sunbury, Delaware county, Ohio, April 15, 1827. He is a farmer; res. Fremont, (May P. O.), Tuscola county, Mich.
Children were as follows, all b. in Delaware county, Ohio:

1. Victor,[8] b. April 13, 1845; d. Jan. 8, 1850.
2. Tilden,[8] b. Oct. 30, 1846; d. Sept. 10, 1848.
3. Fanny Elizabeth,[8] b. March 20, 1848; d. Jan. 10, 1850.
4. Jonas,[8] b. Jan. 18, 1850; d. July 8, 1851.
5. Judson Waterman,[8] b. Oct. 27, 1852, m. in Delaware county, Ohio, Oct. 8, 1872, Lucy Brewster Shade, dau. of Elijah and Emeline (Potter) Shade. She was b. in Logan county, Ohio, Sept. 25, 1852. He is a farmer; res. May P. O., Mich. Children: 1. Hilliard De Wayne,[9] b. May 3, 1875. 2. Bertha Emeline,[9] b. April 11, 1877.
6. Ella,[8] b. April 13, 1855.
7. Ida,[8] b May 20, 1858, m. in Fremont, Tuscola county, Mich., Dec. 24, 1877, Ralph Immer Smith, son of Rodney and Delilah (Reynolds) Smith. He was b. in Berlin, Delaware county, Ohio, Sept. 4, 1856. Farmer; res. Alum Creek, Delaware county, Ohio. No children.

John K. Hovey,[7] third son and fourth child of John F. and Elizabeth (Hill) Hovey, b. in Milton, Vt., March 3, 1821, m. in Brighton, Ohio, March 23, 1843, Mary Elvira Bunce, dau. of William and Sarah

(Hamilton) Bunce. She was b. in Hanover, Chautauqua county, N. Y., July 10, 1821. He is a farmer; res. Townville, Crawford county, Pa.
Children:

1. Edwin Hamilton,[8] (Rev.), b. in Brighton, Ohio, June 26, 1844, m. first, in Randolph, Pa., Sept. 24,1865, Diantha Hunt, dau. of Horace and Eliza (Hatch) Hunt. She was b. in Randolph, Pa., June 22, 1845; d. there, Dec. 4, 1867. He m. second, near Lancaster, Grant county, Wis., May 3, 1871, Mary Jane Rice, dau. of Franklin Rice. She was b. in the State of Vermont, Sept. 16, 1841. He is a Baptist minister; res. Stoneboro, Pa. Children: 1. Mary Eliza,[9] b. Dec. 3, 1867; d. Dec. 3, 1867. 2. Mary Addie,[9] b. March —, 1872; d. March —, 1872. 3. Iona Estelle,[9] b. Aug. 8, 1874; d. July —, 1875. 4. John Franklin,[9] b. June 22, 1876.
2. Laura Jane,[8] b. in Freedonia, Wis., Oct. 2, 1846; d. in Camden, Ohio, Dec. 22, 1852.
3. Sarah Elizabeth,[8] b. in Freedonia, Wis., Jan. 29, 1849.
4. Ellen Janette,[8] b. in Freedonia, Wis., July 4, 1851, m. in Randolph, Pa., Sept. 1, 1872, Enos Ames Scott, son of Daniel and Roby Ann (Ames) Scott. He was b. in Rockdale, Pa., Feb. 11, 1849. Farmer; res. ———. Children: 1. Jennie May,[9] b. July 4, 1873; d. Nov. 15, 1878. 2. Carrie Elizabeth,[9] b. June 20, 1876.
5. Harriet Emelia,[8] b. in Richmond, Pa., May 22, 1853; d. in Randolph, Pa., April 7, 1857.

Alvan S. Hovey,[7] fourth son and fifth child of John F. and Elizabeth (Hill) Hovey, b. in Milton, Vt., March 31, 1823, m. in Birmingham, Erie county, Ohio, Oct. 28, 1849, Sarah Ann Cook, dau. of Newell and Esther L. (Shattuck) Cook. She was b. in Scriba, Oswego county, N. Y., Jan. 13, 1831. He is a farmer; res. Holland, Lucas county, Ohio.
Children, all b. in Lorain county, Ohio:

1. Luella Clarette,[8] b. June 22, 1852, m. in Holland, Ohio, Nov. 15. 1876, William Washington Thomas, son of Geo. Points and Mary Ann Thomas. He was b. in Centerville, Allegany county, N. Y., April 27, 1853. Farmer; res. Farmersville, Cattaraugus county, N. Y. Child: 1. Clarence Hovey,[9] b. July 8, 1878.
2. George Elbert,[8] b. Nov. 24, 1855, m. Jan. 1, 1878, Adelaide Louise Bamsey, dau. of John and Rosette (Ackland) Bamsey. She was b. in Richfield, Lucas county, Ohio. Child: 1. Mabel Ellen,[9] b. Oct. 9, 1878.

Philemon H. Hovey,[7] fifth son and sixth child of John F. and Elizabeth (Hill) Hovey, b. March 17, 1826, m. in Paris, Tenn., Oct. 12, 1854, Rachel Ruthea Indman, dau. of Ezekiel and Martha (Beck) Indman. She was b. in Pleasant Garden, Burke county, N. C., May 8, 1826. He is a farmer; res. Union City, Obion county, Tenn.
Children:

1. Sarah Pauline,[8] b. in Henry county, Tenn., Aug. 19, 1855.
2. Joseph Newton,[8] b. in Henry county, Tenn., Jan. 20, 1858.
3. Martha Ann Eudora,[8] b. in Henry county, Tenn., Feb. 4, 1860.
4. Henry Horace,[8] b. in Metropolis City, Massac county, Ill., Nov. 12, 1861.
5. John William,[8] b. in Metropolis City, Ill., Dec. 14, 1863.
6. Mary Elizabeth,[8] b. in Camden, Lorain county, Ohio, July 20, 1865.
7. James Alvin,[8] b. in Metropolis City, Ill., Aug. 6, 1871.

Daniel H. Hovey,[7] sixth son and seventh child of John F. and Elizabeth (Hill) Hovey, b. March 23, 1828, m. in Sandusky, Ohio, Nov. 8, 1851, Jane Ellis, dau. of Cornelius and Eliza (Walker) Ellis. She was b. in Florence, Erie county, Ohio, Sept. 11, 1830. He is a farmer; res. McPherson, Kansas.
Children:
1. Edgar Willis,[8] b. in Eden, Delaware county, Ohio, March 8, 1853.
2. Mary Elizabeth,[8] b. in Wakeman, Huron county, Ohio, Feb. 8, 1856, m. in Harper, McPherson county, Kan., Feb. 20, 1875, Simon Peter Fisher, son of Isaac D. and Keturah (Rhoadermel) Fisher. He was b. in Northumberland county, Pa., Sept. 9, 1848. Farmer; res. Lindsburg, McPherson county, Kan. Children: 1. Maud Alice,[9] b. Sept. 7, 1876. 2. Lottie,[9] b. April 18, 1878.
3. James Andrew,[8] b. in Ottumwa, Coffey county, Kan., April 27, 1860.
4. John Cornelius,[8] b. in Ottumwa, Kan., April 1, 1862.
5. Ida May,[8] b. in Ottumwa, Kan., Jan 25, 1866.
6. Eva Ellen,[8] b. in Ottumwa, Kan., Feb. 17, 1868.

James Monroe P. Hovey,[7] eighth son and ninth child of John F. and Elizabeth (Hill) Hovey, b. Oct. 29, 1833, m. in Clarksfield, Ohio, June 15, 1856, Nancy Melissa Cook, dau. of Newell and Esther Lucinda (Shattuck) Cook. She was b. in Scriba, Oswego county, N. Y., March 22, 1834. He d. in Clarksfield, Ohio, June 14, 1877. She is living (1879) in Clarksfield, Ohio.
Children:
1. Wilbert Newell,[8] b. Jan. 30, 1860.
2. Esther Elizabeth,[8] b. Dec. 19, 1870.

Abigail R. Howes,[7] eldest daughter and second child of Lucius and Lucy (Hovey) Howes, b. in Chelsea, Vt., Sept. 15, 1814, m. in Chelsea, Vt., Nov. 23, 1831, Worcester Bugbee, son of Pelatiah and Sally (Cook) Bugbee. He was b. in Chelsea, Vt., Feb. 5, 1805. Carriage maker; res. Lowell, Mass.
Children, both born in Chelsea, Vt.:
1. Charles Henry,[8] b. July 4, 1832, m. first, in Lowell, Mass., March 23, 1859, Mary Ann Dixon. Divorced. He m. second, in Lowell, Mass., Jan. 1, 1870, Mary Lovina Wheeler, dau. of Thomas and Dorcas (Sherman) Wheeler. She was b. in Wayland, Mass., Feb. 24, 1835. Child, by wife Mary Ann: 1. Charles Albert,[9] b. Jan. 8, 1860.
2. Albert Volney,[8] b. March 26, 1834, m. in Lowell, Mass., Aug. 31, 1851, Emily Susan Johnson, dau. of Perkins and Loretta (Flanders) Johnson. She was b. in Vershire, Vt., Nov. 5, 1831. Res. Lowell, Mass. Children: 1. Emma A.,[9] b. in Lawrence, Mass., Jan. 15, 1854. 2. Frank Perkins,[9] b. in Lawrence, Mass., Dec. 28, 1871.

Caroline M. Howes,[7] second daughter and third child of Lucius and Lucy (Hovey) Howes, b. in Chelsea, Vt., Jan. 26, 1817, m. first, in Lowell, Mass., May 18, 1839, Joseph Moore, son of Joseph and Mary (Sherman) Moore. He was b. in Wayland, Mass., Feb. 15, 1812; d. in Lowell,

Mass., Nov. 11, 1876. Engineer. They had no children. She m. second, in Lowell, Mass., June —, 1878, Anford Coburn, parentage, etc., not ascertained. Res. Lowell, Mass.

Nancy A. Howes,[7] youngest daughter and fourth child of Lucius and Lucy (Hovey) Howes, b. in Randolph, Vt., Nov. 13, 1819, m. in Lowell, Mass., March 10, 1843, Ora Kimball Goodale, son of Amos and Eunice (Crane) Goodale. He was b. in Stoddard, N. H., Dec. 20, 1814; d. in Medford, Mass., Jan. 14, 1871. She is living (1878) in Medford.
Children were two only, both born in Lowell, Mass.:
1. George Lucius,[8] b. March 7, 1844, m. in Medford, Mass., Jan. 7, 1868, Mary Susan Goldthwait, dau. of Joseph Lorraine and Lydia Ann (Newcomb) Goldthwait. She was b. in Chelsea, Vt., May 20, 1845. He is a book-keeper, with Joseph Nickerson & Co., Boston; res. Medford, Mass. Children: 1. Agnes Goldthwait,[9] b. in Medford, June 20, 1871. 2. Carrie Louise,[9] b. in Medford, Jan. 8, 1876. 3. and 4. (twins.) Joseph Goldthwait,[9] b. May 16, 1879; d. same day. George Mortimer,[9] b. May 16, 1879.
2. Joseph Moore,[5] b. Dec. 17, 1848, m. in Medford, Mass., Feb. 19, 1873, Carrie Almedia Floyd, dau. of Joshua Gleason and Susan (Peirce) Floyd. She was b. in Medford, March 25, 1847. He is a book-keeper, in Boston; res. Medford, Mass. Child: 1. Marion Floyd,[9] b. in Medford, Feb. 15, 1875.

Lucius E. Howes,[7] youngest son and child of Lucius and Lucy (Hovey) Howes, b. in Chelsea, Vt., Sept. 30, 1823, m. in Swanton, Franklin county, Vt., Jan. 22, 1843, Emily Melissa French, dau. of Isaac Hurd and Sarah (Bowers) French. She was b. in Swanton, Franklin county, Vt., June 27, 1823. He is a painter; res. Maquoketa, Iowa.
Children:
1. Silas Conant,[8] b. in Swanton, Vt., Oct. 19, 1843, m. in Maquoketa, Iowa, Feb. 8, 1863, Elizabeth Miller Rice, dau. of Andrew Benedict and Lucy Ann (Manning) Rice. She was b. in Hamburg, N.Y., Feb. 28, 1845. He is a printer. Children: 1. George Gebhart,[9] b. Aug. 11, 1864. 2. Willis Edson,[9] b. Aug. 2, 1869. 3. Son,[9] b. Aug. 25, 1875; d. Aug. 25, 1875.
2. Alonzo Ora,[8] b. Sept. 1, 1854; d. March 25, 1855.
3. Carrie Amanda,[8] b. Aug. 11, 1860, m. in Maquoketa, Iowa, Oct. 5, 1876, Arthur Percival Farr, son of Harry and Mary Ann (Crane) Farr. He was b. in Maquoketa, Iowa, Oct. 1, 1858. Shoemaker; res. Maquoketa, Iowa. No children.

The subjoined sketch of the maternal grandparents of Mrs. Ruth Hovey Sprague concludes Appendix E:

"To rescue from oblivion, even for a brief period, the memory of those we love, is a solace and a pleasure. This sentiment prompts me to pen a brief sketch of my grandmother, Abigail Cleveland, wife of Rev. Samuel Hovey. She was born in Connecticut about the year 1746, and married at the early age of seventeen, her husband being three years her senior. Their first children were born in Canterbury, Conn., from which place they removed to Lyme, N. H., and on Grant's Island, in Connecticut river, several of the youngest of thirteen children were born, and here her aged parents found a home and that tender care which only a devoted daughter can bestow.

"In 1791, the family removed to Norwich, Vt., and one year thereafter her aged mother died.

"In 1794, they removed to Brookfield, Vt., bringing with them her aged and infirm father, for whom she filially cared till his death in 1797. Few daughters have been privileged to care for a parent as she for her father, his state of mind and body requiring almost constant attention, which was given lovingly and cheerfully. Her husband was much from home, laboring with the churches in adjoining towns, holding meetings in school houses, dwelling houses and barns, for church edifices were in that new country few and far between. Her large family, which sometimes numbered sixteen persons, with the labor of clearing away forests and cultivating a large farm, manufacturing woolen and linen cloth for the family, was directed by her and her children. They planted a very large orchard, which remains to this day, built the first cider mill, and literally made the desert blossom. Many are the times she, her neighbors, and her children, have, on Sunday mornings, dressed themselves in their clean homespun clothing, and, taking their shoes in their hands, walked barefoot for miles to some neighboring town to join in public worship under the preaching of the husband, father and neighbor. No such thing as a carriage, or scarcely a decent carriage-road, was then and there known. 'Elder Hovey' never made charges for preaching, and sometimes when a nice little present was given him, he would ride his old horse towards home till he came to a home poorer than his own, then the present was sure to be left. In process of years the original log house gave place to a 'framed' one, a better barn was built, a school house soon followed, and thrifty New England homes multiplied on every side.

"Their two oldest sons they left settled in New Hampshire, and those who came as little children married and settled around them, till all the twelve (one died in infancy) had gone from their home. Subsequently two daughters and one son removed to Ohio, and one son to Indiana; three sons—Rufus C., Samuel and Alvan—settled on farms adjoining their parents; and two daughters, Abigail and Elizabeth, married brothers, Oliver and Gurdon Hibbard, and also resided near.

"Having reared all their children in habits of industry, morality and Christian principles, their old age is quiet and peaceful, as they sit in their snug little cottage, enjoying the fruit of their labor.

"Mrs. Hovey was eminently a woman of peace, possessing 'the soft answer that turneth away wrath,' always excusing when others accused; one of those who never have an enemy.

"Samuel Hovey, Esq., their sixth child, cared for them many years of their advanced age, providing them a cottage and sending their meals prepared for the table, and finally hiring a young woman (who afterwards married his son) to supply those attentions their increasing infirmities required. She often said, 'Samuel's wife could not be kinder to me if she were my own daughter.' On one occasion, their school house having been burned, a school meeting was held in her dwelling house to agree upon a site for rebuilding. In the course of some controversy on the subject her son Abiel exclaimed, 'It makes my blood boil!' 'Ah!' said his mother, 'It is Hovey: he can't help it.'

"Elder Hovey continued to preach to extreme old age, and I have his picture distinctly before my mind's eye, standing behind a table in our school house, his white hair falling over his shoulders, his ruddy face and full blue eyes; preaching to an assembly perhaps half of whom were his children and grandchildren; his little old lady of a wife sitting near him in the only chair the room could boast of, wearing her blue print dress—the best the times afforded—wearing her black bonnet, and gently waving a large black fan; the audience seated on long benches around the room. She died at the age of about 87, and he at the age of 91. The church edifice and cemetery occupy a part of what was the farm he bought on coming to Brookfield. In that most pleasant of rural burial places they sleep side by side; here sleep four of their children, and almost a multitude of their grandchildren and other relatives.

RUTH H. SPRAGUE."

F.

The following letter from Rev. C. P. Wing, D. D., of Carlisle, Pa., is given entire, hoping that its publication may lead to the discovery of these "lost tribes":

"CARLISLE, Sept. 12, 1877.

"H. G. CLEAVELAND:

"*Sir*—Yours of Aug. 30 reached my home while I was absent. I returned this week, and after consulting my notes relating to family history, I can find no one of the name of Cleaveland who has married into the Wing connection, and yet I have a vague recollection of meeting with some record of the kind among the letters in my possession. If on resuming the writing of our family history, (a work which I am expecting at some indefinite day), I should find anything on the subject, I will bear it in mind, and send you an account of it. The name of Burgess (of Maine, 1790,) occurs once or twice with respect to some distant connection. The name of *Freeman* often occurs in our genealogies. It was derived first from the Freeman family of Orleans on Cape Cod, who removed to Rochester, N. Y., which married into ours. My father, who was born at Conway, Hampshire county, Mass., had a half-brother named Freeman (by a third wife named Jane Trescott,) who settled early in life at La Mine, near Boonville, Cooper Co., Missouri, married there and had seven sons and five daughters, an account of whom I have. I had also a brother named Freeman Snow, (who was drowned in a well at Phelps, N. Y., at about the age of 22), whom my father named after the half-brother above named, and his grandmother of the Snow family. I had an uncle who resided awhile at *Wilmington*, Vermont, and afterwards at Charlemont, Franklin Co., Mass. Another uncle (James) lived at Hinsdale, Berkshire Co., Mass., who was the father of Dr. Joel Wing, an eminent physician in Albany, N. Y., who died a few years since, leaving children and grandchildren there. These are all whom I find in my notes, corresponding in any way to the "*hints*" you wrote me, and which offer anything on which to pursue the investigation. I have, however, a mass of letters and papers, that on reperusal may give some further hints, which I will give you when obtained. Should you be able to trace connection with any of those I have mentioned, or with the Wings of *Conneaut*, Ohio, of *Monroe*, Michigan, or of *Phelps*, Ontario county, New York, I should be pleased to have it communicated to me, as I am collecting all I can obtain of family history.

Yours very truly, C. P. WING."

"P. S. My mother's name was Mary Oliver, whom my father married at Conway, Mass., and who died at a town up the Muskingum, twelve miles from Marietta, Ohio, where my father then resided, but from which he removed to Phelps, N. Y., about 1815. C. P. W."

In the "Cushman family" Genealogy there is a statement that one William Cushman, son of William and Mary (Weaver) Cushman—b. in Castleton, Vt., March 6, 1772—m. in Coxsackie, Greene county, N. Y., *Betsey Cleveland*. Her parentage, however, or date and place of birth, is not given. This William Cushman was a blacksmith, and died in Castleton, Vt., in 1850, without children. His wife, after the death of her husband, went to her friends in the State of Pennsylvania, but exactly where they resided is not learned. Though possible, it is not probable, that this Betsey Cleveland was the daughter of Zenas and Eunice (Ludington) Cleveland. The compiler examined the old records of Brookfield, Vt., and in reference to Zenas Cleveland,[5] it appears that he had a son *James*, b. there, Oct. 30, 1784, and who died Aug. 10, 1786—also a daughter *Anna* (birth not recorded), who died Aug. 5, 1786; these are the "two youngest children" of Zenas, whose deaths are referred to in the letter of "Benjamin and Rachel Cleaveland" on page 10.

It also appears by the records at Brookfield, Vt., that one Zenas Cleveland sold and conveyed to Francis Thompson, Jan. 19, 1790, 74 acres of land "for the consideration of Forty pounds L. M." [lawful money.] And also, on the 8th of March, 1791, he sold and conveyed to Joseph Collins, physician, of Berlin, Vt., 160 acres of land "for the consideration of One hundred and fifty pounds L. M."

As before stated, from this date all traces of Zenas[5] and his family are lost until accidentally found by his nephew, James C. Cleveland, about 1811, in Sullivan county, N. Y. The descendants of Zenas,[5] so far as found, I was sorry to observe, had very little knowledge of even their near relatives, much less of their ancestors, paternal or maternal.

Mr. Thomas Acklam, a merchant in Bethel, Sullivan county, N. Y., writes as follows (Jan. 3, 1877), in reference to inquiries concerning the family of Zenas Cleveland, who once lived in that neighborhood: "I learn from Joseph Peck, who is 79 years old, that William Peck, his father, who has been dead nearly 40 years, leased a piece of land to Zenas Cleveland, and after remaining on it a short time, he left and went West. He recollects very well, he says, when Cleveland left, for his father bought Cleveland's horse. As to the family he thinks Cleveland had two daughters. He also says, that Zenas Cleveland worked for his father, William Peck, one summer."

Later, (Feb. 16, 1877), Mr. Acklam writes: "In regard to Zenas Cleveland, I think I have given you all the information I can. Mr. Peck says that Cleveland was a lame shoemaker, and that he had two children. Mrs. Charles DeKay, a very old lady and resident here, says she was acquainted with the family, and that Zenas Cleveland was lame and a shoemaker, had a wife and two children—a boy and a girl—and thinks the girl's name was Flora, the name of the boy she does not remember. She recollects of the family leaving for the West, but don't know to what place they went. It would appear that there was no one here they ever corresponded with. This has left it so it is difficult, if not impossible, to get any trace of descendants of the family. If you can think of anything more that I can do for you, let me know and I will attend to it."

In reference to the supposed daughter Flora, the compiler thinks it possible there were other children born to Zenas Cleveland, by wife Eunice, than those given on page 21. But bereavements and frequent removals, loss of property and straitened circumstances, operated to scatter and gradually alienate the children of this unfortunate couple, and it is almost impossible now to gather and restore the broken links of this genealogical chain worn and rusty with the dreary waste of many years. Any additional information concerning this branch, however, will be thankfully received and acknowledged by the writer.

G.

Thomas Burgess,[1] the pioneer ancestor of the "Burgess" families in New England, arrived in Salem, Mass., from England, with a young family about the year 1630, and lodged for a time at Lynn. A section of land was assigned him, July 3, 1637, in that part of Plymouth called Duxbury, but this section of land being forfeited by his removal to Sandwich the same year, it was assigned to Nicholas Robbins, Nov. 5, 1638, who made to the former occupant some remuneration for fences and culture.

In process of time he became a large landholder, and with advancing age he was called Goodman Burgess. He served the town in every office humble or honorable, from road-surveyor to deputy to the Court at Plymouth, for several successive years.

There is a charm in the fact that the patriarchal estate has never been alienated from the family. Benjamin—the founder of the commercial house of Benjamin Burgess & Sons, Boston—a lineal descendant of the sixth generation, held it in his possession, and in 1863 could point out the old cellar in which Thomas stored his fruits, and the bubbling fountain from which he drank for forty-eight years—dying Feb. 13, 1685, aged 82 years. His grave was honored with a monument slab, imported from England: "This was the only monument," says Amos Otis, Esq., "set up for any pilgrim of the first generation. Dorothy, his wife, also died in Sandwich, Mass., Feb. 27, 1687.

The descendants of Thomas Burgess, thousands in number, are dispersed from Maine to California. They are chiefly devoted to agricultural pursuits, many navigate the seas. Some are employed in the mechanic arts, and others are found in the medical, clerical and legal professions. As a race they hold fast their moral and religious integrity.—(Extracts from "*Burgess Family Genealogy*.")

The children of Thomas and Dorothy Burgess were five in number, as follows:

1. Thomas,[2] b. about 1626; d. ——.
2. John,[2] b. about 1628; d. ——, 1701.
3. Elizabeth,[2] b. about 1630; d. Sept. 26, 1717.
4. Jacob,[2] b. about 1632; d. March 17, 1719.
5. Joseph,[2] b. about 1634; d. Aug. —, 1695.

Jacob Burgess,[2] the third son of Thomas[1] helped to repair the meeting-house in 1654, and was early a member of the church. He served the town for many years in the subordinate offices of surveyor, constable, and grand juror. He took the oath of allegiance in 1657. He inherited, in behalf of his son Thomas,[3] the paternal estate in Sandwich, while the other brothers removed, Thomas,[2] to Newport, John,[2] to Yarmouth, and Joseph,[2] to Rochester. He was one of the executors of his father's will. He m. Mary, daughter of Benjamin Nye, June 1, 1670, who died June 23, 1706. He d. March 17, 1719.

Children:

1. Samuel,[3] b. March 8, 1671.
2. Ebenezer,[3] b. Oct. 2, 1673; d. May 22, 1750.
3. Jacob,[3] b. Oct. 18, 1676; d. ——, 1769.
4. Thomas,[3] b. March —, 1680; d. (probably) in 1757.
5. Benjamin,[3] b. (probably) in 1682; d. at Martha's Vineyard, in 1753.
6. Mary,[3] b. (probably) in 1684, m. Christopher Gifford, of Conway.

Ebenezer Burgess,[3] son of Jacob,[2] and Mary (Nye) Burgess, of Sandwich, Mass., b. Oct. 2, 1673, m. Mercy Lombard, dau. of Benjamin and Jane (Warren) Lombard, of Barnstable, who was b. Nov. 2, 1673, and d. Dec. 6, 1753, aged 80 years. He removed to that part of Plymouth afterwards called Wareham, and d. May 22, 1750, aged 77 years. [Jane Warren, the mother of Mercy Lombard, was the daughter of Nathaniel Warren, Esq., of Plymouth. Nath. Warren, Jr., Esq., in his will, in 1707, makes bequests to several of his kindred, among others to his niece, Mercy Lombard, wife of Ebenezer Burgess.]

Children:
1. Elizabeth,[4] b. about 1698; m. —— Jenkins.
2. Samuel,[4] b. about 1700; date of death not given.
3. Thankful,[4] b. about 1702; m. Cornelius Briggs, Dec. 29, 1729.
4. Nathaniel,[4] b. about 1704; d. young.
5. Ebenezer,[4] b. ——, 1406; d. Dec. 11, 1768, aged 62 years.
6. Benjamin,[4] b. ——, 1708; d. Sept. 18, 1748, aged 40 years.

Samuel Burgess,[4] son of Ebenezer[3] and Mercy (Lombard) Burgess, of Wareham, Mass., m. first, Jedidah Gibbs, March 30, 1732, who d. March 10, 1752. He m. second, Deborah Besse, Nov. 7, 1754.

Children, by wife Jedidah:
1. Jabez,[5] bapt. March 24, 1744.
2. Elisha,[5] bapt. March 24, 1744.
3. Abigail,[5] bapt. Jan. 3, 1745; m. E. Sampson.
4. Jedidah,[5] } bapt. Aug. 28, 1747; m. David Besse.
5. Samuel,[5] } bapt. Aug. 28, 1747; d. May 15, 1783.
6. Benjamin,[5] bapt. Jan. 25, 1749.
7. James.[6]
8. Theophilus,[6] d. in prison-ship during Revolutionary war.

by wife Deborah:
9. Deborah.[5]
10. Thankful,[5] m. John Mendall; removed to Fairfield, Me.
11. David,[5] m. Sylvia Gibbs, Oct. 3, 1797; removed to Fairfield, Me.
12. Mary,[5] m. —— Thomas.

Samuel Burgess,[5] the third son of Samuel[4] and Jedidah (Gibbs) Burgess, bapt. Aug. 28, 1747, m. Hannah Sturtevant, Jan. 8, 1771, and d. in Middleborough, Plymouth county, Mass., May 15, 1783.

Children:
1. Caleb,[6] b. about 1774; removed to Woodstock, Conn., and m. Eleanor Cleveland,[6] dau. of Zenas[5] and Eunice (Ludington) Cleveland.
2. Seth,[6] b. Feb. 12, 1776; m. Joanna Raymond.
3. Asa,[6] b. about 1779; removed to Woodstock, Conn.
4. Sarah,[6] b. about 1782; removed to Woodstock, Conn.

As will be perceived, those that now follow are descendants of Zenas Cleveland,[5] son of Benjamin Cleveland.[4]

Samuel Burgess,[1] eldest son and child of Caleb and Eleanor (Cleveland) Burgess, b. in Woodstock, Conn., Aug. 29, 1801, m. first, in Ithaca, Tompkins county, N. Y., in 1830, Hannah Loder. Parentage and date and place of birth not ascertained. She d. in 1832, and he m. second, in Bedford, Bedford county, Pa., in 1834, Elizabeth Dougherty, a native of Philadelphia, b. in 1805; d. in Belle Vernon, Fayette county, Pa., Aug. 7, 1875. He d. in Allen township, Washington county, Pa., Feb. 8, 1870. No children by second wife.

Children, by wife Hannah:

1. Diana,[8] b. ———, 1830, m. in 1845, Elisha Jenks, Jr., and had a family of six children. Both parents d. about 1859, and the children were cared for by the friends of the family in the neighborhood. 1. Park Marion,[9] b. Oct. 7, 1846, m. in Newark Valley, Tioga county, N. Y., May 18, 1866, Frances Augusta Blair, dau. of Winslow and Mary Jane (Dean) Blair. She was b. in Sullivan county, Pa., Aug. 31, 1847. He is a lumber dealer; res. Alta, Iowa. No children. 2. Sylvanus,[9] b. Sept. 10, 1848; d. Dec. 12, 1863. 3. Charles Franklin," b. Oct. 15, 1850. Salesman; res. Williamsport, Pa. 4. Celia Ann," b. July 20, 1852; m. Lorenzo F. Rockwood. Merchant; res. Berkshire, Tioga county, N. Y. 5. Amy Jane,[9] b. March 4, 1854, m. F. A. Jenks, and resides in San Francisco, Cal. 6. Elisha,[9] b. Nov. 30, 1856; d. Jan. 14, 1857.
2. Harriet," b. July 5, 1832, m. in Litchfield, Bradford county, Pa., Dec. 1, 1849, John Crotsley, son of John and Sally (Mills) Crotsley. He was b. in Barton, Tioga county, N. Y., June 17, 1825; d. in Sheshequin, Bradford county, Pa., Aug. 21, 1874. She d. in Sheshequin, Pa., Nov. 1, 1851. Child: 1. Son,[9] b. April 25, 1851; d. soon.

James Burgess,[7] second son and child of Caleb and Eleanor (Cleveland) Burgess, b. in Woodstock, Conn., April 20, 1803, m. in Ithaca, N. Y., Sept. 20, 1825, Rachel Bellows, dau. of Phillip and Elizabeth (Deshong) Bellows. She was b. in Ithaca, N. Y., Jan. 2, 1806; d. in Greenwich, Huron county, Ohio, Sept. 21, 1865. He d. in same place, Aug. 27, 1866. Farmer.

Children:

1. Harriet," b. June 20, 1838, m. in Greenwich, Huron county, Ohio, Sept. 27, 1857, Thomas Calvin Robinson, son of James and Rebecca (Jacobs) Robinson. He was b. in Bloomingdale, Richland county, Ohio, June 19, 1836. Farmer; res. Hillsdale county (White P. O.) Mich. Children: 1. Rebecca Ann,[9] b. Aug. 31, 1859. 2. Thomas Holland,[9] b. Oct. 23, 1861. 3. James Burgess,[9] b. Dec. 30, 1864. 4. William Orval," b. June 27, 1873.
2. Adaline,[8] b. June 13, 1842, m. in Mansfield, Richland county, Ohio, Oct. 31, 1861, William Stahl, son of John and Catherine (Folmer) Stahl. He was b. in Ashland county, Ohio, May 5, 1840. Farmer; res. Hillsdale county, (White P. O.) Mich. No children.
3. Emeline,[8] b. Jan. 17, 1846, m. in Ashland, Ashland county, Ohio, Oct. 28, 1865, Jacob Wiedler, son of John and Susan (Croup) Wiedler. He was b. in Clarence, Erie county, N. Y., Oct. 18, 1843. Farmer; res. Camden, Hillsdale county, Mich. Children: 1. Francis Elbert,[9] b. Oct. 17, 1866. 2. Addie May," b. Feb. 2, 1873.
4. Sarah Ann,[8] b. April 24, 1848; d. Feb. 10, 1866.

Eunice Burgess,[7] the second daughter and fourth child of Caleb and Eleanor (Cleveland) Burgess, b. in Hartford, Conn., July 20, 1808, m. in Bainbridge, Chenango county, N. Y., May 30, 1826, Hiram Hallett, son of Solomon and Phebe (Mosier) Hallett. He was b. in Schoharie, N. Y., Dec. 1, 1805; d. in Lycoming county, Pa., Feb. 11, 1856. She is living (1878) in White Pine, Lycoming county, Pa.

Children:

1. Didama,[8] b. in Bainbridge, Chenango county, N. Y., Jan. 19, 1828, m. in Ithaca, N. Y., July 4, 1845, Benjamin Jennings Williams, son of Nelson and Abiah (Jennings) Williams. He was b. in Danby, N. Y., April 10, 1824; d. in Danby, N. Y., Aug. —, 1877. She d. in Cuyahoga Falls, Ohio, Nov. 9, 1849. Child: 1. George,[9] b. Nov. 5, 1849; d. Feb. —, 1850. (A Mr. Powell, who knew the family, states that the infant lived only *seven days*.)
2. Son,[8] b. Aug. 12, 1830; d. Aug. 12, 1830.
3. Rosalia,[8] b. in Sidney, N. Y., May 16, 1832, m. in Ithaca, N. Y., Dec. 15, 1851, William S. Cronk, son of Timothy and Elizabeth (Gould) Cronk. He was b. in Ulysses, Tompkins county, N. Y., Dec. 19, 1827. She d. in Ithaca, N. Y., March 1, 1854. He is living (1878) in San Buenaventura, Ventura county, Cal. Child: 1. Homer Gerard,[9] b. in Ithaca, N. Y., Oct. 5, 1852.
4. Harriet,[8] b. in Jackson, Tioga county, Pa., Oct. 12, 1833, m. in Candor, Tioga county, N. Y., Feb. 2, 1850, James Edmund McLoskey, son of Zopher Tidd and Catherine Elizabeth (Boyce) McLoskey. He was b. in Slaterville, Tompkins county, N. Y., June 11, 1829. Blacksmith; res. Beaver Dams, Schuyler county, N. Y. Child: 1. Frances Evelyn,[9] b. Oct. 31, 1857.
5. Arthur,[8] b. in Jackson, Tioga county, Pa., July 15, 1835, m. in Liberty, Tioga county, Pa., July 5, 1857, Margaret Magdalena Gluckner, dau. of Jacob and Catherine Gluckner. She was b. in Liberty township, Pa., June 26, 1835. Children: 1. Charlotte Eveline,[9] b. Jan. 13, 1858, m. in Lycoming county, Pa., March 4, 1876, Ellis Mesner, son of John and Minerva (Ellis) Mesner. He was b. in Tioga county, Pa., Nov. 13, 1854. Child: 1. Madie Minerva,[10] b. Dec. 30, 1876. 2. Clarence Eugene,[9] b. Oct. 28, 1859. 3. William Ellsworth,[9] b. May 10, 1864. 4. Minnie Gay,[9] b. Jan. 4, 1866. 5. Franklin May,[9] b. Nov. 1, 1870.
6. Harvey,[8] b. in Jackson, Tioga county, Pa., March 26, 1837, m. in ———, Mary Shoup, parentage, birth, etc., unknown, or present residence. He resided for some time in Butler, Pa., and then left there for Petrolia, Pa., since which nothing has been heard from him. They have one child, name not ascertained.
   Inman,[8] b. in Jackson, Tioga county, Pa., Aug. 7, 1838, m. in Oil City, Venango county, Pa., Oct. 20, 1865, Katherine Saddler, parentage unlearned. She was b. in Slippery Rock township, Butler county, Pa., March 2, 1844. Res. Oil City, Pa. Children: 1. William Henry,[9] b. Aug. 26, 1866; d. Jan. 28, 1868. 2. Emma Jane,[9] b. Jan. 23, 1869. 3. Hiram Harvey,[9] b. Feb. 11, 1871. 4. Nancy Ann,[9] b. Sept. 14, 1873. 5. and 6. (twins.) Maggie Lydia,[9] and Rosie Lavinia,[9] b. March 4, 1876; the latter d. Jan. 6, 1877.
   Eleanor,[8] b. in Jackson, Tioga county, Pa., March 26, 1840; m. in Jersey Shore township, Lycoming county, Pa., June 17, 1857, Joseph McCollum, son of Joseph and Elizabeth (Douglass) McCollum. He was b. in Chester county, Pa., Oct. 24, 1831. Res. Watsonville, Santa Cruz county, Cal. Children: 1. John Wesley,[9] b. April 8, 1858. 2. Edward Douglass,[9] b. Sept. 29, 1860. 3. Eleanor Cleveland,[9] b. Jan. 4, 1864.

9. Newton,[8] b. in Ithaca, Tompkins county, N. Y., April 16, 1842, m. in Pittsburgh, Pa., Aug. 13, 1868, Margaret Gill, dau. of James and Martha (Dalzell) Gill. She was b. in Indiana township, Alleghany county, Pa., Dec. 2, 1845. Res. Sharpsburg, Pa. Children: 1. James Edwin,[9] b. April 12, 1869. 2. Samuel Harvey,[9] b. March 16, 1871. 3. Son,[9] b. Feb. 21, 1873; d. Feb. 21, 1873. 4. Robert Newton,[9] b. April 18, 1874. 5. Alice May,[9] b. Aug. 9, 1876.
10. Jane,[8] b. in Danby, N. Y., Feb. 26, 1844, m. in Salladyburgh, Lycoming county, Pa., Feb. 26, 1862, Godfrey Decker, son of Frederic and Elizabeth Decker. He was b. in Rugel, Germany, Nov. 15, 1840. Farmer; res. White Pine, Lycoming county, Pa. Children: 1. Eugene Alberto,[9] b. May 4, 1865. 2. Maud Mary,[9] b. Dec. 25, 1868. 3. Frederic,[9] b. July 8, 1871. 4. Anna May,[9] b. Sept. 8, 1873. 5. Arthur Godfrey,[9] b. July 8, 1875.
11. Ann Eliza,[8] b. in Spencer, Tompkins county, N. Y., Feb. 8, 1846, m. in Salladyburgh, Pa., Nov. 2, 1863, George Henry Sellinger, son of Barnhardt and Matilda (Young) Sellinger. He was b. in Lycoming county, Pa., July 31, 1840. Res. Grand Rapids, Mich. Children: 1. Cora Belle,[9] b. Aug. 26, 1864. 2. Elmer Mechlin,[9] b. Sept. 6, 1869. 3. Flora Delia,[9] b. Aug. 21, 1871.

Hannah Burgess,[7] third daughter and fifth child of Caleb and Eleanor (Cleveland) Burgess, b. in Hartford, Conn., Aug. 24, 1811, m. first, in Ithaca, N. Y., April 19, 1834, John DeGraw, son of John and Margaret (Benjamin) DeGraw. He was b. in New York City, Oct. 4, 1807. Occupation, hatter. Divorced in 1865. She m. second, in Hudson, Summit county, Ohio, Nov. 28, 1865, Moses Draper, son of Jonathan and Patience (Benjamin) Draper. He was b. in Whitehall, Washington county, N. Y., May 3, 1796; d. in Hudson, Ohio, July 7, 1873. Farmer. She is living (1878) in Hudson, Ohio.
Children, by first husband, John DeGraw:
1. Emeline,[8] b. in Ithaca, N. Y., June 19, 1835; d. Feb. 14, 1866, unm.
2. Eleanor,[8] b. in Ithaca, N. Y., Jan. 29, 1837. Dressmaker; res. Hudson, Ohio.
3. Margaret,[8] b. in Ithaca, N. Y., Aug. 29, 1838; d. July 26, 1840.
4. Elenora,[8] b. in Ithaca, N. Y., June 8, 1840.
5. Charles Henry,[8] b. in Owasco, N. Y., Aug. 16, 1842, m. in Sharon, Mercer county, Pa., July 27, 1870, Maria Davis, dau. of David and Mary (Davis) Davis. She was b. in Fallston, Beaver county, Pa., Oct. 17, 1849. He is a shoemaker; res. Mercer, Pa. (He served in the 38rd Regt. N. Y. V. M., and was discharged July 26, 1863.) Children, all born in Sharon, Pa. 1. Maud Ellen,[9] b. May 1, 1872. 2. Clifton Evelyn,[9] b. April 23, 1874. 3. William Jesse,[9] b. March 18, 1876; d. May 7, 1876.
6. Orpha Ann,[8] b. in Mount Morris, N. Y., Feb. 28, 1844, m. in Oakland, N. Y., Oct. 26, 1860, George Benjamin, son of Samuel and Jane (DeGraw) Benjamin. He was b. in Paterson, N. J., May 10, 1821. Cabinet maker; res. Brownsville, Ohio. Children: 1. Willard Washington,[9] b. in Hudson, Ohio, Feb. 22, 1863. 2. Charles Clifford,[9] b. in Millersburg, Ohio, Jan. 23, 1866. 3. Edward John,[9] b. in Cleveland, Ohio, March 25, 1872. 4. Eliza Mary,[9] b. in Brownsville, Ohio, March 22, 1874.
7. Martha Jane,[8] b. in Nunda, N. Y., Jan. 16, 1846, m. in Hudson, Ohio, Aug. 18, 1869, Edward Blackman, son of Joseph and Ann (Phillips) Blackman. He was b. in Mount Vernon, Knox county, Ohio, April 29, 1843. Merchant's clerk and salesman; res. Hudson, Ohio. Children: 1. Frederic William,[9] b. Aug. 8, 1870. 2. Grace Maud,[9] b. June 24, 1874. 3. Charles Edward,[9] b. July 2, 1877.

8. William Willis,² b. in Jamestown, N. Y., July 30, 1849.
9. Mary Geneva,³ b. in Jamestown, N. Y., July 4, 1851.
10. George Hamilton,³ b. in Warsaw, N. Y., July 21, 1853.

William C. Burgess,⁷ third son and sixth child of Caleb and Eleanor (Cleveland) Burgess, b. in Ithaca, Tompkins county, N. Y., Oct. 14, 1813, m. in Springfield, Bradford county, Pa., May 1, 1834, Mariette Burgess, dau. of Charles and Anna (Parmenter) Burgess. She was b. in Bridgeport, Susquehanna county, Pa., Nov. 13, 1815. He is a lumber dealer, etc.; res. Springfield, Pa.

Children, all b. in Springfield:

1. Nancy Amelia,⁸ b. July 25, 1840, m. in Springfield, Pa., Dec. 28, 1858, Orrin Clark Horton, son of Hiram and Hannah (Hovey) Horton. He was b. in Ulster, Bradford county, Pa., March 1, 1835. She d. in Mainesburgh, Pa., July 16, 1873. He is living in Hammond, Pa. Miller. Children: 1. Frank Ellsworth,⁹ b. in Burlington, Pa., June 12, 1861. 2. Frederic Arthur,⁹ b. in Burlington, Pa., Nov. 17, 1863; d. young. 3. Orrin Ardell,⁹ b. in Canton, Pa., Aug. 16, 1865. 4. Clarence Edward,⁹ b. in Canton, Pa., Oct. 18, 1867. 5. Martha Ellen,⁹ b. in Lockington, Ohio, March 25, 1872; d. young.
2. Eleanor Ann,⁸ b. Jan. 11, 1843, m. in Rossville, Bradford county, Pa., Aug. 18, 1861, Miles Brunson Potter, son of Elisha and Minerva (Moore) Potter. He was b. in Columbia, Pa., Sept. 29, 1841. Cabinet maker; res. Hood River, Wasco county, Oregon. Children: 1. Ida May,⁹ b. in Springfield, Pa., July 7, 1862. 2. William Burgess,⁹ b. in Canton, Pa., Jan. 29, 1870. 3. Harriet Minerva,⁹ b. in Canton, Pa., June 15, 1873.
3. Edward Parmenter,⁸ b. April 23, 1845; d. March 5, 1865.

Eleanor Burgess,⁷ youngest daughter and child of Caleb and Eleanor (Cleveland) Burgess, b. in Ithaca, Tompkins county, N. Y., May 29, 1819, m. in Litchfield, Bradford county, Pa., Aug. 23, 1834, Frederic Swartwood, son of James and Mary (Schoonover) Swartwood. He was b. in Owego, Tioga county, N. Y., March 20, 1813; d. in Mitchell Creek township, Tioga county, Pa., Dec. 26, 1877. She is living (1878) in Mitchell creek, Pa.

Children:

1. Julia Ellen,⁸ b. in Athens, Pa., Nov. 23, 1836, m. in Erwin, Steuben county, N. Y., Sept. 17, 1853, Julius Emmer Kirkendall, son of Henry Peter and Amanda (Ellston) Kirkendall. He was b. in Barton, Tioga county, N. Y., Sept. 30, 1831. Farmer; res. Somers Lane, Pa. Children, all b. in Lawrence, Pa.: 1. Mary Belle,⁹ b. July 18, 1861. 2. Frederic Henry,⁹ b. Aug. 2, 1866. 3. Daniel Keep,⁹ b. Aug. 29, 1868. 4. Herbert Lee,⁹ b. Sept. 26, 1872.
2. Emily,⁸ b. in Tioga, N. Y., Jan. 6, 1838, m. in Erwin (Painted Post) Steuben county, N. Y., Dec. 31, 1857, Erastus Kirkendall, son of Henry Peter and Amanda (Ellston) Kirkendall. He was b. in Barton, Tioga county, N. Y., Sept. 4, 1836. Carpenter; res. Corning, N. Y. Children: 1. Martha Annette,⁹ b. in Lawrence, Pa., Aug. 30, 1860; d. Jan. 24, 1864. 2. Albert Erastus,⁹ b. in Tioga, Pa., July 24, 1862; d. Feb. 15, 1864. 3. Florence Actell,⁹ b. June 30, 1865; d. Feb. 24, 1872. 4. Rufus Elmer,⁹ b. Sept. 6, 1867. 5. Miles Henry,⁹ b. Jan. 1, 1872; d. March 15, 1873. 6. Horace Cassady,⁹ b. July 31, 1875.

3. Lucetta,[7] b. in Tioga, N. Y., March 17, 1841, m. in Bradford, McKean county, Pa., Nov. 10, 1861, Charles Henry Carleton, son of Philo N. and Rachel (Thompson) Carleton. He was b. in Spafford, Onondaga county, N. Y., Feb. 15, 1840. Carpenter; res. Mitchell Creek, Pa. Children: 1. Jessie May,[9] b. in Corning, N. Y., Aug. 5, 1866. 2. Arthur Henry,[9] b. in Middleton, Pa., March 29, 1871. 3. Frank,[9] b. in Mitchell Creek, Pa., May 24, 1878.
4. Jane,[8] b. in Tioga, N. Y., May 9, 1844, m. in Wellsboro', Pa., Oct. 26, 1867, DeVere Shappee, son of Abner and Mary (Parker) Shappee. He was b. in Jackson, Tioga county, Pa., Feb. 12, 1848. Painter; res. Tioga, Pa. Children: 1. Howard Abner,[9] b. Nov. 8, 1868. 2. Grace Myrtle,[9] b. Sept. 13, 1871; d. Nov. 3, 1874. 3. Carrie May,[9] b. Feb. 21, 1874. 4. Leon Delos,[9] b. June 4, 1876.
5. Ruth,[8] b. in Burlington, Bradford county, Pa., Oct. 12, 1846, m. in Hornellsville, Steuben county, N. Y., July 3, 1868, Schuyler Beers, son of Joseph Husten and Maria (Beers) Beers. He was b. in Wells, Bradford county, Pa., Jan. 13, 1842. Railroad employe; res. Mitchell Creek, Pa. Children: 1. Frederic Husten,[9] b. May 13, 1870; d. Sept. 9, 1874. 2. Ella Maria,[9] b. March 2, 1873.
6. Horace Frederic,[8] b. in Lawrence, Pa., March 16, 1849, m. in Corning, N. Y., Dec. 23, 1872, Fannie Jane Gregory, dau. of Daniel Warner and Emeline Joanna (Hayford) Gregory. She was b. in Kanona, Steuben county, N. Y., April 5, 1856. He is a farmer; res. Tioga, Pa. Child: 1. Sidney,[9] b. May 9, 1877.
7. Harriet,[8] b. in Tioga, Pa., Aug. 14, 1853; d. Feb. 28, 1864.
8. Henry Burgess,[8] b. in Tioga, Pa., Oct. 5, 1861; d. March 10, 1864.

Miriam Hallett,[7] eldest daughter and child of Solomon and Eleanor (Cleveland) [Burgess] Hallett, b. in Bainbridge, Chenango county, N. Y., Jan. 31, 1822, m. in Afton, Chenango county, N. Y., Oct. 5, 1848, Albert Rounds, son of Phillip and Betsey (Smith) Rounds. He was b. in Foster, Providence county, R. I., Jan. 14, 1810. Farmer; res. Afton, Chenango county, N. Y.
Children :

1. Alvah Bush,[8] b. in Afton, N. Y., Jan. 9, 1850, m. in Binghamton, N. Y., Aug. 14, 1874, Catherine Owens, dau. of John J. and Catherine (Snyder) Owens. She was b. in Vallonia Springs, Broome county, N. Y., June 14, 1859. Children: 1. Jessie,[9] b. Aug. 16, 1875; d. Sept. 15, 1875. 2. Arthur,[9] b. March 5, 1877.
2. Ellen Josephine,[8] b. April 15, 1853.
3. Mary Ann,[8] b. Dec. 29, 1857.

Sarah Jane Hallett,[7] youngest child of Solomon and Eleanor (Cleveland [Burgess] Hallett, b. in Bainbridge, Chenango county, N. Y., July 14, 1828, m. in Bainbridge, N. Y., Nov. 2, 1848, Nelson Cook, son of John and Rhoda (Woodruff) Cook. He was b. in Franklin, Delaware county, N. Y., Aug. 28, 1812; d. in Afton, N. Y., May 29, 1873.
Children :

1. Austin,[8] b. Jan. 18, 1850 ; d. March 1, 1850.
2. William,[8] b. June 30, 1853.
3. James,[8] b. July 22, 1867.

H.

Roswell Shepard,[1] eldest son and child of Roswell and Polly (Hamblin) Shepard, b. in Brookfield, Vt., July 9, 1799, m. in Lowell, Vt., Dec. 6, 1821, Lydia Sprague, dau. of Hosea and Elizabeth (Charles) Sprague. She was b. in Brimfield, Mass., July 28, 1798. He d. in Palestine, Pickaway county, Ohio, Sept. 4, 1851. She is living (1878) with her son Henry, in Shadesville, Franklin county, Ohio.

Children:

1. Hamblin,[8] b. in Lowell, Vt., Sept. 3, 1822, m. in Strawtown, Hamilton county, Ind., Dec. 9, 1855, Eliza Reynolds, dau. of Francis Garner and Jane (Lutz) Reynolds. She was b. near Urbana, Champaign county, Ohio, Sept. 12, 1831. He was murdered at Elysian Grove Plantation, in Shreveport, La., Feb. 27, 1867. Merchant. His widow is living (1877) in Noblesville, Ind. Children, all b. near Perkinsville, Hamilton county, Ind.: 1. Alma Elizabeth,[9] b. Oct. 6, 1856; d. in Noblesville, Ind., Oct. 16, 1873. 2. Son,[9] b. July 20, 1858; d. July 20, 1858. 3. Son,[9] b. Sept. 29, 1860; d. Sept. 29, 1860. 4. Eva Belle,[9] b. May 7, 1862.
2. Matilda Elizabeth,[8] b. in Montpelier, Vt., Sept. 30, 1824, m. in Homer, Courtland county, N. Y., July 19, 1847, George Hetherington, son of John and Jane (Coffman) Hetherington. He was b. in Hardy county, Va., June 28, 1818. Farmer; was Auditor of Pickaway county, Ohio, for several years, and now Auditor of Moultrie county, Ill.; res. Lovington, Ill. Children: 1. Charles Shepard,[9] b. July 8, 1848; d. Aug. 12, 1848. 2. Henry Shepard,[9] b. Oct. 20, 1849; d. Aug. 9, 1871.
3. Henry Campbell,[8] b. in Montpelier, Vt., May 11, 1826, m. in Columbus, Ohio, Dec. 11, 1862, Jennie Armstrong, dau. of William and Jane (Delano) Armstrong. She was b. in Columbus, Ohio, Dec. 3, 1835; d. in Pine Grove, Pickaway county, Ohio, Aug. 22, 1867. He resides in Shadesville, Ohio. Children: 1. Henry Delano,[9] b. April 13, 1864. 2. William Armstrong,[9] b. Oct. 19, 1866.
4. Newman Sprague,[8] b. in Barre, Vt., July 19, 1828; d. in Barre, Vt., March 20, 1830.
5. Charles Sprague,[8] b. in Barre, Vt., Sept. 7, 1830, m. in Mt. Sterling, Madison county, Ohio, July 1, 1851, Sarah Margaret Creath, dau. of William and Mary (Monohon) Creath. She was b. near Mt. Sterling, Ohio, Dec. 22, 1831. He is a farmer; res. Sullivan, Ill. Children: 1. Matilda Elizabeth,[9] b. in Pickaway county, Ohio, March 7, 1853; d. in Washington county, Iowa, June 20, 1858. 2. Mary Arabella,[9] b. in Pickaway county, Ohio, May 20, 1855. 3. Henry Sprague,[9] b. in Washington county, Iowa, Feb. 11, 1858. 4. William Langdon,[9] b. in Washington county, Iowa, Nov. 16, 1859. 5. Fannie May,[9] b. in Washington county, Iowa, Aug. 1, 1861. 6. Ann Elma,[9] b. in Washington county, Iowa, March 20, 1863. 7. Charles Hamblin,[9] b. in Washington county, Iowa, Nov. 1, 1864. 8. Lydia Ellen,[9] b. in Washington county, Iowa, May 15, 1866. 9. John Creath,[9] b. in Washington county, Iowa, March 4, 1868. 10. Solomon White,[9] b. in Washington county, Iowa, Oct. 24, 1870. 11. Sarah Margaret,[9] b. in Washington county, Iowa, Oct. 8, 1871.

Betsey H. Shepard,[1] eldest daughter and second child of Roswell and Polly (Hamblin) Shepard, b. in Brookfield, Vt., June 1, 1801, m. in

Alstead, N. H., June 10, 1827, Wilson Darte, son of Jesse and Susan (Capen) Darte. He was b. in Keene, Essex county, N. Y., Sept. 18, 1805. Farmer; res. Hardwick (Greenwich P. O.). Mass.
Children, all b. in Alstead, N. H.:

1. Mary Julia,[8] b. Sept. 20, 1828, m. in Hardwick, Mass., March 10, 1847, Albert Alvin Cleveland, son of Joseph and Bathsheba (Burgess) Cleveland. He was b. in Hardwick, Mass., May 22, 1821. Farmer; res. Barre, Mass. Children: 1. Wilson Albert,[9] b. in Hardwick, Mass., May 18, 1848, m. in Barre, Mass., Feb. 28, 1865, Laura Jane Watson, dau. of Charles Henry and Jane Elizabeth (Prior) Watson. She was b. in Pensacola, Fla., Aug. 5, 1847. Children: 1. Lena Maria,[10] b. in New Salem, Mass., Nov. 10, 1866. 2. Charles Wilson,[10] b. in Perth Amboy, N. J., Dec. 14, 1869; d. Feb. 8, 1870. 3. Henry Warren Sumner,[10] b. in Hardwick, Mass., Aug. 15, 1871. 4. Minnie Ethel,[10] b. in Staten Island, N. Y., Sept. 8, 1875. 2. Vernett Elijah,[9] b. in Barre, Mass., Oct. 11, 1857. 3. Louella Julia,[9] b. in Barre, Mass., June 9, 1867.
2. William Elliott,[8] b. Aug. 16, 1830, m. in Enfield, Mass., March 31, 1858, Charlotte Sabin Whipple, dau. of Joel and Eunice (Richardson) Whipple. She was b. in Greenwich, Mass., Jan. 4, 1838. He is a farmer; res. Hardwick, Mass. No children.
3. Sumner Luman,[8] b. Aug. 22, 1833, m. in Enfield, Mass., Feb. 22, 1854, Harriet E. Woods, dau. of Aaron and Caroline M. (Ellis) Woods. She was b. in Enfield, Mass., Feb. 28, 1830. He d. June 9, 1858. Farmer. No children.
4. Alvin Wilson,[8] b. Oct. 24, 1842, m. in Petersham, Worcester county, Mass., May 27, 1874, Sarah Jane Cook, dau. of Ellison and Mary (Loring) Cook. She was b. in Petersham, Mass., Nov. 25, 1847. He is a farmer; res. Petersham, Mass. No children.

Hiram Shepard,[7] second son and third child of Roswell and Polly (Hamblin) Shepard, b. in Brookfield, Vt., July 4, 1803, m. first, in Chelsea, Vt., Dec. 3, 1829, Harriet Spiller, dau. of Joseph and Dorothy (Stevens) Spiller. She was b. in Chelsea, Vt., Aug. 8, 1810; d. in Barre, Vt., Feb. 17, 1843. He m. second, in Chelsea, Vt., Feb. 18, 1845, Lura Bixby, dau. of Ichabod and Susan (Lewis) Bixby. She was b. in Chelsea, Vt., May 27, 1814. He is a farmer; res. Barre, Vt.
Children, by wife Harriet:

1. Harriet,[8] b. Oct. 14, 1830; d. March 18, 1834.
2. George Newcomb,[8] b. Jan. 14, 1835; d. May 14, 1855.
3. Mary Ann,[8] b. Dec. 10, 1837; d. Feb. 21, 1839.

   by wife Lura:

4. Wilbur,[8] b. Aug. 13, 1848, m. in Barre, Vt., Dec. 6, 1871, Ida Jerusha Woods, dau. of Luther Prentiss and Edna (Town) Woods. She was b. in Barre, Vt., May 24, 1849. Child: 1. George Dan,[9] b. Nov. 4, 1876; d. Nov. 9, 1876.

Simeon Shepard,[7] third son and fourth child of Roswell and Polly (Hamblin) Shepard, b. in Brookfield, Vt., Jan. 4, 1806, m. first, in Brookfield, April 12, 1834, Roxana Paine, dau. of Storrs and Sally (Green) Paine. She was b. in Brookfield, Dec. 28, 1811; d. in Barre, Vt., Dec. 1, 1838. He m. second, in Williamstown, Vt., March 31, 1839, Harriet Martin, dau. of Gurdon and Sarah (Wise) Martin. She was b. in

Williamstown, Vt., Feb. 21, 1814. He d. in Barre, Vt., Dec. 31, 1873. Farmer. She is living in Barre, Vt.

Children:

1. Roxana Lucy,[5] b. Aug. 10, 1840; d. Sept. 10, 1860.
2. Lydia Martin,[5] b. June 18, 1844, m. in Barre, Vt., March 10, 1869, Harrison Bancroft, son of Chester and Susannah (Rice) Bancroft. He was b. in Barre, Sept. 28, 1829. Farmer; res. Barre, Vt. Children: 1. Ellen Frances,[9] b. Nov. 24, 1871; d. Nov. 16, 1876. 2. Harriet Sarah,[9] b. June 23, 1873.
3. Almon Clark,[5] b. Sept. 8, 1848, m. in Williamstown, Vt., Dec. 8, 1875, Alice Celecta Smith, dau. of Hiram Fish and Susan Cordelia (Edson) Smith. She was b. in Barre, Vt., Nov. 8, 1859. Res. Barre, Vt.

Joel H. Shepard,[7] youngest son and child of Roswell and Polly (Hamblin) Shepard, b. in Brookfield, Vt., Feb. 13, 1808, m. in Williamstown, Vt., June 22, 1830, Clarissa Martin, dau. of Jonathan and Susanna (Martyn) Martin. She was b. in Williamstown, Vt., Feb. 11, 1810. He is a farmer, and a prominent citizen of Williamstown, Vt.

Children, all b. in Williamstown:

1. William,[8] b. Feb. 22, 1832, m. in Barre, Vt., Dec. 8, 1858, Frances Rebecca Waterman, dau. of Lewis and Fanny (Averill) Waterman. She was b. in Barre, Vt., Oct. 29, 1834. He d. in Williamstown, Vt., Jan. 10, 1865. No children.
2. Eunice,[8] b. Nov. 18, 1836, m. in Williamstown, Vt., Dec. 10, 1854, Crawford Henry Jackson, son of Henry and Abigail (Bruce) Jackson. He was b. in Troy, Cheshire county, N. H., April 7, 1830. Farmer; res. Barre, Vt. Children: 1. Clara Abbie,[9] b. in Williamstown, Vt., Oct. 5, 1857. 2. Frank William,[9] b. in Barre, Vt., July 23, 1866. 3. Ellen Eliza,[9] b. in Williamstown, Vt., Jan. 31, 1872. 4. Ida May,[9] b. in Barre, Vt., Feb. 9, 1875.
3. Rosina,[8] b. Dec. 12, 1845, m. in Williamstown, Vt., Oct. 22, 1867, Gilbert Orman Smith, son of Alvin Fuller and Susan (Lewis) Smith. He was b. in Northfield, Vt., Nov. 13, 1843. Farmer; res. Williamstown, Vt. Children, all b. in Williamstown: 1. Bertie Leon,[9] b. Jan. 1, 1869; d. Jan. 22, 1869. 2. Nettie Lillian,[9] b. Dec. 12, 1871; d. Dec. 27, 1871. 3. Arthur Gilbert,[9] b. April 15, 1873.

Elijah M. Clifford,[7] eldest son of Samuel and Betsey (Hamblin) Clifford, b. in Danbury, N. H., April 24, 1807, m. first, in Hollister, Mass., Mrs. Julia (Moore) Leland, dau. of William and Sally (Rice) Moore. She was b. in Rutland, Mass., ———, 1810; date of death not learned. He m. second, in Warren, Mass., May 2, 1855, Mrs. Cornelia (Nutting) Shaw, dau. of James and Rachel (Ward) Nutting. She was b. in Brimfield, Mass., Feb. 7, 1821, and is living (1877) in Alton, Ill. He d. in Alton, of pneumonia, Sept. 23, 1875. No children.

Oliver H. Clifford,[7] second son and child of Samuel and Betsey (Hamblin) Clifford, b. in Danbury, N. H., Jan. 18, 1809, m. in Medfield, Mass., Sept. 29, 1838, Elizabeth Mason, dau. of Joseph and Sally

(Foster) Mason. She was b. in Princeton, Mass., Jan. 20, 1816. Res. Medfield, Mass.
Children, all b. in Medfield:
1. Joseph Clark,[8] b. Sept. 10, 1839, m. in Deerfield, Mass., Sept. 10. 1862, Mary Elizabeth Conditt, dau. of Uzziel Wade and Martha Emeline (Van Houten) Conditt. She was b. in Orange, N. J., June 12, 1840. Res. Rock Island, Ill. Child: 1. Charles Conditt,[9] b. in Fortress Monroe, Va., Feb. 17, 1866.
2. Alfred,[8] b. Feb. 11, 1845, m. in St. Louis, Mo., Nov. 20, 1877, Mary Frances Morton, dau. of Hon. John Tillson and Mary Frances (Wyman) Morton, of Topeka, Kan. She was b. in Mount Pleasant, Iowa, April 7, 1850. He is Secretary of the Ludlow-Saylor Wire Company. Res. St. Louis, Mo.

William P. Clifford,[7] third son and fifth child of Samuel and Betsey (Hamblin) Clifford, b. in Danbury, N. H., Sept. 24, 1814. m. first, in Ware, Mass., April 18, 1849, Abigail Green, dau. of John A. and Abigail (Maynard) Green. She was b. in Warwick, Mass., Dec. 9, 1820; d. in Ashland, Mass., June 4, 1850. He m. second, in Ware, Mass., Jan. 7, 1851, Sarah Croft, dau. of Joseph and Chloe (Collins) Croft. She was b. in Warren, Mass., Oct. 14, 1815. He is a carpenter; res. Ware, Mass. No children.

Lorena Clifford,[7] fourth daughter and youngest child of Samuel and Betsey (Hamblin) Clifford, b. in Danbury, N. H., July 4, 1825, m. in Framingham, Mass., Sept. 6, 1851, Luke Wilbur Dean, son of Colburn and Mary (Wilbur) Dean. He was b. in Framingham, Mass., May 27, 1827. Mechanic; res. Waltham, Mass. No children.

Orilla Hamblin,[7] eldest daughter and child of Joel and Phila (Maxfield) Hamblin, b. in Brookfield, Vt., Jan. 6, 1837, m. in Montpelier, Vt., Jan. 25, 1855, Geo. W. Freeman, son of Ralph and Electa C. (Hawes) Freeman. He was b. in Brookfield, Vt., Dec. 3, 1830. Farmer; res. North Montpelier, Vt. No children. Theodotia Hamblin[6] is living (1879) with this family, in her 95th year.

Ellen Hamblin,[7] youngest daughter and child of Joel and Phila (Maxfield) Hamblin, b. in Brookfield, Vt., May 30, 1839, m. in Hardwick, Vt., Oct. 17, 1862, Isadore Fox, son of John and Ellen (Riley) Fox. He was b. in Plattsburg, N. Y., Feb. 6, 1836. Farmer; res. Boonsboro', Iowa. No children.

James M. Hamblin,[7] only son of James and Lovisa (Bigelow) Hamblin, b. in Brookfield, Vt., April 30, 1829, m. first, in Brookfield, Vt., Feb. 27, 1856, Caroline Annis, dau. of Jesse and Charity (Spiller) Annis. She was b. in Chelsea, Vt., Feb. 14, 1832; d. in Brookfield, Vt., Sept. 30, 1863. He m. second, in Brookfield, Vt., Sept. 17, 1866, Calista Lucina Thayer, dau. of Theron and Rebecca (Whitney) Thayer.

She was b. in Brookfield, Vt., Dec. 18, 1833. He is a farmer; res. Brookfield, Vt. No children by second wife.
Child, by wife Caroline:
1. Walter Monroe,[8] b. in Brookfield, Vt., Jan. 25, 1857.

This father and son are the only living descendants of Oliver and Rachel (Cleveland) Hamblin, bearing the family name.

Lovisa Bean,[7] eldest daughter and child of Folsom and Nancy (Hamblin) Bean, b. in Danbury, N. H., Sept. 8, 1815, m. in Danbury, N. H., Jan. 1, 1846, William Small Curtice, son of Stephen and Lydia (McClintock) Curtice. He was b. in Windsor, N. H., April 17, 1814; d. in Concord, N. H., Aug. 4, 1875. She is living (1877) in Concord.
Children, all b. in Danbury, N. H.:
1. Son,[8] b. Nov. 19, 1848; d. Nov. 19, 1848.
2. William Austin,[8] b. Dec. 17, 1849, m. in Geneva, Ohio, Jan. 26, 1874, Emma Miriam Austin; parentage unknown. She was b. in Geneva, Ashtabula county, Ohio, March 28, 1847. He is a farmer; res. Red Oak, Iowa. No children.
3. Nancy Emma,[8] b. April 8, 1852; d. May 26, 1852.
4. Nancy Velona,[8] b. May 24, 1853.
5. Emma Oliver,[8] b. March 16, 1856.
6. Son,[8] b. May 25, 1858; d. May 25, 1858.

Elvira Bean,[7] second daughter and child of Folsom and Nancy (Hamblin) Bean, b. in Danbury, N. H., Dec. 22, 1816, m. in Danbury, N. H., Feb. 1, 1838, Asa Martin Whittier, son of Richard and Lettie (Phillips) Whittier. He was b. in Grafton, N. H., March 12, 1814. She d. in Rock Bluff, Cass county, Neb., April 27, 1864. He is living (1877) in Empire City, Minn.
Children:
1. Ellen Hastings,[8] b. Feb. 16, 1839, m. in Tipton, Iowa, Feb. 27, 1857, Dr. Hiram Latham. Parentage and place and date of birth not learned. Children: 1. Charles Whittier,[9] b. in St. Louis, March 16, 1859. 2. Arthur Bean,[9] b. in St. Louis, April 2, 1861.
2. Oscar Pulaski,[8] b. July 27, 1844, m. in Frankfort, Iowa, Nov. 15, 1862, Amanda Strait. Parentage and place and date of birth not learned. Children: 1. Thaddeus Strait,[9] b. in Rock Bluff, Neb., May 25, 1864. 2. Elvira Anna,[9] b. in Red Oak, Iowa, March 18, 1867.
3. Frank Bean,[8] b. Sept. 27, 1849.

Abigail H. Bean,[7] third daughter and child of Folsom and Nancy (Hamblin) Bean, b. in Danbury, N. H., Aug. 24, 1818, m. in same place, Oct. 30, 1853, Alfred Huse, son of John and Mary (Currier) Huse. He was b. in Enfield, N. H., Oct. 1, 1811. Farmer; res. Enfield, N. H. No children.

Joel H. Bean,[7] eldest son and fourth child of Folsom and Nancy (Hamblin) Bean, b. in Danbury, N. H., Aug. 11, 1821, m. in Macedon,

N. Y., Nov. 4, 1852, Celia Anthony, dau. of John and Susan (Cypher) Anthony. She was b. in Milton, Ulster county, N. Y., Aug. 7, 1827. He is a merchant ; res. Hawleyville, Iowa.
Children :

1. Alice Lavinia,[8] b. in Macedon, N. Y., May 27, 1854, m. in Hawleyville, Iowa, May 24, 1875, John McGuire. Parentage and place and date of birth not learned. Child: 1. Son,[9] b. Dec. —, 1877.
2. Mabel Anthony,[8] b. in Douglass, Iowa, Nov. 11, 1859.
3. Jesse Cass,[8] b. in Douglass, Iowa, Dec. 15, 1861.

Lovina H. Bean,[7] fourth daughter and fifth child of Folsom and Nancy (Hamblin) Bean, b. in Danbury, N. H., Aug. 1, 1823, m. in Danbury, N. H., June 7, 1846, Daniel Flanders, son of Caleb and Mehetabel (Searls) Flanders. He was b. in Danbury, N. H., March 24, 1818.
Child :

1. Henry Willis,[8] b. Dec. 27, 1855.

Susan C. Bean,[7] fifth daughter and sixth child of Folsom and Nancy (Hamblin) Bean, b. in Danbury, N. H., April 30, 1829, m. in same place, Dec. 22, 1860, George Perly Mason, son of Perly and Ruth (Padelford) Mason. He was b. in Danbury, N. H., April 5, 1828. Res. Frankfort, Iowa.
Children :

1. Ida Candice,[8] b. Nov. 18, 1861.
2. Cora Kent,[8] b. June 10, 1864.

Frank G. Bean,[7] youngest son and child of Folsom and Nancy (Hamblin) Bean, b. in Danbury, N. H., Feb. 17, 1831, m. in Douglass, Iowa, Sept. 15, 1861, Abbie Mansfield, dau. of George and Abby (Lane) Mansfield. She was b. in Glenwood, Iowa, May 6, 1830. He is a farmer ; res. Wallace, Montgomery county, Iowa.
Children, all b. in Douglass, Iowa :

1. Oscar Whittier,[8] b. Aug. 8, 1862.
2. Cora Amanda,[8] b. March 16, 1867.

The following, from a daughter of Folsom and Nancy (Hamblin) Bean, should have a place in these records:

"ENFIELD, N. H., April 20, 1878.

DEAR COUSIN:

"Many thanks for your photograph. We prize it highly, and hope to see the original as soon as you can spare the time to visit us. I will now endeavor to give you what information I can concerning my mother's parents, Oliver and Rachel (Cleveland) Hamblin.

"My grandfather Hamblin moved from Connecticut to Vermont. He, with two other men and their families, were the first settlers in the eastern part of Brookfield, on "the Branch," as it was called. Soon after, the Indians became very troublesome, and the men always worked together, as they did not consider it safe to work alone. Grandmother was very timid. She took off her gold beads and her ear ornaments and put them into a pewter porringer and buried them in the cellar for fear the Indians would tear the rings from her ears. She lived in great fear of being taken by them. Indeed, she learned subsequently they had a narrow escape on one occasion. A man by the name of Johnson being captured by the Indians was held in custody for several months, and the chief of the tribe gave Johnson charge of some braves while on a scouting expedition. They saw grandfather and the other men at work while concealed on a hill above them, and begged of Johnson permission to go and kill the men, but he managed to restrain them. Soon after, the Indians burnt Royalton, and grandfather and the others with their families started for Lebanon, N. H., some fifty miles distant. While making the hurried journey, they saw cattle with their tongues cut out and otherwise barbarously injured; feather beds emptied and burnt to a crisp; and two men murdered, whom they buried under an old log. But the party arrived safely at last in Lebanon, and staid there two years before it was deemed safe to return. A few years after grandfather's return he sold out the place and moved to a hill farm, where he and grandmother remained till their death. They were both hard-working, industrious people, and accumulated a good property.

"My grandmother was a good-looking woman, rather stout, and was greatly beloved by all who knew her. I well remember the linen thread she used to spin; it was as white as snow, and exquisitely fine. She used to make her muslin caps with it. She made me a present of some; and I still have one pair of linen pillow slips made from the linen she spun and wove, all her own handiwork, and I shall always keep them. She was an excellent butter and cheese maker, and took care of the milk from ten cows the summer she was eighty, but after that she commenced to fail. She nearly lost her mind before her death at the age of 86. She was one of those cheerful, happy women—it was all sunshine with her. My mother resembled her very much in appearance, both having dark hair and blue eyes.

"I presume you have got your book almost completed, and I have no doubt it will be very interesting to us all. Send me a copy and tell me the price, and I will gladly send you the money for it.

Very truly, etc, ABIGAIL H. HUSE."

The following, from Mrs. Ruth H. Sprague, concerning the Hamblins, is subjoined. Strange to say, this conveys the first intimation to the compiler that any one of the daughters of James and Lovisa (Bigelow) Hamblin was married. Unfortunately the information comes too late to be available in this edition of the work.

"I can remember Rachel Cleveland, wife of Oliver Hamblin, as a thrifty housewife, doing the work for her son Joel (who was at that time a bachelor), with the help of 'Dotia, her deaf and dumb daughter. In visiting with my mother she talked of her success in making butter and cheese, and I have heard the neighbors say no one ever called on them without having food offered in token of true hospitality. I was never acquainted with her married daughters, they having died or removed from the State before my remembrance. Her two sons James and Joel settled in our town, were for many years prosperous farmers, professors of Christianity, and bore an honorable part in the public business of the community. Five of the eldest daughters of James were among my valued friends, having been for a considerable part of several years among my dearest pupils. They were the victims of consumption, and died early, only one of the seven having married. Some were unusually precocious and talented. Joel cared for his parents and sister 'Dotia, and on all occasions of public worship in the school-house he was sure to be there with his family, 'Dotia included. He removed from the place some years before his death, after which my acquaintance with his family ceased."

I.

Hannah Payne,[7] eldest daughter and child of James and Mercy (Goddard) Payne, b. in Montague, Mass., May 1, 1799, m. in Eaton, Madison county, N. Y., Jan. 28, 1823, Walter Menter, son of Richard and Cynthia (Clough) Menter. He was b. in Vermont, date not given; d. in Friendship, Fond du Lac county, Wis., July 24, 1865. Farmer. She is living (1878) with her son in Friendship, Wis.
Children:
1. Harriet Maria,[8] b. in Eaton, N. Y., March 20, 1825, m. in Richland, N. Y., June 19, 1845, Seneca David Moore, son of David and Elizabeth Moore. The date and place of his birth unknown. She d. in Richland, N. Y., Nov. 26, 1848. He m. again; res. Daysville, N. Y. Children: 1. Duane Fernando,[9] b. in Richland, N. Y., Oct. 21, 1846; d. June 20, 1858. 2. Harriet Adell,[9] b. in Richland, N. Y., Aug. 30, 1848, m. in Friendship, Wis., March 15, 1866, Henry William James, parentage, etc., not learned. Farmer; res. Jenny, Lincoln county, Wis. Children: 1. Frank,[10] b. May 2, 1869. 2 Jerry Willis,[10] b. Aug. —, 1872. 3. Walter,[10] b. Feb. —, 1876.
2. Hannah,[8] b. in Eaton, N. Y., Oct. 1, 1827; d. Feb. 18, 1829.
3. Hannah Sophia,[8] b. in Eaton, N. Y., June 1, 1830, m. in Richland, N. Y., Dec. 1, 1852, Volney Charles Chapman, son of Zenas L. and Abigail Chapman. The date and place of his birth not given. She d. Oct. 25, 1854. No children.
4. Lovina Lucinda,[8] b. in Richland, N. Y., March 23, 1832, m. first, in Richland, N. Y., Feb. 22, 1849, Henry L. Pettingill, parentage, etc., unknown. He was a cooper. She m. second, July 3, 1863, William A. Anderson, parentage, etc., not learned. Millwright; res. Fond du Lac, Wis. No children.
5. Walter Samuel,[8] b. in Richland, N. Y., Sept. 28, 1836, m. in Fond du Lac, Wis., Feb. 20, 1860, Mary Prosser, dau. of Jeremiah and Gertrude Prosser. She was b. in Rochester, N. Y., April 12, 1836. He is a farmer; res. Friendship, Wis. Child: 1 Duane Franklin,[9] b. April 7, 1867.

Brigham Payne,[7] eldest son and second child of James and Mercy (Goddard) Payne, b. in Montague, Mass., Jan. 3, 1801, m. first, date and place not learned, Julia Ann Chapman parentage or date and place of birth not given. She d. in Kansas, about 1868, exact date unknown, and he m. second, a lady (name unknown) with whom he did not live happily. He d., it is believed, in Garnett, Anderson county, Kansas, about 1876, but whether his last wife survives him, is not ascertained. Having so far been unable to get communication with his children, the following very unsatisfactory sketch, gathered from other sources, is all the compiler can present:
1. Marvin Henry,[8] date and place of b. unknown, m. a lady in Wisconsin, and moved to Kansas about 1858, and subsequently to California. Number and names, etc., of children, if any, not learned.
2. Julia Elizabeth,[8] the date and place of birth unknown, m. a Mr. Pritchard, removed to Kansas, and from there to California. Names of children, if any, etc., not known.

3. Edward Wyman,[s] date and place of birth unknown, said to be living when last heard from, in one of the Territories.
4. James Andrews,[s] date and place of birth unknown, said to be with his brother Edward, probably in Idaho.
5. Albert Levant,[s] date and place of birth unknown, or anything about his family, if any.
6. Savilla Antoinette,[s] date and place of birth unknown, or if married or single.
7. Alice May,[s] date and place of birth unknown, or if married or single. The last three are supposed by my correspondent to be still living in Garnett, Kansas, but as no attention has been paid to my letters, and the Postmaster there can give no account of them, it is probable they have all removed from the place, though it is very strange that no one should know whither.

Sophia Payne,[7] second daughter and third child of James and Mercy (Goddard) Payne, b. in Montague, Mass., July 5, 1804, m. in Eaton, Madison county, N. Y., about 1822, Rev. Joel Wilson Nye, son of Bonham and Anna (Record) Nye. He was b. in Eaton, N. Y., date not known ; d. in Iowa, about 1853. He was a Baptist minister. She d. in Mexico, Oswego county, N. Y., Jan. 31, 1833. [His second wife, m. in Richland, N. Y., in 1834, was Nancy Melvina Ferris, dau. of Rev. Enoch Ferris, a Baptist minister, and by whom he had a son and a daughter.]

Children, so far as learned, were three in number :

1. Melissa Bloomfield,[8] b. in Eaton, N. Y., Feb. 15, 1823, m. in Stockbridge, Oneida county, N. Y., Dec. 6, 1849, Rufus Leverett Dimmock, Jr., son of Rufus L. and Ruhama (Cady) Dimmock. He was b. in Westminster, Windham county, Conn., date of birth and death not given. She is living (1879) at 43 Leroy Street, New York City. Children : 1. Leverett Nye,[9] b. in Waterford, New London county, Conn., Jan. 29, 1851, m. in same place, Sept. —, 1873, Mary Florine Parker, parentage, etc., not given. He is a farmer; res. Waterford, Conn. Children : 1. Clarence Parker,[10] b. June 7, 1876. 2. Frank Leverett,[10] b. July 1, 1878. 2. Melissa Cornelia,[9] b. in Waterford, Conn., Oct. 29, 1856. She is a teacher of vocal and instrumental music, and resides with her mother at 43 Leroy Street, New York City.
2. Alonzo Harrington,[8] b. in Nelson, Madison county, N. Y., ——, 1831. A harness maker by trade; went to Kansas, and is supposed to be living there yet, and m. to a widow with five children. Was driving stage when last heard from, some fifteen years ago.
3. Joel Watts,[8] (Rev.) b. in Mexico, Oswego county, N. Y., Jan. 22, 1833, m. in Lawrenceville, Dearborn county, Ind., July 3, 1855, Margaret Showalter, dau. of Abraham and Christina (Kile) Showalter. She was b. in Lawrenceville, Ind., Jan. 8, 1839; res. Vermillion, Edgar county, Ill. He is a presiding elder in that district, of the United Brethren. Children : 1. Edwin Alonzo,[9] b. in Lawrenceville, Ind., June 24, 1856. 2. Etta Louisa Melissa,[9] b. in Vermillion, Ill., Oct. 7, 1861; d. Aug. 16, 1876, while a student at Green Hill Seminary, Warren county, Ind. 3. Ida May,[9] b. in Vermillion, Ill., April 7, 1864. 4. Charles Leverett,[9] b. in Vermillion, Ill., Dec. 29, 1866; d. Jan. 7, 1870. 5. Lena Centennia,[9] b. in Green Hill, Warren county, Ind., April 13, 1876.

Lucinda Payne,[7] third daughter and fourth child of James and Mercy (Goddard) Payne, b. in Montague, Mass., May 16, 1806, m. in Eaton, Madison county, N. Y., May 27, 1824, William Menter, son of William

and Cynthia (Hopkins) Menter. He was b. in Hebron, Washington county, N. Y., April 7, 1802; d. in Fond du Lac, Wis., Nov. 9, 1867. She d. in same place, June 21, 1861.
  Children:
  1. William James,[5] b. in Eaton, N. Y., Jan. 1, 1826, m. in Mexico, N. Y., Jan. 26, 1848, Alma Everts, dau. of Samuel and Lucinda (Slack) Everts. She was b. in Mexico, N. Y., Nov. 7, 1826. He is a farmer; res. Mexico, Oswego county, N. Y. No children.
  2. Lyman Payne,[8] b. in Eaton, N. Y., Aug. 29, 1830; d. Sept. 2, 1830.
  3. Son,[8] b. in Richland, N. Y., May 27, 1832; d. May 27, 1832.
  4. Lucinda Jane,[8] b. in Richland, N. Y., July 13, 1835, m. first, in Fond du Lac, Wis., Dec. 11, 1859, Alexander Clendenning, son of Charles and Elizabeth (Johnson) Clendenning. He was b. in Niagara county, N. Y., Feb. 25, 1836; d. in the Army, at Pittsburgh Landing, Tenn., June 4, 1862. Carpenter. She m. second, in Fond du Lac, Wis., June 23, 1864, John Monk, son of Caspar and Hannah (Hesler) Monk. He was b. in Fort Plain, Montgomery county, N. Y., Jan. 8, 1819. Carpenter; res. St. Cloud, Wis. Children, by husband, Alex. Clendening: 1. Ella Lucinda,[9] b. in Eden, Fond du Lac county, Wis., March 1, 1861, m. in Greenbush, Sheboygan county, Wis., Sept. 5, 1878, Alton Lawrence, son of William and Charlotte (Mills) Lawrence. He was b. in ———. Telegraph operator; res. St. Cloud, Wis. By husband, John Monk: 2. Robert William,[8] b. in Friendship, Wis., March 28, 1866. 3. Verna Luetta,[9] b. in Greenbush, Wis., April 7, 1871.
  5. Robert Henry,[8] b. in Richland, N. Y., June 26, 1842; d. June 11, 1869, unm.

Samuel S. Payne,[7] second son and fifth child of James and Mercy (Goddard) Payne, b. in Montague, Mass., June 21, 1808, m. in Van Buren, Onondaga county, N. Y., Aug. 21, 1832, Sarah Ann Goddard, dau. of Ebal and Esther (Earle) Goddard. She was b. in Van Buren, N. Y., Aug. 20, 1813; d. in Van Buren, N. Y., April 2, 1846. He d. in Richland, Oswego county, N. Y., April 24, 1834.
  Child:
  1. Esther Ann,[8] b. in Baldwinsville, Onondaga county, N. Y., July 3, 1833, m. in South Richland, Oswego county, N. Y., March 24, 1850, George Palmerton, son of Lyman and Esther (Brayton) Palmerton. He was b. in Wilna, Jefferson county, N. Y., July 9, 1827. Farmer; res. Pulaski, N. Y. Children: 1. Robert Edwin,[9] b. in South Richland, N. Y., Dec. 25, 1851; drowned Oct. 18, 1870. 2. George Davis,[9] b. Aug. 21, 1866.

Persis Payne,[7] fourth daughter and sixth child of James and Mercy (Goddard) Payne, b. in Eaton, Madison county, N. Y., April 20, 1810, m. in Richland, Oswego county, N. Y., June 22, 1834, Levi Keith, son of Lincoln and Submit (Doolittle) Keith. He was b. in Nelson, Madison county, N. Y., Sept. 7, 1809. Farmer; res. Nelson, N. Y.
  Child:
  1. Mary Jane,[9] b. in Nelson, N. Y., Aug. 3, 1847, m. in same place, Oct. 12, 1876, David Walton Jones, son of Thomas and Hannah (Jones) Jones. He was b. in Carmarthenshire, (Wales,) Eng., April 1, 1849. Farmer; res. Nelson, N. Y. No children.

James Payne,[7] third son and seventh child of James and Mercy (Goddard) Payne, b. in Eaton, Madison county, N. Y., March 24, 1812, m. in Richland, Oswego county, N. Y., April 17, 1842, Abby Fenner Southworth, dau. of Royal and Phebe (Gleason) Southworth. She was b. in Mendon, Worcester county, Mass., Aug. 26, 1824, and is living (1878) with her second husband, William Porter, in Allegan, Mich. Her first husband d. in Richland, N. Y., May 7, 1855. Farmer.
Children:

1. James Barney,[8] b. in Pineville, Oswego county, N. Y., March 29, 1844, m. in Fort Wayne, Ind., Feb. 20, 1871, Myra Ross, dau. of Seneca and Cornelia Pamela (Dow) Ross. She was b. in Burr Oak, Mich., Nov. 19, 1842; res. South Bosque, McClellan county, Texas. Child: 1. James Barney,[9] b. Sept. 20, 1873.
2. Emogene Lora,[8] b. in Litchfield, Hillsdale county, Mich., Oct. 15, 1850, m. in Trowbridge, Mich., Nov. 15 1867, Seth Orr, of Decatur, Mich., son of James Madison and Martha (Wilson) Orr. He was b. in Meredith, Delaware county, N. Y., June 19, 1835. Farmer; res. Trowbridge, Mich. Children: 1. Abbie Myra,[9] b. Sept. 10, 1869. 2. Bertha Ethnel,[9] b. May —, 1877. 3. Blanche Leona,[9] b. April 3, 1879.

Henrietta Payne,[7] fifth daughter and ninth child of James and Mercy (Goddard) Payne, b. in Eaton, Madison county, N. Y., June 18, 1816, m. in Richland, Oswego county, N. Y., Jan. 10, 1836, Robert Gillespie, son of Robert and Martha (Johnson) Gillespie. He was b. in Richland, N. Y., May 15, 1816. Farmer; res. Daysville, Oswego county, N. Y.
Child:

1. Nettie,[8] b. June 25, 1854.

Selina Payne,[7] sixth daughter and tenth child of James and Mercy (Goddard) Payne, b. in Eaton, Madison county, N. Y., April 6, 1819, m. in Richland, Oswego county, N. Y., Nov. 28, 1841, Nathan Harrison Soule, son of Constant and Lucena (Brace) Soule. He was b. in Richland, N. Y., July 30, 1818; d. in Burr Oak, St. Joseph county, Mich., May 1, 1870. Farmer. She is living (1878) in Burr Oak, Mich.
Children, both b. in Richland, N. Y.:

1. Melvina Henrietta,[8] b. Dec. 13, 1842, m. in Burr Oak, Mich., March 7, 1865, Erastus George, son of Isaac and Sally (Purdy) George. He was b. in Ashtabula county, Ohio, April 7, 1837. Merchant; res. Burr Oak, Mich. Children: 1. Carrie Eliza,[9] b. May 10, 1866. 2. Florence Persis,[9] b. Jan. 28, 1872.
2. Marcellus Fayette,[8] b. Jan. 29, 1845, m. in Fort Wayne, Ind., Sept. 10, 1872, Helen Martha Jones, dau. of Amos Clark and Martha Ann (Smith) Jones. She was b. in Nunda, Livingston county, N. Y., April 8, 1850. He is a salesman; res. Burr Oak, Mich. Children: 1. Charles Wayne,[9] b. in Sturgis, Mich., Nov. 26, 1873. 2. Edith Jane,[9] b. in Camden, Jay county, Ind., Oct. 5, 1875. 3. Harry Fayette,[9] b. in Burr Oak, Mich., Sept. 20, 1878.

Lyman Payne,[7] youngest son and child of James and Mercy (Goddard) Payne, b. in Nelson, Madison county, N. Y., May 23, 1822, m. in

Mexico, Oswego county, N. Y., Oct. 20, 1847, Matilda Everts, dau. of Samuel and Lucinda (Slack) Everts. She was b. in Mexico, N. Y., May 31, 1824. He is a farmer; res. Mexico, N. Y. No children.

Mary Payne,[7] eldest daughter and child of Edward and Susan (Bancroft) Payne, b. in Montague, Mass., Nov. 9, 1809, m. in Wendell, Mass., June 25, 1838, John Watt Brewer, son of Samuel and Fanny (Watt) Brewer. He was b. in Wendell, Mass., Nov. 7, 1812; d. in Montague, Mass., Oct. 3, 1876. No children.

Nathan C. Payne,[7] eldest son and second child of Edward and Susan (Bancroft) Payne, b. in Montague, Mass., Nov. 5, 1812, m. in Wendell, Mass., Nov. 8, 1836, Sarah Brewer, dau. of Samuel and Fanny (Watt) Brewer. She was b. in Wendell, Mass., April 6, 1817; d. in Montague, Mass., Feb. 5, 1870. He d. in Montague, Aug. 24, 1856. Farmer.

Children, all b. in Montague, Mass.:

1. Henry Welford,[8] b. March 15, 1838, m. in same place, Jan. 1, 1861, Maria Louise Clapp, dau. of Martin Harvey and Maria (Russell) Clapp. She was b. in Montague, Jan. 4, 1840. Res. Springfield, Mass. Children: 1. George Henry,[9] b. May 2, 1868. 2. Lucius Lee,[9] b. Nov. 21, 1869.
2. Susan Fanny,[8] b. Sept. 8, 1840; d. March 18, 1842.
3. Julia Bancroft,[8] b. April 14, 1842, m. in Dayton, Ohio, June 2, 1866, Asa Burton Closson, Jr., son of Asa Burton and Caroline (Taylor) Closson. He was b. in Norwich, Vt., June 27, 1837. Dealer in artists' materials, etc., 186 West Fourth Street, Cincinnati, Ohio. Children: 1. Fanny Agnes,[9] b. in Cincinnati, Ohio, Dec. 12, 1867. 2. Henry Burton,[9] b. in Cincinnati, Ohio, May 2, 1871. 3. Alice Helen,[9] b. in Ludlow, Ky., July 20, 1873.
4. Samuel Brewer,[8] b. Dec. 6, 1843, m. first, in Montague, Mass., Nov. 22, 1864, Myra M. Sherwood, dau. of Cephas G. and Diadama M. (Brown) Sherwood. She was b. in Montague, Dec. 27, 1844; d. in Montague, March 11, 1869. He m. second, in Fisherville, Mass., Dec. 7, 1870, Eva C. Hough, dau. of Daniel and Caroline Y. (Merrill) Hough. She was b. in Boston, Mass., June 10, 1850. He is a harness maker; res. Greenfield, Mass. No children by first wife. By wife Eva: 1. Herbert B.,[9] b. Nov. 16, 1871. 2. Frederic H.,[9] b. Nov. 10, 1876.
5. Freeman Edward,[8] b. Feb. 8, 1847, m. in Bernardston, Mass., Oct. 26, 1869, Ella C. Slate, dau. of Jonathan L. and Electa (Marsh) Slate. She was b. in Amherst, Mass., Aug. 31, 1847. He is a harness maker; res. Greenfield, Mass. Child: 1. Florence Isabel,[9] b. in Greenfield, Mass., Nov. 5, 1876.
6. Fannie Caroline,[8] b. Dec. 18, 1849, m. in Greenfield, Mass., Oct. 4, 1871, John Thaxter Shaw, son of Thaxter and Eliza Ann (Wilson) Shaw. He was b. in Colerain, Franklin county, Mass., Aug. 17, 1848. Farmer; res. Montague, Mass. Child: 1. Edith Lulu,[9] b. in Montague, June 7, 1874.
7. Charles Nathan,[8] b. July 24, 1852, m. in Springfield, Mass., Nov. 17, 1875, M. Lulu Bugbee, dau. of Samuel A. and Orrie L. (Miller) Bugbee. She was b. in Ticonderoga, Essex county, N. Y., May 4, 1853. He is a druggist; res. Greenfield, Mass.

John F. Payne,[1] second son and third child of Edward and Susan (Bancroft) Payne, b. in Montague, Mass., Aug. 13, 1815, m. in Wendell, Mass., Aug. 15, 1837, Mary Brewer, dau. of Samuel and Fanny (Watt) Brewer. She was b. in Wendell, Mass., Aug. 3, 1819. He is a farmer, but carried on boot and shoe making in early life; res. Montague, Mass.
Children, all b. in Montague :

1. Ellen Aurelia,[8] b. July 13, 1838, m. in Montague, Mass., May 1, 1860, Henry Belden Cook, son of Zenas and Lucy (Russell) Cook. He was b. in Hadley, Mass., March 15, 1833. Res. Orange, Mass. Children, all b. in Montague: 1. Carrie Lida,[9] b. July 9, 1861; d. May 28, 1864. 2. Edward Henry,[9] b. May 21, 1866. 3. Frank Payne,[9] b. Oct. 5, 1870. 4. Mary Ellen,[9] b. Aug. 5, 1872; d. Oct. 28, 1873. 5. Alice Louisa,[9] b. Aug. 2, 1874.
2. Edward Samuel,[8] b. Aug. 11, 1840; d. Sept. 10, 1841.
3. George Dwight,[8] b. Oct. 15, 1843, m. first, in Montague, Mass., Nov. 24, 1864, Lucy Arabella Shaw, dau. of Roland and Britannia (Johnson) Shaw. She was b. in Montague, Mass., Jan. 20, 1843 ; d. in same place, Aug. 27, 1868. He m. second, in Hartford, Conn., March 28, 1876, Vesta Noyes, dau. of Jason and Nancy (Shaw) Noyes. She was b. in Plainfield, Mass., Oct. 26, 1846. Child, by wife Lucy: 1. Carrie Dell,[9] b. July 21, 1868; d. June 7, 1869.
4. Abby Louise,[8] b. Oct. 14, 1849, m. in Montague, Mass., March 1, 1871, Horatio Mann, son of William and Abigail (Cook) Mann. He was b. in Petersham, Mass., Jan. 28, 1841. Farmer; res. West Roxbury, Mass. Child: 1. Jennie Dell,[9] b. in Petersham, Mass., April 17, 1872.

Melona Martin,[7] eldest daughter and child of Eluna and Persis (Payne) Martin, b. in Franklin county, Mass., March 2, 1809, m. in Morrisville, Madison county, N. Y., Oct. 9, 1843, Myranda Seymour, son of Silas and Sally (Gilbert) Seymour. He was b. in Lebanon, Madison county, N. Y., Sept. 12, 1806. Farmer; res. Oneida, Madison county, N. Y.
Children :

1. Charles Myranda,[8] b. in Lebanon, N. Y., July 26, 1844, m. in same place, Jan. 8, 1868, Mary Janette King, dau. of Davis T. and Janette (Leland) King. She was b. in Sangerfield, Oneida county, N. Y., May 5, 1848. He is a merchant, firm of Storrs & Seymour, dry goods, groceries, etc.; res. Morrisville, N. Y. Children, both born in Morrisville: 1. Florence,[9] b. Nov. 5, 1871. 2. Laura,[9] b. Feb. 9, 1874.
2. Henry Franklin,[8] b. in Lebanon, N. Y., Dec. 16, 1845, m. in Greece, Monroe county, April 30, 1868, Florence Matilda Mahon, dau. of Archibald and Mahala (Dodge) Mahon. She was b. in Mahon, Huntington county, Ind., May 13, 1846; d. in Rochester, N. Y., Feb. 15, 1875. He is a farmer and dairyman; res. Rochester, N. Y. Children: 1. Annie,[9] b. in Oneida, Madison county, N. Y., May 1, 1869. 2. Katie,[9] b. in Oneida, Madison county, N. Y., Feb. —, 1871. 3. Fannie,[9] b. in Rochester, N. Y., Sept. —, 1873. 4 Florence,[9] b. in Rochester, N. Y., Feb. 5, 1875.

Eluna Martin,[7] eldest son and second child of Eluna and Persis (Payne) Martin, b. in Franklin county, Mass., Nov. 17, 1810, m. in

Morrisville, N. Y., April 20, 1859, Ellen Hitchcock, dau. of Joseph and Catherine Hitchcock. Date and place of her birth not learned. He d. in Morrisville, Dec. 16, 1868.
Children:
1. Lizzie,[8] b. Sept. 23, 1861.
2. Sidney,[8] b. March 14, 1863.

Adaline Martin,[7] second daughter and third child of Eluna and Persis (Payne) Martin, b. in Morrisville, N. Y., Aug. 20, 1812, m. in ——, April 16, 1833, Elisha Crane Topliff, son of Elisha and Zilpha (Crane) Topliff. He was b. in Vermont, June 11, 1807. She d. in Morrisville, N. Y., Nov. 26, 1865. No children.

Hibbard Martin,[7] second son and fourth child of Eluna and Persis (Payne) Martin, b. in Morrisville, N. Y., Aug. 17, 1814, m. in Madison, N. Y., Jan. 21, 1841, Elvisa Tracy Smith, dau. of Zenas and Sally (Reed) Smith. She was b. in Madison, N. Y., May 3, 1822. Res. Morrisville, N. Y.
Child:
1. Mary Emogene,[8] b. in Morrisville, N. Y., Sept. 10, 1843, m. in same place, Dec. 26, 1861, Edwin Gregg Adams, son of William Lawson and Araminta D. (Platt) Adams. He was b. in Cohoes, Albany county, N. Y., Feb. 28, 1835. Res. Cohoes, Albany county, N. Y., and member of the firm of S. & E. G. Adams, wholesale meats and vegetables, Cohoes, N. Y. Children: 1. Clara Hattie,[9] b. in Cohoes, N. Y., Oct. 21, 1862. 2. Nellie Fidelia,[9] b. in Troy, N. Y., Nov. 23, 1864. 3. Mary Elizabeth,[9] b. in Troy, N. Y., Feb. 24, 1867. 4. Edwin,[9] b. in Lansingburgh, N. Y., Aug. 23, 1870. 5. Florence,[9] b. in Lansingburgh, N. Y., March 14, 1873.

Susan Martin,[7] third daughter and fifth child of Eluna and Persis (Payne) Martin, b. in Morrisville, N. Y., July 11, 1816, m. in same place, Feb. 16, 1837, James H. Curtiss, son of Abel and Anna (Donahue) Curtiss. He was b. in Ballston, Saratoga county, N. Y., July 9, 1814. Farmer; res. Spencerport, N. Y.
Children:
1. George Martin,[8] b. in Perrington, Monroe county, N. Y., Jan. 25, 1838, m. in Peterboro', Madison county, N. Y., Aug. 2, 1865, Mary Elizabeth Campbell, dau. of John and Maria (Rich) Campbell. She was b. in Peterboro', N. Y., Aug. 26, 1835. He is a farmer; res. Gates, Monroe county, N. Y. Children: 1. Clifton Campbell,[9] b. July 9, 1866; d. April 14, 1871. 2. John Gerritt Henry,[9] b. Aug. 8, 1870. 3. Florence Maria,[9] b. Aug. 30, 1872. 4. Mary Isabel,[9] b. Nov. 5, 1875.
2. Adaline Topliff,[8] b. in Perrington, N. Y., Sept. 16, 1841, m. in Gates, N. Y., Dec. 14, 1859, Hezekiah Raney Dewey, son of Joseph and Maria (Raney) Dewey. Date and place of birth not given. She d. in Hardin county, Iowa, April 7, 1863. He is a farmer; res. Grand Blanc, Mich. Children: 1. Kittie,[9] b. in Ogden, Monroe county, N. Y., Oct. 11, 1860. 2. Willie,[9] b. in Gates, Monroe county, N. Y., Nov. 16, 1861. 3. Minnie,[9] b. in Hardin county, Iowa, Dec. —, 1862; d. ——, 1865.

3. Mary Harriet,[8] b. in Perrington, N. Y., Jan. 25, 1844, m. in Penfield, Monroe county, N. Y., Aug. 5, 1862, Thomas D. Dewey, son of Joseph and Maria (Raney) Dewey. Date and place of birth not given. Res. Marshalltown, Iowa. Children: 1. Eva,[9] b. ——. 2. Minnie,[9] b. ——. 3. Alice,[9] b. ——. 4. Martha,[9] b. ——. 5. Harry,[9] b. ——.
4. Seymour Henry,[8] b. in Peterboro', N. Y., Dec. 30, 1851, and writes (1879) he is *engaged* to be married on the 18th of September, 1879, to Miss Nellie S. Gott, dau. of Oscar F. and Martha Gott. The compiler tenders in advance his best wishes for the happiness and prosperity of the young couple.

Alexa Martin,[7] fourth daughter and sixth child of Eluna and Persis (Payne) Martin, b. in Morrisville, N. Y., June 20, 1820, m. in same place, Oct. 12, 1844, John Marble, date and place of birth and parentage unknown. She d. in Venango county, (Cherry Tree Township) Pa., July 15, 1845.
Child:
1. Ann Amelia,[8] b. in Venango county, Pa., July 4, 1845, m. in Morrisville, Madison county, N. Y., April 9, 1873, George Hockridge, of whom or of his family nothing further is known, except that he resides at Morrisville, N. Y.

Charles H. Payne,[7] eldest son and second child of Dr. John and Elizabeth S. (Nelson) Payne, b. in Morrisville, Madison county, N. Y., April 15, 1830, m. in Janesville, Wis., July 11, 1872, Eunice Preston. dau. of Charles and Betsey (Blaudin) Preston. She was b. in Hopewell, Ontario county, N. Y., July 1, 1827. He is a mechanic; res. Janesville, Wis. No children.

Sarah S. Payne,[7] second daughter and third child of Dr. John and Elizabeth S. (Nelson) Payne, b. in Morrisville, N. Y., March 31, 1832, m. in Horseheads, Chemung county, N. Y., Jan. 6, 1853, James Wiggins, son of Alexander C. and Rachel C. (Crissy) Wiggins. He was b. in Newburgh, Orange county, N. Y., Jan. 18, 1827. Farmer; res. Footville, Rock county, Wis.
Children:
1. Mary Frances,[8] b. in Elmira, Chemung county, N. Y., March 27, 1854, m. in Chicago, Ill., March 10, 1873, Frank Fayette Ford, son of Elisha E. and Hannah L. (Rice) Ford. He was b. in Rutland, Vt., Jan. 1, 1847. Res. Council Bluffs, Iowa. Child: 1. Grace M.,[9] b. in Janesville, Wis., Feb. 16, 1874.
2. Alice Nelson,[8] b. in Center, Rock county, Wis., May 24, 1857.
3. Herbert Elmer,[8] b. in Center, Wis., May 15, 1862.
4. Willis,[8] b. in Center, Wis., May 12, 1865; d. Nov. 21, 1867.
5. Stella M.,[8] b. in Harmony, Wis., Aug. 7, 1868; d. March 27, 1875.

William H. H. Payne,[7] second son and fourth child of Dr. John and Elizabeth S. (Nelson) Payne, b. in Canastota, Madison county, N. Y., March 14, 1834, m. in Watertown, Wis., Feb. 21, 1870 Mary Calista Albee, dau. of Preserved and Calista Matilda (Nash) Albee. She was b. in Ann Arbor, Mich., June 29, 1840. Res. Sandwich, Ill.

Children :
1. Harry,* b. June 13, 1871; d. Dec. 30, 1871.
2. Edward Ernest,⁸ b. Nov. 14, 1872.
3. Charles Albee,⁸ b. Nov. 21, 1873.
4. Daughter,⁸ b. July 19, 1875; d. July 19, 1875.

Rev. Henry N. Payne,⁷ youngest son and child of Dr. John and Elizabeth S. (Nelson) Payne, b. in Horseheads, Chemung county, N. Y., Nov. 4, 1840, m. in Auburn, N. Y., Sept. 7, 1871, Elizabeth Amelia Porter, dau. of Rev. Lansing and Elizabeth (Curtis) Porter. She was b. in Chicago, Ill., April 15, 1847. He is a Presbyterian minister; res. Oxford, Chenango county, N. Y.

Children :
1. Annie Elizabeth,* b. in Minneapolis, Minn., Aug. 20, 1872.
2. Charles Lansing,⁸ b. in Minneapolis, Minn., July 27, 1874; d. in Onondaga Valley, Onondaga county, N. Y., June 17, 1876.
3. Porter,⁸ b. in Lima, Livingston county, N. Y., Dec. 15, 1877.

Mr. Payne furnishes the following letter by request of the compiler, in reference to his ministerial labors, etc. :

" As for my ministerial record, etc., for which you ask, it is briefly as follows— (I think you have my military record):

" My literary course was pursued in Hamilton College, Clinton, N. Y., from which I graduated with honor, July 16, 1868. After passing a year each in the Chicago Theological Seminary, and the Auburn Theological Seminary, I graduated from Lane Theological Seminary, Cincinnati, Ohio, May 11, 1871. Licensed to preach by Presbytery of Cayuga, April 13, 1870. Ordained to the gospel ministry by Presbytery of St. Paul, at Minneapolis, Minn., Oct. 5, 1871.

" After declining an invitation to the pastorate of the Sixth Presbyterian Church, of Cincinnati, Ohio, I accepted a call to the First Presbyterian Church, of Minneapolis, Minn., July 1, 1870, and was soon after installed as its Pastor. During this pastorate of nearly four years, considerable accessions were made to the church, and a new and commodious edifice erected, (at that time the best belonging to our denomination in the city), at a cost of $12,000. Resigned May 1, 1875.

" From Feb. 1, 1876, to Nov. 12, 1876, had charge of Presbyterian Church, of Onondaga Valley, N. Y. Dec. 1, 1876, became pastor of Presbyterian Church, Lima, N. Y.; resigned Feb. 10, 1879. Feb. 15, 1879, accepted call to pastorate of the Associated Presbyterian Church, of Oxford, N. Y., in which field I am now happily and successfully laboring.

" Thanks for your kind messages to mother. She has failed quite rapidly for a month past, and we hardly expect to keep her with us long.

" Perhaps it may interest you to know that my brother, Wm. H. Payne, of Sandwich, Ill., is the inventor of a very successful Automatic Grain Binder, which is proving a fortune to him.

" I congratulate you on the approaching completion of your work on the Family Record. All branches of the family will owe you thanks for your untiring labor.

" Your Cousin, HENRY NELSON PAYNE."

Miranda Payne,⁷ eldest daughter and child of Ira and Lydia (Makepeace) Payne, b. in Montague, Mass., Nov. 23, 1816, m. in Hinsdale, N. H., Jan. 7, 1837, Samuel Henry Hendrick, son of Jabez and Sally

(Henry) Hendrick. He was b. in Middlebury, Vt., March 8, 1811. Farmer; res. Ripton, Vt.

Children, eldest b. in Middlebury, the others in Ripton, Vt.:
1. Susan,⁸ b. Sept. 29, 1838, unm. and resides in Ripton, Vt.
2. Eliza Jane,⁸ b. Aug. 19, 1840, m. in Ripton, Vt., Nov. 28, 1872, David Hale, son of Benjamin and Lucy (Stebbins) Hale. He was b. in Ripton, Vt., Dec. 22, 1827. Farmer; res. Ripton, Vt. Children: 1. Samuel David,⁹ b. in Granville, Vt., Aug. 23, 1874. 2. Lucy Miranda,⁹ b. in Granville, Vt., Jan. 10, 1876. 3. Susan Roxana,⁹ b. in Ripton, Vt., May 12, 1877. 4. Mary Jane,⁹ b. in Ripton, Vt., March 16, 1879.
3. Luther Henry,⁸ b. Sept. 9, 1842. He entered the Union Army, early in the war, and d. in Emory Hospital, near Washington, D. C., Nov. 19, 1862.
4. Stillman,⁸ b. Sept. 2, 1844; d. April 19, 1846.
5. Laura,⁸ b. April 11, 1847; d. Sept. 10, 1864.
6. Lydia Ann,⁸ b. Nov. 24, 1851; d. Sept. 29, 1853.
7. Jessie Edwina,⁸ b. Nov. 30, 1855, m. in Ripton, Vt., Jan. 19, 1871, George Newell Dow, son of Newell and Almira (Folsom) Dow. He was b. in Ripton, Vt., Dec. 6, 1852. Farmer; res. Ripton, Vt. Child: 1. Ira Luther,⁹ b. April 2, 1872.

Willard Payne,⁷ (not "William," as erroneously given on page 30,) eldest son and third child of Ira and Lydia (Makepeace) Payne, b. in Montague, Mass., Dec. 1, 1820, m. first, in Sunderland, Mass., April 20, 1841, Emily Renfield, dau. of Capt. Renfield, of Sunderland, where she was b. in the year 1811. She d. in Mass., Sept. 15, 1853. He m. second, in Monroe, Wis., Feb. 14, 1854, Lucetta Permelia Witter, dau. of Chester and Emily (Tompkins) Witter. She was b. in Livonia, Livingston county, N. Y., Nov. 18, 1837. He is a farmer; res. Monroe, Wis.

Children, by wife Emily:
1. Sarah Jane,⁸ b. Oct. 19, 1844; d. June 4, 1863.
2. Laura Ann,⁸ b. Dec. 5, 1846, m. in Chicago, Ill., Sept. 15, 1862, Alvin Tompkins Witter, son of Chester and Emily (Tompkins) Witter. He was b. in Mount Morris, Livingston county, N. Y., April 2, 1835. Merchant; res. Monticello, Wis. Children: 1. Willard Mack,⁹ b. in Monroe, Wis., June 9, 1864. 2. Lillie Belle,⁹ b. in Monroe, Wis., Aug. 15, 1866; d. Aug. 26, 1866. 3. Merta Ardell,⁹ b. in Monroe, Wis., May 29, 1868. 4. Daisy Belle,⁹ b. in Monroe, Wis., July 14, 1872. 5. Chester Robert,⁹ b. in Monticello, Wis., Jan. 20, 1877.
3. Ellen Frances,⁸ b. Aug. 3, 1849, m. in Monroe, Wis., June 24, 1866, Stephen Barber Perkins, son of Stephen Barber and Salina (Dorman) Perkins. He was b. in Newtonville, Canada, April 20, 1845. Res. Marion, Crittenden county, Ky. Children, all b. in Monroe, Wis. 1. Grace Emily,⁹ b. June 28, 1868. 2. Laura Selina,⁹ b. July 24, 1871. 3. Edwin Dorman,⁹ b. Dec. 30, 1873. 4. Herman,⁹ b. Sept. 13, 1875.

by wife Lucetta:
4. Lizzie Estella,⁸ b. Aug. 16, 1857.
5. Edward Willard,⁸ b. April 3, 1859.

Calvin Payne,⁷ second son and fourth child of Ira and Lydia (Makepeace) Payne, b. in Montague, Mass., April 4, 1823, m. in same place, Nov. 26, 1846, Lois Emeline Webster, dau. of Francis and Edith (Gold-

thwait) Webster. She was b. in Montague, Mass., Oct. 30, 1826. He is a grocer; res. Monroe, Wis.
Children:
1. Emma,[8] b. Nov. 7, 1850; d. Oct. 20, 1851.
2. Frank Webster,[8] b. July 4, 1860.
3. Frederic,[8] b. Feb. 23, 1863; d. Feb. 27, 1863.

John A. Payne,[7] third son and fifth child of Ira and Lydia (Makepeace) Payne, b. in Montague, Mass., March 30, 1825, m. in same place, Jan. 1, 1852, Maria Lawrence, dau. of Cephas and Olivia (Stratton) Lawrence. She was b. in Montague, Mass., Jan. 22, 1823. He is a farmer; res. Paola, Miami county, Kansas.
Children:
1. Charles Adams,[8] b. in Schoolcraft, Mich., July 5, 1853, m. in Fontana, Miami county, Kansas, Oct. 25, 1876, Fannie Ann DeBall, dau. of Dr. James Montgomery and Hannah Ann (Ballard) De Ball, of Fontana. She was b. in Waco, Texas, Jan. 8, 1855.
2. George Fremont,[8] b. in Monroe, Wis., June 16, 1856.

Susan Payne,[7] third daughter and sixth child of Ira and Lydia (Makepeace) Payne, b. in Montague, Mass., May 14, 1827, m. in same place, March 26, 1860, Adoniram Prentice, son of Nathaniel and Permelia (Warren) Prentice. He was b. in Williamsburgh, Mass., March 24, 1822. Farmer; res. North Hadley, Mass. No children.

Emeline Payne,[7] fourth daughter and seventh child of Ira and Lydia (Makepeace) Payne, b. in Montague, Mass., Nov. 22, 1831, m. in Vernon, Windham county, Vt., April 16, 1849, Charles Willis Peeler, son of David and Nancy (Downs) Peeler. He was b. in Boston, Mass., Oct. 1, 1830. Hatter; res. Orange, Franklin county, Mass.
Children, all b. in Montague, Mass.:
1. Eveline Gertrude,[8] b. Aug. 5, 1850, m. in Vernon, Vt., March 4, 1869, George Luther Wyman, parentage not given. He was b. in Boston, Mass., March 28, 1848. Mechanic; res. Athol, Worcester county, Mass. No children.
2. Charles Abraham,[8] b. July 20, 1854. Mechanic; res. Orange, Mass.
3. Cora Belle,[8] b. July 5, 1862.
4. Oren Ellsworth,[8] b. Sept. 7, 1864; d. Feb. 13, 1866.

Julia A. Payne,[7] youngest daughter and child of Ira and Lydia (Makepeace) Payne, b. in Montague, Mass., Sept. 11, 1833, m. in Vernon, Windham county, Vt., Aug. 2, 1854, John Spaulding Peirce, son of Jacob and Elizabeth (Lamb) Peirce. He was b. in Leverett, Franklin county, Mass., July 2, 1830. Farmer; res. Montague, Mass.
Children:
1. Jennie Maria,[8] b. in Northfield, Mass., Feb. 5, 1856.
2. Susan Ardell,[8] b. in Montague, Mass., July 9, 1863; d. Dec. 11, 1864.
3. Fannie Ardell,[8] b. in Montague, Nov. 15, 1873.

Capt. James Chamberlain, the maternal grandfather of Oren Cleveland,[6] son of Rufus[5] and Mary (Chamberlain) Cleveland, (see page 30,) was a son of Joseph Chamberlain, who was resident in Tolland, Conn., as early as 1737. The following entries appear on the old township records there :

"Colbee, y[e] son of Mr. Joseph Chamberlain, was born y[e] 2[d] day of January, A. D. 1738." [He became a colonel in the Revolutionary war.]

"Jacob, y[e] son of Joseph Chamberlain, was born y[e] 21st day of January, A. D. 1740–41."

"William and Rebecca, y[e] son and daughter of Joseph Chamberlain, were born y[e] 25th day of January, A. D. 1744–45."

These were only those of the family of children born to him after he settled in Tolland, but there were several older children who came with their parents besides James, the subject of this sketch, as the following entries show :

"Joseph Chamberlain, Jr., of Tolland, and Elizabeth Delano, of Coventry, were married, July y[e] 3[d], A. D. 1744," followed by records of the birth of "Susannah, born July 16, 1745," and "Joel, born October 4, 1747." The Coventry (Conn.) records have "Abner Chamberlain, y[e] son of Joseph Chamberlain and Elizabeth his wife, was born November y[e] 14th, A. D. 1751." This Joseph Chamberlain, Jr., was undoubtedly the eldest brother of Capt. James Chamberlain. There were several sisters, names not learned, one of whom married a Chase, another married a Rice, another a Dimmock, another a Benton, another a Delano. One of them married for her second husband a Slosson. John Chase and Adoniram Benton, nephews of Capt. James Chamberlain, were each employed by him upon the extensive farm he owned, and James Chamberlain, Jr. (the only son of the worthy Captain), when he removed to Canaan, Vt., in after years, was accompanied by his "uncle Bill" (Chamberlain) as he was familiarly called, and his cousin, Adoniram Benton. Mr. Rice lived in Mansfield, Conn., and Mr. Dimmock, probably in Willington, Conn., but several of the Chamberlains settled at an early day in "Oblong," now Amenia, Dutchess county, N. Y., and about the year 1802, Oren Cleveland,[6] with his brother Alexander,[6] rode out there on horseback—a day's journey—to visit their relatives. They took dinner en route at some cousins of Rufus Cleveland,[5] by the name of Cobb, and it may be that this was the *family name* of Rachel, the mother of Rufus,[5] and wife of Benjamin Cleveland,[4] or perhaps a sister of the said Rachel had married a Cobb. My father seems quite certain that these Cobbs were his *father's cousins*. Possibly they were children of Dorothy Cleveland,[4] who may have so married. The town where this family of Cobbs resided, is not remembered by my father, but he thinks it was about half way between Winsted, Conn., and Amenia, N. Y.

The compiler has reason to believe that Capt. James Chamberlain was a descendant of Thomas Chamberlain, of Newton, Mass., who it is concluded was a son of "William Chamberlain, of Woburn, Mass., who had, at Concord : 1. Timothy, b. Aug. 13, 1649. 2. Isaac, b. Oct. 1, 1650, d. young; prob. removed to Billerica, Mass., in 1654 ; had there, 3. Sarah, b. Jan. 18, 1656. 4. Jacob, b. Jan. 18, 1658. 5. Thomas, b. Feb. 20, 1659. 6. Edmund, b. July 15, 1660. 7. Rebecca, b. Feb. 25, 1662. 8. Abraham, b. Jan. 6, 1664. 9. Ann, b. March 3, 1666. 10. Clement, b. May 30, 1669. 11. Daniel, b. Sept. 27, 1671 ; and 12. Isaac, b. Jan. 20, 1681. His wife Rebecca, mother of the last four children, perhaps of more, d. Sept. 26, 1692, in prison, on the preposterous charge of witchcraft, and he d. May 31, 1706, aged 85." [The foregoing is from Savage's Gen. Dict. of First Settlers of New England, Vol. I, CHAMBERLAIN, page 352.]

Thomas Chamberlain, of Newton, Mass., it appears, m. April 18, 1682, Elizabeth Hammond, a daughter of Thomas and Elizabeth (Stedman) Hammond. She was b. in Newton, Mass., Nov. 3, 1664. They had : 1. Thomas, b. Sept. 10, 1683. 2. Elizabeth, b. Aug. 1, 1686. 3. Rebecca, b. March 11, 1689. 4. Mary, b. Feb. 11, 1693. 5. Sarah, b. Oct. 18, 1695. 6. John, b. Sept. 26, 1698, and (probably) 7. Joseph, b. about 1700, and 8. William, b. about 1704. Joseph, it is conjectured, was the father of (Capt.) James, but the place of the birth of the latter, which occurred on Feb. 11, 1734, O. S., is not positively learned, though it is thought to have been Mansfield.

The full maiden name of his mother is not found, or remembered by his grandson, Oren Cleveland,[6] but there is little or no reason to doubt her given name was Mary.

By the Coventry (Conn.) records, it appears that "James Chamberlain and the widdow Abigail Palmer, the dafter of Zachariah Bointon,* was married together, January, ye 27, A. D. 1757." By her first husband, John Palmer, she had four children, all b. in Coventry, Conn., as follows :

1. Hannah, b. May 21, 1749, m. in Coventry, Joel Chamberlain, son of Joseph and Elizabeth (Delano) Chamberlain, and dying in child bed March 18, 1769, gave her infant daughter to her mother, then Mrs. Capt. James Chamberlain, to rear, and nurse with her own child, a babe of tender years (Naomi), and so daughter and granddaughter were fed and cradled together. The babe, called Hannah for her mother, grew to womanhood, and m. Dr. Joseph Chamberlain, by whom she had a son named Oren, and they resided in New York State, probably in or near Amenia, Dutchess county.

2. John, b. June 22, 1751, m. in Tolland, Conn., Ruth Chapman, a dau. of Deacon Chapman and sister of Elijah Chapman, Sheriff of Tolland county. He was a tanner ; removed to Charlotte, Vt., where he carried on the business of farming very successfully. He d. there, July 8, 1834, and his wife May 13, 1822. They had a family of six children,

* Zachary Boynton married Sarah Wicom, [Wyckham] a native of England, and had, according to the records in Coventry, seven children, namely: 1. John, b. Oct. 9, 1718. 2. Hannah, b. Dec. 30, 1720. 3. Joshua, b. Feb. 26, 1722. 4. Sarah, b. Oct. 6, 1723; d. Oct. 6, 1724. 5. Mehetabel, b. March 21, 1726. 6. Abigail, b. June 17, 1729. 7. Wicom, b. July 28, 1732.
"Zachary Boynton, of Coventry, Dyed December 30th, A. D. 1750, about 65 years of age," according to the records. Also, "John Palmer and Abigail Boynton, his wife, was married September ye 7th Day, A. D. 1748." John Palmer was son of Benjamin and Rebecca Palmer, and b. in Coventry, Feb. 14, 1725; d. Jan. 26, 1755.

namely : 1. Abigail, the eldest, b. about 1780, m. Edward Allen, both deceased many years since. Two sons, Harmon and Lovatus Allen, are living in Milan, Monroe county, Mich., prominent and influential citizens. Both have been members of the State Legislature. Carlos Allen, M. D., another brother, resides in New Jersey. 2. John, the next child, and eldest son, b. Sept. 5, 1783, m. Lovisa Hill, and had a family of nine children, two are living in Westfield, N. Y., one in Essex, Vt., and others in Charlotte, Vt., one of them A. C. Palmer, my correspondent. 3. Laura, b. about 1785, m. Ahira Hall, and settled in Portland, Chautauqua county, N. Y., where they died, leaving a large and highly respectable family. One son, John P. Hall, an extensive farmer, was a member of the New York Legislature, and spent the winter in Albany, about the year 1848. He d. in Fredonia, N. Y. His brother James Hall, M. D., was surgeon of a brigade during the war, and d. in Brocton, Chautauqua county, N. Y.; another, Rev. Albina Hall, is living in Northeast Pennsylvania ; another, S. P. Hall, resides in Sherman, N. Y. ; and another, Ralph Hall, in Newport, N. H. They had an equal array of sisters. 4. James, the second son, b. in Charlotte, Vt., Feb. 6, 1787, m. Charlotte Catlin, and d. in 1862–3, leaving one son, Olla C. Palmer, and five daughters. 5. Ruth, b. about 1793, m. Annanias Jones. She is. now a widow, living with her son, Rev. N. W. Jones, in Perrysburgh, N. Y. 6. William, b. about 1797, went to St. Lawrence county, N. Y., when young, and married there, but subsequently removed to New Hampshire, where he died, leaving several sons and daughters. His son, Theodore Palmer, resides in Greenfield, Mass., and a daughter, Mrs. M. F. Baldwin, resides in Bridgeport, Conn. 7. Daniel C., b. about 1806, and the youngest child, m. Mahala Eggleston, and both are now living (1877) in Charlotte, Vt., with many sons and daughters married and settled near them.

3. Mehitabel, b. July 13, 1753, m. Andrew West, of Tolland, Conn., a farmer, and removed, it is believed, to Oneida county, N. Y., where they had a family of children. One daughter, Hannah West, was brought to Capt. Chamberlain's, and remained until she married John Barton, son of Col. Barton, Providence, R. I., of Revolutionary fame. Nothing further learned of their children.

4. Abigail, b. July 22, 1755, m. Oliver Edgerton, son of Hezekiah Edgerton, of Tolland, Conn. They came, however, soon after to Warehouse Point, Conn., and he engaged in trade, but his wife dying, he returned to his native place after marrying a widow with considerable property at Amenia, N. Y. His father was at one time a resident of Norwich, Conn., and deeded, Feb. 2, 1775, a farm of 82½ acres in Tolland, to his son Oliver. No children.

The descendants of Abigail (Boynton) Palmer, by second husband, Capt. James Chamberlain, claim more particular attention, and will be next in order.

As before stated, they "were married together, Jan. y⁰ 27, A. D. 1757," in Coventry, Conn., and their children were six in number, as follows, all b. in Coventry, or Tolland, Conn. :

1. Joseph, b. Nov. 4, 1757; d. June 12, 1759.
2. Mary, b. Aug. 7, 1759; d. Nov. 13, 1807.
3. Sally, b. Aug. 12, 1761; d. June 25, 1835.
4. Joseph (again), b. ———, 1763; d. June 3, 1766.
5. James, (Maj.), b. July 24, 1766; d. Feb. 22, 1814.
6. Naomi, b. Nov. 19, 1769; d. April 26, 1867.

It is a notable circumstance that the two little Josephs were each accidentally drowned (in a large kettle used by the family) between the ages of one and a half and three years. They are buried side by side in the old cemetery in Tolland, a double headstone marking the graves with full inscriptions. As will be perceived, three daughters and one son only grew to adult age.

Mary Chamberlain, the eldest daughter and second child of Capt. James and Abigail (Boynton) [Palmer] Chamberlain, b. in Coventry, Conn., Aug. 7, 1759, m. in Ellington, Conn., Sept. 9, 1779, Rufus Cleveland,[5] son of Benjamin[4] and Rachel Cleveland. He was b. in Canterbury, Conn., June 14, 1754; d. in Barkhamstead, Litchfield county, Conn., Feb. 22, 1838. She d. in same place, Nov. 13, 1807. They had a family of fourteen children, records of whom may be found on page 31, and descendants thereafter following to page 65, to which the reader is referred.

Sally Chamberlain, the second daughter and third child of Capt. James and Abigail (Boynton) [Palmer] Chamberlain, was b. in Coventry, Conn., Aug. 12, 1761, m. in Ellington, Conn., ———, 1782, Roswell Paine, son of Stephen and Deborah (Skinner) Paine. He was b. in North Bolton (now Vernon), Conn., Feb. 24, 1756; d. in Amherst, Mass., March 7, 1806. She d. in Hadley, Mass., June 25, 1835. He was a very successful farmer, and in later years the popular landlord of a hotel in Amherst, to which town he removed in 1802. Children:

1. James, b. in Vernon, Conn., June 18, 1784, a cripple from birth; d. in Amherst, Mass., March 22, 1823.
2. Sally, b. in Vernon, Conn., April 14, 1786; d. in Chardon, Geauga county, Ohio, Nov. 24, 1874.
3. Deborah, b. in Vernon, Conn., Aug. 31, 1788; d. in Kingsville, Ashtabula county, Ohio, Aug. 5, 1874.
4. Abigail, b. in Vernon, Conn., July 22, 1790; d. in Parishville, St. Lawrence county, N. Y., Feb. 17, 1871.
5. Henry, (Rev.), b. in Vernon, Conn., Aug. 17, 1793; d. in Rockland, Knox county, Me., of heart disease, March 25, 1877.
6. Roswell, b. in Vernon, Conn., Aug. 4, 1795; d. in Galesburgh, Knox county, Ill., Feb. 1, 1870.
7. Harriet, b. in Vernon, Conn., Nov. 11, 1797; d. in Pacific, Columbia county, Wis., July 7, 1861.
8. Charles, b. in Vernon, Conn., Sept. 29, 1799; d. in Amherst, Mass., Feb. 16, 1817.
9. Julianna, b. in Vernon, Conn., June —, 1801; d. in Amherst, Aug. 31, 1802.
10. Joseph Chamberlain, b. in Amherst, Mass., July 6, 1804; d. in Galva, Henry county, Ill., April 1, 1871.
11. Edward, b. in Amherst, Mass., Oct. 28, 1806; d. in Chardon, Geauga county, Ohio, April 19, 1850.

Hon. L. M. Boltwood, of Hartford, Conn., who has been several years preparing the materials for a history of Amherst, his native place, says, there is the record there of the death of *Robert*, son of Roswell Paine, June 8, 1807. If there was no clerical error about it, and such a son was b. to Roswell Paine by wife Sally, the birth probably occurred early in the year 1803, but the records extant in hands of descendants show but eleven children as given.

James Paine, eldest son and child of Roswell and Sally (Chamberlain) Paine, d. unmarried. My father tells me that the unremitting care and solicitude bestowed upon this unfortunate and almost helpless cripple by his mother, was touching to behold.

Sally Paine, the eldest daughter and second child of Roswell and Sally (Chamberlain) Paine, m. in Amherst, Mass., Sept. 5, 1805, Eli Hastings, son of Thomas and Hannah (Billings) Hastings. He was b. in Amherst, June 1, 1784; d. in Brecksville, Cuyahoga county, Ohio, March 20, 1835. She d. in Chardon, Geauga county, Ohio, Nov. 24, 1874. He was a farmer. Children, all b. in Amherst, Mass.:

1. Juliana, b. Oct. 31, 1806; d. Nov. 12, 1806.
2. George, b. April 12, 1808, m. in Belchertown, Mass., Sept. —, 1829, Betsey Thayer, dau. of John Thayer, date of her birth, etc., not learned, but she d. in Illinoistown, Ill., Sept. 8, 1843. He d. in Alabama, at Bladen Springs, Jan. 31 1859. Children: 1. Ellen Maria, b. ——, 1830; d. ——, 1832. 2. Julia, b. ——, 1832; d. July 12, 1852. 3. ——, b. Feb. 22, 1834; d. March —, 1834. 4. Henry Eli, b. Feb. 12, 1836; d. March —, 1864, unm. 5. ——, b. ——, 1838; d. ——, 1838. 6. Harriet, b. ——, 1840; d. ——, 1840. 7. ——, b. Sept. 6, 1843; d. Sept. 10, 1843.
3. Juliana, (again), b. Nov. 21, 1809; d. May 1, 1810.
4. Nancy, b. March 10, 1811, m. first, in Brooklyn, Ohio, Oct. 20, 1831, her uncle, Edward Paine, son of Roswell and Sally (Chamberlain) Paine. He was b. in Amherst, Mass., Oct. 28, 1806; d. in Chardon, Ohio, April 19, 1850. Clerk and accountant. She m. second, in Chardon, Ohio, Nov. 3, 1850, Samuel Squire, son of Jonathan and Esther (Thusedell) Squire. He was b. in Orange county, N. Y., Oct. 16, 1799; d. in Chardon, Ohio, Nov. 8, 1854. Merchant. She is living (1878) in Chardon, Ohio. Children by first husband, Edward Paine: 1. Sarah Antoinette, b. in Brecksville, Cuyahoga county, Ohio, Jan. 25, 1833; d. in Chardon, Geauga county, Ohio, Dec. 3, 1851. By second husband, Samuel Squire: 2. Sarah Maria, b. in Chardon, Dec. 29, 1852.
5. Daughter, b. Aug. 9, 1814; d. Aug. 21, 1814.
6. Edwin, b. May 16, 1819, m. first, in Louisville, Ky., Sept. 5, 1841. Gulielma Shibel, dau. of John Shibel. She was b. in Louisville, Ky.; d. in St. Clair county, Ill., Sept. 20, 1843. He m. second, in Cap au Gris, Mo., May 15, 1849, Mary Ann Gordon, dau. of Alfred and Maria A. (Wing) Gordon. She was b. in Cap au Gris, Sept. 22, 1830; d. in Kirkwood, Mo., April 25, 1860. He m. third, in Brooklyn, N. Y., April 2, 1868, Charlotte Payne, dau. of John and Mary (Leighton) Payne. She was b. in London, Eng., Sept. 13, 1839. He is a merchant; res. Chardon, Ohio. No children by his first wife. Children, by wife Mary Ann: 1. Henry Bee, b. Aug. 12, 1850; d. June 25, 1853. 2. Georgiana, b. Feb. 10, 1852; d. March 13, 1861. 3. Ella Gordon, b. May 6, 1854. 4. Emma, b. March 15, 1856. 5. Charles Edwin, b. June 28, 1862; d. Aug. 28, 1863. By wife Charlotte: 6. Sally, b. Feb. 5, 1869. 7. Edwin, b. June 27, 1870. 8. Fannie Maud, b. June 6, 1872. 9. Helen, b. Dec. 16, 1873. 10. George, b. July 6, 1875.

Deborah Paine, second daughter and third child of Roswell and Sally (Chamberlain) Paine, m. in Amherst, Mass., Oct. 19, 1809, Horace Merrill, son of Capt. Calvin and Orinda (Rowe) Merrill. He was b. in Amherst, Mass., Aug. 31, 1789; d. in Chardon, Ohio, Sept. 6, 1873. Hatter. She d. in Kingsville, Ohio, Aug. 5, 1874.
Children :
1. Mary Elvira, b. in Amherst, Mass., Nov. 13, 1812, m. in Chardon, Ohio, Oct. 18, 1847, John Nichols, M. D., son of Joshua and Rebecca (Wetherell) Nichols. He was b. in Chesterfield, Mass., Jan. 8, 1816. A druggist; res. Columbus, Ohio. Child: 1. John Merrill, b. in Kirtland, Ohio, Nov. 1, 1851; m. in South Toledo, Ohio, May 4, 1876, Julia Adelaide Baldwin, dau. of Perry C. and Jane (Starkweather) Baldwin. She was b. in Waterville, Ohio, Sept. 13, 1852.
2. Frederic, b. in Amherst, Mass., Sept. 28, 1814; d. Feb. 4, 1817.
3. Julia Ann, b. in Amherst, Mass., Dec. 5, 1816, m. in Chardon, Ohio, July 11, 1839, Roderick King, son of Zadok and Fanny (Collins) King. He was b. in Suffield, Conn., Jan. 20, 1814; d. in Munson, Geauga county, Ohio, April 10, 1857. She is living (1878) in Chardon, Ohio. Children: 1. Mary Eliza, b. July 23, 1845. 2. Horace Merrill, b. Aug. 17, 1847. 3. Rufus Roderick, b. Dec. 11, 1853.
4. Frederic Henry, b. in Amherst, Mass., July 25, 1819, m. in Denny, Warren county, Ill., Oct. 7, 1847, Lucretia Paine, dau. of Charles Henry and Parthenia (Mason) Paine. She was b. in Freedom, Portage county, Ohio, Aug. 27, 1825. He is a merchant; res. Avon, Ill. Children: 1. Mary Emily, b. in Henderson county, Ill., July 4, 1848, m. in Avon, Ill., April 26, 1868, George Albro Johnson, son of Ralph and Clara (Jackson) Johnson. He was b. in Clinton, N. J., Nov. 6, 1845. Child: Harry Gorham, b. in Avon, Ill., Dec. 14, 1868. 2. Charles Henry, b. in Greenbush, Ill., Jan. 11, 1850. 3. Horace, b. in Greenbush, Ill., April 25, 1852; d. May 16, 1852. 4. Effie Maria, b. in Greenbush, Ill., Nov. 19, 1853. 5. John Edward, b. in Greenbush, Ill., Jan. 25, 1857; d. March 15, 1857. 6. Fanny Cornelia, b. in Greenbush, Ill., May 7, 1858; d. May 15, 1859. 7. Frederic Horace, b. in Greenbush, Ill., April 20, 1860. 8. Giles Edward, b. in Greenbush, Ill., Dec. 13, 1862. 9. Cora Eliza, b. in Avon, Ill., April 17, 1865. 10. Frank, b. in Avon, Ill., Oct. 6, 1867. 11. Arthur, b. in Avon, Ill., Nov. 20, 1869.
5. Rufus Rowe, b. in Amherst, Mass., Aug. 31, 1821, m. first, in Monmouth, Ill., about 1848, Hannah Elizabeth Ickus, dau. of Dr. Jonas Ickus, and a native of Bloomfield, Perry county, Pa., where she was b. about 1823. She d. in Monmouth, Ill., in the fall of 1864. He was a young man of ability, studied law in Chardon, Geauga county, Ohio, and was admitted to practice. Shortly after the birth of his first child he went to the Golden State, and remained till he d. suddenly, in Marysville, Cal., Sept. 22, 1874. By his first wife, Hannah Elizabeth, he had one child, a son, Harding Ickus, b. in Monmouth, Ill., Feb. —, 1850, who is now married and resides in Clarion, Sedgwick county, Kansas. By his second wife, m. in Marysville, Cal., who d. within a year after marriage, he had no children, but by a third wife he had two children. The names, etc., of the second and third wives, or of the children by the latter, not ascertained.
6. Nancy Louisa, b. in Amherst, Mass., Jan. 2, 1824, m. in Chardon, Ohio, Nov. 20, 1845, Leverett King, son of George and Nancy King. He was b. in Chardon, Ohio, June 7, 1824. Farmer; res. Chardon, Ohio. Children: 1. Belle, b. Jan. 25, 1848, m. and res. in Chardon. 2. Lizzie Orinda, b. Sept. 28, 1855. 3. Charles Leverett, b. Dec. 16, 1860. 4. William George, b. Feb. 1, 1863.

7. Eliza Orinda, b. in Amherst, Mass., Sept. 9, 1826, m. in Chardon' Geauga county, Ohio, Aug. 23, 1855, Rev. Dormer L. Hickox, son of Thomas and Emeline (Robinson) Hickox. He was b. in Hartwick, Otsego county, N. Y., May 13, 1831. Presbyterian clergyman; res. Talladega, Ala. Children: 1. Howard Merrill, b. May 9, 1859. 2. Mary Eliza, b. May 11, 1861. 3. Emma Paine, b. Nov. 11, 1863. 4. Charles Thomas, b. Nov. 8, 1869. Mr. Hickox was pastor several years in Bloomfield, Trumbull county, Ohio, and subsequently in Kingsville, Ashtabula county, Ohio.
8. Lucy Emily, b. in Amherst, Mass., June 30, 1829, m. in Chardon, Geauga county, Ohio, Aug. 1, 1849, Martin Benjamin Cook, son of Benjamin and Robie (Kelley) Cook. He was b. in Cummington, Mass., Jan. 22, 1830. Children: 1. Emma Julia, b. Jan. 23, 1851; d. unm. Aug. 10, 1875. 2. Ida Eliza, b. July 26, 1853. 3. Fred. Martin, b. Sept. 1, 1856. 4. Willis Merrill, b. July 18, 1859. 5. Charles, b. June 23, 1861; d. Aug. 6, 1862.
9. Charles Chauncey, b. in Orwell, Vt., Sept. 10, 1833, m. in North Bloomfield, Ohio, Aug. 27, 1855, Cornelia Converse Osborn, dau. of Leonard and Amanda (Smith) Osborn. She was b. in Bloomfield, Ohio, Oct. 23, 1833. He is a merchant; res. Galesburgh, Ill. No children.

Abigail Paine, third daughter and fourth child of Roswell and Sally (Chamberlain) Paine, b. in North Bolton, Conn., July 23, 1790, m. in Amherst, Mass., March 1, 1813, Stoughton Cowles, son of Eleazer and Hannah (Stoughton) Cowles. He was b. in Amherst, Jan. 3, 1788; d. in Parishville, N. Y., Oct. 13, 1861. Farmer. She d. in same place, Feb. 17, 1871.
Children:

1. Roswell Paine, b. Dec. 18, 1813; d. Jan. 4, 1814.
2. Harriet Julianna, b. Jan. 3, 1815, (in Salisbury, Vt.), m. in Parishville, N. Y., Feb. 18, 1835, Stephen Freeman Palmer, son of Zuriel and Martha (Morgan) Palmer. He was b. in Hubbardton, Vt., March 6, 1812; res. Madrid, N. Y. Children: 1. Samuel Henry, b. in Colton, N. Y., Aug. 12, 1837, m. in Pierpont, St. Lawrence county, N. Y., June —, 1867, Martha Elizabeth Packard, dau. of Hiram and Caroline (Dimmock) Packard. She was b. in Madrid, N. Y., Feb. 4, 1843. They have four children, all b. in Ogdensburg, N. Y., namely: Martha Henrietta, b. Feb. 27, 1868. Henry Hiram, b. Nov. 1, 1869. Freeman Packard, b. Nov. 10, 1872. Harriet Cowles, b. March 31, 1874. 2. Henrietta, b. in Colton, N. Y., Sept. 25, 1839; d. April 21, 1848. 3. Stephen Freeman, b. in Madrid, N. Y., July 2, 1846, m. in Ogdensburgh, N. Y., May 6, 1874, Josephine Lankton, dau. of Patrick and Melissa (Gardner) Lankton. She was b. in Ogdensburgh, N. Y., Dec. 14, 1851. They have two children, as follows: Charles Clare, b. July 27, 1875; d. March 19, 1876. William Lankton, b. April 7, 1877.
3. Roswell Paine (again), b. July 9, 1816; d. Nov. 24, 1816.
4. Marvin Hastings, b. May 12, 1818, m. in Parishville, N. Y., Oct. 1, 1845, Lucretia Ann Samson, dau. of Levi and Olive (Green) Samson. She was b. in Grand Isle, Vt., Dec. 3, 1824; res. Parishville, Vt. Children: 1. Myron Hastings, b. Sept. 20, 1846; d. Oct. 10, 1860. 2. Harriet Lucretia, b. Nov. 25, 1852. 3. Clark Hastings, b. March 25, 1860.
5. Abigail Paine, b. May 6, 1820; d. March 15, 1843, unm.
6. Rosana Amanda, b. June 20, 1822; d. Dec. 23, 1844, unm.

7. Charles Stoughton Dickinson, b. May 11, 1824, m. in Potsdam, N. Y., June 6, 1848, Abigail Avery Bannister, dau. of Stewart Elkanah and Abigail (Avery) Bannister. She was b. in Potsdam, N. Y., Dec. 20, 1822.: Children, all born in Parishville, N. Y.: 1. Sarah Patience Abigail, b. June 30, 1849, m. in Parishville, Aug. 31, 1871, Oscar Orlando Stone, son of Thomas and Almira (Boland) Stone. He was b. in Parishville, Nov. 16, 1843. Child, Maria Almira, b. Oct. 15, 1876; d. April 29, 1877. 2. George Stoughton Paine, b. Dec. 4, 1854, m. in Parishville, Nov. 15, 1875, Agnes Arabella Ewings, dau. of Oscar Fitzland and Betsey (Willis) Ewings. She was b. in Parishville, Jan. 8, 1853. He d. in same place, March 18, 1877. Child: Mabel Edith, b. Nov. 1, 1876. 3. Isabel Ormanda Avery, b. Oct. 21, 1858; d. March 17, 1877. 4. Eunice Betsey Maria, b. July 21, 1863.
8. Henry Paine, b. Sept. 28, 1826; d. March 14, 1827.
9. Sarah Ann, b. March 23, 1828; d. Dec. 28, 1844.

Henry Paine, second son and fifth child of Roswell and Sally (Chamberlain) Paine, b. in North Bolton, Conn., Aug. 17, 1793, m. in Waterville, Me., Feb. 19, 1827, Evelina Bacon, dau. of Ebenezer and Hannah (Lovejoy) Bacon. She was b. in Waterville, Me., Jan. 22, 1800; d. in Rockland, Me., of heart disease, March 25, 1877. He d. in same place, Nov. 12, 1868. He was licensed to preach by the Baptists in Belchertown, Mass., but devoted his life to the cause of education, principally in the State of Maine, from 1824 till about two weeks before his death. He lived at one time in Monmouth, Me.

Children :

1. Charles Henry, b. Feb. 3, 1826; d. Oct. 1, 1828.
2. Charles Henry (again), b. Jan. 13, 1829, m. in Rockland, Me., Aug. 12, 1852, Alice Drinkwater, dau. of James and Henrietta (Philbrook) Drinkwater. She was b. in Isleborough, Me., Feb. 3, 1830. He is a printer; res. Hallowell, Me. Children: 1. Cora Alecia, b. in Rockland, Me., Jan. 15, 1854. 2. Henry James, b. in Thomaston, Me., Aug. 12, 1856. 3. Eva Havener, b. in Rockland, Me., May 3, 1859. 4. Charles Albert, b. in Bath, Me., Dec. 19, 1861. 5. Alice Louisa, b. in Hallowell, Me., April 24, 1865. 6. William Edward, b. in Hallowell, Me., April 24, 1865. 7. Grace Ellen, b. in Rockland, Me., Feb. 6, 1873.
3. Evelina Maria, b. July 31, 1830, m. in Thomaston, Me., Aug. 29, 1853, Capt. Joseph Havener, son of Joseph and Mary (Brier) Havener. He was b. in Brooks, Waldo county, Me., ——, 1829; d. on his passage home from Callas (South America), to New York, April 19, 1873. She d. in Thomaston, Me., Oct. 27, 1855. They had no children.
4. Lydia Elvira, b. May 19, 1832, m. in Rockland, Me., April 6, 1868, John Sears, son of Dr. John B. and Priscilla (McIntyre) Sears. He was b. in Rockland, Me., ——, 1834. Grain ranche; res. Stockton, Cal. Nothing learned as to family.
5. Louisa Jane, b. March 15, 1835, m. in Rockland, Me., Feb. 9, 1875, Lewis Horan, birth, parentage, etc., unknown, except he was a native of Virginia and b. about the year 1829. Merchant; res. Santa Barbara, San Domingo, W. I. No children.
6. William Edward, b. Dec. 1, 1836; d. in the army.
7. Isabella Marshall, b. Feb. 29, 1840; resides in California. Teacher.

Roswell Paine, third son and sixth child of Roswell and Sally (Chamberlain) Paine, b. in North Bolton, Conn., Aug. 4, 1795, m. in

Bridport, Addison county, Vt., April 27, 1820, Elvira Barbour, dau. of James and Dorcas (Doane) Barbour. She was b. in Bridport, Vt., Jan. 11, 1795; d. in Galesburgh, Ill., June 12, 1867. He d. in same place, Feb. 1, 1870. Farmer.
Children:

1. Roswell Richmond, b. Nov. 14, 1821, m. first, in Boyle county, Ky., (near Danville), Feb. 3, 1853, Georgia Ann Nash, dau. of Marvel Mosely, and Nancy (Vineyard) Nash. She was b. in Lincoln county, Ky., Aug. 20, 1830; d. in or near Danville, Boyle county, Ky., Dec. 24, 1853. He m. second, in Jessamine county, Ky., Sept. 14, 1854, America Smith, dau. of James and Maria (Lockett) [Hawks] Smith. She was b. in Jessamine county, Ky., Aug. 5, 1825. He is a farmer; res. Cambridge, Storey county, Iowa. Children, by wife Georgiana: 1. Daughter, b. Dec. 24, 1853; d. Dec. 24, 1853. By wife America: 2. Nash, b. in Galesburg, Knox county, Ill., Sept. 26, 1855; d. in Cambridge, Iowa, April 12, 1867. 3. Smith, b. in Abingdon, Ill., Dec. 6, 1857. 4. Charles Roswell, b. in same place, July 6, 1859. 5. May, b. in same place, Oct. 23, 1860. 6. Emerson, b. in same place, July 26, 1862. 7. John William, b. in same place, Sept. 6, 1864. 8. Willard Barbour, b. in Cambridge, Iowa, March 23, 1866.
2. Sarah Elvira, b. March 12, 1823, m. in Galesburg, Ill., Dec. 16, 1846, Luzerne Bartholomew, son of Noyes Dana and Elizabeth (Hull) Bartholomew. He was b. in Wallingford, Conn., Feb. 24, 1812; d. in Wallingford, Conn., Feb. 10, 1866. She is living (1878) in Galesburg, Ill. Children: 1. Payne, b. in Byfield, Mass., July 18, 1854; d. July 21, 1854. 2. Minnie Evalena, b. in Elmwood, Ill., Feb. 25, 1856, m. in Galesburg, Ill., Oct. 4, 1877, Cyrus Miner Avery, son of George and Seraphina Princess Mary (Phelps) Avery. He was b. in Galesburg, June 19, 1846. 3. Bessie Helen, b. in Elmwood, Ill., Dec. 7, 1858. 4. Charles Henry, b. in Hogleton, Ill., March 31, 1861; d. Oct. 15, 1861. 5. Daughter, b. Oct. 21, 1863; d. Oct. 23, 1863.
3. Mary Priscilla, b. Jan. 11, 1825, m. in Galesburg, Ill., Sept. 12, 1853, Rev. George Bent, son of Samuel Browning and Catherine (Avery) Bent. He was b. in Middlebury, Vt., March 29, 1827. Congregational clergyman; res. Seneca, Nemaha county, Kansas. Children: 1. George Payne, b. in Dundee, Ill., June 16, 1854, m. in Burr Oak, Iowa, April 26, 1876, Clara A. Wingate, dau. of Henry and Charity Eliza (Willsie) Wingate. She was b. in Hemmingford, Canada, July 24, 1857. Child: Clara Wingate, b. in Chicago, Ill., March 10, 1877. 2. Samuel Browning, b. in Lansing, Iowa, Oct. 27, 1858; d. in Burr Oak, Iowa, Aug. 19, 1861. 3. Charles Avery, b. in Burr Oak, Iowa, Oct. 10, 1860. 4. Mary Catherine, b. in Burr Oak, Iowa, March 31, 1862; d. Aug. 15, 1864. 5. Arthur Sumner, b. in Burr Oak, Iowa, July 17, 1864. 6. Harriet Maria, b. in Burr Oak, Iowa, Aug. 10, 1867.
4. Eliza, b. Feb. 17, 1827; d. June 17, 1828.
5. Charles Henry, b. April 25, 1829, m. in La Fayette, Ill., April 15, 1852, Sarah Ann Reed, dau. of William Allen and Amy (Crandall) Reed. She was b. in Canada Village, Conn., Aug. 12, 1832; res. Otho, Webster county, Iowa. Children: 1. Georgiana, b. Nov. 15, 1853; d. Sept. 17, 1854. 2. Olive Gertrude, b. March 25, 1856; d. July 3, 1856. 3. Frank Roswell, b. Jan. 4, 1857. 4. Frederic Edward, b. Sept. 26, 1858. 5. Charles Albert, b. April 4, 1860. 6. George Harrington, b. Oct. 6, 1864. 7. Henry Bascom, b. Jan. 14, 1867. 8. Walter Wells, b. Jan. 10, 1869. 9. Hattie Amy, b. Oct. 21, 1873.

6. Eliza Juliana, b. Oct. 7, 1830, m. in Fremont, Ill., May 5, 1860, Morton Monroe Eaton, M. D., son of Monroe and Clarissa (Fales) Eaton. He was b. in Pelham, Mass., April 21, 1839. She d. in Seneca, Kansas, Feb. 24, 1878. Res. Cincinnati, O. Children: 1. Alice Augusta, b. in Galesburg, Ill., Feb. 18, 1861; d. June 10, 1861. 2. Daniel Brainard, b. in Peoria, Ill., May 23, 1862; d. June 14, 1862. 3. Lucy Elvira, b. in Peoria, Ill., May 5, 1863 4. Alice Ellen, b. in Peoria, Ill., Oct. 27, 1864. 5. Morton Monroe, b. in Peoria, Ill., Nov. 2, 1866.
7. Edward Nelson, b. July 14, 1832, m. in Burr Oak, Iowa, Jan. 18, 1865, Helen Manning, dau. of Dea. Alpha and Lovina (Van Vliet) Manning. She was b. in Belmont, Canada West, March 24, 1842. He d. in Burr Oak, Iowa, March 13, 1871. She is living (1878) in ——. Children: 1. Harriet Helen, b. in Galesburg, Ill., Feb. 6, 1866. 2. Charlotte Lovina, b. in Otho, Iowa, Feb. 27, 1870. 3. Edward Nelson, b. in Burr Oak, Iowa, Sept. 2, 1871.
8. Martha Laura, b. July 24, 1834, m. in Galesburg, Ill., Jan. 18, 1855, Newell Sapp, M. D., son of Brumel and Elizabeth (Wier) Sapp. He was b. in Salem, N. C., Sept. 20, 1854. Physician and surgeon; res. Plmouth, Ill. Children: 1. Florence Payne, b. in Birmingham, Ill., Dec. 22, 1855; d. Feb. 3, 1856. 2. Harriet Clementine, b. Sept. 2, 1858; d. Dec. 3, 1865. 3. Son, b. Nov. 6, 1861; d. Nov. 6, 1861. 4. Little Joe, b. in Plymouth, Ill., Oct. 11, 1866; d. June 2, 1867. 5. Cora Ellen, b. May 8, 1868.
9. Harriet Lucetta, b. Dec. 24, 1836, m. in Galesburg, Ill., Sept. 29, 1859, Newton Briggs, son of John and Chloe (Northrup) Briggs. He was b. in Weymouth, Medina county, Ohio, April 11, 1830. She d. in Galesburg, Ill., Nov. 30, 1872. Res. Galesburg, Ill. Children: 1. Willis Payne, b. Aug. 11, 1860. 2. Harry Elmer, b. Feb. 18, 1865. 3. Carrie Myrtle, b. Feb. 25, 1867.
10. Ellen Barbour, b. April 27, 1840, m. in Galesburg, Ill., Aug. 23, 1859, Philander James Harrington, son of ——. He was b. in New Berlin, N. Y., Jan. 7, 1834; d. in Philadelphia, Pa., April 22, 1877. She d. in Galesburg, Ill., Jan. 26, 1863. Children: 1. Son, b. ——, 1860; d. ——, 1860. 2. Lucy Ellen, b. May 6, 1862; res. 185 20th Street, Detroit, Mich.

Harriet Paine, fourth daughter and seventh child of Roswell and Sally (Chamberlain) Paine, b. in North Bolton, Conn., Nov. 11, 1797, m. in Amherst, Mass., Jan. 16, 1817, Alpheus Osborn, son of Richard and Isabel (Jones) Osborn. He was b. in Pittsfield, Mass., Dec. 3, 1791; d. in Fairfax, Iowa, Feb. 16, 1874. She d. in Pacific, Wis., July 7, 1861. He was a builder.

Children, all b. in Hadley, Mass.:

1. Charles Paine, b. Nov. 22, 1817, m. in Troy, Walworth county, Wis., May 1, 1844, Harriet Newell Marsh, dau. of Enos and Rebecca (Hawley) Marsh. She was b. in Montague, Mass., Aug. 28, 1823. He is a nurseryman; res. Fairfax, Linn county, Iowa. Children, all b. in La Fayette, Wis.: 1. Dwight Pomeroy, b. April 17, 1845; d. June 9, 1855. 2. Charles Hunt, b. Dec. 16, 1848. 3. Harriet, b. Nov. 8, 1853. 4. Herbert, b. March 19, 1856. 5. George McClellan, b. April 8, 1862.
2. Harriet, b. May 27, 1819, m. in Hadley, Mass., April 30, 1840, Timothy Green Ayres, son of Josiah and Eunice (Green) Ayres. He was b. in Amherst, Mass., Feb. 10, 1816. Farmer; res. Byron, Ogle county, Ill.
3. Eliza, b. Oct. 20, 1820; d. Nov. 29, 1837.

4. Julia, b. July 25, 1822, m. in Hadley, Mass., May 2, 1844, Champion Dickinson, son of Gideon and Demaris (Waite) Dickinson. He was b. in Hatfield, Mass., Dec. 22, 1814; res. Le Roy, N. Y. Children: 1. Alpheus Dwight, b. in Hatfield, Mass., Jan. 6, 1845, m. in Le Roy, N. Y., Jan. 1, 1872, Mary McCarter, and has two children. Carriage painter; res. Le Roy. 2. Harriet Lucelia, b. Nov. 11, 1846; d. April 28, 1848. 3. Edwin Brainard, b. Dec. 23, 1849; d. Sept. 5, 1851. 4. Son, b. Dec. 29, 1851; d. Jan. 1, 1852. 5. Nellie Amelia, b. June 1, 1853, m. in Le Roy, N. Y., Jan. 1, 1872, William Benjamin Wansor, and has three children. Sign and carriage painter. 6. Evelyn Alice, b. Jan. 8, 1856; d. Feb. 19, 1856. 7. Julia Estella, b. July 15, 1859; d. Oct. 1, 1859. 8. Lizzie Osborn, b. Dec. 30, 1857; d. Oct. 6, 1861. 9. Charles Clark, b. June 19, 1863; d. April 23, 1864.

5. Mary, b. Oct. 24, 1823, m. in Brattleboro', Vt., Nov. 30, 1849, Charles Dexter Fairfield, M. D., son of Joel Lee and Rosina (Phelps) Fairfield. He was b. in Belchertown, Mass., May 24, 1825. She d. in Newport, Tenn., July 13, 1861. He is a physician; res. Newport, Tenn. Children: 1. Mary Dexter, b. in Newport, Me., Oct. 11, 1851; d. in Newport, Tenn., Nov. 28, 1864. 2. Charles Lee, b. in Chardon, Ohio, Nov. 6, 1852; d. in Cleveland, Ohio, Nov. 22, 1853. 3. Minnie Gray, b. in Winchester, Ky., Sept. 1, 1854. 4. Shelley, b. in Newport, Tenn., Sept. 22, 1855; d. Oct. 19, 1856. 5. Harriet Augusta, b. Aug. 2, 1856; d. Sept. 11, 1856. 6. Dexter, b. Dec. 13, 1859; d. Oct. 28, 1860. 7. Tennessee, b. June 25, 1861; d. Aug. 15, 1861.

6. Catherine, b. May 6, 1825; d. April 30, 1828.
7. Alpheus Dwight, b. Oct. 22, 1826; d. Nov. 29, 1843.
8. Matthias Lanckton, b. July 25, 1828, m. in Monticello, Ill., ———, 1855, Angeline Branch, dau. of Thomas Anderson and Elizabeth (Robinson) Branch. She was b. in Monroe county, Ky., Jan. 16, 1831. He is a farmer; res. Seymour, Champaign county, Ill. Children: 1. George Henry, b. May 19, 1857; d. Aug. 30, 1857. 2. Douglas, b. Aug. 16, 1858. 3. William, b. March 10, 1860. 4. Lizzie Cowles, b. Feb. 19, 1861; d. Oct. 9, 1863. 5. Eliza Augusta, b. March 13, 1862. 6. Thomas Alpheus, b. June 24, 1863; d. Jan. 12, 1869. 7. Hattie K., b. Jan. 12, 1866. 8. James Lanckton, b. April 27, 1867.
9. Catherine (again), b. March 26, 1830, m. in Holyoke, Mass., Dec. 15, 1859, Isaac Newton Day, son of Jedediah and Phebe (Day) Day. He was b. in Holyoke, Mass., Feb. 8, 1826. Farmer; res. Holyoke, Mass. Children: 1. Irving Newton, b. Nov. 9, 1861. 2. Ernest Osborn, b. April 10, 1863; d. May 28, 1873. 3. Harriet Paine, b. April 20, 1865.
10. Elizabeth Cowles, b. Aug. 2, 1831. Teacher; res. Portage City, Wis.
11. Ellen, b. Dec. 4, 1832; d. in Hatfield, Mass., March 15, 1850.
12. George Henry, b. Dec. 30, 1833, m. in Portage, Wis., —— 1859, Mary Josephine Ketchum, dau. of Reuben Doud and Sarah Jane (Eldridge) Ketchum. She was b. in Stockbridge, Madison county, N. Y., Oct. 27, 1840. He d. of pneumonia, in Stockton, Cal., May 27, 1864. Children, both b. in Portage, Wis.: 1. Carrie Smith, b. Dec. 4, 1860. 2. Allie May, b. April 29, 1863; d. May 9, 1864.
13. Sarah Jane, b. April 30, 1836, m. in Holyoke, Mass., June 22, 1854, Austin Dickinson Hemenway, son of Otis and Elizabeth (Upson) Hemenway. He was b. in Leverett, Mass., Aug. 29, 1831; res. Portage, Wis. Children: 1. George Henry, b. Nov. 9, 1855. 2. Julia Maria, b. June 25, 1857; d. Sept. 28, 1872. 3. Edward Herbert, b. Sept. 20, 1859. 4. Florence Paine, b. Feb. 15, 1862. 5. Gertrude Osborn, b. Nov. 14, 1864; d. Sept. 18, 1865. 6. Mayday, b. May 1, 1866. 7. Harrie Osborn, b. Aug. 6, 1869. 8. Fred. Ritchie, b. March 16, 1874.

14. William White, b. March 18, 1838, m. in Newport, Tenn., Feb. 16, 1869, Eliza Shields Storey, dau. of William C. and Melinda (Kendrick) Storey. She was b. in Newport, Tenn., May 1, 1843; res. Columbia, Tenn. Children, both b. in Columbia: 1. Minni Eliza, b. May 8, 1871. 2. George Henry, b. July 4, 1875.
15. Eliza Augusta, b. Feb. 28, 1840, m. in Portage, Wis., Aug. 31, 1865, Rev. George Thomas Crissman, son of Adam and Nancy (Reighley) Crissman. He was b. in Milroy, Mifflin county, Pa., May 26, 1836; graduated from Miami University, Ohio, in July, 1860; prepared for the ministry in the Western Theological Seminary, at Allegheny City, Pa.; was licensed to preach by Chillicothe Presbytery, Ohio, in April, 1862; and ordained by the Rock River Presbytery, Illinois, in April, 1864. He has continued his labors in the ministry as pastor of the Presbyterian Church in Morrison, Ill., since July, 1863; res. Morrison, Ill. Children: 1. Mary Augusta, b. April 18, 1867. 2. Elizabeth Barrett, b. March 25, 1872.

Joseph C. Paine, fifth son and tenth child of Roswell and Sally (Chamberlain) Paine, b. in Amherst, Mass., July 6, 1804, m. in Palmyra, N. Y., Aug. 3, 1828, Aurelia Buck, dau. of Daniel and Betsey (Thompson) Buck. She was b. in Waterloo, N. Y., April 27, 1811. He d. in Galva, Ill., April 1, 1871. Salesman and auctioneer.
Child:
1. Charles Henry, b. in Palmyra, N. Y., June 30, 1830, m. in Chardon, Geauga county, Ohio, March 9, 1857, Janette Pease, dau. of Joseph and Ellen (Palmer) Pease. She was b. in Hambden, Geauga county, Ohio, April 27, 1837. Divorced. He resides in Galva, Ill. Children: 1. Mary Ellen, b. in Galesburg, Ill., May 12, 1858, m. in Belleville, Ill., May 22, 1876, Simon P. Evans, parentage, birth, etc., unknown. 2. Stella Louisa, b. in Galva, Ill., June 20, 1860. 3. George Wallace, b. in Galva, Ill., Oct. 22, 1861. 4. Rosamond Lydia, b. in Galva, Ill., Dec. 27, 1863.

Edward Paine, youngest son and child of Roswell and Sally (Chamberlain) Paine, b. in Amherst, Mass., Oct. 28, 1806, m. in Brooklyn, Cuyahoga county, Ohio, in 1832, Nancy Hastings, dau. of Eli and Sally (Paine) Hastings. She was b. in Amherst, Mass., March 10, 1811. He d. in Chardon, Ohio, April 19, 1850.
Child:
1. Sarah Antoinette, b. in Brecksville, Ohio, Jan. 25, 1833; d. in Chardon, Ohio, Dec. 3, 1851.

Roswell Paine, the husband of Sally Chamberlain, was an own cousin to Edward Payne, the husband of Persis Cleveland,[5] (see page 26.) Though spelling the name differently, both were descended from Stephen Paine of Rehoboth, Mass., a miller by occupation and the founder of this branch of the *Paine* family. He came from near Hingham, Norfolk county, Eng., in 1638, in the ship *Dilligent* of Ipswich, John Martin, master, bringing his family, consisting of his wife Rose, three sons and four servants, and settled first in Hingham, Plymouth county, Mass. He was made a freeman in 1639, and elected a Representative or Deputy in 1641. Two or three years afterwards, he removed with his family to

"Seekonk" which settlement it was decided, at the suggestion of Rev. Samuel Newman, (who came there from Weymouth, Mass., with the greater part of his congregation), should be called Rehoboth. Mr. Paine became prominent in the affairs of the colony, and held many offices of honor and trust, as shown by the records of the town. He was a man of wealth for those days, his estate being valued in 1643 at £535; the third highest on the list. As indicative of the confidence his townsmen had in his judgment, it may be stated that in 1659, "it is agreed upon between the Town and Lieut. Hunt and William Bucklin, that they is to shingle the new end of the meeting house, and to be done as sufficiently as the new end of Goodman Paynes house," the inference being, of course, that what was good enough for him was good enough for the town. His two sons that grew to manhood and left families were Stephen and Nathaniel; the eldest son of the former, also named Stephen, being the grandfather of Roswell and Edward. A very complete genealogy of the families bearing the name of Payne (or Paine) in this country, may be had by application to Henry D. Paine, M. D., 26 West 30th street, New York.

Maj. James Chamberlain, the third son and fifth child of Capt. James and Abigail (Boynton) [Palmer] Chamberlain, b. in Coventry, Conn., July 24, 1766, m. in East Windsor, Conn., June 25, 1788, Annah Watkins Babcock, dau. of Elijah and Elizabeth (Bassett) Babcock. She was b. in Ashford, Conn., Nov. 7, 1769; d. in Portland, Me., Oct. 2, 1804. He d. in Amherst, Mass., Feb. 22, 1814. He was a merchant in early life, and associated with his father under the style of "James Chamberlain & Son," at Warehouse Point, East Windsor, Conn. He retired from business, and removed to Canaan, Vt., where he engaged in buying and selling horses and cattle. As a horseman he had few if any superiors. While a resident of Vermont, he was elected a member of the Legislature one or two terms, and being fond of and excelling in military drill and exercises, he received from the State his commission as a major in the militia.
Children :
1. Abigail, b. Nov. 28, 1790; d. May 8, 1824.
2. James, b. —— —, 1792; d. Jan. 3, 1794.
3. William, b. Dec. 4, 1796; d. March 11, 1840.
4. Elizabeth, b. Feb. 8, 1799; living (1879) in Canton, Fulton county, Ill.
5. James (again), b. March 4, 1801; d. in March, 1831, unm.
6. Harriet, b. April 3, 1804; d. Aug. 15, 1834.

Abigail Chamberlain, the eldest daughter and child of Major James and Annah W. (Babcock) Chamberlain, b. in East Windsor, Conn., Nov. 28, 1790, m. in Amherst, Mass., Oct. 23, 1815, Rufus Kellogg, son of Daniel and Mary (Eastman) Kellogg. He was b. in Amherst, Nov. 10, 1788, and d. there, Dec. 2, 1833. She d. in same place, May 8, 1824. He was a farmer.
Children :

1. Esther, b. Sept. 10, 1816; d. Feb. 1, 1835, unm.
2. James Chamberlain, b. Oct. 18, 1818; d. Feb. 2, 1819.
3. Daniel, b. Aug. 9, 1820, m. in Hadley, Mass., July 5, 1854, Martha Hunt Kellogg, dau. of Giles C. and Martha H. (Warner) Kellogg. She was b. in Hadley, Mass., Oct. 25, 1823; res. Hadley, Mass. Children: 1. Henry Martin, b. Oct. 2, 1855. 2. Charles Daniel, b. May 20, 1857; d. Jan. 15, 1864. 3. Edward Hunt, b. March 29, 1859; d. April 10, 1874. 4. Giles Melcher, b. Aug. 16, 1863.
4. Henry Martyn, b. April 22, 1823; d. Oct. 10, 1851, unm.

William Chamberlain, second son and third child of Maj. James and Annah W. (Babcock) Chamberlain, b. in East Windsor, Conn., Dec. 4, 1796, m. in Harford county, Md., Oct. 27, 1824, Rachel Ring, dau. of Joshua and Sarah (Phillips) Ring. She was b. in Birmingham, Pa., Oct. 6, 1804; d. in Lapidam, Md., March 12, 1864. He d. in Port Deposit, Md., March 11, 1840.

Children :
1. James Henry, b. July 24, 1825; d. Dec. 20, 1826.
2. Sarah Jane, b. Dec. 25, 1827; d. Oct. 25, 1832.
3. George Washington, b. Feb. 15, 1830, m. in Havre de Grace, Md., June 15, 1854, Mary Ann Carver, dau. of Joseph Cannon and Mary Magdalene (Peterman) Carver. She was b. in Williamsport, Pa., May 26, 1825. He is a hotel keeper; res. Havre de Grace, Md. Children: 1. Benjamin Franklin, b. Jan. 27, 1855; d. Aug. 23, 1855. 2. Elizabeth Carver, b. June 23, 1856. 3. Caroline Virginia, b. March 14, 1858. 4. Joseph William, b. July 27, 1860. 5. Mary Katherine, b. Oct. 18, 1862; d. Aug. 10, 1863. 6. George Washington, b. June 29, 1864. 7. Henry Hopkins, b. Nov. 14, 1866.
4. Margaret Ann, b. Jan. 1, 1833, m. in Port Deposit, Md., Nov. 1, 1855, Samuel Morton Clendman Nesbitt, son of Samuel and Hannah (Lyons) Nesbitt. He was b. in Port Deposit, Md., May 18, 1833; d. there, Feb. 7, 1872, and his wife, Nov. 17, 1874. Children: 1. Laura Virginia, b. March 1, 1857. 2. Edwin Rinehart, b. Aug. 2, 1859. 3. Charles Haines, b. Jan. 14, 1863. 4. Paul, b. Sept. 29, 1866; d. July 29, 1867.
5. Joshua Ring, b. Jan. 17, 1836; d. March 8, 1836.
6. Hannah Ring, b. Feb. 23, 1837, m. first, in Port Deposit, Md., Dec. 7, 1854, Edwin Lybran Morgan, son of Edwin and Martha (Gibson) Morgan. He was b. in Port Deposit, Md., Jan. 31, 1831; d. in same place, Aug. 17, 1862. She m. second, in Port Deposit, April 2, 1865, Joseph Woodward Abrahams, son of Woodward and Hannah (Willey) Abrahams. He was b. in Baltimore, Md., July 30, 1808. Merchant; res. Port Deposit, Md. Children, by husband, Edwin L. Morgan: 1. Ida May, b. Sept. 17, 1855; d. June 20, 1875. 2. Franklin Evan, b. Aug. 10, 1858, m. in Port Deposit, June 20, 1877, Annie Eliza Wilson, dau. of John and Eliza Wilson. She was b. in Port Deposit, June 22, 1859. Child: Blanche Eliza, b. Sept 20, 1878. 3. Edwin Lybran, b. July 17, 1861; d. Jan. 15, 1862. By husband, Joseph W. Abrahams: 4. Emma, b. Aug. 14, 1866. 5. Caroline, b. Feb. 7, 1869. 6. Lucy, b. Nov. 7, 1872.
7. Elizabeth Stevens, b. July 10, 1839, m. in Harford county, Md., Nov. 17, 1859, John Jacob Hunt, son of Elias and Mary (Riker) Hunt. He was b. in White Plains, Westchester county, N. Y., Sept. 3, 1835. Carpenter; res. Baltimore, Md. She d. in Port Deposit, Md., Aug. 14, 1876. Children, all b. in Port Deposit: 1. Benjamin Franklin, b. Aug. 29, 1860. 2. John Milton, b. April 26, 1865; d. June 22, 1866. 3. John Jamar, b. June 13, 1867. 4. Anna Martin, b. Oct. 8, 1872.

Elizabeth Chamberlain, second daughter and fourth child of Maj. James and Annah W. (Babcock) Chamberlain, b. in East Windsor, Conn., Feb. 8, 1799, m. in Milo, Yates county, N. Y., June 14, 1827, Francis Stevens, son of Roswell and Lucy (Carey) Stevens. He was b. in Grafton, Vt., March 9, 1790; d. in Bath, Steuben county, N. Y., Oct. 21, 1871. She is living (1878) in Canton, Fulton county, Ill.
Children:

1. Francis Augustus, b. in Painted Post, Steuben county, N. Y., June 10, 1829; d. in Campbelltown, Steuben county, N. Y., Feb. 22, 1833.
2. Arabella Augusta, b. in Campbelltown, N. Y., March 17, 1832, m. in Canton, Ill., April 24, 1850, Stodard Christopher Tuell, son of Charles and Olive (Paine) Tuell. He was b. in Westmoreland, Cheshire county, N. H., Oct. 17, 1821. Grocer; res. Canton, Ill. Children: 1. Francis, b. April 24, 1854; d. May 1, 1854. 2. Lucie Florence, b. Sept. 6, 1856. 3. Mabel Blanche, b. Feb. 5, 1859. 4. William Clarence, b. March 24, 1861. 5. Charles Everett, b. Jan. 17, 1864. 6. Elizabeth Chamberlain, b. June 10, 1868. 7. Frederic, b. Feb. 7, 1874.

Harriet Chamberlain, third daughter and youngest child of Maj. James and Annah W. (Babcock) Chamberlain, b. in Portland, Me., April 3, 1804, m. in Steuben county, N. Y., May 24, 1824, John Dobson Dent, son of Thomas and Ann (Head) Dent. He was b. in Kirby-Stephen, Westmoreland, England, June 21, 1801; d. in Embro, Ontario, Canada, Sept. 21, 1875. She d. in Camboro', Ontario, Aug. 15, 1834.
Children:

1. Thomas Harrison, b. in Steuben county, N. Y., Feb. 28, 1825; d. in Oxford county, Ont. ——, 1835.
2. Richard Rudd, b. in Steuben county, N. Y., Feb. 23, 1827, m. in Embro, Ont., May 5, 1849, Elizabeth Matteson, dau. of Hugh and Sarah (McGregor) Matteson. She was b. in Suthernshire, Scotland, Jan. 9, 1829. He is the proprietor of the hotel, Woodstock, Ont. Children, all b. in Embro, Ont.: 1. John Dobson, b. May 15, 1851, m. in Detroit, Mich., Nov. —, 1873, Annie Grant, dau. of F. D. and Mary (Campbell) Grant. She was b. in Detroit, March 20, 1854. Child: Annie, b. Nov. 10, 1874. 2. Thomas Harrison, b. June 10, 1853. 3. James, b. Dec. 25, 1855. 4. and 5. (twins), Richard Rudd and Harriet Elizabeth, b. Nov. 7, 1856. She m. in Woodstock, Ont., June 12, 1878, Frank Williams, a native of England. He was b. June —, 1851. Res. Toronto, Ont. 6. Annie, b. Nov. 5, 1858, m. in Woodstock, Ont., April 24, 1877, John G. Mackey, parentage, etc., unknown: Child: John G., b. April 6, 1878. 7. Angus, b. Oct. 18, 1861.
3. Edwin, b. in Steuben county, N. Y., Nov. 20, 1829, m. in Mitchell, Ont., Jan. 14, 1851, Elizabeth Kingsmill, eldest daughter of George and Lydia (Dudley) Kingsmill. She was b. in Toronto, Ont., March 31, 1831, and is living (1878) in Stratford, Ont. He d. in Stratford, Oct 5, 1877. Children: 1. Mary Elizabeth, b. in Mitchell, Ont., Jan. 23, 1852. 2. William Frederic, b. in same place, Oct. 21, 1854. 3. Lydia Caroline, b. in Stratford, Ont., Nov. 1, 1856. 4. Bessie Harriet Jane, b. in same place, May 15, 1859.

4. James, b. in Steuben county, N. Y., Sept. 1, 1831, m. in Embro, Ont., Feb. 23, 1852, Elvira Saunders, dau. of Asa and Nancy (Reynolds) Saunders. She was b. in Erie county, N. Y., Sept. 12, 1831. He d. in Embro, Ont., May 3, 1854. Child: 1. James, b. April 20, 1853; resides in Alpena, Mich. [His mother m. second, W. McDonald, of Embro, Ont.]

5. Elizabeth Ann, b. in Camboro', Ont., July 1, 1833; d. ——, 1834.

Concerning the *Babcocks*, the following may be of interest to the descendants of Maj. James and Annah W. (Babcock) Chamberlain:

"CEDAR RAPIDS, IOWA, Jan. 6, 1879.

"DEAR SIR: About the beginning of the eighteenth century my great grandfather, Amos Babcock, came over from England and settled in Providence, R. I., and, tradition says, two brothers, Stephen and Timothy, came with him. Timothy took an active part in the Indian wars; but Stephen was a person of literary tastes and habits, who considered "the pen mightier than the sword." My grandfather was also named Amos, and was born about 1715 to 1718; was sent to England to finish his education; returned to Providence about 1735 to 1740; married Miss Annah Watkins; settled in Ashford, Windham county, Conn., and had a family of children as follows: 1. Stephen, who m. Prudence ——. 2. Elijah, who m. for his first wife Elizabeth Bassett. 3. Sally, who m. Shubal Gear. 4. William, who d. in his sixth year. 5. Amos, who m. Peggy Peabody. 6. Horace, who m. a Miss Berry. 7. Roswell, who m. a Miss Holt. 8. Miriam, who m. a Mr. Keyes. 9. Annah W., who m. a Mr. Wales.

"Elijah Babcock, the second son and child, b. in Ashford, Conn., about 1745, m. first, about 1762-3, Elizabeth Bassett, by whom he had, in Ashford, Conn.: 1. Roxana, who m. Col. Jacob Newkirk. 2. Linda, who m. Peter Campbell. 3. Hettie, who m. Col. Baldwin. 4. Annah Watkins, who m. Maj. Chamberlain. 5. William, who m. Rhoda Hull. 6. Elizabeth, who m. George Steele, 7. Ralph, who d. July 15, 1859, unmarried. 8. Prudence, who also m. George Steele, husband of her sister Elizabeth, deceased. And by second wife, Ruhama Hare: 9. Annah Watkins (again), who m. Dr. Harvey Burritt, and d. in South Toledo, Ohio, Feb. 4, 1879, aged about 70. 10. Amos, who was b. Oct. 22, 1811, m. Caroline Lucas, and resides (1879) in Cedar Rapids, Iowa.

"It is related of my grandfather, that while attending college in England, and on a wager with his fellow students, he threw one of the king's guards off his horse, mounted the animal and made his escape. On another occasion, at the queen's levee she held out her hand for the students to kiss as they passed by, but he audaciously kissed her cheek. The offense was forgiven on his assurance that the salutation was according to the mode adopted in the Colonies.

"When he returned to Providence he began to pay his addresses to Miss Annah Watkins, whose father, a proud old Englishman, claiming royal blood in his veins, promptly forbade him his house, and shut his daughter up in the second story. But grandfather, illustrating the adage that "love laughs at locksmiths," stole away with his sweetheart on horseback to Connecticut, married her, and became a prominent man in Windham county. Was a representative for twenty-six years in the Colonial Legislature, and a Selectman, Deacon and Judge. I remember well the "coat of arms" painted on the back of our "old shay"—two fighting cocks in the act of sparring.

"My father, Elijah Babcock, went to Vermont in 1775, joined Gen. Ethan Allen, and helped take Fort Ticonderoga; continued a soldier through the war; was captain of a company of men he raised in Connecticut, who marched under Gen. Arnold to Quebec; was the last man Gen. Montgomery spoke to just before the fatal bullet struck him; and was present at the surrender of Cornwallis.

"I never heard that my great grandfather had any other children than my grandfather, but suppose he probably raised a large family.

"Respectfully submitted,
"AMOS BABCOCK.

"To A. H. BABCOCK, Esq., Des Moines, Iowa."

Naomi Chamberlain, third daughter and youngest child of Capt. James and Abigail (Boynton) [Palmer] Chamberlain, b. in Coventry, Conn., Nov. 19, 1769, m. in East Windsor, Conn., ——, 1787, Joseph Hilliard, son of Capt. Miner and Marian (Barnes) Hilliard. He was b. in Tolland county, Conn., Aug. 18, 1765; d. in Colebrook, N. H., Nov. 22, 1830. She d. in Canaan, Vt., April 26, 1867, in her 98th year.

Children:

1. Charles, b. in East Windsor, Conn., July 29, 1788; d. in Canaan, Vt., June 5, 1874. He was an expert hunter and trapper, and his rifle was his constant companion. He never married.
2. James, b. in East Windsor, Conn., April 17, 1796; d. Aug. 12, 1801, from a terrible wound in the abdomen, inflicted by a scythe, in the hands of a lad, who thoughtlessly swung it while he was standing near him in the hay-field.
3. Barnes, b. in East Windsor, Conn., Aug. 10, 1798; d. in Colebrook, N. H., Dec. 9, 1869.
4. James Miner, b. in Colebrook, N. H., Oct. 13, 1801; d. in same place, July 7, 1870.
5. Miriam, b. in Colebrook, N. H., May 30, 1804; d. July 15, 1805.
6. Oren, b. in Colebrook, N. H., July 12, 1806, where he still resides; a tanner by occupation.
7. Gennett, b. in Colebrook, N. H., Jan. 8, 1810, and resides in Canaan, Vt.

Joseph Hilliard in early life was a saddle-tree maker in Tolland; but after coming to Warehouse Point, in East Windsor, he built, in connection with his father-in-law, Capt. Chamberlain, a vessel called a "coaster," and loaded it with merchandise for Charleston, S. C., James Chamberlain, Jr., going as the supercargo. My father states that Joseph Hilliard was a tall and well proportioned man, favoring his mother physically, who was an unusually tall woman, and that the family came to Connecticut from the region of Cape Cod, Massachusetts.

Barnes Hilliard, third son and child of Joseph and Naomi (Chamberlain) Hilliard, b. in East Windsor, Conn., Aug. 10, 1798, m. in Canaan, Vt., Dec. 22, 1820, Judith Weeks, dau. of Samuel and Abigail (Moody) Weeks. She was b. in Gilmanton, N. H., May 19, 1797; d. in Stewartstown, N. H., Sept. 10, 1874. He d. in Colebrook, N. H., Dec. 9, 1869. Farmer.

Children, all b. in Colebrook, N. H.:

1. Abigail, b. Dec. 16, 1821, m. in Colebrook, N. H., June 15, 1845, Asahel Brainard, son of Barzillai and Mehetabel Farnham) Brainard. He was b. in Stewartstown, N. H., March 28, 1816. Res. Colebrook, N. H. No children.
2. Melinda Louisa, b. Jan. 17, 1823, m. in Canterbury, N. H., Dec. 24, 1846, John Ingalls, son of Nathaniel P. and Polly (Haines) Ingalls. He was b. in Canterbury, N. H., Oct. 16, 1820. Carpenter; res. Canterbury, N. H. Children, all b. in Canterbury: 1. Arianna Barron, b. Jan. 24, 1848; d. Jan. 15, 1872. 2. Oriella Melinda, b. May 14, 1849. 3. Frank Barnes, b. Dec. 8, 1854; d. April 18, 1867. 4. Helen Clark, b. Sept. 4, 1859. 5. John Elmer, b. Aug. 15, 1861; d. June 16, 1870.

3. Ira, b. Sept. 28, 1824, m. in Wyoming county, Pa. ——, 1858, Emily Carr, dau. of Caleb and Hannah (Gardner) Carr. She was b. in Clinton, Wyoming county, Pa., April 30, 1836. He is a farmer; res. Webster City, Iowa. Children: 1. Lewis, b. Sept. 7, 1861. 2. Archibald, b. July 17, 1863.
4. John Moody, b. June 25, 1826, m. in West Stewartstown, N. H., Nov. —, 1856, Mary Ann Hibbard, dau. of Stirling S. and Rachel F. (Rogers) Hibbard. She was b. in Hereford, P. Q., (Canada), Oct. 10, 1836. He d. June 5, 1874, and his widow is now wife of Geo. Chamberlain, Esq., of West Stewartstown, N. H. Children: 1. Charles Fred, b. July 24, 1856; d. Aug. 6, 1861. 2. Belle Lavinia, b. Nov. 2, 1858. 3. Elsie Ermina, b. Oct. 20, 1860. 4. Mary Eliza, b. April 8, 1862. 5. James Fred, b. April 11, 1864; d. Dec. 20, 1865. 6. John Stirling, b. Aug. 28, 1866; d. Oct. 15, 1875. 7. Anna Bawn, b. Jan. 3, 1868; d. May 14, 1874. 8. Ira Elwin, b. May 3, 1870. 9. Frank Moody, b. Sept. 12, 1873; d. May 18, 1874.
5. James Barnes, b. March 16, 1828, m. in Stewartstown, N. H., Dec. 14, 1852, Lucy Ann Neal, dau. of John and Lucy B. (Morgan) Neal. She was b. in Hereford, Lower Canada, date not given. He enlisted and d. in battle at Buzzard's Prairie, La., Nov. 3, 1863. Child: Ivo Herbert, b. in Canaan, Vt., Aug. 29, 1854; d. in Brookline, Mass., Dec. 20, 1872.
6. Persis, b. Jan. 25, 1830, m. in Colebrook, N. H., May 8, 1870, Joseph Drew Little, son of Ebenezer and Thirza Mason (Carr) Little. He was b. in Colebrook, N. H. ——, 1833. Farmer; res. Colebrook, N. H. Children: 1. ——, b. March 24, 1871; d. March 24, 1871. 2. Irving Drew, b. Sept. 26, 1872. 3. Etta May, b. June 29, 1875.
7. Laurinda, b. Dec. 10, 1831, m. in Canterbury, Merrimac county, N. H., Jan. 7, 1855, Matthias Weeks, son of Stephen and Betsey (Weed) Weeks. He was b. in Gilmanton, N. H., Nov. 15, 1824. Farmer; res. Gilmanton, N. H. Children: 1. Ermina, b. July 8, 1856. 2. Jesse Fremont, b. Nov 1, 1857. 3. Lorrain Edwin, b. Sept. 17, 1859. 4. Albert Matthias, b. June 9, 1861. 5. James Henry, b. March 9, 1865. 6. Ann Eliza, b. March 27, 1867. 7. Stephen Leavitt, b. Oct. 30, 1870. 8. John Moody, b. Dec. 15, 1871. 9. Mary Ellen, b. May 27, 1874.
8. Sarah, b. Jan. 29, 1834, m. in Northumberland, N. H., Dec. 25, 1851, Nicholas Oren Tuttle, son of Nicholas and Celia (Stillings) Tuttle. He was b. in Hart's location, N. H., Sept. 27, 1825. No children.
9. Martha Macknight, b. Oct. 30, 1836, m. in Stewartstown, N. H., July 5, 1853, Othniel Stillings, parentage not given; b. in Bartlett, N. H., March 16, 1827. She d. in Stewartstown, N. H., July 5, 1877. Children: 1. Flora, b. in Lancaster, N. H., May 18, 1855, m. Nov. —, 1873, Joseph Sullivan, and have, Cora Ellen, b. March 16, 1874; Arthur Willard, b. Sept. 3, 1877. 2. Charles Herbert, b. in Lancaster, N. H., May 24, 1857. 3. Edith, b. in Lancaster, N. H., April 14, 1862. 4. Byron Barnes, b. in Jefferson, N. H., July 18, 1865. 5. William, b. in Stewartstown, N. H., June 6, 1869; d. July 5, 1870. 6. Mabel, b. in Stewartstown, N. H., May 12, 1872. 7. Hattie, b. in Stewartstown, N. H., Nov. 26, 1874. 8. Albert, b. in Stewartstown, N. H., June 14, 1877; d. Aug. 23, 1877.
10. Lovina Weeks, b. April 14, 1838, m. in Stewartstown, N. H., Feb. 3, 1863, James Carr Little, son of Ebenezer and Tirza (Carr) Little. Date of his birth not given. She d. in Colebrook, N. H., Oct. 25, 1870. No children.
11. Fidelia, b. Sept. 28, 1839; res. Colebrook, N. H.; unm.

12. Susan Eliza, b. July 14, 1842, m. in Stewartstown, N. H., Jan. 22, 1870, Osman Baker Forrest, son of Emanuel Swett and Mary (Edmunds) Forrest. He was b. in Stewartstown, N. H., June 27, 1842. Farmer; res. Stewartstown, N. H.

James M. Hilliard, fourth son and child of Joseph and Naomi (Chamberlain) Hilliard, b. in Colebrook, N. H., Oct. 13, 1801, m. in Lemington, Essex county, Vt., Oct. 21, 1829, Susan Bailey, dau. of Timothy and Lydia (Abbott) Bailey. She was b. in Eaton, Province of Quebec, Dec. 30, 1805. He d. in Colebrook, N. H., July 7, 1870. She is living (1878) in Canaan, Vt.

Children, all b. in Colebrook, N. H.:

1. James Miner, b. Aug. 15, 1830; d. Dec. 2, 1849.
2. Mary, b. March 31, 1832, m. in Stewartstown, N. H., May 4, 1851, Ira Young Brainard, son of Barzillai and Lucy (Beecher) Brainard. He was b. in Stewartstown, N. H., July 5, 1828. Lumberman; res. Pittsburg, N. H. Children: 1. Minetta Mary, b. in Stewartstown, N. H., Oct. 27, 1851; d. July 1, 1854. 2. Henrietta, b. in Canaan, Vt., May 2, 1855. 3. Charles Hilliard, b. in Canaan, Vt., Nov. 20, 1857; d. Nov. 16, 1858. 4. Charles Ira, b. in Canaan, Vt., Nov. 2, 1859. 5. Carrie Minetta, b. in Pittsburg, N. H., March 26, 1862. 6. Jennie, b. in Pittsburg, N. H., Feb. 12, 1865. 7. Frank Hilliard, b. in Pittsburg, N. H., Aug. 4, 1869. 8. Son, b. in Pittsburg, N. H., Oct. 8, 1873; d. April 14, 1874.
3. Susan Elvira, b. Oct. 28, 1833; d. May 16, 1835.
4. Charles, b. March 19, 1836; d. Nov. 7, 1856.
5. Henry Schoff, b. Dec. 19, 1837, m. in Pittsburg, N. H., July 15, 1870, Alma Persis Jacobs, dau. of Fernando Cortes and Julia Ann (Cooper) Jacobs. She was b. in Canaan, Vt., Oct. 25, 1846. Dealer in lumber, etc.; res. Lancaster, N. H. Children: 1. Harry DeForest, b. in Canaan, Vt., Jan. 31, 1871. 2. Nellie, b. in Lancaster, N. H., Jan. 3, 1873. 3. Anna, b. in Lancaster, N. H., June 24, 1877.
6. Warren, b. Nov. 19, 1839; drowned April 25, 1869.
7. Joseph, b. Jan. 7, 1842; d. Sept. 27, 1861.
8. Hiram, b. Oct. 15, 1843, m. in Colebrook, N. H., July 11, 1865, Alma Rowena White, dau. of Richard Russell and Hannah (Frissell) White. She was b. in Canaan, Vt., Oct. 9, 1847. Res. Pittsburg, N. H. Child: James Irving, b. May 29, 1868.
9. George, b. Oct. 15, 1845, m. in Stewartstown, N. H., Jan. 8, 1870, Hannah Flanders, dau. of Nehemiah and Polly (Colby) Flanders. She was b. in Stewartstown, N. H., Aug. 30, 1851. Res. Canaan, Vt. Children: 1. Everett, b. May 4, 1871. 2. Susan Estella, b. June 20, 1872. 3. Alice, b. June 15, 1874. 4. and 5. (twins), Lewis and Lawrence, b. May 22, 1876, the latter d. Oct. 28, 1876. 6. Mary Ellen, b. March 9, 1878.
10. Frank, b. Sept. 9, 1848; d. Nov. 9, 1869.
11. Ellen Arabella, b. Aug. 18, 1850; d. Aug. 24, 1866.
12. James Edward, b. March 5, 1853, m. in Stewartstown, N. H., Oct. 20, 1877, Mary Jane Dorman, dau. of Thomas and Caroline (Parsons) Dorman. She was b. in Bury, Province of Quebec, June 2, 1859.

Oren Hilliard, fifth son and sixth child of Joseph and Naomi (Chamberlain) Hilliard, b. in Colebrook, N. H., July 12, 1806, m. in Hartford, Conn., May 15, 1832, Catherine Dalliber, dau. of Samuel and Minerva

(Marshall) Dalliber. She was b. in Torrington, Litchfield county, Conn., Oct. 17, 1808. He is a tanner; res. Colebrook, N. H.
Children :

1. Mary Jane, b. in Colebrook, Conn., June 22, 1834; d. Dec. 15, 1834.
2. Mary Catherine, b. in Hartford, Conn., Jan. 11, 1839. Res. Colebrook, N. H.
3. James Raphael, b. in Hartford, Conn., Jan. 5, 1842; d. Jan. 23, 1844.
4. Robert, b. in Hartford, Conn., Jan. 10, 1845, m. Bridget Shaller. Works in a factory in Providence, R. I. Nothing further concerning his family ascertained.

Gennett Hilliard, second daughter and youngest child of Joseph and Naomi (Chamberlain) Hilliard, b. in Colebrook, N. H., Jan. 8, 1810, m. in Colebrook, March 9, 1829, Samuel Weeks, son of Samuel and Abigail (Moody) Weeks. He was b. in Gilmanton, Belknap county, N. H., Nov. 10, 1804. Farmer; res. Canaan, Vt.
Children:

1. Ann Maria, b. in Canaan, Essex county, Vt., Nov 10, 1829, m. in Canaan, Feb. 24, 1849, John J. Martin, son of Moses and Dorcas (Holmes) Martin. He was b. in Stewartstown, N. H., July 29, 1830, entered the Union army and served in the late war. He d. from disease contracted in the service, Aug. 29, 1877. Farmer; res. West Stewartstown, N. H. Children: 1. Melvin Moses, b. July 6, 1851; d. July 3, 1874, unm. 2. Frank P., b. Dec. 22, 1853; d. Aug. 17, 1854. 3. Charles Wesley, b. March 16, 1855, m. in Stewartstown, N. H., Nov. 28, 1878, Harriet Tyler. 4. Albert, b. March 11, 1859. 5. Genette E., b. April 27, 1861. 6. Jennie E., b. Dec. 3, 1867. 7. Samuel John, b. March 14, 1869.
2. Charles Hilliard, b. in Canaan, Vt., Feb. 17, 1833, m. in Canaan, April 15, 1872, Mrs. Elizabeth (Emery) Fletcher, dau. of Joshua and Hannah (Wentworth) Emery. Date of birth not given. She was a native of Shelburne, Coos county, N. H. He is a farmer; res. Canaan, Vt. Children: 1. Hannah Jane, b. June 23, 1874. 2. Gertrude Elizabeth, b. Sept. 26, 1875.
3. James Albert, b. in Colebrook, N. H., April 14, 1835, m. in Loon Bay, up the St. Croix river, Maine, July 9, 1863, Caroline Maria Rideout, dau. of James Augustus and Sarah Jane (Walker) Rideout. She was b. in St. George, N. B., Aug. 27, 1844. He is a farmer; res. Canaan, Vt. Children: 1. Josephine, b. in Loon Bay, Me., May 18, 1864, d. in Canaan, Vt., Dec. 23, 1865. 2. Charles Freeman, b. in Canaan, Vt., Jan. 28, 1866. 3. Bertha May, b. in West Stewartstown, N. H., April 29, 1867. 4. Sarah Adelia, b. in West Stewartstown, April 27, 1869. 5. James Augustus, b. in Canaan, Vt., July 20, 1871. 6. Lizzie Belle, b. in Canaan, Jan. 6, 1874. 7. Carrie Janette, b. in Canaan, Oct. 17, 1876. 8. Samuel Albert, b. in Canaan, March 20, 1879.
4. Emma Jane, b. in Stewartstown, N. H., April 23, 1846, m. in Canaan, Vt., July 12, 1869, Daniel Heath, son of Thomas B. and Laura M. (Farnham) Heath. He was b. in Hereford, P. Q., (Canada), Jan. 10, 1847. Farmer; res. Canaan, Vt. Children: 1. Samuel Thomas, b. in Canaan, Dec. 3, 1869. 2. Ada Mabel, b. in Canaan, Nov. 29, 1875. 3. Daniel Webster, b. in Stewartstown, N. H., July 4, 1878.

Captain James Chamberlain was a man of large stature (being six feet in his stockings, and weighing over 250 pounds avoirdupois), of fine personal appearance, and well known throughout the Colony and State of Connecticut in his day. He became dissatisfied with the Congregationalism of that period, and with Gen. Jenks, Wm. C. Warner, and others of like mind, organized a church parish for worship according to the forms of the mother Church of England, and was a devout and consistent Churchman until his death. He was noted as a peacemaker, and was often selected as an umpire or arbitrator to settle differences; and belligerent parties would end their quarrels by agreeing to leave the matter in dispute to "Cap'n Chamberlain," as he was familiarly known. Many pages might be filled with anecdotes concerning him and his bustling, kind-hearted little wife, but the compiler has not space for them in this volume. The following from the "Early History of Tolland," page 77, in reference to his civil and military services concludes Appendix J.

"James Chamberlain commanded a company of cavalry one or two tours of duty during the War of the Revolution. He came to Tolland from Coventry about the year 1772, and removed to East Windsor before the year 1782. While in this town he lived at the extreme southeast part of it on a farm lying east of the one lately owned by Jesse West. He was one of the representatives in the General Assembly, October session, 1775."

K.

Samuel[1] Allen came from Braintree, Essex county, England. He was born about the year 1588, in the reign of Queen Elizabeth. He came to Cambridge, Mass., in 1632; was brother of Col. Matthew Allyn, of Cambridge, Mass., afterwards of Windsor and Hartford, Conn., and Dea. Thomas Allyn, of Middletown, Conn. He removed to Connecticut in 1635, and settled in Windsor. He was a juryman March 5, 1644, and was by occupation a farmer. From the Windsor, Conn., land records we have the following:

"January 27, 1640, Samuel Allen hath granted from the Plantation at Windsor, Conn. 1st. An house lott being six acres, three roods, ten poles, bounded from the rivulet [Farmington River] to the West, by Rodger Ludlow on the South; by Thomas Marshall on the North; and runs in length to the West into a highway laid out unto some part of the lot of the said Rodger Ludlow and him the said Samuel Allen. 2nd. In Plymouth meadow Four acres, bounded by Bray Rossiter on the North; and a rivulet that runs into the great [Connecticut] River on the South. 3rd. Toward Hartford Nineteen acres more or less, and runs in length to the Great River to the West one hundred and thirty and four rods, and is bounded by John Witchfield on the North, and Thomas Marshfield on the South. 4th. Over the Great River next to the same, fifteen rods in breadth, in the length to the East three miles; bounded by Joseph Lummus on the South; John Hurd on the North."

The fourth division was undoubtedly within the present limits of South Windsor. Samuel Allen was a man of public spirit, and was honored by his fellow citizens with positions of trust. He d. in Windsor, Conn., and was buried April 28, 1648, aged 60 years, leaving a widow

ALLEN.

and six children. His widow, Ann Allen, removed to Northampton, Mass., where she m. second, William Hurlbut. Ann (Allen) Hurlbut d. in Northampton, Mass., Nov. 13, 1687.

"Windsor, 8th September, 1648.
"An Inventory of the estate of Samuel Allen, late of Windsor, deceased:

	£	s.	d.
Impr: the housing and home lottes 11.£: It. 4 acres of meadow 7£,	18	00	0
It: 15 acres over the Great River,	15	00	0
It: 15 acres of upland,	4	10	0
It: In goods one bed with furniture,	5	00	0
It: two beds more, &c.,	2	14	0
It: One pillow beere, one table cloath & napkins,		10	8
It: his wearing aparrell,	5	05	0
It: Iron pots 2l. 5s.; in brass 1l. 10s.; in pewter 1l.,	4	15	0
It: in hogsheads, payles, tubbs and earthenware,		19	0
It: 2 spinning wheels,		07	0
It: in crooks, Grid iron, fire pan and tongs,		13	0
It: his working tooles 2l. 2s.,	2	02	0
It: a muskitt and sworde 13s.,		13	0
It: a table and forme, and other lumber,		10	0
It: in cattle, one cowe, one heifer, one yearling,	12	00	0
It: two swynes,	4	00	0
	£76	18	8

HENRY CLARK.
DAVID WILTON."

The children of Samuel and Ann Allen were:

1. Samuel,[2] b. 1634, m. Nov. 29, 1659, Hannah Woodford, dau. of Thomas and Mary (Blott) Woodford. Was a freeman in 1683. He had a grant of land from the Town of Northampton, Mass., Dec. 17, 1657. He d. in Northampton, Mass., Oct. 18, 1718, or 1719. They had, among other children:
   Samuel,[3] b. in Northampton, Mass., July 6, 1675, m. in 1699, Sarah Rust, dau. of Israel Rust. She was b. May 29, 1675. He d. in Northampton, Mass., March 29, 1739; was a Deacon in Rev. Jonathan Edwards' church in Northampton, Mass. They had, among other children:
   Joseph,[4] b. in Northampton, Mass., April 5, 1712, m. Nov. 22, 1733, Elizabeth Parsons, dau. of Noah and Mindwell (Edwards) Parsons. She was b. in Northampton, Mass., March 25, 1716; d. in Northampton, Mass., Jan. 9, 1800. He d. in Northampton, Dec. 30, 1779. They had, among other children:
   Rev. Thomas,[5] b. in Northampton, Mass., Jan. 17, 1743; m. Feb. 18, 1768, Elizabeth Lee, dau. of Rev. Jonathan and Elizabeth (Metcalf) Lee. She was b. Sept. 4, 1747; d. in Pittsfield, Mass., March 31, 1830. He d. in Pittsfield, Mass., Feb. 10, 1810. First minister of Pittsfield. Ordained April 18, 1764. Harvard, 1762. They had, among other children:
   Rev. William,[6] b. in Pittsfield, Mass., Jan. 2, 1784, m. first, Jan. 28, 1813, Maria Mallaville Wheelock, only dau. of John and Maria (Suhn) Wheelock. She was b. Feb. 3, 1788; d. in Brunswick, Me., June 3, 1828. He m. second, Dec. 2, 1831, Sarah Johnson Breed, dau. of John McLaren and Rebecca (Walker) Breed. She was b. Jan. 11, 1789; d. Feb. 25, 1848. He d. in Northampton, Mass., July 16, 1868. Had eight children. He was the author of the American Biographical Dictionary.

2. Nehemiah,[2] m. Sept. 21, 1664, Sarah Woodford, dau. of Thomas and Mary (Blott) Woodford. She was b. in Hartford, Conn., Sept. 2, 1649; d. in Northampton, Mass., March 31, 1712-13. He d. in Northampton, 1684. [She m. second, in Northampton, Sept. 1, 1687, Richard Burk. She m. third, in Northampton, July 11, 1706, Judah Wright.] He settled in Salisbury, Conn. They had, among other children:

    Samuel,[3] b. in Northampton, Mass., Jan. 3, 1666, m. Mercy Wright, dau. of Samuel and Elizabeth (Burt) Wright. She was b. in Northampton, Mass., March 14, 1669; d. in Litchfield, Conn., Feb. 5, 1728. They had, among other children:

    Joseph,[4] b. in Deerfield, Mass., Oct. 14, 1708, m. in Woodbury, Conn., March 11, 1736–37, Mary Baker, dau. of John Baker. He d. in Cornwall, Conn., April 4, 1755. They had, among other children:

    Gen. Ethan,[5] of Revolutionary fame, b. in Litchfield (?), Conn., Jan. 10, 1737, m. first, in Woodbury, Conn., by Rev. Daniel Brinsmade, of (Judea Parish) Woodbury, Conn., June 23, 1762, Mary Bronson, dau. of Richard Bronson. She d. in Sunderland, Vt., 1783; buried in Arlington, Vt. He m. second, in Westminster, Vt., Feb. 9, 1784, Mrs. Frances Buchanan. She was b. April 4, 1760. He d. in Burlington, Vt., Feb. 12, 1789. He had five children by first wife and three by second. Gen. Allen paid Rev. Mr. Brinsmade four shillings as a marriage fee.

3. John.[2]
4. Rebecca.[2]
5. Mary.[2]
6. Obadiah,[2] d. in Middletown, Conn., April 7, 1723; m. first, Oct. 23, 1669, Elizabeth Sanford, of Milford, Conn. He m. second, Mary (Savage) Whetmore, widow of John Whetmore and dau. of John Savage. She d. in Middletown, Oct. 20, 1723.

    Soon after the decease of his father, he was adopted by his uncle, Deacon Thomas Allyn, of Middletown, where he resided, and after his uncle's death (Oct. 16, 1688,) inherited most of his estate. He was admitted to the first Church, Middletown, by certificate from the church in Windsor, Conn., May 2, 1669, but owned the covenant Nov. 9, 1668, and was chosen Deacon May 31, 1704.

John[2] (Samuel[1]), m. Dec. 8, 1669, Mary Hannum, dau. of William and Honor Hannum. She was b. April 5, 1650. He was killed by the Indians at the battle of Bloody Brook, Deerfield, Mass., Sept. 18, 1675.
Children:
1. John, b. Sept. 30, 1670; d. in Enfield, Nov. 3, 1739.
2. Samuel, b. Feb. 5, 1673; d. in Enfield, 1735.
3. Hannah, b. in Northampton, Mass., May, 1675; bapt. June 20, 1675.

John[3] (John,[2] Samuel[1]), b. in Northampton, Mass., Sept. 30, 1670, m. first, May 3, 1694, Bridget Booth, dau. of Simeon and Rebecca Booth. She was b. in Enfield, Conn., 1670; d. in Enfield, Sept. 5, 1714. He m. second, Elizabeth Gardner, of Gardner's Island. She d. in Enfield, Feb. 27, 1759, and he d. there, Nov. 3, 1739. He removed from Deerfield, Mass., to King Street, Enfield, Conn., to escape the Indians, about 1690. Farmer; lived in Enfield on the old Abiel Pease place. The following autobiography of John Allen is furnished through the kindness of Solomon Allen, Esq., of Enfield, Conn.:

"I was b. in Northampton, Mass., September 30, 1670. After awhile my father went to live at Deerfield, where he continued till the town broke up, and at Lathrop's fight my father was slain. My mother was left a widow with three small children, myself the oldest of them, and not above five years old. She was left in a low state, for she had lost the greater part of what she had. I have taken an account of the most remarkable fits of sickness that I have been visited with in all my lifetime. My mother tells me of one very sore fit of sickness of malignant fever when I was about three years old, when she did not expect my life for three weeks together. I was very bad. Another fit of the chicken pox when I was about eight years old; another form of sickness when I was about twelve or thirteen years old, with a pain in my side. I had the measles when I was about seventeen or eighteen years old; another fit of sore sickness when I was about nineteen years old. In the years when the great fever was about, I had a long and lingering sickness, twenty-two and three years old. I had the [illegible] a long sore weak time in the year 1696. I had a fit of sickness at Wethersfield when I was about twenty-six years old, and so continued weakly sometime. Mr. Mix at Wethersfield admitted me 4 o'clock into the church August 2d day, 1696, sacrament day.

JOHN ALLEN."

Children, all born in Enfield, Conn., by wife Bridget, were :

1. Mary, b. Feb. 26, 1696; d. in Enfield, Conn., Aug. 16, 1778, unm.
2. Elizabeth, b. April 21, 1698, m. Nov. 20, 1717, Samuel Ellsworth, of East Windsor, Conn., son of Josiah and Martha (Taylor) Ellsworth, Jr. He was b. July 18, 1697. Lived in East Windsor. Had five sons.
3. Azariah, b. May 14, 1701; d. in Enfield, Conn., April 3, 1787.
4. John, b. Sept. 13, 1703; drowned in the Connecticut river at Enfield, about 1721.
5. Israel, b. March 18, 1705; d. in Enfield, March 24, 1712.
6. Patience, b. May 22, 1709, m. first, a Mr. Bement, of Suffield; m. second, a Mr. Pease. She d. in Suffield, Conn.
7. Ebenezer, b. Feb. 10, 1711-12; d. in Enfield, June 25, 1795.

Azariah[4] (John,[3] John,[2] Samuel[1]), b. in Enfield, Conn., May 14, 1701, m. in Longmeadow, Mass., Dec. 3, 1727, Martha Burt. She was born in Longmeadow, 1706; d. in Enfield, Oct. 12, 1782. He d. in Enfield, April 3, 1787. Farmer.

Children, all born in Enfield, Conn., were :

1. Martha, b. Dec. 25, 1728, m. first, in Enfield, Aug. 12, 1749, David Chapin 2nd, of New Hartford, Conn.; m. second, in New Hartford, about 1772, Joseph Merrills.
2. Rebecca, b. Nov. 13, 1730, m. first, Oct. 17, 1751, Maj. Benjamin Parsons, of Somers, Conn. He was b. in Enfield, Jan. 24, 1724; d. April 8, 1818. She m. second, Thomas Hale, of Enfield. She d. June 10, 1793. Had eight children.
3. Moses, b. Oct. 12, 1732; d. in Enfield, Sept 30, 1741.
4. Jemima, b. July 15, 1734; d. in Enfield, Sept. 14, 1741.
5. Abigail, b. April 21, 1736; d. in Enfield, Sept. 13, 1738.
6. Eunice, b. March 30, 1738, m. in Enfield, April 24, 1755, Nathaniel Pease, of Enfield, son of Samuel and Elizabeth (Warner) Pease. He was b. in Enfield, Sept. 20, 1728; d. in Norfolk, Conn , March 28, 1818. She d. in Norfolk, March 21, 1807. Resided at Norfolk. They had thirteen children.
7. Abigail, b. July 5, 1740; d. in Enfield, Oct. 15, 1741.
8. Submit, b. May 14, 1742, m. Elisha Brown, of Canton, Conn. He d. in Canton, March 27, 1824. She d. in Canton, May 30, 1807. They resided at Canton (Collinsville), Conn. Had five children.
9. Jemima, b. Aug. 21, 1744; d. in Enfield, Oct. 14, 1767.
10. Moses, b. May 14, 1746; d. in Enfield, Sept. 26, 1826.

Moses[5] (Azariah,[4] John,[3] John,[2] Samuel[1]), b. in Enfield, Conn., May 14, 1746, m. in Warehouse Point, Conn., May 1, 1766, Mary Adams, dau. of Thomas and Mary (Hammond) [Vallet] Adams. She was b. in East Windsor, Conn., Sept. 21, 1745; d. in Enfield, Oct. 9, 1805. He m. second, in Enfield, Feb. 16, 1807, Mrs. Mary Pease, widow of James Pease, of Enfield, and dau. of Thomas and Mercy (Hall) Pease. She was b. in Enfield, and d. there, Feb. 6, 1814. He died in Enfield, Sept. 26, 1826. Farmer. Lived in Enfield.

Children, all born in Enfield, Conn., by wife Mary Adams, were:

1. Mary, b. Feb. 3, 1767, m. in Enfield, June 15, 1786, Samuel Allen, Jr., of East Windsor, son of Samuel and Elizabeth (Wells) Allen. He was born in East Windsor, June 16, 1764; d. in East Windsor, Oct. 11, 1841. She d. in East Windsor, May 21, 1823. Resided in East Windsor.
2. Moses, b. Feb. 10, 1769; d. in Enfield, Nov. 17, 1833.
3. George, b. Oct. 24, 1770; d. in Enfield, Sept. 1, 1833.
4. Anson, b. July 20, 1772; d. in Enfield, July 10, 1832.
5. Isaiah, b. July 8, 1774; d. in Enfield, May 7, 1845.
6. Jemima, b. Aug. 16, 1776; d. in Enfield, July 22, 1820, unm.
7. Rubie, b. May 14, 1778, m. in Enfield, Nov. 10, 1795, Erastus Eldridge, of Ellington, Conn. He was b. in Willington, Conn., April 3, 1775; d. in Springfield, Mass., May 6, 1820. She d. in Enfield, Conn., Sept. 15, 1844. He worked in the U. S. Armory, Springfield, Mass. Had ten children.
8. Luther, b. June 11, 1780; d. in Ithaca, N. Y., Nov. 7, 1821.
9. Son, b. Oct. 27, 1782; d. in Enfield, Oct. 31, 1782.
10. Esther, b. Aug. 26, 1783; d. in Enfield, Nov. 15, 1783.
11. Esther, b. Sept. 24, 1785; m. in Enfield, March 7, 1806, Oren Cleveland, of East Windsor, son of Rufus and Mary (Chamberlain) Cleveland. He was b. in East Windsor, May 3, 1785. She d. in Huntsburgh, Ohio, May 21, 1869. He is living in Cleveland, Ohio. Had eleven children.
12. Sabra, b. Jan. 18, 1788, m. in Enfield, Dec. 17, 1805, Sylvanus Olmstead, of Enfield, son of Simeon and Roxalana (Abbe) Olmstead. He was b. in Enfield, July 16, 1783; d. in Enfield, Feb. 6, 1826. She d. in Enfield, June 1, 1865. Had five children.

Those who desire to further trace the descendants of Samuel Allen,[1] are referred to Willard S. Allen, Esq., clerk of the Municipal Court in East Boston, Mass., and compiler of the "Genealogy of the Allen family" in this country, from which the foregoing is taken. He resides at 88 Lexington Street, East Boston, Mass.

Concerning the Adams branch of my ancestry on the maternal side, it may be traced with confidence to Thomas Adams* of Colchester,

---

* Thomas Adams was undoubtedly descended from "Henry Adams, who emigrated to this country in 1632, from Essex county, Eng., and settled in Braintree, Mass., and who was the ancestor of the patriots, Samuel and John Adams—the latter second President of the United States. Thomas Adams, son of Henry Adams, of Braintree, Mass., made freeman May 10, 1643. By wife Mary ——, had Mary, b. July 24, 1643; d. soon; removed to Concord, Mass., there had Jonathan and Pelatiah (twins), b. March 6, 1646; Timothy, b. April 2, 1648; George, b. May 29, 1650; Samuel b. ——, 1652; Thomas, b. ——, 1655; removed to Chelmsford, Mass., there had Rebecca, b. Sept. 18, 1657; Elizabeth, b. Oct. 21, 1659; and Mary (again), b. Oct. 29, 1664. Was town clerk, selectman, representative at second session 1673, and d. July 20, 1688, aged 76." [Savage, Gen. Dict.]

Conn., who had, according to the old records there, a family of ten children, as follows :

1. Sarah, b. Feb. 1, 1717.
2. Abigail, b. March 3, 1718.
3. Thomas, b. Aug. 30, 1719.
4. Elizabeth, b. Nov. 3, 1720.
5. Hannah, b. July 4, 1722.
6. Elijah, b. May 30, 1724.
7. Mary, } b. March 17, 1727.
8. Martha, } b. March 17, 1727.
9. Lydia, b. July 16, 1729.
10. Elisha, b. Sept. 28, 1732.

Thomas Adams, the eldest son, b. Aug. 30, 1719, was, I conjecture from the perpetuation of family given names (as will appear), the father of Mary Adams, wife of Moses Allen. The romantic circumstances of his marriage in 1744, to Mrs. Mary (Hammond) Vallett, of Montville, Conn., must be briefly narrated. About the year 1736, Jeremiah Vallett, a worthy sea captain, courted and married Miss Mary Hammond.* She bore him a son who was named Jeremiah, for his father. One day, some three years after his marriage, Capt. Vallett, leaving his snug little home well stored with the necessaries of life, bade his wife an affectionate farewell, kissed little "Jerry," his only son and heir, and joined his vessel for a short cruise. The time came around for his promised return, but no tidings of the ship or its captain. Weeks and months passed by, and the disconsolate wife anxiously watched and waited for some message from the absent husband and father. At length the report came that the ship had been lost at sea with all on board, and the "widow Vallett" put on mourning for the prescribed period. At the expiration of the time, but with no unseemly haste, she accepted the hand of Thomas Adams, a young and active ship carpenter at that time, and her junior by a few years only. Her former husband's estate being administered upon, as any dead man's should be, the newly married couple settled down to domestic happiness in the comfortable home of "the late" Capt. Vallett.

Everything was going on swimmingly enough when, to the consternation of all, Capt. Vallett himself appeared at the door of his former domicil, and the consequent surprise and astonishment may be imagined better than described. But under the laws of the colony no wrong had been done or intended, and a consultation was held without delay, with the good minister of the place who had tied the second knot, and a magistrate of the law as the legal counselor, to effect an amicable arrangement among the parties so deeply interested. It was agreed that the wife should herself say which husband she preferred, and she unhesitatingly

* Mary Hammond was, without doubt, a descendant of "Thomas Hammond, of Hingham, Mass., 1636, who came from Lavenham, Suffolk county, Eng. He was made a freeman March 9, 1637. By wife Elizabeth, m. (probably in England), Nov. 12, 1623, who d. before him, brought children Elizabeth and Thomas; had Sarah, baptized Sept. 13, 1640, and Nathaniel, March 12, 1643; removed to Watertown, Mass., thence across the river in 1650 to Cambridge village, purchased a large farm with Vincent Druce, and d. Sept. 30, 1675, aged 88 years. His will names all these children: Elizabeth, (who m. Aug. 17, 1659, George Woodward,) Thomas and Nathaniel, all then married, and Sarah, probably wife of Nathaniel Stedman, as deceased, but her children, Sarah and Elizabeth to be heirs. He had a very good estate." [*Savage, Gen. Dict.*]

chose the second one, undoubtedly, from her past experience, being more in favor of a land lubber on shore, than the best sailor man in the world afloat.

So the Captain graciously accepted the situation, with the stipulation, however, that young Adams and his wife should depart from that neighborhood a considerable distance, little " Jerry," of course, to remain with his father.

Thomas Adams and his wife removed to East Windsor, and settled at Warehouse Point, on the Connecticut river, following his occupation of ship carpenter. Subsequently he kept the public house there, and died about November, 1767, in his 49th year. She married third, Gen. Wolcott, and went to reside in Springfield, Mass.; but not living happily with her third husband, they mutually consented to a separation, and she afterwards resided with one of her daughters till she died. She was a woman above the medium height, and was very fleshy in the later years of her life. The children and grandchildren were accustomed to go occasionally and visit "Cousin Jerry" Vallett, and were always cordially received and entertained with the utmost hospitality. But this intercourse, I understoood from my informant, was after the worthy Captain's death.

Children of Thomas and Mary (Hammond) [Vallett] Adams, as far as known, were eight in number, as follows, all b. in East Windsor, Conn.:

1. Mary, b. Sept. 21, 1745.
2. Lydia, b. about 1747.
3. Elijah,) b. about 1749; d. young.
4. Elisha,) b. about 1749; d. young.
5. Thomas, b. Jan. —, 1752.
6. Sarah, b. Sept. 16, 1753.
7. Abigail, b. about 1755.
8. Lucy, b. about 1757.

Mary Adams, the eldest daughter and child of Thomas and Mary (Hammond) [Vallett] Adams, b. in East Windsor, (or possibly in Montville) Conn., Sept. 21, 1745, m. in Enfield, Conn., May 1, 1766, Moses Allen, son of Azariah and Martha (Burt) Allen. He was b. in Enfield, Conn., May 14, 1746; d. in Enfield, Conn., Sept. 26, 1826. She d. in Enfield, Conn., Oct. 3, 1805. He was a farmer, and much respected by his townsmen for his undoubted piety and uprightness of character.

Children, all b. in Enfield:

1. Mary, b. Feb. 3, 1767, m. in Enfield, June 15, 1786, Samuel Allen, Jr., son of Samuel and Elizabeth (Wells) Allen. He was b. in East Windsor, Conn., June 16, 1764; d. in same place, Oct. 11, 1841. She d. there also, May 21, 1823. He was a farmer. Children: 1. Samuel, b. March 21, 1787; d. May 26, 1787. 2. Mary, b. Dec. 29, 1788, m. Jabez Phelps; d. May 5, 1841. 3. Samuel (again), b. Nov. 28, 1790, m. Jane Allen; d. Nov. 10, 1836. 4. Harvey, b. March 16, 1794, m. Mary Parsons; d. Sept 4, 1865. 5. Roswell, b. Jan. 2, 1798, m. Beulah Chapin; d. in Belchertown, Mass., April 28, 1868. 6. Cynthia, b. Oct. 25, 1800, m. Levi Parsons; d. April 30, 1844. 7. Laura, b. July 16, 1804, m. Horace Phelps; d. Sept. 17, 1870.

2. Moses, (Maj.), b. Feb. 10, 1769. m. in Enfield, Nov. 1, 1789, Esther Chapin, dau. of Nathaniel and Sybil (Terry) Chapin. She was b. in Enfield, Jan. 20, 1771; d. there, Oct. 28, 1857. He d. there, Nov. 17, 1833. He kept a public house in Enfield for many years. Children: 1. Moses, b. Sept. 24, 1790, m. Nancy Kingsbury; d. Jan. 16, 1816. 2. Esther, b. Nov. 6, 1792, m. Sept. 18, 1814, Jabez Terry Taylor. 3. Hermonie, b. Aug. 16, 1796, m. Harris Meacham; d. in Hartford, Conn., July 10, 1859. 4 Lucinda, b. July 30, 1798, m. Dr. Homer Holland; d. in Westfield, Mass., July 11, 1853. 5. Gilbert, b. Nov. 29, 1800, m. Caroline Owen; was Sheriff of Hartford county; d. in Enfield, Conn., Oct. 30, 1856. 6. Clarendon, b. Feb. 6, 1804; d. April 9, 1837. 7. Olcott, b. Oct. 13, 1806, m. first, Mary Spaulding; second, Lucy Ann Parsons. Treasurer of the Hartford Savings Bank; d. Oct. 24, 1872. 8. Roderick, b. June 17, 1810, m. Sophronia Rebecca Pease; d. in Hartford, Conn., Sept. 4, 1840.

3. George, b. Oct. 24, 1770. m. in Enfield, Conn., March 1, 1793, Betsey Rich, of Haddam, Conn. She was b. in Haddam, March 6, 1778; d. in Enfield, Nov. 6, 1864. He d. in Enfield, Sept. 1, 1833. Her father was a sea captain, and she was brought up by Mr. Meacham, of Enfield. Children: 1. George, b. Dec. 11, 1795, m. first, Fannie Smith; second, Theodotia Smith; res. Hadley, Mass. 2. Betsey, b. Feb. 16, 1798, m. Henry Augustus Abbee; d. April 1, 1849. 3. Norman, b. Oct. 18, 1800, m. Mary Robinson; d. May 12, 1860. 4. Henry, b. Jan. 15, 1803, m. Mary Patten; d. July 13, 1867. 5. Clarissa Maria, b. Aug. 5, 1812, m. Norton Olmstead; res. Enfield, Conn.

4. Anson, b. July 20, 1772, m. in Enfield, Conn., Feb. 26, 1792, Rebecca Nichols, of Enfield, Conn. She was b. in 1774, and was brought up by Dea. Levi Booth; d. in Enfield, Jan. 25, 1821. He d. in same place, July 10, 1832; was a great mathematician and astronomer, and supplied all the New England States with Almanacs for a number of years. Children: 1. Anson, b. Sept. 19, 1792; d. in Havana, Cuba, 1811. 2. Rebecca, b. Aug. 18, 1794, m. William Chapman; d. 1836, in Argyle, N. Y. 3. Son, b. Sept. 18, 1796; d. Oct.—, 1796. 4. Almira, b. July 9, 1799, m. William C. Warner; d. Dec.—, 1857. 5. Emily, b. Sept. 20, 1801; m. Gibbons Lay; of (Feeding Hills) Agawam, Mass.

5. Isaiah, b. July 8, 1774, m. in Enfield, Conn., Dec. 24, 1794, Martha Pease, dau. of William and Martha (Webster) Pease. She was b. in Enfield, Oct. 31, 1771, and d. there, June 26, 1850. He d. there, also, May 7, 1845. Farmer and carpenter. Children: 1. Isaiah, b. March 19, 1796, m. first, Deborah Pease; second, Mrs. Bellisene (Emmons) Fudge. Farmer and carpenter. 2. Martha, b. July 24, 1798; d. unm., Feb. 19, 1868. 3. Minerva, b. Feb. 23, 1800, m. Heber Pease; d. Feb. 13, 1868. 4. Jeremiah Vallett, b. Dec. 7, 1801, m. Emily Pease; d. Aug. 28, 1866. 5. Thomas Adams, b. June 18, 1805; d. Nov. 10, 1805. 6. Mary Ann, b. Dec. 4, 1806. 7. Carlos, b. March 19, 1809; m. Laura Brooks; d. Oct. 14, 1874. 8. and 9. Job Beckwith and Josiah Bennett (twins), b. June 23, 1813. The former m. Mary Pease; res. Thompsonville, Conn.; the latter, a man of wonderful ingenuity, d. unm., Aug. 9, 1870. He was a manufacturer of musical and astronomical instruments of the most perfect design and workmanship, in Springfield, Mass., for many years and accumulated a handsome competency. A violin which he made and presented to his twin brother was a marvelous specimen of excellence in tone and finish. His delight in the later years of his life, after he removed from Springfield to Thompsonville, was to entertain his relatives and friends with views of the "starry heavens" through a telescope of his own manufacture.

6. Jemima, b. Aug. 16, 1776; d. July 22, 1820, unm.

7. Rubie, b. May 14, 1778, m. in Enfield, Conn., Nov. 10, 1795, Erastus Eldridge, son of Azoath and Elizabeth (Pearl) Eldridge. He was b. in Willington, Conn., April 3, 1775; d. in Springfield, Mass., May 6, 1820. Mechanic. She d. in Whitehall, N. Y., Sept. 14, 1841, and was buried in Castleton, Vt. Children: 1. Rubie Allen, b. in Enfield, Jan. 29, 1797, m. Samuel Bliss; d. in Springfield, Feb. 13, 1877. 2. Elizabeth, b. in Enfield, Oct. 26, 1798, m. Horace Wright; d. in Middlefield, Conn., Oct. 31, 1825. 3. Mary Adams, b. in Enfield, Aug. 26, 1800; d. unm. 1878. 4. Erastus, b. in Enfield, July 25, 1802, m. Julia Hosmer; d. in Independence, Ohio, July 6, 1877. 5. Esther Allen, b. in Enfield, Nov. 21, 1804, m. Edmund Austin; resides (1879) in Hartford, Conn. 6. Moses Allen, b. in Enfield, Feb. 28, 1807, m. Elizabeth Jane Stebbins; his res. not known. 7. Elijah, b. in Springfield, Mass., Jan. 19, 1809; d. April 22, 1829. 8. Harriet, b. in Springfield, April 7, 1812, m. Dr. Jonathan Don Woodward; d. Sept. 6, 1867. 9. Albert Gallatin, b. in Springfield, Nov. 20, 1815, m. Nancy Younglove McLean; res. Washington, D. C. 10. Adaline, b. in Springfield, April 30, 1817; d. Aug. 21, 1865, unm.

8. Luther, b. June 11, 1780, m. in Enfield, Conn., Nov. 17, 1803, Sally Pease Abbe, dau. of Daniel and Sally Pease (Bartlett) Abbe. She was b. in Enfield, March 28, 1783; d. in Ithaca, N. Y., Oct. 27, 1820. He d. in Ithaca, N. Y., Nov. 27, 1821. He was an engraver and portrait painter, and also an accomplished violinist. He was the composer of the well-known contra-dance tune, "The Opera Reel," and taught both music and dancing for many years. Children: 1. Sarah Abbe, b. in Enfield, Aug. 31, 1804, m. Walter Huntington Mead; res. Rochelle, Ill. 2. Luther Adams, b. in Enfield, Sept. 10, 1806, m. Mrs. Margaret Drake (Stringham) Chapin; res. Springfield, Ill. 3. Eliza Matilda, b. in Enfield, Nov. 19, 1808; d. in Cortland, N. Y., unm., Dec. 15, 1870. 4. Caroline, b. in Enfield, Jan. 16, 1811, m. William Tanner; res. Groton, N. Y. 5. Moses David, b. in Ithaca, N. Y., Oct. 6, 1821; d. in Albion, Mich., unm., Oct. 4, 1850.

9. Son, b. Oct. 27, 1782; d. in Enfield, Oct. 31, 1782.

10. Esther, b. Aug. 26, 1783; d. in Enfield, Nov. 15, 1783.

11. Esther, (again), b. Sept. 24, 1785, m. in Enfield, Conn., March 7, 1806, Oren Cleveland, of East Windsor, Conn., son of Rufus and Mary (Chamberlain) Cleveland. He was b. in East Windsor, May 3, 1785. She d. in Huntsburgh, Ohio, May 21, 1869. He is living with his youngest son, in Cleveland, Ohio. (See pages 42 to 51.)

12. Sabra, b. Jan. 18, 1788, m. first, in Enfield, Conn., Dec. 17, 1805, Sylvanus Olmstead, son of Simeon and Roxalana (Abbe) Olmstead. He was b. in Enfield, July 18, 1783; d. in Enfield, Feb. 6, 1826. She d. there, June 1, 1865. [Her second husband was a Goudy, from whom she separated by mutual agreement.] Children: 1. Roxalana, b. ——, 1807; d. June 22, 1809. 2. Sabra, b. Jan. 9, 1809, m. Asahel Robinson; resides near Lockport, N. Y. 3. Sylvanus, b. Feb. 18, 1811, (non compos). 4. William, b. Feb. 28, 1814, m. first, Caroline Ingraham; second, Sarah M. Lord; third, Catherine D. Benton; resides in Thompsonville, Conn. Probate Judge. 5. Roxa Abbe, b. Nov. 8, 1816, m. Lewis Joy; d. Nov. 7, 1863.

Lydia Adams, the second daughter and child of Thomas and Mary (Hammond) [Vallett] Adams, b. in East Windsor, Conn., about 1747, m. in Enfield, Conn., Nov. 16, 1769, Dennis Bement, son of Dennis (?) and Mary (Abbe) Bement. The date and place of his birth and death not learned, or of the death of his wife.

Children :
1. Lydia, b. Jan. 31, 1772, m. Jamin Parsons, of Somers, Conn. They had six children, names, etc., not learned.
2. Dennis, b. Jan. 18, 1774; d. Oct. 19, 1775.
3. Elizabeth, b. Aug. 18, 1775, m. Dr. Arnold Hamilton, of Somers, Conn., and had three children, names, etc., not given. She d. Dec. 28, 1859.
4. Mary, b. about 1777, m. Obadiah Olmstead, of Enfield, Conn. She d. without issue, Dec. 24, 1865.
5. Pina, b. about 1780, m. Seth Alden, of Enfield, and had two sons and four daughters. She d. April 11, 1832.
6. Dennis (again), b. Aug. 24, 1782, m. Huldah Hawkins, of Enfield, and had three children. He d. Sept. 23, 1828.
7. Delight, b. Aug. 5, 1784, m. Oct. 29, 1808, Roderick White. He was b. in Enfield, Feb. 24, 1784. She d. April 17, 1875. Children: 1. Roderick Adams, b. Oct. 24, 1809, m. Elizabeth W. Hungerford, of Wolcottville, Conn. He is a physician; res. Simsbury, Conn. 2. Mary, b. about 1812, m. Luke B. Case. 3. Delia, b. about 1815; d. Feb. 11, 1877, unm. 4. Caroline, b. about 1818.
8. Charlotte, b. March 5, 1788, m. Richard Abbe, of Enfield, Conn. She d. Sept. 25, 1874. They had four children.

Thomas Adams, third son and fifth child of Thomas and Mary (Hammond) [Vallett] Adams, b. in East Windsor, Conn., Jan. —, 1752.

F. N. Allen, Esq., of Hartford, Conn., writes, July 27, 1878, and gives copy of an entry found on the Probate Records of Hartford county, as follows :

"2 Day of February, 1768. It was certified to this Court by Ephraim Terry, a justice of the peace, that Thomas Adams, a minor, aged sixteen years, son of Thomas Adams, late of Windsor, deceased, appeared before him on the 1st day of December last, and made choice of Moses Allyn, of Enfield, to be his guardian; which choice the Court accepts. And the said Moses appeared before the Court, and acknowledged himself bound to the Judge of this Court or his successor in a recog. of £100 money, that he will faithfully discharge the trust of guardian to said minor, during his minority, according to law."

Mr. Allen further writes :

"This is all that I could find on the records. The Judge says that probably there was no will, and that the property of Thomas Adams was all personal and no inventory was made. We examined the books, thinking there might appear a copy of a will, or names of legally appointed administrators; but this is all we could find. It may be concluded, I think, that Thomas Adams, Sr., died about the latter part of November, 1767, and that this was his only minor child."

Another correspondent on the subject, has an impression of hearing it said that he enlisted in the army when the Revolutionary war commenced, was severely wounded, remained in a hospital until convalescent, and came home an emaciated cripple. He probably did not survive many years, and it is believed died unmarried.

Sarah Adams, third daughter and sixth child of Thomas and Mary (Hammond) [Vallett] Adams, b. in East Windsor, Conn., April 16, 1753, m. in East Windsor, Jan. 1, 1776, Jonathan Allen, son of Ebenezer and Rebecca (Bartlett) Allen. He was b. in Enfield, June 22, 1775 ; d. there, Aug. 22, 1803. Farmer. She d. in Springfield, Mass., Jan. 2, 1844.

Children, all b. in Enfield :

1. Jonathan, b. Oct. 27, 1776, m. first, Mary Pease, dau. of James and Mary (Larkham) Pease. She was b. in Enfield, March 20, 1774; d. in Hambden, Ohio, June 20, 1818. He m. second, Miriam Kibbe; and third, Mary Sawings, who d. in Illinois, in 1858. He d. in Vernon, Trumbull county, Ohio, July 15, 1826. Children, by wife Mary Pease: 1. Mary, b. Oct. 2, 1798, m. Park Swift. 2. Jonathan Pease, b. March 7, 1801; d. unm., 1826. 3. Peter, b. ——, 1803; d. in ten days. 4. Cynthia, b. Nov. 2, 1804, m. Walter Thorington. 5. Harriet, b. May 22, 1806, m. Sheridan Roberts 6. Sally Janette, b Jan. 7, 1808, m. Royal Pease. 7. Elbridge Gerry, (M. D.), b. April 7, 1811, m. Pamelia Roberts. By wife Mary Sawings: 8. Jane, b. March 22, 1823, m. Myron Burnett. 9. Rufus Selden, b. Oct. 2, 1825, m. Janette Fuller.

2. Obadiah, b. Aug. 6, 1783, m. in Enfield, March 5, 1801, Lydia Bush, dau. of Rufus and Huldah (Alden) Bush. She was b. in Enfield, July 28, 1782; d. in Springfield, Mass., Dec. 14, 1850. He d. in Springfield, Mass., Nov. 7, 1859. He was foreman in the U. S. armory, Springfield, Mass. Children: 1. Lydia, b. in Enfield, Conn., May 17, 1802; d. Sept. 9, 1803. 2. Lemira Bush, b. in Enfield, Oct. 27, 1804. 3. Euphrasia Maria, b. in Enfield, Oct. 28, 1806. 4. Erskine Selenca, b. in Enfield, Feb. 3, 1809, m. Fidelia Van Horn; res. Springfield, Mass.; Master armorer in the United States Armory there. 5. Lucina Columba, b. in Enfield, Jan. 30, 1811. 6. William Bainbridge, b. March 15, 1813; d. Aug. 1, 1836. 7. Delia Lucinda, b. Dec. 3, 1815, m. Rev. Mosely Dwight 8. Laura Angelina, b. June 12, 1818. 9. Huldah Volusia, b. June 2, 1822, m. Col H. C. Lee; d. March 5, 1868. 10. Delius, b. Nov. 14, 1824. 11. Joseph Warren, b. in Springfield, Mass., Aug. 12, 1827; d. there, Jan. 8, 1828.

3. Sally, b. Jan. 9, 1786, m. in Enfield, Conn., March 1, 1801, Rufus Bush, Jr., son of Rufus and Huldah (Alden) Bush. They had three children.

4. David, b. Sept. 18, 1793, m. ——, and had three children: George, Selden, and Gates. His wife d. in Enfield, Dec. 16, 1834, and he d. there, Feb. 13, 1834. Nothing further learned of this family.

Abigail Adams, fourth daughter and seventh child of Thomas and Mary (Hammond) [Vallett] Adams, b. about 1755, m. in Enfield, Conn., about 1777, John French, of whom nothing is learned, except that he inherited or acquired a handsome property; but in consequence of the depreciation of the Continental money, he became greatly disheartened, and finally somewhat intemperate. In the records of Enfield births, is an entry as follows :

1. Anna, b. Jan. 18, 1779.

But who she m. or what became of her, has not yet been ascertained.

Lucy Adams, youngest daughter and child of Thomas and Mary (Hammond) [Vallett] Adams, b. in East Windsor, Conn., about 1757. m. first, a Mr. Ward, and after his death, a Mr. McWhalen. Of her descendants no trace has been found, though she is known to have had two or three children at least.

L.

Marcius Sutherland,[1] eldest son and child of Benjamin and Anna (Pearson) Sutherland, b. in Manchester, Vt., Nov. 18, 1801, m. in Perry, Wyoming county, N. Y., March 30, 1830, Mary Taylor, dau. of Dennis and Martha (Egbertson) Taylor. She was b. in Scipio, Cayuga county, N. Y., March 12, 1810. Res. Allegan, Mich.
Children, all b. in Perry, Wyoming county, N. Y.:

1. Dennis Taylor,[8] b. June 19, 1831, m. first, in Perry, N. Y., Dec. 24, 1851, Mary A. Gardner, dau. of Alanson and Mariliaette (Truesdell) Gardner. She was b. in Perry, N. Y., Aug. 19, 1831; d. in Allegan, Mich., Dec. 17, 1872. He m. second, in Allegan, Mich., April 28, 1875, Mrs. Charlotte Hollenbeck, dau. of Elias and Clarissa (Ward) Bathrick. She was b. in Perry, Wyoming county, N. Y., Aug. 25, 1829. He is a farmer; resides in Allegan, Mich. Child, by wife Mary: 1. James,[9] b. in Allegan, Mich., July 4, 1871; d. July 4, 1871.
2. Cyrenius Marcius,[8] b. Jan. 20, 1837; d. April 26, 1858, unm.
3. William Henry,[8] b. Aug. 10, 1840, m. first, in Kalamazoo, Mich., Sept. 21, 1864, Emily Celia Fisher, dau. of Reuben and Lavinia (Knox) Fisher. She was b. in Stark county, Ohio, March 23, 1841; d. in Kalamazoo, Mich., March 12, 1875. He m. second, in Kalamazoo, Mich., March 23, 1876, Mrs. Crista Eliza (McArthur) Simex, dau. of Archibald and Ann Maria (Saunders) McArthur. She was b. in Marshall, Mich., April 26, 1843. No children.

Julia Sutherland,[1] eldest daughter and second child of Benjamin and Anna (Pearson) Sutherland, b. in Manchester, Vt., June 6, 1803, m. in Manchester, Vt., Dec. 25, 1827, Lewis Brown, son of Oliver and Betsey (Estee) Brown. He was b. in Salem, Washington county, N. Y., Dec. 2, 1791; d. in Salem, N. Y., Dec. 19, 1830. She d. in Lawrence, Kansas, Sept. 24, 1867.
Children, all b. in Salem, N. Y.:

1. Henry,[8] b. Dec. 15, 1828, m. in Chicago, Ill., Feb. 1, 1857, Rhoda Anna Stevens, dau. of Lawrence and Eve Ann (Statts) Stevens. She was born in Glenville, Schenectady county, N. Y., May 28, 1834, and d. in Lawrence, Kan., July 30, 1871. He is living in South Pueblo, Col. Merchant. Children: 1. Lewis,[9] b. Oct. 24, 1862. 2. Addison,[9] b. Jan. 30, 1866. 3. Everett Lawrence,[9] b. Oct. 28, 1868; d. July 11, 1870.
2. Lewis,[8] b. May 12, 1831, m. in Hudson, Wis., Nov. 20, 1855, Frances Jane Simonds, daughter of Samuel Curtis and Mary (Coit) Simonds. She was b. in Charlestown, Mass., Feb. 15, 1835. He d. in Lawrence, Kan., Feb. 10, 1869. She is living in Hudson, Wis. Children: 1. Annie Simonds,[9] b. May 12, 1857; d. Oct. 3, 1865. 2 Ada Frances,[9] b. May 31, 1861. 3. Mary Coit,[9] b. April 30, 1864; d. Aug. 15, 1870. 4. Frank Lewis,[9] b. Oct. 28, 1866; d. Aug. 10, 1870.

Delia Sutherland,[1] second daughter and third child of Benjamin and Anna (Pearson) Sutherland, b. in Manchester, Vt., Oct. 22, 1804, m. in Manchester, Vt., Sept. 7, 1834, Hymen Burgess, son of Ebenezer and Hannah (Gibbs) Burgess. He was b. in Grafton, Vt., Jan. 26, 1788,

and d. in Grafton, Vt., Feb. 24, 1869. She is living (1877) in Grafton, Vt., a lady of much intelligence and culture.
Children, all b. in Grafton, Vt.:

1. Gustavus Willard,[8] b. Oct. 25, 1835, m. in Rockport, Me., Jan. 24, 1870, Sophia Carey, dau. of Charles Caleb and Ruth Robbins (Richards) Carey. She was b. in La Harpe, Ill., Feb. 11, 1843. He d. in Yokohama, Japan, Dec. 15, 1872. She is living in Rockport, Me. No children.
2. Lucy Arabella,[8] b. Dec. 29, 1838, m. in Grafton, Vt., Sept. 7, 1859, John Syng Dorsey Taylor, son of Dr. Jonathan and Asenath (Little) Taylor. He was b. in Sudbury, Vt., Oct. 5, 1818; d. in St. Albans, Vt., Aug. 20, 1873. Lawyer; but devoted his time to teaching and the cause of popular education. The last three years of his life was editor and proprietor of the St. Albans Messenger. They had: 1. William Belcher,[9] b. in Plattsburgh, N. Y., June 9, 1860. 2. Lucy Burgess,[9] b. in St. Albans, Vt., June 23, 1865. 3. John Burnham,[9] b. in St. Albans, Vt., Dec. 25, 1871.
3. Albert Hymen,[8] b. May 19, 1843, m. in Grafton, Vt., June 9, 1864, Rose Emeline Eaton, dau. of Stillman and Mehitabel (Watson) Eaton. She was b. in Stoddard, N. H., April 19, 1844; d. in Grafton, Vt., Sept. 15, 1877. Child: Mary Eaton,[9] b. in Grafton, Vt., Oct. 27, 1866.

Mary P. Sutherland,[7] third daughter and fourth child of Benjamin and Anna (Pearson) Sutherland, b. in Manchester, Vt., April 26, 1806, m. first, in Battle Creek, Mich., Oct. 27, 1856, Truman Martin Watrous, son of Josiah and Mary (Pearson) Watrous. He was b. in Avon, Livingston county, N. Y., May 8, 1807; d. in Tuscola, Mich., Feb. 20, 1857. She m. second, in Tuscola, Mich., Nov. 23, 1861, William Slafter, son of John and Persis (Grow) Slafter. He was b. in Norwich, Vt., Oct. 1, 1807. She d. in Tuscola, Mich., Dec. 4, 1865. Her last husband is living (1877) in Tuscola, Mich. No children.

Ammi Sutherland,[7] second son and fifth child of Benjamin and Anna (Pearson) Sutherland, b. in Manchester, Vt., Jan. 11, 1808, m. first, in Manchester, Vt., Aug. 20, 1831, Elizabeth Wheaton, dau. of James Seth and Sarah (Thomas) Wheaton. She was b. in Manchester, Vt., July 23, 1808; d. in Springfield, Erie Co., Pa., May 3, 1838. He m. second, in Springfield, Pa., Aug. 12, 1838, Melinda Raymond, dau. of Jacob and Elizabeth (Webster) Raymond. She was b. in Salem, Washington county, N. Y., June 4, 1811. He is a farmer; res. Sharon, Wis.

Children, by wife Elizabeth:

1. Mary Frances,[8] b. in Manchester, Vt., April 7, 1834, m. in Chemung, McHenry county, Ill., Feb. 20, 1867, Samuel Allen Freeman, son of Walter and Mary (Olin) Freeman. He was b. in Essex, Vt., March 14, 1820. No children.
2. James Wheaton,[8] b. in Springfield, Pa., April 23, 1837, m. in Atchison, Kan., May 15, 1860, Ellen Adella Raymond, dau. of Dr. David Webster and Frances Jane (Chester) Raymond. She was b. in Conneaut, Ohio, May 4, 1839. No children. Occupation unknown; res. Neodesha, Kan.

Edgar Sutherland,[7] third son and sixth child of Benjamin and Anna (Pearson) Sutherland, b. in Manchester, Vt., June 22, 1809, m. in Salem, Washington county, N. Y., May 9, 1833, Annie Rice, dau. of Daniel and Rosina (Kidder) Rice. She was b. in White Creek, N. Y., Oct. 8, 1808. He d. in Shushan, N. Y., Oct. 22, 1877. She is living (1878) in Shushan, N. Y.

Children :
1. Orrin Kidder,[8] b. in Shushan, N. Y., Oct. 15, 1841; resides in Shushan, N. Y.; unm.
2. Mary Augusta,[8] b. in Warensburg, N. Y., June 9, 1845, m. in Shushan, N. Y., Dec. 9, 1875, George Edward Andrews, son of William and Annie (Randall) Andrews. He was b. in Shushan, Washington county, N. Y., Nov. 19, 1845. Res. Shushan, N. Y.

Samuel Sutherland,[7] fifth son and eighth child of Benjamin and Anna (Pearson) Sutherland, b. in Manchester, Vt., Feb. 8, 1813, m. in Rockville, Scioto county, Ohio, Jan. 28, 1840, Thermuthis Mitchell, dau. of David and Mary (Stockham) Mitchell. She was b. in Rockville, Ohio, Aug. 4, 1820. He d. in Lawrence, Kan., June 2, 1857. She is living (1878) in Lawrence, Kan.

Children :
1. Samuel Mitchell,[8] b. in Rockville, Ohio, Feb. 19, 1841; d. in Lawrence, Kan., Dec. 3, 1856.
2. David Morrison,[8] b. in Rockville, Ohio, April 15, 1843, m. in Brodhead, Wis., Nov. 21, 1871, Annie Cleveland Goodhue, dau. of William P. and Sarah (Fletcher) Goodhue. She was b. in Chelsea, Mass., Oct. 28, 1847; d. in Great Bend, Kan., July 4, 1876. They had: 1. Paul,[9] b. Oct. 7, 1874. 2. Annie,[9] b. July 2, 1876; d. July 21, 1876.
3. Rezin Wilcoxon,[8] b. in Rockville, Ohio, Nov. 1, 1845; d. in St. Louis, Mo., Dec. 10, 1863.
4. William Hardy,[8] b. in Cedarville, Ill., May 22, 1849; d. in Cedarville, Oct. 11, 1850.
5. Mary Mitchell,[8] b. in Cedarville, Ill., June 17, 1851.
6. Martha Cyrinda,[8] b. in Cedarville, Ill., Sept. 15, 1854; d. in Cedarville, Ill., Sept. 19, 1855.
7. Samuel Henry,[8] b. in Lawrence, Kan., Jan. 2, 1858.

Elon Galusha Sutherland,[7] sixth son and ninth child of Benjamin and Anna (Pearson) Sutherland, was b. in Manchester, Vt., Jan. 23, 1815. All that can be ascertained concerning him is that he married, in 1836, a Miss Sarah Ann Stillman, dau. of Nathaniel and Mary (Thompson) Stillman, of New London, Conn., and that she d. in Buffalo or Chicago in 1837. He was a sailor on the lakes in early life, and the last known of him by any of his relatives was that he went to Lake Nicaragua.

They had one child :
1. Daughter,[8] b. in 1837; d. at the age of six months.

Jonah Sutherland,[7] seventh son and tenth child of Benjamin and Anna (Pearson) Sutherland, b. in Manchester, Vt., March 10, 1817, m. in Pomfret, Vt., Feb. 1, 1840, Martha Perrin, dau. of Epaphras and Esther (Chamberlain) Perrin. She was b. in Pomfret, Vt., April 1, 1810. He is a farmer ; res. Waucoma, Iowa.

Children :
1. Delia,* b. Nov. 2, 1840; d. April 10, 1842.
2. Albert,* b. Aug. 8, 1843, m. in Eden, Fayette county, Iowa, March 13, 1864, Mary Ann House, daughter of John Nelson and Dency (Hunt) House. She was born in Palatine, Cook county, Ill., Oct. 13, 1849. He has been auditor of Fayette county for six years; res. West Union, Iowa. Children: 1. Lee Nelson,[9] b. Aug. 22, 1865. 2. John Ammi,[9] b. Jan. 25, 1867. 3. Albert,[9] b. Feb. 12, 1869. 4. Clarence Marshall,[9] b. Jan. 18, 1871.
3. Herbert,* b. April 29, 1851.

William Sutherland,[7] (M. D.), eighth son and twelfth child of Benjamin and Anna (Pearson) Sutherland, b. in Manchester, Vt., Feb. 28, 1820, m. first, in Lewis county, Ky., June 20, 1844, Elizabeth Beacum Hughes, dau. of Jesse and Priscilla (Parker) Hughes. She was b. in Nicholas county, Ky., March 18, 1825 ; d. in Lewis county, Ky., July 24, 1845. He m. second, in Nicholas county, Ky., March 11, 1847, Jane Purie Hughes, (sister to his first wife). She was b. in Nicholas county, Ky., June 12, 1817. He is a surgeon and physician ; res. Victoria, Texas.

Children, by wife Elizabeth :
1. Walter Scott,* b. in Lewis county, Ky., May 11, 1845, m. in Wilson county, Texas, Dec. 19, 1872, Ann Peacock, dau. of Thomas and Salina (Steele) Peacock. She was b. in Fayette county, Texas, May 30, 1852. He is a wool grower; res. Victoria, Texas. Children: 1. and 2. (twins). Jesse,[9] and Jane,[9] b. in Wilson county, Texas, Oct. 3, 1873.

by wife Jane :
2. Mary Elizabeth,* b. in Bourbon county, Ky., Sept. 24, 1848, m. in Wilson county, Texas, March 23, 1870, Jack Sutherland, son of John and Ann Bryan (Lane) Sutherland. He was b. in Wharton county, Texas, Jan. 26, 1838. Merchant; res. Sutherland Springs, Texas. Children: 1. Mary Jane,[9] b. in Wilson county, Texas, July 2, 1872. 2. Anna Bryan,[9] b. in Wilson county, Texas, Feb. 27, 1874. 3. Jack,[9] b. in Wilson county, Texas, Jan. 1, 1876. 4. Agnes,[9] born in Wilson county, Texas, Nov. 6, 1877.
3. William Hughes,* b. in Bourbon county, Ky., June 8, 1851.
4. Anna Priscilla,* b. in Bourbon county, Ky., Feb. 9, 1852.

Benjamin Sutherland,[7] youngest son and child of Benjamin and Anna (Pearson) Sutherland, b. in Manchester, Vt., Nov. 19, 1821, m. in Van Buren, Hancock county, Ohio, Feb. 22, 1850, Mary Elizabeth Phillips, dau. of Samuel and Sarah Jane (Shotta) [or Shatta] Phillips. She was b. in Canfield, Mahoning county, Ohio, Jan. 12, 1831. He is a farmer and lawyer ; res. Jerry City, Wood county, Ohio.

Their children are as follows :
1. Susan,* b. March 4, 1851.
2. Benjamin,* b. July 30, 1853, m. in Wood county, Ohio, Sept. 17, 1874, Eveline Evelsinger, dau. of George and Katherine (Worthington) Evelsinger. She was b. in Henry, Wood county, Ohio, Aug. 14, 1860. He d. in Jerry City, Ohio, Feb. 19, 1876. She is living in Jerry City, Ohio. Child: Benjamin,[9] b. Aug. 4, 1875.

Walter Sutherland,[1] eldest son and child of Jonah and Mary (Pearson) Sutherland, b. in Manchester, Vt., Aug. 12, 1807, m. first, in Edmeston, Otsego county, N. Y., Jan. 1, 1830, Almira Swan, dau. of Gurdon and Lucy (Palmer) Swan. She was b. in Exeter, Otsego county, N. Y., Jan. 13, 1812; d. in Edmeston, N. Y., Nov. 25, 1841. He m. second, in Sangerfield, Oneida county, N. Y., Jan. 1, 1843, Ruth Berry, dau. of Ephraim and Lydia (Wheaton) Berry. She was born in Sangerfield, N. Y., April 30, 1813; d. in Wheeling, Ill., Sept. 9, 1863. He m. third, in Chicago, Ill., Nov. 13, 1864, Mrs. Miriam Austin, dau. of Aaron and Rebecca (Jackson) Davis. She was b. in Belchertown, Mass., May 1, 1816. [Her first husband was Reuben M. Mellen, and her second husband was William H. Austin.] Res. Dunton, Ill.

Children, by wife Almira:

1. Son,[8] b. Jan. 1, 1831; d. Jan. 1, 1831.
2. Miranda,[8] b. May 22, 1832, m. in ——, Reuben Cross Beard, a son of John Beard. He was b. in Otsego county, N. Y., June 12, 1832. Res. Golden City, Mo., when last heard from. Nothing learned of the family further, as they evidently do not communicate with even their nearest relatives, for reasons unexplained.
3. Mary Ann,[8] b. Oct. 22, 1833, m. in Vernon, Lake county, Ill., Oct. 10, 1852, Osman David Dana, son of Francis and Harriet (Nutting) Dana. He was b. in Dickinson, Franklin county, N. Y., July 8, 1831. Farmer; res. Nashua, Iowa. Children: 1. Marvin Le Roy,[9] b. in Deerfield, Ill., Feb. 4, 1854, m. in Douglass, Bremer county, Iowa, April 15, 1875, Alice Louise Jeffers, dau. of James Foote and Hannah (Rhinehart) Jeffers. She was b. Dec. 24, 1855. Have two children; names and dates of birth not received. 2. Helen Marion,[9] b. in Deerfield, Ill., Sept. 24, 1856. 3. Adaline,[9] b. in Wheeling, Ill., July 16, 1859. 4. Ettie,[9] b. in Polk, Iowa, Dec. 29, 1862. 5. Emma,[9] b. in Walworth, Wis., Sept. 21, 1866. 6. Carrie,[9] b. in Douglass, Iowa, Aug. 20, 1871.

by wife Ruth:

4. Walter,[8] b. in Edmeston, N. Y., Jan. 4, 1844, m. in Dunton, Ill., Feb. 9, 1865, Jemima Adaline Blackman, dau. of Zenas and Elvira (Mitchell) Blackman. She was born in Streetsville, Canada, July 2, 1841. Res. Prescott, Linn county, Kan. Children: 1. Harriet Ruth,[9] b. in Whiting, Ill., Feb. 25, 1866. 2. Zenas William,[9] b. in Sheridan, Kan., April 23, 1871. 3. Walter Mason,[9] b. in Sheridan, Kan., Aug. 15, 1873. 4. Clara Elvira,[9] b. in Prescott, Kan., July 10, 1875. 5. James,[9] b. in Prescott, Kan. Sept. 3, 1877.
5. Adelia Louisa,[8] b. in Wheeling, Ill., March 11, 1847, m. in Franklin Grove, Lee county, Ill., Dec. 8, 1870 Johnson Earl, son of Luther and Ellen (Ready) Earl. He was b. in Augusta, Ont., Dec. 27, 1845. Is a contractor and builder; res. Austin, Ill. Child: 1. Mary Edna,[9] b. in Austin, Nov. 19, 1873.
6. Byron,[8] b. in Wheeling, Ill., July 20, 1848, m. in Racine, Wis., Dec. 24, 1874, Clara Cornelia Gear, dau. of Henry Austin and Cornelia (Gouff) Gear. She was b. in Racine, Wis., Nov. 9, 1856. He is a harness-maker; res. Racine, Wis. Child: 1. Minnie Ruth,[9] b. Nov. 20, 1875.

Benjamin Sutherland,[1] second son and fourth child of Jonah and Mary (Pearson) Sutherland, b. in Manchester, Vt., Dec. 1, 1813, m. in Edmeston, N. Y., March 15, 1839, Fidelia Bennett, dau. of Benjamin and Fanny (Ladd) Bennett. She was b. in Burlington, Otsego county,

N. Y., Dec. 1, 1819; d. in Jefferson, Ill., March 5, 1847. He d. in Pueblo, Col., July 13, 1877.

Children, all b. in Jefferson, Ill.:
1. Morris Scott,[8] b. Dec. 19, 1842, m. in Marengo, Ill., March 31, 1875, Amelia Elizabeth Talbot, dau. of Jacob and Ruth Permelia (Cole) Talbot. She was b. in West Edmeston, N. Y., Feb. 20, 1845. No children.
2. Orlando Bennett,[8] b. Nov. 16, 1844; unm. Res. Towanda, Kan.

Giles Sutherland,[7] the next son of Jonah and Mary (Pearson) Sutherland, b. in Manchester, Vt., March 25, 1815, m. in Burlington, N. Y., April 3, 1839, Ruth Sheldon, dau. of Timothy and Lucinda (Hulbert) Sheldon. She was b. in Burlington, N. Y., July 20, 1816, died in Exeter, Otsego county, N. Y., Jan. 23, 1864. He died in Oneonta, N. Y., Oct. 5, 1867.

Children:
1. Maria Lucinda,[8] b. Oct. 6, 1843, m. in Exeter, N. Y., March 6, 1866, Charles T. Munson, son of George and Phebe (Robinson) Munson. He was b. in Plainfield, Otsego county, N. Y., Dec. 8, 1841. Res. Burlington, N. Y. Child: 1. Ethel, b. Oct. 15, 1874.
2. Cornelia Amanda,[8] b. March 6, 1850.

Charles Sutherland,[7] the next son of Jonah and Mary (Pearson) Sutherland, b. in Edmeston, N. Y., Nov. 4, 1816, m. in West Edmeston, N. Y., May 7, 1844, Frances Elizabeth Burdick, dau. of Ichabod and Frances (Greene) Burdick. She was b. in Hopkinton, R. I., Feb. 22, 1824. He is a farmer; res. Sharon, Wis.

Children:
1. Mary Jane,[8] b. Jan. 20, 1845, m. in Walworth, Wis., April 27, 1864, David William Hulbert, son of Silas and Polly (Shepard) Hulbert. He was b. in Cohocton, Steuben county, N. Y., Aug. 2, 1838; served in the late war. Res. Covert, Mich. Children: 1. Ellen Mowry,[9] b. in Geneva, Kane county, Ill., Dec. 8, 1866; d. in Rockford, Kan., Nov. 2, 1871. 2. Eulalia Cassie,[9] b. in Walworth, Wis., April 20, 1869.
2. Ichabod Ellis,[8] b. Aug. 24, 1847, m. in Sharon, Wis., Dec. 28, 1870, Emma Adelia Peirce, dau. of Delos and Theodosia (Collins) Peirce. She was b. in Plainfield, N. Y., Aug. 23, 1848. No children. Res. Walworth, Wis.
3. George Herbert Eugene,[8] b. May 8, 1853.
4. Charlie Frank,[8] b. Feb. 26, 1856.

Mark Sutherland,[7] the next son of Jonah and Mary (Pearson) Sutherland, b. in Edmeston, N. Y., June 28, 1819, m. in Walworth, Wis., Nov. 27, 1844, Mary Coon, dau. of Daniel and Esther (Clark) Coon. She was born in Plainfield, Otsego county, N. Y., Sept. 11, 1818. He is a farmer; res. Horton, Bremer county, Iowa.

Children:
1. James Monroe,[8] b. in Lyme, Wis., Aug. 5, 1845; d. Jan. 16, 1867.
2. Mary Maria,[8] b. in Lyme, Wis., Sept. 8, 1848, m. in Waverly, Bremer county, Iowa, Oct. 2, 1870, Azro Edson Dana, son of Francis and Harriet (Nutting) Dana. He was b. in Dickinson, Franklin county, N. Y., June 27, 1845. Livery; res. Nashua, Iowa. Children: 1. Cyron Jay,[9] b. in Douglass, Iowa, Sept. 25, 1872. 2. Howard Victor,[9] b. in Lafayette, Iowa, April 26, 1874. 3. Frederic Clarke,[9] b. in Lafayette, Iowa, Feb. 24, 1876.

3. Emily De Ette,[8] b. in Lyme, Wis., Aug. 5, 1851; d. Nov. 1, 1853.
4. Alonzo Lafayette,[8] b. in Walworth, Wis., Nov. 4, 1853.
5. Alice Medora,[8] b. in Walworth, Wis., July 25, 1856.

Albert Sutherland,[7] the next son of Jonah and Mary (Pearson) Sutherland, b. in Edmeston, N. Y., Nov. 16, 1821, m. first, in Edmeston, N. Y., Jan. 1, 1846, Irene Bennett, dau. of Benjamin and Fanny (Ladd) Bennett. She was b. in New Lisbon, Otsego county, N. Y., Sept. 21, 1823, and d. in Edmeston, N. Y., Aug. 25, 1874. He m. second, in Edmeston, N. Y., Dec. 16, 1877, Mrs. Betsey Jane (Rainey) White, dau. of John and Betsey (Welch) Rainey. She was b. in Brookfield, Madison county, N. Y., Oct. 6, 1827. He is a farmer; res. West Edmeston, N. Y.

Children, by wife Irene :

1. Charles Henry,[8] b. June 21, 1847; m. in Fairfield, Breckenridge county, Va., Dec. 18, 1872, Mary Ann Taylor, dau. of Gabriel and Jane (Smith) Taylor. She was born in Allegheny county, Va., July 23, 1852. Res. Brownsburgh, Va. Children: 1. Walter Elmer,[9] b. Oct. 30, 1873. 2. Son, b. Nov. 7, 1874 ; d. ——. 3. Otis Tilden,[9] b. March 25, 1876.
2. Adelbert Irving,[8] b. April 5, 1850.
3. Hermon Albertis,[8] b. Jan. 7, 1853.
4. Elmer,[8]) b. March 9, 1856; d. April 5, 1860.
5. Elwin,[8]) b. March 9, 1856.
6. Fannie Fidelia Theresa,[8] b. Feb. 22, 1859.
7. Ella Jane,[8] b. June 29, 1861.
8. Mary Annie DeEtta,[8] b. Aug. 23, 1866.

Alonzo W. Sutherland,[7] the youngest son and child of Jonah and Mary (Pearson) Sutherland, b. in Edmeston, N. Y., Jan. 12, 1827, m. in Edmeston, N. Y., July 4, 1848, Harriet Mitchell, dau. of George and Mary (Colgrove) Mitchell. She was b. in Edmeston, N. Y., Oct. 22, 1829. He is a farmer; res. Edmeston, N. Y.

Children :

1. Emeline Amelia,[8] b. March 3, 1849, m. in Edmeston, N. Y., Sept. 17, 1867, William Henry Northrup, son of Nicholas and Sarah (Medbury) Northrup. He was b. in Pittsfield, Otsego county, N. Y., Jan. 1, 1838. Mechanic; res. Edmeston, N. Y. Child : 1. Clark,[9] b. July 12, 1872.
2. Helen Maria,[8] b. Oct. 15, 1854, m. in Edmeston, N. Y., Nov. 12, 1876, Reuben Talbot, son of Hiram and Silvia (Cutter) Talbot. He was b. in Edmeston, N. Y., April 3, 1855. Farmer; res. Edmeston, N. Y.

James Eaton,[7] eldest son and child of DeEstaing and Eunice (Pearson) Eaton, b. in Manchester, Vt., March 24, 1805, m. in Sangerfield, Oneida county, N. Y., March 24, 1825, Mary Stockwell, dau. of Asa and Sally (Tuttle) Stockwell. She was b. in Sangerfield, Oneida county, N. Y., June 23, 1807; d. ——. He died in New Berlin, N. Y., April 20, 1872.

Children :
  1. Philander DeEstaing,[8] b. in Brookfield, N. Y., Nov. 15, 1830, m. in Toddsville, Otsego county, N. Y., March 28, 1852, Abigail Burke, dau. of Daniel and Maria (McCreery) Burke. She was b. in Hardwick, Otsego county, N. Y., Jan. 9, 1834. He d. in Mohawk, Herkimer county, N. Y., Nov. 8, 1866. Child: 1. Ida May,[9] b. in Moravia, Cayuga county, N. Y., June 19, 1859.
  2. Maria Almira,[8] b. in Sangerfield, N. Y., Nov. 10, 1839, m. in West Edmeston, N. Y., Aug. 7, 1859, George Sumner Sheldon, son of Jonathan H. and Eliza (Thompson) Sheldon. He was b. in Jamestown, Chautauqua county, N. Y., Oct. 13, 1837. Res. Morris, N. Y. Children : 1. Ella Maria,[9] b. in New Berlin, N.Y., April 9, 1861. 2. Mary Eliza,[9] b. in Burlington, N. Y., March 29, 1863.
  3. Francis Marion,[8] b. in Sangerfield, N. Y., June 22, 1842, m. in Burlington Flats, N. Y., Aug. 4, 1861, Sarah Jane Pope, dau. of Charles and Sarah (Payne) Pope. She was b. in New Berlin, N. Y., Nov. 29, 1844. He is a farmer; res. Morris, N. Y. Children : 1. Lelia Maria,[9] b. in New Berlin, N.Y., Nov. 4, 1865. 2. James Orville,[9] b. in New Berlin, N. Y., Sept. 4, 1869.

Nancy Eaton,[7] second child of DeEstaing and Eunice (Pearson) Eaton, b. in Sherburne, N. Y., May 8, 1807, m. in Brookfield, Madison county, N. Y., Dec. 15, 1825, Saxton Berry, son of Ephraim and Lydia (Wheaton) Berry. He was b. in Pomfret, Conn., May 19, 1804 ; d. in Sangerfield, N. Y., Sept. 7, 1876. She is living in Sangerfield, Oneida county, N. Y.

  Children, all born in Brookfield, N. Y. :
  1. Adelia Jane,[8] b. June 19, 1827, m. in Brookfield, N. Y., Oct. 19, 1842, Edwin Walter Beebe, son of Pliny and Hannah (Stetson) Beebe. He was b. in Sangerfield, N. Y., April 21, 1823. Children, all b. in Sangerfield, N. Y.: 1. La Motte,[9] b. May 7, 1848, m. in Conestota, Madison county, N. Y., Nov. 26, 1867, Helen Mary Gleason, dau. of Alfred William and Mary Helen (Glass) Gleason. She was b. in Bridgeport, N. Y., Nov. 26, 1849. Child : Edwin Alfred,[10] b. in Sangerfield, N. Y., March 12, 1870. 2. Ellen Louisa,[9] b. July 8, 1852, m. in Sangerfield, N.Y., Nov. 3, 1870, George Gleason, son of Alfred William and Mary Helen (Glass) Gleason. He was b. in Bridgeport, N. Y., Jan. 10, 1848. She d. in Sangerfield, N. Y., May 22, 1876.
  2. Alphonso Eaton,[8] born Oct. 2, 1830, m. in New Berlin, N. Y., May 18, 1851, Maria Clark, dau. of James and Sarah (Boone) Clark. She was b. in Brookfield, N. Y., Feb. 5, 1831. He d. in Sangerfield, N. Y., March 3, 1873. Children, all b. in Sangerfield, N. Y.: 1. Emma Jane,[9] b. May 4, 1854, m. in Sangerfield, N. Y., Oct. 25, 1871, Ezra Seymour Brainard, son of Diodate and Amy (Aldridge) Brainard. He was b. in Hamilton, N. Y., March 4, 1849. Child : Milo Clark,[10] b. Oct. 28, 1872. 2. Saxton Scott,[9] b. Aug. 20, 1856, m. in Sangerfield, N. Y., Aug. 7, 1874, Alta Eliza Gleason, dau. of Alfred W. and Mary H. (Glass) Gleason. She was b. in Sullivan, N. Y., Sept. 13, 1858.

Nathan Eaton,[7] third child of DeEstaing and Eunice (Pearson) Eaton, b. in Brookfield, N. Y., Aug. 30, 1815, m. in Brookfield, N. Y., April 14, 1835, Mary Clarke, dau. of James and Sarah (Boone) Clarke. She was b. in Brookfield, N. Y., April 5, 1815; d. in New Berlin, N. Y., April 9, 1856. He d. in New Berlin, N. Y., March 2, 1856.

Children :
1. Clarke Alvinza,[8] b. in Brookfield, N. Y., Jan. 23, 1837, m. in ——, Oct. 13, 1858, Emma Elizabeth Kinney, dau. of Roger and Mary Ann (Bates) Kinney. She was b. in ——, Feb. —, 1840. He d. in New Berlin, N. Y., July 15, 1860.
2. Louisa Adelaide,[8] b. in Augusta, N. Y., Dec. 26, 1839, m. in Sangerfield, N. Y., Nov. 2, 1859, LeGrande Lacy Colburn, son of George and Sally Ann (Medbury) Colburn. He was b. in Pittsfield, Otsego county, N. Y., April 18, 1839. Res. New Berlin, N. Y. Child: 1. Willis Lee,[9] b. Dec. 12, 1864.
3. Willis Delos,[8] b. in New Berlin, N. Y., Jan. 26, 1844, m. in New Berlin, Chenango county, N. Y., July 19, 1863, Harriet Annette White, dau. of William Avery and Nancy (Wolcott) White. She was b. in New Berlin, N. Y., April 14, 1839. Res. New Berlin, N. Y. Child: 1. Nathan Clark,[9] b. Feb. 3, 1871; d. April 18, 1872.
4. Lewis Nathan,[8] b. in New Berlin, N. Y., Aug. 12, 1845, m. in Hamilton, N. Y., June 7, 1870, Ella May Penner, dau. of Joseph and Mary (Fisher) Penner. She was born in Sangerfield, N. Y., March 10, 1855. Res. Cherry Creek, N. Y. Child: 1. Nathan De Estaing,[9] b. July 8, 1875.
5. Mary Lorinda,[8] b. in New Berlin, N. Y., Nov. 7, 1850, m. in New Berlin, N. Y., Jan. 3, 1871, William Francis Stetson, son of Francis Marion and Sarah Gennette (Wells) Stetson. He was b. in Sangerfield, N. Y., June 19, 1850. Child: 1. Genevra Louisa,[9] b. May 3, 1875.

John Eaton,[7] fourth child of DeEstaing and Eunice (Pearson) Eaton, b. in Brookfield, Otsego county, N. Y., Feb. 15, 1818, m. in Marshall, Oneida county, N. Y., Sept. 13, 1838, Lucina Green, dau. of Perry and Hannah (Tooley) Green. She was b. in Springville, Erie county, N. Y., July 19, 1817.

Child:
1. Nancy Polleesa,[8] b. in Brookfield, N. Y., Nov. 11, 1842, m. in Pittsfield, Pike county, Ill., Dec. 5, 1876, Eugene Toles, son of Orson and Emeline (Farnham) Toles. He was b. in Pittsfield, N. Y., May 22, 1845. Res. Sangerfield, N. Y. No children.

Joseph Eaton,[7] youngest child of DeEstaing and Eunice (Pearson) Eaton, m. first, in Brookfield, Madison county, N. Y., Dec. 29, 1839, Elmina Read, dau. of Lemuel and Sarah (Clarke) Read. She was b. in Brookfield, N. Y., Dec. 28, 1824; d. in Brookfield, N. Y., Aug. 7, 1856. He m. second, in Battle Creek, Mich., Nellie Lewis, birth and parentage unknown, who d. (without issue) in Chicago, Ill., Nov. 26, 1866. He m. third, in Highland, Pike county, Ill., Jan. 2, 1870, Mary Ann Beaven, dau. of Charles and Mary (Middleton) Beaven. She was b. in Highland, Ill., April 2, 1841. He is a carpenter ; res. Pittsfield, Pike county, Ill.

Children, by wife Elmina, all b. in Brookfield, N. Y. :
1. Cyrenius Read,[8] b. Aug. 27, 1842; d. in Kendallville, Ind., March 9, 1862, unm.
2. Elmira Cerina,[8] b. Sept. 4, 1844, m. in Pittsfield, Pike county, Ill., April 2, 1867, Marshall Long Chambers, son of William and Cynthia (Long) Chambers. He was b. in Muscatine, Iowa, Nov. 6, 1847. She d. in Muscatine, Iowa, Jan. 22, 1870. He resides in Muscatine, Iowa. Child: 1. Scott Wike,[9] b. Dec. 12, 1869.

by wife Mary Ann, all b. in Pittsfield, Ill.:
3. Nellie Elmina,[6] b. Jan. 5, 1874.
4. Mary Luellie,[8] b. June 28, 1876.

Phebe C. Pearson,[7] eldest daughter and child of Jacob and Rhoda (Ewers) Pearson, b. in Leroy, Genesee county, N. Y., May 26, 1813, m. in Waterville, Oneida county, N. Y., Nov. 3, 1859, Orenzo Barnard, son of Benjamin and Polly (Murray) Barnard. He was b. in Hardwick, Mass., Aug. 18, 1804; d. in Waterville, N. Y., June 16, 1873. A builder by occupation. She is living (1878) in Waterville, N. Y. They had no children.

Elizabeth B. Pearson,[7] second daughter and child of Jacob and Rhoda (Ewers) Pearson, b. in Brookfield, N. Y., July 25, 1815, m. in Akron, O., Jan. 1, 1846, Porter Cunningham Rector, son of John and Tamasin Mary (Dana) Rector, of Albany, N. Y. He was b. in Manlius, Onondaga county, N. Y., Feb. 3, 1815, and is now residing in Oakland, Cal. A miller by occupation. She d. in Akron, Ohio, Aug. 14, 1871.
Children :
1. Alice Logenia,[8] b. in Copley, Ohio, Feb. 22, 1848; d. Feb. 13, 1853.
2. Emma,[8] b. in Akron, Ohio, Oct. 10, 1849; d. Jan. 4, 1850.
3. Henrietta,[8] b. in Warsaw, Ohio, Dec. 4, 1851; d. March 5, 1854.

Josiah M. Pearson,[7] eldest son and third child of Jacob and Rhoda (Ewers) Pearson, b. in Brookfield, Madison county, N. Y., April 25, 1817, m. in Rome, Oneida county, N. Y., Dec. 29, 1839, Tryphena Bitgood, dau. of Varnum and Abbie (Comstock) Bitgood. She was b. in Massachusetts, March 4, 1820. He is a farmer; res. Martinton, Ill.
Children :
1. George Hough,[8] b. June 12, 1841; d. July 28, 1867.
2. Henry,[8] b. Oct. 4, 1847, m. in Watseca, Iroquois county, Ill., June 28, 1872, Love Peirce, dau. of Nathaniel and Mary Eliza (Simmons) Peirce. She was b. in Adams, La Salle county, Ill., April 21, 1849. He is a farmer; res. Martinton, Ill. Children: 1. Emery La Forest,[9] b. Dec. 20, 1873. 2. George Herbert,[9] b. April 25, 1875; d. Oct. 8, 1875. 3. Josiah Nathaniel,[9] b. April 5, 1876. 4. Jennie Morton,[9] b. March 25, 1877.
3. Adaline,[8] b. Nov. 4, 1849, m. in Watseca, Ill., July 29, 1869, Alvin Milton Miller, son of Worthington and Harriet (Everett) Miller. He was b. in Algonquin, McHenry county, Ill., April 30, 1844. Farmer; res. Martinton, Ill. Children: 1. Melvin La Forest,[9] b. April 19, 1871. 2. Daughter,[9] b. Nov. 24, 1874; d. Nov. 24, 1874. 3. Georgia Alice,[9] b. July 15, 1876.
4. Hermon Clark,[8] b. May 10, 1855.

Adaline Pearson,[7] third daughter and fourth child of Jacob and Rhoda (Ewers) Pearson, b. in Brookfield, N. Y., July 22, 1820, m. first, in Akron, Summit county, Ohio, March 7, 1842, William Charles Augustus Emil Rausch, son of Henry Phillip and Emily Christiana Thomasine (Steinbach) Rausch. He was b. in Hesse Cassel, Germany, Sept. 7,

1807. (Divorced.) He is living in Toledo, Ohio. She m. second, in Akron, Ohio, March 27, 1852, Julio Ralph Newman, son of William Ralph and Eleanor (Shannon) Newman. He was b. in Chester, N. S., July 10, 1817; d. in Alden, Iowa, Oct. 19, 1877. She is living in Cuyahoga Falls, Ohio.

Children, by husband, William C. A. E. Rausch:

1. Caroline Emelia Elizabeth,[8] b. Dec. 13, 1842, m. in Akron, Ohio, Jan. 8, 1866, Addison John Farrand, son of Jared and Sally (Randall) Farrand. He was b. in Dover, Ohio, May 20, 1839. Grocer; res. Linndale, Ohio. Children, all b. in Brooklyn, (Linndale), Ohio: 1. Arthur Monroe,[9] b. Aug. 28, 1875; d. in Martinton, Ill., Nov. 7, 1876. 2. Walter Cleveland,[9] b. Dec. 21, 1877.
2. Adaline Augusta,[8] b. Jan. 26, 1845, m. in Cuyahoga Falls, Ohio, Jan. 8, 1872, Monroe Bradley Camp, son of Matthew and Ann Eliza (Estey) Camp. He was b. in Dundas, C. W., Jan. 3, 1845. Farmer; res. Streator, La Salle county, Ill. Children: 1. Grace Ella,[9] b. Oct. 9, 1872. 2. Josephine Belle,[9] b. Dec. 9, 1874.

by husband, J. Ralph Newman:

3. Lauretta Selby,[8] b. April 1, 1853; d. July 5, 1866.
4. Esther Henrietta,[8] b. Sept. 23, 1855; d. June 2, 1874.

Ephraim J. Pearson,[7] third son and sixth child of Jacob and Rhoda (Ewers) Pearson, b. in Brookfield, N. Y., Oct. 28, 1825, m. in Salt Lake City, Utah, Dec. 5, 1848, Nancy Ann Foutz, dau. of Jacob and Margaret (Munn) Foutz. She was b. in Jemper City, Franklin county, Pa., May 21, 1826. He is a farmer; res. Pleasant Grove City, Utah.

Children:

1. Ephraim,[8] b. in Salt Lake City, Sept. 1, 1849; d. young.
2. Ann Sophia,[8] b. in Salt Lake City, Nov. 3, 1850; d. young.
3. Hyrum,[8] b. in Pleasant Grove City, Jan. 5, 1852.
4. Louisa,[8] b. in Pleasant Grove City, June 10, 1854.
5. Phebe Elizabeth,[8] b. in Pleasant Grove City, Aug. 12, 1855, m. in Salt Lake City, Utah, Oct. 13, 1873, John Albert Robison, son of Lewis and Clarissa (Duzette) Robison. He was b. in Salt Lake City, Jan. 29, 1850. Res. Georgetown, Idaho. Children: 1. John Albert,[9] b. in Pleasant Grove City, May 24, 1875. 2. Gove Benjamin,[9] b. in Georgetown, Idaho, Aug. 27, 1877.
6. Benjamin,[8] b. in Pleasant Grove City, Nov. 29, 1857.
7. George,[8] b. in Pleasant Grove City, March 3, 1859; d. young.
8. Lewis Heber,[8] b. in Pleasant Grove City, July 6, 1861.

Elias F. Pearson,[7] fourth son and seventh child of Jacob and Rhoda (Ewers) Pearson, b. in Brookfield, N. Y., July 9, 1827, m. in Provo City, Utah, July 8, 1855, Minerva Lucinda Eaton, dau. of Joseph and Minerva (Sagars) Eaton. She was b. in Lorain county, Ohio, June 8, 1836. He is a miner; res. Circleville, Utah.

Children:

1. Rhoda Minerva,[8] b. in Pleasant Grove City, Utah, July 2, 1856, m. in Glenwood, Utah, Jan. 10, 1876, Henry A. Zufelt, son of Henry and Louise Zufelt. He was b. in Germany, May 10, 1853.
2. Rosetta Adaline,[8] b. in Ophir, Placer county, Cal., Jan. 10, 1858, m. in Circleville, Utah, Oct. 22, 1877, James Abiel Stark, son of Abiel and Jane Alice (Ely) Stark. He was b. in Lyme, New London county, Conn., May 3, 1843.

3. Henrietta Adelaide,⁸ b. in Beaver City, Utah, Nov. 22, 1859.
4. Elias Frasier,⁸ b. in Scipio, Millard county, Utah, Dec. 23, 1861.
5. Joseph Henry,⁸ b. in Scipio, Millard county, Utah, Aug. 24, 1864.
6. John Riley,⁸ b. in Gunnison, Utah, April 18, 1867.
7. Phebe Alverta,⁸ b. in Ephraim City, Utah, Oct. 15, 1869; d. Aug. 23, 1871.
8. George Washington,⁸ b. in Glenwood, Utah, April 28, 1872.
9. Mayetta,⁸ b. in Glenwood, Utah, Jan. 31, 1875.
10. Eugene,⁸ b. in Circleville, Utah, Feb. 25, 1877.

James A. C. O'Brien,⁷ eldest child and only son of Timothy and Mary (Chase) O'Brien, b. in Sherburne, Chenango county, N. Y., Nov. 11, 1823, m. in Sherburne, Chenango county, N. Y., Feb. 7, 1844, Adaline Louisa Gritman, dau. of Solomon and Lydia (Wickwire) Gritman. She was b. in Pharsalia, Chenango county, N. Y., Jan. 28, 1825. He d. in Edmeston, N. Y., April 15, 1871. She is living (1878) in Edmeston. He was a farmer.

Children:

1. Daughter,⁸ b. in Hamilton, N. Y., Nov. 15, 1844; d. Nov. 15, 1844.
2. Lydia Almira,⁸ b. in Hamilton, N. Y., Oct. 25, 1845, m. in New Berlin, N. Y., April 5, 1866, Henry Adelbert Hunt, son of Boylston and Eliza Ann (Staples) Hunt. He was b. in Hamilton, N. Y., Jan. 9, 1842. Farmer; res. Hamilton, N. Y. Child: 1. Roy,⁹ b. April 6, 1871.
3. Mary Almena,⁸ b. in Brookfield, N. Y., Oct. 14, 1850, m. in Earlville, N. Y., Dec. 15, 1873, Lyman Barrett, son of Daniel Rockwell and Serene (Coombs) Barrett. She was b. in Edmeston, N. Y., May 8, 1849. No children. Res. Edmeston Centre, N. Y.
4. Albert Jay,⁸ b. in Brookfield, N. Y., Aug. 27, 1855.

Almira J. O'Brien,⁷ youngest child and only daughter of Timothy and Mary (Chase) O'Brien, b. in Norwich, N. Y., Nov. 29, 1824, m. in Hamilton, N. Y., Aug. 24, 1845, Chauncey Palmer, M. D., son of Calvin and Abigail Peabody (Sumner) Palmer. He was b. in Pomfret, Windham county, Conn., March 24, 1818; d. in Norwich, N. Y., Nov. 14, 1875. He practiced medicine for over thirty years in Chenango and adjoining counties with marked success. His widow is living (1878) in Earlville, N. Y.

Children:

1. Mary Theresa,⁸ b. in Pitcher Springs, N. Y., Dec. 3, 1846, m. in Sherburne, N. Y., Jan. 14, 1869, David Jerome Preston, son of William and Harriet (Beach) Preston. He was b. in Hamilton, N. Y., Dec. 25, 1843; d. in Sherburne, N. Y., from the effects of an accident while driving his horses, April 8, 1876. He was a farmer. His widow is living (1878) near Poolville, N. Y. Child: 1. Clara Louise,⁹ b. Nov. 10, 1873.
2. Abigail Althea,⁸ b. in Pitcher Springs, N. Y., Sept. 20, 1848.
3. James Sumner,⁸ b. in Hamilton, N. Y., Oct. 12, 1850; d. Aug. 29, 1861.
4. Milton Chase,⁸ b. April 7, 1853.
5. Emma Jane,⁸ b. Feb. 17, 1855; d. March 26, 1855.
6. Omer,⁸ b. March 24, 1857.
7. Chauncey,⁸ b. March 8, 1862.

Sarah C. M. Reese,[7] eldest daughter and child of Simeon G. and Drusilla (O'Brien) Reese, b. in Berkshire, Tioga county, N. Y., Feb. 24, 1825, m. in Sherburne, N. Y., Nov. 27, 1842, Alfred Parsons, son of John and Flavia (Billings) Parsons. He was b. in Smyrna, Chenango county, N. Y., Sept. 23, 1815. Farmer; res. Earlville, N. Y.
Children, all b. in Earlville:
1. Delphurnia Adelia,[8] b. Nov. 5, 1843, m. in Smyrna, N. Y., June 12, 1866, Nathan Albert Turner, son of Horace and Marinda (Randall) Turner. He was b. in New Hartford, N. Y., Nov. 12, 1840. Farmer; res. New Dort, Richmond county, N. Y. Children: 1. Minnie,[9] b. April 8, 1867. 2. Alfred Parsons,[9] b. Jan. 8, 1869. 3. Caressa,[9] b. Jan. 6, 1875. 4. Nathan Albert,[9] b. Nov. 1, 1876.
2. DeForrest,[8] b. Nov. 15, 1844, m. in Earlville, N. Y., Jan. 7, 1875, Mary Clarke, dau. of David and Experience (Merrick) Clarke. She was b. in Lebanon, N. Y., Nov. 22, 1842. He is a farmer; res. Earlville, N. Y. No children.
3. John Reese,[8] b. Feb. 21, 1856. Is a teacher; res. Earlville.

Simeon DeW. C. Reese,[7] eldest son and second child of Simeon G. and Drusilla (O'Brien) Reese, b. April 23, 1827, m. in Hamilton, N. Y., March 20, 1856, Ellen Adelia Chappell, dau. of Peter and Marcia (Gardner) Chappell. She was b. in Hamilton, N. Y., Sept. 6, 1837. He is a farmer; res. South Hamilton, N. Y.
Children:
1. Clara Marcia,[8] b. July 5, 1861.
2. Chappell DeWitt,[8] b. June 9, 1864.
3. Nora Ellen,[8] b. Sept. 4, 1868.
4. Peter Gardner,[8] b. Feb. 27, 1872.
5. Jennie Marilla,[8] b. Nov. 8, 1875.

Rachel E. C. Reese,[7] second daughter and third child of Simeon G. and Drusilla (O'Brien) Reese, b. Aug. 31, 1829, m. in Hamilton, N. Y., April 18, 1852, George Edmund Baker, son of Edmund and Betsey (Baker) Baker. He was b. in Danbury, N. H., Oct. 23, 1823, and was well known as one of the "Baker Family" vocalists. She traveled and sang with them for several years, and d. in Waukegan, Lake county, Ill., Aug. 11, 1858. No children.

Haskell G. C. Reese,[7] second son and fourth child of Simeon G. and Drusilla (O'Brien) Reese, b. April 19, 1832, m. in Hamilton, N. Y., April 29, 1855, Lovina Adelaide Riddell, dau. of David and Polly (Parkes) Riddell. She was b. in Hamilton, N. Y., May 23, 1839. He is a farmer; res. near Earlville, N. Y.
Children:
1. Anna Drusilla,[8] b. June 3, 1856.
2. Frank DeWitt,[8] b. July 8, 1858.

Jacob G. Reese,[7] third son and fifth child of Simeon G. and Drusilla (O'Brien) Reese, b. Dec. 26, 1833, m. in Sherburne, N. Y., Feb. 14, 1866, Lucy Orcelia Miller, dau. of Lyman Onslow and Rachel Emeline (Burdick) Miller. She was b. in Sherburne, N. Y., May 11, 1844. He is a farmer; res. near Earlville, N. Y.
Children:
1. David Miller,[8] b. Dec. 27, 1866.
2. Simeon Gillett,[8] b. April 2, 1875.

Phebe L. Stetson,[1] eldest daughter and child of Ezra and Sarah (O'Brien) Stetson, b. April 9, 1828, m. in Sangerfield, N. Y., Nov. 25, 1851, James Graham Burlingame, son of Harry and Elmina (Frisbie) Burlingame. He was b. in Lenox, Madison county, N. Y., Dec. 4, 1827. Farmer; res. Sangerfield, N. Y.

Children, all b. in Sangerfield:

1. Willis Clifton,[8] b. July 27, 1855, m. in Marshall, Mich., April 11, 1877, Janette Gage Bull, dau. of William Augustus and Juelma Maria (Sayles) Bull. She was b. in Portage, Ind., Sept. 26, 1854.
2. Frederic Jay,[8] b. March 21, 1857.
3. Scott Harry,[8] b. May 3, 1865.
4. Maria Adelia,[8] b. Dec. 30, 1867.
5. Clara Sarah,[8] b. April 21, 1871.

Egbert J. Stetson,[7] eldest son and second child of Ezra and Sarah (O'Brien) Stetson, b. Nov. 29, 1833, m. in Sangerfield, N. Y., April 8, 1856, Louisa Marcia Burlingame, dau. of Harry and Elmina (Frisbie) Burlingame. She was b. in Lenox, N. Y., March 14, 1832. He is a farmer; res. Sangerfield, N. Y.

Children, all b. in Sangerfield:

1. Scott Egbert,[8] b. Dec. 28, 1859; d. Aug. 19, 1863.
2. Frank Cleveland,[8] b. May 20, 1864.
3. Kirk Alvin,[8] b. Nov. 27, 1867.

Adelia D. Stetson,[7] youngest daughter and child of Ezra and Sarah (O'Brien) Stetson, b. July 3, 1840, m. in Wolcott, Wayne county, N. Y., Oct. 12, 1866, Henry Loomis Day, son of Lyman and Maria (Preston) Day. He was b. in Sangerfield, N. Y., Aug. 3, 1834. Farmer; res. Marshall, Mich. No children.

KNAPP — BARNUM.

(SEE PAGE 50.)

The Knapps in this country, or at least in the New England States, are undoubtedly largely descended from Nicholas Knap, who came from Sussex, Eng., about A. D. 1630, and settled in Watertown, Mass. By first wife, Elinor, he had: 1. Jonathan, (who was buried Dec. 27, 1631); 2. Timothy, b. Dec. 14, 1632; 3. Joshua, b. Jan. 5, 1635; 4. Caleb, b. Jan. 20, 1637; 5. Sarah, b. Jan. 5, 1639; 6. Ruth, b. Jan. 6, 1641; 7. Hannah, b. March 6, 1643. Removed to Stamford, Conn., and there had: 8. Moses, b. ——, 1645; 9. Lydia, b. ——, 1647. His wife Elinor d. Aug. 16, 1658, and he m. second, March 9, 1659, Mrs. Unity, widow of Peter Brown, and who had been widow of Clement Buxton. He d. April, 1670. His will of April 15, 1670, names four sons, Caleb, Joshua, Moses, Timothy; and four daughters, Sarah, Hannah, Lydia, Ruth.

Timothy, second son of Nicholas Knap, was representative for Rye in 1670, and was living in Greenwich, 1697.

Joshua, third son of Nicholas Knap, was of Greenwich, 1670; m. in Stamford, June 9, 1657, Hannah Close; d. Oct. 27, 1684, leaving a good estate by inventory of 1685; and children: Hannah, aged 25; Joshua, 22; Joseph, 20; Ruth, 18; Timothy, 16; Benjamin, 10; Caleb, 7; Jonathan, 5. His widow m. John Bowers.

Caleb, fourth son of Nicholas Knap, was of Stamford, 1670, made his will Dec. 11, 1674, and names wife Hannah, and children, Caleb, John, Moses, Samuel, Sarah and Hannah.

Sarah, eldest daughter of Nicholas Knap, m. Sept. 6, 1667, Peter Disbrough; and Ruth, the second daughter, m. Nov. 20, 1667, Joseph Ferris.

Moses, the youngest son of Nicholas Knap, was of Greenwich, 1670, but perhaps only a landholder, and never lived there but at Stamford, as early as 1667, and there his father gave him land by his will; m. about 1669, Abigail, daughter of Richard Wescoat. Whether he had children is not learned, but he was living certainly at Stamford up to 1701, perhaps later. The name is now generally spelled with two p's.

The compiler has no good reason to doubt that *John Knap*, second son of Caleb and Hannah Knap, and grandson of Nicholas and Elinor Knap, was the grandfather (or great grandfather) of John Knapp, of Danbury, Conn., who m. Ruth Gregory, and had:

1. Samuel, b. about 1760, m. Mary Lindsley.
2. Elizabeth, b. about 1763, m. Ezra Nichols.
3. Jehu, b. Nov. 17, 1767, m. Lois Wood.
4. Ruth, b. about 1770, m. Baker Bass.
5. John, b. May 13, 1772, m. first, Lucy Merwin.
6. Chloe, b. about 1774, m. Joseph Mansfield.
7. Levi, b. May 1, 1777, m. Elizabeth Hamilton.

Of this family and descendants the following sketch, hastily prepared and necessarily very imperfect in dates, etc., is given, for preservation and future reference:

Samuel Knapp, the eldest son and child of John and Ruth (Gregory) Knapp, by wife Mary Lindsley had:

1. Polly, who m. James Disbrow, and had Orville, Perry, Rachel, James and Samuel.
2. William, who d. unmarried.
3. Samuel, who m. Mary Mack. No children.
4. Lucy, who m. Zadoc Green. No children.
5. Shubal, who m. Eliza Tuttle, and had a son Lemuel.
6. Stephen, who m. Grace Johnson, and had William, Charles, Lucy, Harriet, Sally, Julius, Van Buren, Helen, Ephraim, Caroline and Charlotte.
7. Lewis, who d. unmarried.
8. Ephraim, who d. unmarried.

Elizabeth Knapp, the eldest daughter and second child of John and Ruth (Gregory) Knapp, by husband Ezra Nichols had:

1. Sarah, who m. Whitman Bryant, and had Zachariah, Ezra, John, Polly, Sally, James and Sophia.

2. John, who m. Laura Hamilton, and had Susan, Sarah, Clarinda and Lucinda.
3. Daniel, who m. Amy Disbrow, and had Lura, Fanny, Sally and Spicer.
4. Chloe, who m. Francis Dixon, and had Elizabeth, Alfred, Eli, Russell and Almon. She d. in Huntsburgh, Geauga county, Ohio.
5. Eli, who m. Clarissa Munson, and had Clarinda, Sarah, John, Ezra and Angeline.
6. Clemens, who m. Mary Peirce, and had Elizabeth, Adeline, Clemens and Horace.

Jehu Knapp, the second son and third child of John and Ruth (Gregory) Knapp, by wife Lois Wood had :
1. Noah, b. about 1793; d. March 30, 1866. By wife ——, had Laura, John, Clarissa, Lucy, Hannah, Mary, Levi, Emeline, Charlotte, and (twins) Cornelius and Cornelia.
2. Lucy, b. about 1795; now deceased. By husband —— Kirkpatrick, had two children, names not given.
3. Levi, b. about 1797; had a son named Levi, it is said, living in Eugene, Iowa.
4. Lucinda, b. about 1799, m. a Mr. Haines, and had a son, Austin Haines, in Panama, N. Y. She died about 1849.
5. Nancy, b. about 1800; deceased. She m. a Mr. Joslyn, and had two sons, Frank and Fred, living, it is stated, near Conneautville, Pa.
6. Jehu, b. about 1802; d. in Auburn, N. Y., leaving one daughter, Ann Eliza, present residence not learned.
7. Darius, b. April 24, 1805, m. Polly Edwards, dau. of Ebenezer and Sybil (Seeley) Edwards. She was b. Nov. 3, 1807; d. Dec. 5, 1877. He d. Jan. 24, 1866. Children : 1. Ebenezer, b. April 19, 1831; d. Aug. 7, 1831. 2. Elpha, b. Aug. 8, 1834; d. March 24, 1835. 3. Charles, b. May 16, 1838, m. Alice Barry; d. Sept. 10, 1868. 4. Mary, b. May 31, 1840, m. Henry C. Stewart. 5. James, b. Sept. 23, 1841, m. Ellen Lewis. Resides in Panama, Chautauqua county, N. Y.
8. Orrin, b. about 1806, and supposed to be still living (1879) in Sheridan, Montcalm county, Mich., with his family.
9. Cyrus, b. about 1808; killed by falling from a tree near Panama, N. Y., at the age of 18.
10. Harriet, b. about 1810, m. Hiram Smith, who is supposed to be still living. She d. near Conneautville, Pa.

Ruth Knapp, second daughter and fourth child of John and Ruth (Gregory) Knapp, m. Baker Bass, and had a daughter:
1. Sylvia, who died in early womanhood, unmarried.

John Knapp, third son and fifth child of John and Ruth (Gregory) Knapp, m. first, in Danbury, Conn., 1796, Lucy Merwin, who d. about 1827, and he m. second, Feb., 1829, Albacinda Barnum, dau. of Capt. Azor and Anna (Sweet) Barnum. She was b. in South East, Putnam county, N. Y., May 12, 1790; d. in Huntsburgh, Ohio, at the residence of her daughter, Mrs. F. C. Conley, Oct. 2, 1867. He d. in Huntsburgh, July 11, 1850. Farmer and shoemaker.

Children, by wife Lucy :
1. Betsey, b. Aug. 18, 1797; d. March 17, 1862.
2. David, b. Jan. 27, 1800; d. June 13, 1873.
3. John, b. Nov. 6, 1801; d. Nov. 1, 1869.
4. Nathan, b. Feb. 17, 1803.

5. Reuben, b. April 15, 1805; d. Feb. —, 1827.
6. Philo, b. May 21, 1806; d. Sept. —, 1824.
7. Polly, b. Sept. 5, 1807.
8. Hiram, b. Dec. 28, 1808.
9. Levi, b. May 5, 1810; d. Jan. —, 1838.
10. Amelia, b. March 18, 1812.
11. Ruth, b. June 1, 1813.
12. Son, b. April 17, 1814; d. April 17, 1814.
13. Lucy, b. May 4, 1815.
14. Susannah, b March 22, 1817.
15. Ezra, b. Sept. 10, 1818 ; d. Aug. 1, 1819.
16. Ezra Russell, b. Sept. 14, 1820.
17. Eliza, b. July 28, 1822.
18. Lydia, b. Sept. 8, 1826; d. Oct. 24, 1846.

by wife Albacinda :
19. Reuben Barnum, b. Nov. 23, 1829; d. April 16, 1865.
20. Anna Maria, b. Nov. 15, 1831.
21. Lucinda Althea, b. Jan. 26, 1834.
22. Laura Marilla, b. April 17, 1837; d. Jan. —, 1843.

Betsey, the eldest child, m. John Graham Scott, and had : 1. Susan Jane, b. Dec. 3, 1828, m. Riley S. Root, of Middlefield, Ohio, by whom she had Ernest and Alice. 2. Sarah Maria, b. July —, 1830, m. Eddy Kile, of Huntsburgh, Ohio, by whom she had Alvin, John and Lucena, and d. in California, in 1864. 3. Lucy Eliza, b. June 30, 1832, m. first, Leander Bigelow, and had dau. Sarah, who m. George Peckham, in California. After divorce from Bigelow, she went to live with her sister, Mrs. Kile, in California, where she soon m. Walter Barnes, son of Zenas and Flora (Goodwin) Barnes, of Huntsburgh, Ohio, and by whom she had one child that d. young. Her husband d. soon after, and she m. third, a Mr. Swayne, by whom she has a dau. Lucy, a cripple.

David, the second child, m. his cousin, Sarah Nichols, widow of Whitman Bryant, by whom he had : 1. Polly Ann, b. Jan. —, 1822, who m. Joseph Eggleston, and had Emma, Everett and Elbert. 2. Solomon, b. —, 1824, who m. Sophia Munn, and had Lovias and Lydia Ann. 3. Cyrus, b. —, 1826, who m. Mary Jane Fields, of Middlefield, Ohio, and had Reuben, Eugene, Flora, Clemens, Leni Leoti, and Ellen. 4. Susan, b. March 2, 1829, who m. John Roe, and had Addison and Jennie.

John, the third child, m. Dec. 18, 1823, Sally Hubbard, in Danbury, Conn. She was b. April 10, 1804; d. Nov. 11, 1873. Children were : 1. Philo Asa, b. Dec. 31, 1824, m. Mary Hoyt, dau. of Horatio and Ann (Knapp) Hoyt. Have buried several children, one daughter living. 2. Harmon, b. Jan. 14, 1828, m. Rachel Mahala Bartow. No children. 3. Anna, b. March 13, 1830, m. Robert James Van Dusen, and resides in Harpersfield, N. Y. 4. John, b. Feb. 1, 1832, m. Nancy Young. 5. Ira Stephen, b. May 2, 1834, m. Sophia Augusta Disbrow. 6. Isaac Hubbard, b. Dec. 19, 1836; d. June 11, 1839. 7. Michael F., b. Oct. 29, 1838, m. Mary Baxter; d. in the Union army, Aug. 14, 1863. 8. Isaac Hubbard, b. Feb. 26, 1841, unm. 9. Ezra P., b. Feb. 11, 1843, m. Sarah Jane Meeker. 10. Abijah O., b. Sept. 16, 1844, m. Lucy Sherman. 11. Sarah Elizabeth, b. April 16, 1847; d. Jan. 2, 1863.

Nathan, the fourth child, m. Sally Peirce, and became residents in Fall River, Mass. Nothing heard of him since he left home in 1850. Children were: 1. James, b. Sept. 30, 1825. 2. Sarah, b. ——. 3. Lucy, b. ——. 4. John, b. ——.

Polly, the seventh child, m. Isaac G. Washburn, and had: 1. Jane Ann, b. Jan. —, 1836; d. ——, 1854. 2. Susan Eliza, b. Aug. —, 1840. 3. Mary, b. Feb. 9, 1845, m. a Mr. Hawley. Res. Danbury, Conn.

Hiram, the eighth child, m. Sally Ann Wilsey, and had: 1. Silas. 2. Annette. 3. David. 4. Hiram. 5. Lucy. He is a farmer; res. Munson, Geauga county, Ohio.

Levi, the ninth child, m. Mary Brackett, sister to Judge Brackett, of Huntsburgh, Ohio, and d. at twenty-eight. No children.

Amelia, the tenth child, m. Harmon Locy, and had: 1. Sally Ann, who m. Howard Hues. 2. Maria, who m. first, David Conley, and second, a Mr. Rogers. 3. Levi Knapp. 4. Mary Amelia. Res. Ashtabula, Ohio.

Ruth, the eleventh child, m. Alvord Church, son of Asa and Cynthia Church, and had: 1. Cynthia Maria, b. Aug. 20, 1842; d. in 1843. 2. Cynthia Maria, (again), b. Aug. 21, 1844, m. Marcus Florence Roberts, son of Lyman Roberts. 3. John Asa, b. Feb. 5, 1857. Res. Munson, Ohio.

Lucy, the thirteenth child, m. first, Stephen Gates, and had: 1. Levi. 2. Mary. 3. Sarah M. 4. Hiram L. 5. John. Mr. Gates d. in Huntsburgh, Ohio, of a cancer; and she m. second, in LaGrange, Ohio, Dec. 10, 1850, her cousin, James Disbrow, and had: 6., Louis Kossuth. 7. Horace E. 8. Mary E. Mr. Disbrow d. Feb. 7, 1859.

Susannah, the fourteenth child, m. Jesse Morehouse, and had: 1. Susan Elizabeth, b. June 23, 1838, m. a Mr. Heath, and resides in Danbury, Conn. 2. Aaron, b. Sept. 11, 1841. 3. Emma, b. Oct. 3, 1843. 4. Jesse, b. Nov. 4, 1845; d. May 27, 1846. 5. Annette, b. April 1, 1847; d. June 7, 1857. 6. Martha, b. March 29, 1850. 7. Ella, b. May 18, 1852. 8. Daniel, b. April 28, 1854. 9. Flora, b. Sept. 6, 1855; d. July 15, 1856. Res. Danbury, Conn.

Ezra Russell, (Rev.), the sixteenth child, m. in Huntsburgh, Ohio, Minerva Clarinda Starkey, dau. of William Starkey, and had: 1. Melissa Minerva, b. Oct. 13, 1842. 2. Mary Charlotte, b. Sept. 17, 1847; d. Feb. 16, 1850. 3. William Ezra, b. Nov. 4, 1849; d. Dec. 19, 1849. 4. Charles Edward, b. June 8, 1851; d. Feb. 1, 1858. 5. John Wesley, b. Aug. 18, 1854. 6. Charles Henry, b. July 4, 1859. 7. Frederic Reuben, b. Sept. 27, 1861. 8. Clara Maria, b. July 29, 1866; d. Oct. 15, 1866. Res. Clarion, Pa.

Eliza, the seventeenth child, m. Dr. Lemuel Atwood, and had: 1. Daughter, b. June —, 1849; d. soon. 2. Frank, b. Dec. 24, 1858. Res. Pentwater, Mich.

Lydia, the eighteenth child, m. Dec. —, 1845, David Roe, and d. without issue the following year.

Reuben Barnum, the nineteenth child, m. in Hartsgrove, Ashtabula county, Ohio, Nov. 22, 1850, Mary Hercelia Pinney, dau. of Philo and Delia (Griswold) Pinney. She was b. in Conn., April 18, 1831, and now resides in Geneva, Ohio. Children: 1. Mary Maria, b. Feb. 1, 1852, m. Dr. Almon Lionel Bennett, of Chardon, Ohio. 2. Martha Cornelia, b. Dec. 8, 1854, m. Geo. M. Cone, of Geneva, Ohio. 3. Edwin Armine, b. Feb. 20, 1859. 4. Mila Lucinda, b. Feb. 20, 1864. He was a builder and contractor. He enlisted in the Union army, and d. in Camp Chase, Columbus, Ohio, Easter Sunday, April 16, 1865.

Anna Maria, the twentieth child, m. in Huntsburgh, Ohio, 1853, Horace Gillette Cleveland, son of Oren and Esther (Allen) Cleveland. He was b. in Winchester, Conn., Jan. 3, 1832. Merchant; res. Cleveland, Ohio. Children: 1. Esther Maria, b. Jan. 19, 1854, m. Prof. Floyd Baker Wilson. Res. Chicago, Ill. 2. Edward Horace, b. Sept. 24, 1855. A graduate of Racine College, class of 1878; now (1879) a student at the General Theological Seminary, New York City. 3. Charles Luther, b. July 5, 1857; now at Racine College, class of 1881.

Lucinda Althea, the twenty-first child, m. in East Claridon, Geauga county, Ohio, Nov. 11, 1852, Fernando Cortes Conley, son of Patrick and Abigail (La Vallet) Conley. He was b. in Jefferson, Schoharie county, N. Y., Oct. 26, 1826. Builder; res. Chardon, Ohio. Children: 1. Son, b. May 12, 1854; d. May 12, 1854. 2. Ella Maria, b. Aug. 28, 1855, m. in 1872, Lewis Melvin Moffett, of Chardon, Ohio. 3. Horace Fernando, b. April 27, 1858. 4. Arvilla May, b. March 2, 1862. 5. Carrie, b. Aug. 2, 1867. 6. Son, b. July 17, 1871; d. July 17, 1871.

Chloe Knapp, the third daughter and sixth child of John and Ruth (Gregory) Knapp, by husband Joseph Mansfield had:
1. Laura, who m. Ira Wildman, and had Smith, Levi, Jerusha and Ezra.
2. Oliver, who m. Esther Beers, and had Lucy, Chloe and Fairchild.
3. Polly, who m. first, —— Monroe, and had Mary and Henry; and m. second, —— Birch, and had Samuel.
4. David, who m. Sally Thomas, and had Levi, David and two daughters, names not learned.
5. Fanny, who m. —— Sherman, and had a family of children, names not given.
6. Alfred, who m. Abigail Knapp. No children.
7. Betsey, who m. —— Chichester, and had a daughter, name not learned.
8. Joseph, who m. ——, but names of wife and children unknown.
9. Julia, who m. John Plough, and had a daughter, Frances, and perhaps other children.

Levi Knapp, youngest son and child of John and Ruth (Gregory) Knapp, by wife Elizabeth Hamilton, b. May 29, 1781, (sister of Eli Hamilton, who m. Hannah Barnum), had, in Danbury, Conn.:
1. Florinda, b. April 26, 1802, m. William Putnam, and had a son, William.

2. Maria, b. May 22, 1804, m. Othniel Knapp, and had Elizabeth, Silas, James, Daniel, Sylvanus and Robert.
3. Anna, b. Dec. 10, 1806, m. Horatio Hoyt, and had Mary (who m. Philo Knapp), Lucius (who d. in California), and Elizabeth.
4. Ruth, b. Oct. 10, 1808, who m. Ezra Hamilton. No children.
5. Son, b. Dec. 29, 1810; d. July 31, 1811.
6. John, b. Aug. 7, 1813, m. Minerva Morehouse (sister of Jesse Morehouse), and had George and Florinda (twins), Susannah and Eliza.
7. Laura, b. June 21, 1816, m. George W. Hamilton, son of Eli and Hannah (Barnum) Hamilton. He resides in Pembroke (Danbury), Conn. Has been Judge of Probate. No children.
8. James H., b. July 7, 1818, m. Susan Hopkins, and have a daughter, Sophronia.
9. Levi Gregory, b. May 29, 1821, m. Angeline Sturtevant. No children living.
10. Alexander, b. Aug. 9, 1828, m. Mary E. Disbrow. Have five children: 1. Phebe Augusta. 2. Mary Ella. 3. Levi Gregory. 4. Frances Elizabeth. 5. Willie N. (the only one now living).

The family of Knapps is traced back for twenty or more generations, and derive from Roger de Knap, who figured in English history, sometime in the 12th century; and descendants in almost every town and village in the United States are of a direct line, and entitled to the family coat of arms.

The ancestry of Capt. Azor Barnum, the maternal grandfather of Anna M. Knapp (see page 50), may be traced to Thomas Barnum, of Norwalk, Conn., 1662, and before that at Fairfield, and after at Danbury. He had: Thomas, b. July 9, 1663; John, b. Feb. 24, 1678; Hannah, b. Oct. 14, 1680; and Ebenezer, b. May 19, 1682; but six more children he had, two sons and four daughters, yet at Norwalk are no more recorded, nor can I find (says Savage) the names of these six or either of them, or either of two wives, one of whom outlived him, who d. 1695.

From surviving descendants of Capt. Azor Barnum, however, it is ascertained that he was a son of Joshua Barnum, and a grandson of Thomas Barnum, Jr., though no further particulars of names and dates have been gathered.

The children of Capt. Azor Barnum, by wife Anna Sweet, were at least seven in number, all b. in South East, Putnam county, N. Y., as follows:

1. Azor, b. about 1772, m. first, ———, who d. soon, and he m. second, Sally Bradley, by whom he had two daughters, Sally and Julia. It is not known if any descendants are living.

2. Rebecca, b. about 1774, who m. a Mr. Lewis, and lived in Poughkeepsie, N. Y., and had George, Azor, Ann Maria, Sally, and Julia.

3. Elizabeth, b. July 6, 1776, m. first, Henry Thomas, b. June 8, 1773. Children: 1. Orange B., b. May 24, 1797. 2. Norris A., b. Dec. 26, 1798; d. March 25, 1825. 3. Sally B., b. June 18, 1802, who m. David Mansfield, and had George, Mary, Hannah, David, and Levi. 4. Naomi M., b. Feb. 14, 1807. 5. Azor Hart, b. Feb. 18, 1815.

4. Daniel, b. Oct. 8, 1778, m. Urania Hoyt, dau. of Thaddeus and Keziah Hoyt. She was b. in Danbury, Conn., Dec. 16, 1780; d. in Illinois, April 28, 1849. He d. Oct. 28, 1870. Children: 1. Adelia, b. Jan. 29, 1808. 2. Maria, b. Feb. 20, 1811, m. Oct., 1839, Phineas Howes, and had Ella C., b. Jan., 1848, Herbert H., b. Dec. 10, 1853, and Cora, b. April, 1857. She d. Dec. 10, 1877. 3. Emily, b. Oct. 23, 1813; d. June 30, 1838, unm. 4. Daniel Hoyt, b. Feb. 12, 1816, m. Feb. 22, 1870, Harriet Goodhue; no children. 5. Harris, b. Sept. 8, 1819, m. Jan. 13, 1870, Emma M. Moffett, and have Alta, b. June 13, 1872, and Blanche, b. July 27, 1874. He is a banker; res. Rockford, Ill. 6. Cynthia Ann, b. Sept. 8, 1821.

5. Caleb, b. Jan. 8, 1781, m. first, in South East, Putnam county, N. Y., Sept. 22, 1810, Loretta Richards, dau. of Moses and Mary (Paddock) Richards. He was b. in South East, N. Y., Aug. 25, 1791; d. March 7, 1830. He m. second, Oct. 7, 1830, a sister of his first wife, Maria Matilda Richards, b. Aug. 27, 1794, and who d. Sept. 12, 1870. He d. in Junius, Seneca county, N. Y., Oct. 5, 1868. Farmer. Children: 1. David Paddock, b. in South East, N. Y., July 3, 1811, m. Oct. 25, 1849, Catherine Burch, and have three daughters, namely, Laura Maria, Mary, and Ora Anna. Res. Junius, N. Y. 2. Azor, b. in South East, N. Y., April 4, 1813, m. April 18, 1838, Louisa French, of Junius, N. Y. He d. there, July 23, 1861, leaving a widow and seven children, namely, George Belden, Joseph Edwin, James Paddock, Nathaniel French, Mary Loretta, Caleb Azor, and Clarence Adelbert. 3. Mary M., b. in South East, N. Y., Feb. 20, 1815; d. in Junius, N. Y., June 10, 1821. 4. Daniel Belden, b. in Junius, N. Y., June 29, 1820. In the spring of 1852 he went to California, where he still resides with wife and three children, the eldest about twelve or thirteen years of age. 5. Moses Richards, b. in Junius, N. Y., June 23, 1824, m. there, Oct. 24, 1849, Harriet Mills Fancher. He d. in Junius, May 28, 1853. They had one son, Elbert Eugene, now an M. D. in Ann Arbor, Mich. 6. Joseph M., b. in Junius, N. Y., Jan. 23, 1830, m. in same place, Nov. 7, 1858, Julia Fidelia Bridges, dau. of Alonzo and Fidelia (Barber) Bridges, of Milford, Otsego county, N. Y. Farmer; res. Laporte, Ind. Children: Edwin Alonzo, b. in Junius, N. Y., Sept. 15, 1859, and Clara Elizabeth, b. in Junius, N. Y., May 26, 1866.

6. Hannah, b. about 1783, m. April 16, 1806, Eli Hamilton, of Danbury, Conn. They had: 1. Norman, b. Jan. 21, 1807; d. Jan. —, 1873, leaving a wife and children. 2. George Washington, b. April 19, 1813, m. his cousin Laura Knapp, dau. of Levi and Elizabeth (Hamilton) Knapp. No children. 3. Philander, b. Aug. 4, 1819; d. Oct. 15, 1868, leaving a widow who has since married again.

7. Albacinda, b. May 12, 1790, m. Feb. —, 1829, John Knapp, son of John and Ruth (Gregory) Knapp, of Danbury, Conn., by whom she had four children, namely: 1. Reuben Barnum, b. in Danbury, Conn., Nov. 23, 1829, a builder and contractor, m. in Hartsgrove, Ashtabula county, Ohio, Nov. 22, 1850, Mary Hercelia Pinney, dau. of

Philo and Delia (Griswold) Pinney. She was b. in Conn., April 18, 1831. He d. in Camp Chase, Columbus, Ohio, Easter Sunday, April 16, 1865. His widow is living (1879) in Geneva, Ashtabula county, Ohio. Children : Mary Maria, b. in Huntsburgh, Ohio, Feb. 1, 1852, m. in East Trumbull, Ashtabula county, Ohio, July 31, 1872, Dr. Almon Lionel Bennett, son of Dr. Lionel and Sophronia (Fowler) Bennett. He was b. in Harpersfield, Ashtabula county, Ohio, April 22, 1851. Res. Chardon, Geauga county, Ohio. Have two children, namely, Nathan George, b. in Harpersfield, Ohio, May 19, 1873; Mabel Jean, b. in Morgan, Ohio, Oct. 5, 1875. Martha Cornelia, b. in Huntsburgh, Ohio, Dec. 8, 1854, m. in Geneva, Ohio, Nov. 7, 1874, George Millard Cone, son of Edwin and Lorinda (Huntoon) Cone. He was b. in Leroy, Lake county, Ohio, March 8, 1848. They have one or two children. He was formerly a grain dealer in Chicago, Ill., but now resides in Geneva, Ohio. Edwin Armine, b. in Hartsgrove, Ohio, Feb. 20, 1859. Mila Lucinda, b. in Hartsgrove, Ohio, Feb. 20, 1864. 2. Anna Maria, b. in Danbury, Conn., Nov. 15, 1831, m. in Huntsburgh, Ohio, Jan. 5, 1853, Horace Gillette Cleveland, son of Oren and Esther (Allen) Cleveland. He was b. in Winchester, Litchfield county, Conn., Jan. 3, 1832. Iron merchant, in Cleveland, Ohio, and Chicago, Ill. Res. 74 Hamilton Street, Cleveland, Ohio. Children, all b. in Cleveland : Esther Maria, b. Jan. 19, 1854, m. in Grace Church, Cleveland, Ohio, July 28, 1874, Prof. Floyd Baker Wilson, son of William Henry and Eveline (Weaver) Wilson. He was b. in Watervliet, Albany county, N. Y., June 23, 1845. Children : Ethel Maude, b. Aug. 30, 1875 ; Coral Eveline, b. May 25, 1878. Attorney at Law, etc., 24 Portland Block ; res. 33 Winthrop Place, Chicago, Ill. Edward Horace, b. Sept. 24, 1855, grad. of Racine College, class of '78. Charles Luther, b. July 5, 1857; student of medicine. 3. Lucinda Althea, b. in Danbury, Conn., Jan. 26, 1834, m. in East Claridon, Ohio, Nov. 11, 1852, Fernando Cortes Conley, son of Patrick and Abigail (La Vallett) Conley. He was b. in Jefferson, Schoharie county, N. Y., Oct. 26, 1826. Builder and contractor ; res. Chardon, Ohio. Children, all b. in Huntsburgh, Ohio : Son, b. May 12, 1854; d. May 12, 1854. Ella Maria, b. Aug. 28, 1855, m. in 1872, Lewis Melvin Moffettt, son of Marcus and Rachel (Chapman) Moffett. He was b. in Claridon, Geauga county, Ohio, Aug. 25, 1849. Builder, etc.; res. Chardon, Ohio. Have two children, namely, Horace Marcus, b. July 10, 1873; Susie May, b. July 9, 1876. Horace Fernando, b. April 17, 1858, clerk in store of Cleveland, Brown & Co., Cleveland, Ohio. Arvilla May, b. March 2, 1862. Carrie, b. Aug. 2, 1867. Son, b. July 17, 1871; d. July 17, 1871. 4. Laura Marilla, b. in Huntsburgh, Ohio, April 17, 1837; d. in same place, Jan. —, 1843.

The descendants of the senior Thomas Barnum are scattered in all directions over the New England and other States, though the orthography of the name is sometimes changed to *Burnham*. The distinguished iron master, Hon. William H. Barnum, late United States Senator from Connecticut, as well as the "great American showman," Phineas Taylor Barnum, of Bridgeport, Conn., are both descendants of the aforesaid common ancestor, Thomas Barnum, of Fairfield, Conn.

FROM THE TOWNSHIP RECORDS OF WOBURN, MASS.

Moses Cleavland and Ann Winn married ye 26th of ye 7th month, 1648.
Moses, son of Moses Cleavland, born ye 1st of ye 7th month, 1651.
Hannah, daughter of Moses Cleavland, born ye 4th of ye 6th month, 1653.
Aaron, son of Moses Cleavland, born ye 10th of ye 11th month, 1654.
Samuel, son of Moses Cleavland, born ye 9th of ye 4th month, 1657.
Miriam, daughter of Moses Cleavland, born ye 10th of ye 5th month, 1659.
Joanna, daughter of Moses Cleavland, born ye 19th of ye 7th month, 1661.
Edward, son of Moses Cleavland, born ye 20th of ye 3rd month, 1664.
Josiah, son of Moses Cleavland, born ye 26th of ye 12th month, 1666.
Joanna, daughter of Moses Cleavland, died ye 12th of ye 1st month,* 1667.
Isaac, son of Moses Cleavland, born ye 13th of ye 6th month,† 1669.
Joanna, daughter of Moses Cleavland, born ye 5th day of ye 2d month, 1670.
Enoch, son of Moses Cleavland, born ye 1st day of ye 6th month, 1671.

Aaron Cleavland and Dorcas Wilson married ye 26th of ye 7th month, 1675.
Dorcas, daughter of Aaron Cleavland, born ye 29th of ye 8th month, 1676.
Hannah, daughter of Aaron Cleavland, born ye 18th of ye 9th month, 1678.
Hannah, died ye 13th of ye 4th month, 1679.
Aaron, son of Aaron Cleavland, born ye 9th of July, 1680.
Hannah, daughter of Aaron and Dorcas Cleavland, born ye 7th of June, 1687.
Moses, son of Aaron Cleavland, born ye 24th of February, 1689.
Sarah, daughter of Aaron and Dorcas Cleavland, born ye 5th of March, 1692.
Meriam, daughter of Aaron and Dorcas Cleavland, born 9th of July, 1694.
Isabell, daughter of Aaron and Dorcas Cleavland, born 6th of April, 1697.
Benjamin, son of Aaron and Dorcas Cleavland, born 16th of May, 1701.
Isabell, died December 7th, 1714.
Dorcas, wife of Aaron Cleavland, died November 29th, 1714.

Moses Cleavland and Ruth Norton married ye 4th of ye 8th month, 1676.
Annah, daughter of Moses and Ruth Cleavland, born ye 7th of ye 9th month, 1677.
Joseph, son of Moses and Ruth Cleavland, born ye 31st of March, 1686.
Moses Cleavland, Sen., died 9th of January, 1701-2.
Aaron, son of Aaron and Abigail Cleavland, born 20th of October, 1702.
Samuel, son of Aaron and Abigail Cleavland, born 17th of April, 1704.
Aaron Cleavland, died 14th of September, 1716.

Thomas Hensher [Henshaw] and Hannah Cleavland married ye 2d of ye 7th month, 1677.

---

* This would make the date of her death March 12, 1667, whereas, in Sewall's History of Woburn (page 600), it is given "July 2, 1667."

† This would be *August*, and not "May" as given by Mr. Sewall in his History of Woburn, page 600. The Compiler is disposed, however, to consider Mr. Sewall's dates correct, and adopted them in preference to the list furnished by the town clerk.

Elizabeth, daughter of Samuel and Peircess [Persis] Cleavland, born 26th June, 1693.

FROM THE TOWNSHIP RECORDS OF CHELMSFORD, MASS.

Samuel, son of Moses Cleveland, of Woburn, and Jane, daughter of Solomon Keyes, were joyned in marriage May 17, 1680.
Jane, wife of Samuel Cleveland, died November 14, 1681.
Samuel Cleveland and Persis, daughter of Richard Hildreth, were joyned in marriage May 23, 1682.
Persis, daughter to Samuel and Persis Cleveland, was born April 21, 1683.
Samuel, son to Samuel and Persis Cleveland, was born Jan. 12, 1685.
Joseph, son to Samuel and Persis Cleveland, was born July 18, 1689.
Joseph Keyes and Joanna Cleveland entered into a covenant of marriage May 28, 1690.

Children to Joseph and Joanna Keyes:
Joanna, born Feb. 10, 1695.
Joseph, born May 1, 1698.

Children to Josiah and Mary Cleveland — [no record of marriage found]:
Josiah, born October 7, 1690.
Joseph, born June 13, 1692.
Mary, born March 17, 1693.
John, born June 28, 1696.
Jonathan, born March 2, 1698.
Jonathan, died April 5, 1698.
Henry, born —— 22, 1699.

FROM THE SUDBURY (MASS.) RECORDS.

Sarah, daughter of Enoch and Elizabeth Cleveland, born May 26, 1701.
Enoch, son of Enoch and Elizabeth Cleveland, born July 2, 1703.
James, son of Enoch and Elizabeth Cleveland, born Oct. 31, 1706.
Jonathan, son of Enoch and Elizabeth Cleveland, born March —, 1708.

FROM THE TOWNSHIP RECORDS OF CANTERBURY, CONN.

MARRIAGES — MALES.

Isaac Cleaveland and Elizabeth Curtis, m. July 17, 1699.
Samuel Cleaveland and widow Margaret Fish, m. July 25, 1699.
Josiah Cleaveland and Abigail Paine, m. Aug. 7, 1710.
Joseph Cleaveland and Abigail Hyde, m. Feb. 7, 1710–11.
Edward Cleaveland, Jr., and Rebekah Paine, m. April 17, 1717.
Moses Cleaveland and Mary Johnson, m. Oct. 19, 1717.
Joseph Cleaveland and Deborah Butterfield, m. May 19, 1718.
Samuel Cleaveland and Sarah Buswell, m. Dec. 10, 1719.

Joseph Cleaveland and Sarah Ensworth, m. March 31, 1725.
Joseph Cleaveland and Mary Woodward, m. June 24, 1725.
Deliverance Cleaveland and Kesiah Eaton, m. Jan. 20, 1731-2.
Josiah Cleaveland, Jr., and Sarah Lawrence, m. Oct. 15, 1735.
David Cleaveland and Eunice Backus, m. June 25, 1744.
Deliverance Cleaveland and Rebecca Paine, m. July 4, 1744.
Aaron Cleaveland and Thankful Paine, m. June 7, 1748.
Solomon Cleaveland and Abiel [Abiah?] Baker, m. Oct. 3, 1748.
Eleazer Cleaveland and Anne Bradford, m. April 25, 1750.
Silas Cleaveland and Elizabeth Hyde, m. May 10, 1750.
David Cleaveland and Rebecca Tracy, of Preston, m. Aug. 15, 1750.
Samuel Cleaveland and Ruth Darbe, m. May 7, 1751.
Hopestill Cleaveland and Patience Benjamin, m. May 9, 1754.
Josiah Cleaveland and Joanna Brewster, m. June 5, 1755.
Paine Cleaveland and Prudence Buzwell, m. Jan. 18, 1757.
Timothy Cleaveland and Esther Fish, m. Jan. 30, 1760.
Paine Cleaveland and Susannah Falkner, m. March 10, 1761.
John Cleaveland and Betsey Downer, m. Nov. 17, 1762.
Ephraim Cleaveland and Mary Griffin, of Windham, m. March 6, 1766.
Paine Cleaveland and Sarah Church, m. April 16, 1767.
Moses Cleaveland and Azuba Kendall, m. March 24, 1768.
Shubael Cleaveland and Eunice Luce, m. March 30, 1769.
John Cleaveland, Jr., and Abigail Adams, m. Feb. 2, 1773.
Tracy Cleaveland and Phebe Hyde, m. April 25, 1773.
Aaron Cleaveland, Jr., and Jemima Robinson, m. June 12, 1777.
Josiah Cleaveland and Alice Dyar, m. June 3, 1778.
Eliphas Cleaveland and Anne Pellett, m. Sept. 5, 1784.
Col. Moses Cleaveland and Esther Champion, m. March 21, 1794.
Bethabra Cleaveland and Margaret Pellett, m. Dec. 31, 1794.
Wm. Pitt Cleaveland and Mary Bacon, m. Feb. 2, 1796.

MARRIAGES — FEMALES.

Mary Cleaveland and Richard Smith, m. Jan. 30, 1715-16.
Elizabeth Cleaveland and John Ensworth, m. April 2, 1717.
Mary Cleaveland and Joseph Ensworth, m. Oct. 5, 1719.
Mary Cleaveland and Robert Buswell, m. Jan. 22, 1721-22.
Lydia Cleaveland and Obadiah Johnson, m. Nov. 6, 1723.
Mary Cleaveland and Richard Adams, m. March 30, 1730.
Mary Cleaveland and William Bradford, m. April 6, 1743.
Hetty Cleaveland and Faxon Dean, m. Oct. 15, 1746.
Deliverance Cleaveland and Josiah Baker, m. Sept. 16, 1747.
Elizabeth Cleaveland and Elihu Paine, m. Nov. 24, 1748.
Experience Cleaveland and Jabez Holmes, m. May 2, 1749.
Abigail Cleaveland and William Darbe, m. Nov. 9, 1749.
Zipporah Cleaveland and Francis Simonds, m. Nov. 19, 1750.
Margaret Cleaveland and Samuel Woodward, m. Jan. 13, 1751.
Penelope Cleaveland and Ezekiel Park, m. Nov. 7, 1753.
Lucretia Cleaveland and Jedediah Darbe, m. Jan. 2, 1755.
Elizabeth Cleaveland and Nathan Kimball, m. Aug. 28, 1755.

Rachel Cleaveland and George Austin, m. Jan. 18, 1758.
Sarah Cleaveland and Peter Stanton, m. Sept. 21, 1763.
Keziah Cleaveland and Levi Downing, m. Nov. 21, 1771.
Sarah Cleaveland and Samuel Ensworth, m. May 28, 1772.
Anna Cleaveland and Joshua Bradford, m. Feb. 9, 1775.
Sarah Cleaveland and Joseph Butt, m. April 11, 1776.
Mary Cleaveland and Silas Allen, m. May 16, 1776.
Abigail Cleaveland and John Hebbard, m. March 17, 1777.
Joanna Cleaveland and Jedediah Ensworth, m. Nov. 15, 1819.

BIRTHS.

Mary, dau. of Samuel and Persis Cleaveland, b. June 14, 1696.
Abigail, dau. of Samuel and Margaret Cleaveland, b. April 23, 1700.
Curtis, son of Isaac and Elizabeth Cleaveland, b. Jan. 23, 1701.
Timothy, son of Samuel and Margaret Cleaveland, b. Aug. 25, 1702.
Anne, dau. of Isaac and Elizabeth Cleaveland, b. June 6, 1703.
Lydia, dau. of Josiah and Mary Cleaveland, b. Dec. 7, 1704.
Miriam, dau. of Isaac and Elizabeth Cleaveland, b. July 4, 1705.
Deliverance, son of Josiah and Mary Cleaveland, b. July 13, 1707.
Abiel, dau. of Josiah and Mary Cleaveland, b. Oct. 9, 1709.
Keziah, dau. of Josiah and Abigail Cleaveland, b. Nov. 26, 1711.
Ephraim, son of Joseph and Abigail Cleaveland, b. Feb. 3, 1712.
Josiah, son of Josiah and Abigail Cleaveland, b. April 4, 1713.
Jonathan, son of Joseph and Abigail Cleaveland, b. May 9, 1713.
Benjamin, son of Joseph and Abigail Cleaveland, b. May 20, 1714.
Abigail, dau. of Josiah and Abigail Cleaveland, b. June 3, 1715.
Dorothy, dau. of Joseph and Abigail Cleaveland, b. March 31, 1716.
Elisha, son of Josiah and Abigail Cleaveland, b. Jan. 7, 1717.
Johannah, dau. of Edward and Rebecca Cleaveland, b. July 22, 1717.
Jonas, son of Joseph and Deborah Cleaveland, b. Oct. 16, 1718.
Aaron, son of Aaron and Mercy Cleaveland, b. Dec. 7, 1718.
Lois, dau. of Josiah and Abigail Cleaveland, b. Dec. 11, 1718.
Sybil, dau. of Joseph and Deborah Cleaveland, b. Jan. 7, 1719.
Miriam, dau. of Moses and Mary Cleaveland, b. Jan. 30, 1719.
Rebecca, dau. of Edward and Rebecca Cleaveland, b. March 16, 1719.
William, son of Henry and Lucy Cleaveland, b. July 7, 1719.
Solomon, son of Edward and Rebecca Cleaveland, b. June 1, 1720.
Mary, dau. of Josiah and Abigail Cleaveland, b. June 29, 1720.
Elijah, son of Joseph and Abigail Cleaveland, b. Jan. 5, 1721.
Hannah, dau. of Moses and Sarah Cleaveland, b. May 5, 1721.
Dorcas, dau. of Moses and Mary Cleaveland, b. May 9, 1721.
Nehemiah, son of Henry and Lucy Cleaveland, b. July 30, 1721.
John, son of Joseph and Deborah Cleaveland, b. Dec. 31, 1721.
Palmer, son of Edward and Rebecca Cleaveland, b. Jan. 29, 1722.
John, son of Josiah and Abigail Cleaveland, b. April 12, 1722.
Eleazer, son of Samuel and Sarah Cleaveland, b. May 26, 1722.
Johnson, son of Isaac and Susannah Cleaveland, b. Oct. 29, 1722.
Deliverance, dau. of Edward and Rebecca Cleaveland, b. March 10, 1723.
Obadiah, son of Moses and Mary Cleaveland, b. Sept. 16, 1723.

Lydia, dau. of Josiah and Abigail Cleaveland, b. Feb. 16, 1724.
Lucy, dau. of Henry and Lucy Cleaveland, b. March 2, 1724.
David, son of Samuel and Sarah Cleaveland, b. June 1, 1724.
Lemuel, son of Isaac and Susannah Cleaveland, b. Aug. 13, 1725.
Anne, dau. of Moses and Mary Cleaveland, b. Aug. 15, 1725.
Ebenezer, son of Josiah and Abigail Cleaveland, b. Dec. 25, 1725.
Hopestill, son of Samuel and Sarah Cleaveland, b. April 17, 1726.
Silas, son of Edward and Rebecca Cleaveland, b. May 28, 1726.
Deborah, dau. of Joseph and Mary Cleaveland, b. Aug. 11, 1726.
Phineas, son of Samuel and Mary Cleaveland, b. Oct. 19, 1727.
Esther, dau. of Benjamin and Anne Cleaveland, b. Nov. 5, 1727.
Aaron, son of Josiah and Abigail Cleaveland, b. Nov. 27, 1727.
Mehitabel, dau. of Sarah (relict of Sam'l) Cleaveland, b. Feb. 16, 1728.
Abigail, dau. of Timothy and Abigail Cleaveland, b. March 27, 1728.
Bridget, dau. of Joseph and Mary Cleaveland, b. Aug. 12, 1728.
Experience, dau. of Edward and Rebecca Cleaveland, b. Sept. 5, 1728.
Deliverance, dau. of Isaac and Susannah Cleaveland, b. April 2, 1729.
Zipporah, dau. of Timothy and Dorothy Cleaveland, b. Sept. 4, 1729.
Joseph, son of Joseph and Mary Cleaveland, b. Jan. 19, 1730.
Moses, son of Josiah and Abigail Cleaveland, b. April 18, 1730.
Aaron, son of Benjamin and Anne Cleaveland, b. June 3, 1730.
Samuel, son of Joseph and Sarah Cleaveland, b. June 7, 1730.
Rebecca, dau. of Moses and Mary Cleaveland, b. June 28, 1730.
James, son of Samuel and Mary Cleaveland, b. July 3, 1730.
Mary, dau. of Isaac and Susannah Cleaveland, b. Jan. 10, 1731.
Mary, dau. of Joseph and Mary Cleaveland, b. April 19, 1731.
Paine, son of Edward and Rebecca Cleaveland, b. Aug. 30, 1731.
Anne, dau. of Benjamin and Anne Cleaveland, b. March 23, 1732.
Susannah, dau. of Eleazer and Anne Cleaveland, b. July 29, 1732.
Hannah, dau. of Joseph and Mary Cleaveland, b. Nov. 2, 1732.
Amy, dau. of David and Rebecca Cleaveland, b. Jan. 14, 1733.
Penelope, dau. of Deliverance and Kesiah Cleaveland, b. May 7, 1733.
Betty, dau. of Isaac and Susannah Cleaveland, b. June 11, 1733.
Timothy, son of Timothy and Dorothy Cleaveland, b. Dec. 29, 1734.
John, son of Abigail Cleaveland, b. Feb. 27, 1735.
Shubael, son of Deliverance and Kesiah Cleaveland, b. March 29, 1735.
Isaac, son of Isaac and Susannah Cleaveland, b. May 13, 1735.
Rachel, dau. of Capt. Joseph and Mary Cleaveland, b. March 3, 1736.
Asa, son of Josiah and Sarah Cleaveland, b. Aug. 1, 1736.
Lucretia, dau. of Timothy and Dorothy Cleaveland, b. Feb. 2, 1737.
Joseph, son of Benjamin and Rachel Cleaveland, b. May 14, 1737.
Jabez, son of Henry and Lucy Cleaveland, b. Nov. 4, 1737.
Jonathan, son of Capt. Joseph and Mary Cleaveland, b. Nov. 24, 1737.
Rachel, dau. of Deliverance and Kesiah Cleaveland, b. Oct. 29, 1738.
Samuel, son of Timothy and Dorothy Cleaveland, b. Feb. 23, 1739.
Jesse, son of Joseph and Mary Cleaveland, b. Oct. 20, 1739.
Kesiah, dau. of Deliverance and Kesiah Cleaveland, b. April 6, 1740.
Alice, dau. of William and Rachel Cleaveland, b. July 21, 1740.
Ephraim, son of Timothy and Dorothy Cleaveland, b. Aug. 20, 1740.

Appendix.

Mary, dau. of Joseph and Mary Cleaveland, b. Aug. 5, 1742.
Cyrus, son of Timothy and Dorothy Cleaveland, b. Oct. 2, 1743.
Dorothy, dau. of Benjamin and Rachel Cleaveland, b. June 10, 1744.
Moses, son of Josiah and Sarah Cleaveland, b. June 26, 1744.
Sarah, dau. of David and Eunice Cleaveland, b. Sept. 3, 1744.
Sarah, dau. of Deliverance and Rebecca Cleaveland, b. June 15, 1745.
Abigail, dau. of Benjamin and Rachel Cleaveland, b. Aug. 13, 1746.
Lydia, dau. of Ebenezer and Abigail Cleaveland, b. March 29, 1747.
Samuel, son of David and Eunice Cleaveland, b. Sept. 18, 1747.
Mary, dau. of Josiah and Sarah Cleaveland, b. Jan. 6, 1748.
Ezra, son of Ezra and Jerusha Cleaveland, b. June 22, 1748.
Zenas, son of Benjamin and Rachel Cleaveland, b. Sept. 21, 1748.
Olive, dau. of Ebenezer and Abigail Cleaveland, b. Feb. 17, 1749.
Tyxhall, son of Ezra and Jerusha Cleaveland, b. April 26, 1750.
Rachel, dau. of Benjamin and Rachel Cleaveland, b. May 18, 1750.
Aaron, son of Aaron and Thankful Cleaveland, b. June 18, 1750.
Anne, dau. of Eleazer and Anna Cleaveland, b. Nov. 3, 1750.
Tracy, son of David and Rebecca Cleaveland, b. May 8, 1751.
Lydia, dau. of Josiah and Sarah Cleaveland, b. May 25, 1751.
Rebecca, dau. of Solomon and Abigail Cleaveland, b. July 6, 1751.
Mary, dau. of Silas and Elizabeth Cleaveland, b. Jan. 22, 1752.
Joseph, son of Samuel and Ruth Cleaveland, b. Feb. 7, 1752.
Thomas, son of Ezra and Jerusha Cleaveland, b. March 25, 1752.
Persis, dau. of Benjamin and Rachel Cleaveland, b. June 18, 1752.
Susannah, dau of Eleazer and Anna Cleaveland, b. July 29, 1752.
Josiah, son of Josiah and Sarah Cleaveland, b. Dec. 3, 1753.
Moses, son of Aaron and Thankful Cleaveland, b. Jan. 29, 1754.
Mary, dau. of Samuel and Ruth Cleaveland, b. Feb. 12, 1754.
Solomon, son of Enoch and Deborah Cleaveland, b. Feb. 27, 1754.
Solomon, son of Silas and Elizabeth Cleaveland, b. April 21, 1754.
Rufus, son of Benjamin and Rachel Cleaveland, b. June 14, 1754.
Squier, son of Eleazer and Anna Cleaveland, b. July 29, 1754.
Sarah, dau. of Ezra and Jerusha Cleaveland, b. Oct. 29, 1754.
Silas, son of Silas and Elizabeth Cleaveland, b. March 17, 1756.
Mary, dau. of Benjamin and Rachel Cleaveland, b. April 14, 1756.
Jedediah, son of Samuel and Ruth Cleaveland, b. May 8, 1756.
Mehitabel, dau. of Eleazer and Anna Cleaveland, b. July 14, 1756.
Ann, dau. of Aaron and Thankful Cleaveland, b. Aug. 29, 1756.
Anna, dau. of Enoch and Deborah Cleaveland, b. Oct. 15, 1756.
Newcomb, son of Ezra and Jerusha Cleaveland, b. Nov. 6, 1756.
Patience, dau. of Hopestill and Patience Cleaveland, b. Jan. 12, 1757.
Ticia [Letitia], dau. of Josiah and Joanna Cleaveland, b. Feb. 13, 1757.
Elizabeth, dau. of Silas and Elizabeth Cleaveland, b. April 30, 1758.
Phebe, dau. of Benjamin and Rachel Cleaveland, b. June 25, 1758.
John, son of Eleazer and Anna Cleaveland, b. June 29, 1758.
Abigail, dau. of Samuel and Ruth Cleaveland, b. Aug. 6, 1758.
Jerusha, dau. of Ezra and Jerusha Cleaveland, b. Aug. 31, 1758.
Abigail, dau. of Aaron and Thankful Cleaveland, b. Aug. 5, 1759.
Thankful, dau. of Josiah and Joanna Cleaveland, b. Dec. 30, 1759.

Appendix. 243

Perez, son of Eleazer and Anna Cleaveland, b. July 17, 1760.
Zeruah, dau. of Samuel and Ruth Cleaveland, b. Feb. 19, 1761.
Jacob, son of Timothy and Esther Cleaveland, b. March 6, 1761.
Lurenah, dau. of Silas and Elizabeth Cleaveland, b. May 15, 1761.
Edward, son of Paine and Susannah Cleaveland, b. Nov. 19, 1761.
Abigail, dau. of Josiah and Joanna Cleaveland, b. Feb. 10, 1762.
John, son of Aaron and Thankful Cleaveland, b. June 28, 1762.
Polly, dau. of Eleazer and Anna Cleaveland, b. Aug. 19, 1762.
Palmer, son of Silas and Elizabeth Cleaveland, b. Sept. 17, 1762.
Asena, dau. of Ezra and Jerusha Cleaveland, b. May 16, 1763.
Martha, dau. of John and Betsey Cleaveland, b. May 17, 1763.
Samuel, son of Samuel and Ruth Cleaveland, b. Aug. 7, 1763.
Bethabra, son of Timothy and Esther Cleaveland, b. Oct. 31, 1763.
John, son of John and Betsey Cleaveland, b. Aug. 13, 1764.
Bradford, son of Eleazer and Anna Cleaveland, b. Sept. 9, 1764.
Stephen, son of Paine and Susannah Cleaveland, b. Oct. 9, 1764.
Zeruiah, son of Ezra and Jerusha Cleaveland, b. March 6, 1765.
Clarrissa, dau. of Silas and Elizabeth Cleaveland, b. June 14, 1765.
Mary, dau. of Aaron and Thankful Cleaveland, b. July 3, 1765.
David, son of Hopestill and Patience Cleaveland, b. July 9, 1765.
Susannah, dau. of Paine and Susannah Cleaveland, b. Jan. 26, 1766.
William Darbee, son of Samuel and Ruth Cleaveland, b. Feb. 8, 1766.
Cyrus, son of Timothy and Esther Cleaveland, b. May 12, 1766.
Abigail, dau. of John and Betty Cleaveland, b. May 18, 1766.
Esther, dau. of Hopestill and Patience Cleaveland, b. June 30, 1767.
Daniel, son of Silas and Elizabeth Cleaveland, b. July 6, 1767.
Dorothy, dau. of Ezra and Jerusha Cleaveland, b. Sept. 14, 1767.
Alice, dau of Eleazer and Anna Cleaveland, b. Dec. 16, 1767.
Downer, son of John and Betty Cleaveland, b. Feb. 10, 1768.
Paine, son of Aaron and Thankful Cleaveland, b. March 20, 1768.
Arunah, son of Samuel and Ruth Cleaveland, b. March 21, 1768.
Jeptha, son of Timothy and Esther Cleaveland, b. Oct. 7, 1768.
Calvin, son of Moses and Azubah Cleaveland, b. Feb. 3, 1769.
Caleb, son of John and Betty Cleaveland, b. Feb. 9, 1770.
Kesiah, dau. of Shubael and Eunice Cleaveland, b. Sept. 24, 1770.
Prudence, dau. of Paine and Sarah Cleaveland, b. Oct. 13, 1770.
William Pitt, son of Aaron and Thankful Cleaveland, b. Dec. 18, 1770.
William, 10th child of Eleazer and Anna Cleaveland, b. Feb. 22, 1771.
Chester, son of Samuel and Ruth Cleaveland, b. March 28, 1771.
Luther, son of Moses and Azubah Cleaveland, b. July 22, 1771.
Dorothy, dau. of Timothy, Jr., and Esther Cleaveland, b. May 30, 1772.
Deliverance, dau. of Paine and Sarah Cleaveland, b. May 30, 1772.
Anson, son of John and Betty Cleaveland, b. Aug. 4, 1772.
Thankful, 9th child of Aaron and Thankful Cleaveland, b. Oct. 29, 1773.
Luther, son of Moses and Azubah Cleaveland, b. Jan. 14, 1774.
Wealthy, dau. of Tracy and Phebe Cleaveland, b. Feb. 4, 1774.
Sarah, dau. of Paine and Sarah Cleaveland, b. May 22, 1774.
Mary, dau. of Timothy and Esther Cleaveland, b. Nov. 6, 1774.
David, son of Tracy and Phebe Cleaveland, b. Dec. 16, 1775.

Arubah, dau. of Tracy and Phebe Cleaveland, b. Dec. 25, 1775.
Anne, dau. of Aaron, Jr., and Jemima Cleaveland, b. Jan. 18, 1778.
A male child of Tracy and Phebe Cleaveland, b. Feb. 20, 1778.
Augustus, son of Moses and Azubah Cleaveland, b. March 29, 1778.
Camden, son of Aaron and Thankful Cleaveland, b. April 8, 1778.
'Vester, son of Samuel and Ruth Cleaveland, b. Aug. 22, 1778.
Dorothy, dau. of Timothy, Jr., and Esther Cleaveland, b. Oct. 12, 1779.
Dyar, son of Josiah, Jr., and Alice Cleaveland, b. March 3, 1780.
Rebekah, dau. of Tracy and Phebe Cleaveland, b. July 18, 1780.
Josiah, son of Josiah, Jr., and Alice Cleaveland, b. Jan. 10, 1782.
Elkanah, son of Timothy and Esther Cleaveland, b. June 9, 1782.
Abigail, dau. of Eliphas and Anna Cleaveland, b. Nov. 22, 1784.
Elijah, son of Josiah, Jr., and Alice Cleaveland, b. Jan. 28, 1788.
Rebecca, dau. of Perez and Betsey Cleaveland, b. Nov. 6, 1790.
Sophia, dau. of Perez and Betsey Cleaveland, b. Feb. 17, 1793.
Julian, son of Eliphas and Anna Cleaveland, b. Oct. 21, 1793.
Marvin, son of Perez and Betsey Cleaveland, b. May 8, 1795.
Mary Esther, dau. of Moses and Esther Cleaveland, b. May 14, 1795.
Nancy, dau. of Bethabra and Margaret Cleaveland, b. Sept. 4, 1795.
William Pitt, son of William P. and Mary Cleaveland, b. May 14, 1797.
Francis Moses, son of Moses and Esther Cleaveland, b. Sept. 25, 1797.
Anna, dau. of Eliphas and Anna Cleaveland, b. Oct. 20, 1797.
Hiram, son of Bethabra and Margery Cleaveland, b. Jan. 8, 1798.
Perez Franklin, son of Perez and Betsey Cleaveland, b. May 29, 1798.
Caroline, dau. of William P. and Mary Cleaveland, b. Aug. 18, 1799.
Moses, son of Perez and Betsey Cleaveland, b. June 10, 1800.
Thomas, son of Bethabra and Margery Cleaveland, b. Sept. 14, 1801.
Lucius, son of Perez and Betsey Cleaveland, b. July 29, 1803.
Mary, dau. of Bethabra and Margery Cleaveland, b. Aug. 26, 1803.
Julius Moses, son of Moses and Esther Cleaveland, b. May 21, 1805.
Betsey Ann, dau. of Perez and Betsey Cleaveland, b. June 12, 1805.
Louisa, (Aspinwell,) dau. of Dorothy Cleaveland, (a single woman,) b. Feb. 16, 1806.
Luther, son of Bethabra and Margery Cleaveland, b. Oct. 25, 1806.
Emeline, dau. of Bethabra and Margery Cleaveland, b. Sept. 25, 1809.

DEATHS.

Persis, wife of Samuel Cleaveland, d. Feb. 22, 1698.
Josiah Cleaveland, Sen., d. April 26, 1709.
Ephraim Cleaveland, d. March 13, 1711.
Jonathan Cleaveland, d. July 15, 1713.
Deliverance, wife of Edward Cleaveland, d. June 7, 1717.
Abigail, dau. of Samuel and Margaret Cleaveland, d. Feb. 23, 1718.
John, son of Josiah and Mary Cleaveland, d. July 11, 1718.
Deborah, wife of Joseph Cleaveland, Jr., d. Nov. 14, 1724.
Abigail, wife of Joseph Cleaveland, d. Dec. 16, 1724.
Samuel Cleaveland, Jr., d. Oct. 1, 1727.
John, son of Capt. Joseph Cleaveland, d. March 5, 1734.
Jonathan, son of Capt. Joseph Cleaveland, d. March 19, 1734.

Lydia, dau. of Josiah and Sarah Cleaveland, d. Sept. 30, 1734.
Rebecca, wife of David Cleaveland, d. Nov. 30, 1734.
Sarah, wife of Josiah Cleaveland, d. Feb. 6, 1735.
Samuel Cleaveland, d. March 12, 1736.
Lois Cleaveland, d. Sept. 29, 1736.
Abijah, son of Capt. Joseph Cleaveland, d. Nov. 3, 1736.
Rachel, dau. of Capt. Joseph Cleaveland, d. Nov. 4, 1736.
Hannah, dau. of Capt. Joseph Cleaveland, d. Nov. 5, 1736.
Mary, dau. of Capt. Joseph Cleaveland, d. Nov. 8, 1736.
Jabez, son of Henry and Lucy Cleaveland, d. Nov. 13, 1736.
Moses, son of Josiah and Abigail Cleaveland, d. Jan. 1, 1741.
Mary, dau. of Joseph and Mary Cleaveland, d. Aug. 21, 1742.
Kesiah, wife of Deliverance Cleaveland, d. Sept. 19, 1742.
    (The infant of Deliverance was b. Aug. 20, and d. Sept. 21, 1742.)
Lydia, dau. of Josiah and Abigail Cleaveland, d. March 26, 1745.
Cyrus, son of Timothy and Dorothy Cleaveland, d. Feb. 23, 1749.
Eunice, wife of David Cleaveland, d. Oct. 5, 1749.
Dorothy, dau. of Benjamin and Rachel Cleaveland, d. Nov. 12, 1749.
Joseph, son of Benjamin and Rachel Cleaveland, d. Nov. 17, 1749.
Benjamin, son of Benjamin and Rachel Cleaveland, d. Nov. 25, 1749.
Josiah Cleaveland, d. Feb. 9, 1750.
Solomon Cleaveland, d. March 14, 1752.
Capt. Joseph Cleaveland, d. May 12, 1752.
Prudence, wife of Paine Cleaveland, and her infant, d. June 30, 1758.
Ann, dau. of Aaron and Thankful Cleaveland, d. March 11, 1759.
Sarah, wife of Joseph Cleaveland, d. June 21, 1761.
Mary, dau. of Benjamin and Rachel Cleaveland, d. Jan. 27, 1763.
Susannah, wife of Paine Cleaveland, d. Jan. 26, 1766.
Joseph Cleaveland, (aged 76), d. March 11, 1766.
Zeruiah, dau. of Samuel and Ruth Cleaveland, d. Oct. 25, 1766.
Dorothy, wife of Capt. Timothy Cleaveland, d. Aug. 19, 1769.
Luther, son of Moses and Azubah Cleaveland, d. Aug. 4, 1771.
Edward Cleaveland, d. Nov. 3, 1771.
Aruna, son of Samuel and Ruth Cleaveland, d. Aug. 17, 1773.
Paine Cleaveland, d. Nov. 25, 1773.
Molly, dau. of Aaron and Thankful Cleaveland, d. Oct. 12, 1775.
An infant male child of Tracy and Phebe Cleaveland, d. Feb. 24, 1778, aged 4 days.
Elkanah, son of Timothy and Esther Cleaveland, d. June 21, 1782.
Timothy Cleaveland, (aged 84), d. Jan. 19, 1784.
Wid. Rebecca Cleaveland, d. Feb. —, 1784.
Sarah, dau. of Capt. Josiah Cleaveland, d. April 23, 1784.
Caroline, dau. of Wm. Pitt and Mary Cleaveland, d. Feb. 28, 1800.
Moses, son of Perez and Betsey Cleaveland, d. ———.
Hiram, son of Samuel Cleaveland, d. ———.
Timothy Cleaveland, d. Oct. 27, 1804.
Esther, wife of Timothy Cleaveland, d. Nov. 3, 1804.
Gen. Moses Cleaveland, d. Nov. 16, 1806.

EPITAPHS, ETC.,

FROM THE OLD CEMETERY, CANTERBURY, CONN.

"Moses Cleaveland, Esq., died Nov. 16, 1806, aged 52."

"Esther, relict of Moses Cleaveland, Esq., died Jany. 17, 1840, aged 74."
"Jesus said unto her, ' I am the resurrection and the life; he that believeth on me, though he were dead, yet shall he live.' "

"In memory of Col. Aaron Cleaveland, who died in a fit of apoplexy, on the 14th day of April, 1785, aet. 57. Born the 7th day of December, 1727. On the 17th June, A. D. 1782, when in the bloom of health and prime of life, was struck with the numb palsy. From that time to his death, had upwards of sixty fits of the palsy and apoplexy. He was employed in sundry honorable offices, both civil and military."

> "Calm and composed my soul her journey takes,
> No guilt that troubles, and no heart that aches,—
> Adieu, thou son: all bright like thee arise,
> Adieu, dear friends, and all that 's good and wise."

"Thankful Cleaveland, relict of Colonel Aaron Cleaveland. Born March, A. D. 1738; died Septmr 29, A. D. 1827, aged eighty-nine years."

"In memory of Mr. Shubael Cleaveland, who died April 25th, 1795, aged 60 years."

"Capt. Josiah Cleaveland, departed this life, May 7th, 1793, in ye 81st year of his age. Beloved in life, lamented in death, he calmly bid adieu to this world, with a pleasing hope of life immortal beyond the grave."

"In memory of Mrs. Joanna Cleaveland, wife of Capt. Josiah Cleaveland. She died Apl. 4th, 1803, in ye 80th year of her age."

> "Here let me rest my weary^d head,
> Till Christ the Lord shall raise the dead."

"In memory of Capt. Jacob Cleaveland, who died July 26th, 1826, aged 65 years."

"In memory of Mrs. Rebecca, wife of Capt. Jacob Cleaveland, who died Sept. 30, 1825, aged 59 years."

"In memory of Lieut. Timothy Cleaveland, who died Oct. 27th, 1804, in ye 70th year of his age.

"In memory of Mrs. Esther, wife of Lieut. Timothy Cleaveland, who died Novr 3d, 1804, in ye 60th year of her age."

"Bethabra Cleaveland, died at Ware, Mass., April 17, 1835, aged 71 years."

"Margery, wife of Bethabra Cleaveland, died in Ware, Mass., May 11, 1847, aged 77."

"Dolly Cleaveland, died March 3d, 1862, aged 76 years."

"In memory of Nancy Cleaveland, who died April 15th, 1863, aged 67."

The last two seem to be the *latest* interments in the old cemetery of Canterbury, and the foregoing are all the inscriptions where the name of Cleaveland appears.

FROM THE TOWNSHIP RECORDS OF BROOKLYN, CONN.

Brooklyn, Conn., was made a town in 1786, but I find births recorded dating back to 1758.

MARRIAGES.

Isaac Cleveland and Abigail Brown, m. Jan. 18, 1808.
Samuel Cleveland and Lucy Jones, m. April 17, 1820.
Colbe C. Cleveland and Flora Farnham, m. Sept. 19, 1825.
Olive Cleveland and Lester Burnett, m. June 1, 1828.
Lucius Cleveland and Sarah Cady, m. May 23, 1830.
Lucy Cleveland and Charles Cady, m. Aug. 4, 1845.
Harry P. Cleveland and Mary M. Rogers, m. Jan. 14, 1848.
Jane F. Cleveland and Lewis Searls, m. Dec. 12, 1853.
  (Jane F. Cleveland is a daughter of Colby C. Cleveland.)
Henry M. Cleveland and Mary C. Welch, m. Sept. 27, 1854.
Stephen Cleveland and Isabella M. Tarbox, m. March 10, 1858.
William B. Cleveland and Mary Ann Lyon, m. Jan. 29, 1864.
  (William B. Cleveland is a son of Colby C. Cleveland.)
Vernet E. Cleveland and Lucy D. Stetson, m. Sept. 17, 1868.

BIRTHS.

Aaron Augustus, son of John and Polly Cleveland, b. Jan. 21, 1797.
Harriet, dau. of John and Polly Cleveland, b. March 10, 1799.
Olive Brown, dau. of Isaac and Abigail Cleveland, b. Oct. 13, 1809.
Nancy Juliet, dau. of Isaac and Abigail Cleveland, b. Aug. 17, 1813.
James Hervey, son of Isaac and Abigail Cleveland, b. Jan. 3, 1816.
Henry Clarence, son of Henry P. and Mary Cleveland, b. Dec. 26, 1852.
  (Henry P. is son of Colby C. Cleveland, now living here.)
Addie L., dau. of Charles and Juliet Cleveland, b. Feb. 27, 1853.
  (Charles is another son of Colby C. Cleveland.)
Lewis B., son of Henry M. and Mary Cleveland, b. June 30, 1855.
  (Henry M. is son of Mason Cleveland, Hampton, Conn.)
Eliza P., dau. of Henry M. and Mary Cleveland, b. Sept. 30, 1857.
Gertrude, dau. of Charles and Juliet Cleveland, b. Oct. 25, 1857.
Mary A., dau. of Henry M. and Mary Cleveland, b. May 27, 1862.
Anna M., dau. of Charles and Juliet Cleveland, b. May 8, 1864.
Daughter (no name) of Charles and Juliet Cleveland, b. Feb. 16, 1865.
  (Charles Cleveland resides in Norwich, Conn.)
Henry Mason, son of Henry M. and Mary Cleveland, b. Aug. 26, 1866.

From a separate record overlooked:

Eva Ophelia, dau. of Charles and Juliet Cleveland, b. Oct. 21, 1847.
Alice, dau. of Charles and Juliet Cleveland, b. April 4, 1851.

DEATHS.

Capt. Joseph Cleveland, d. Feb. 9, 1795.
Olive Cleveland, widow of Capt. Joseph Cleveland, d. March 20, 1820.

In the cemetery is an obelisk with the following names and dates upon it:

Capt. Davis Cleveland, d. March 17, 1805, aged 39.
Mrs. Lydia Cleveland, d. May 24, 1810, aged 40.
Harriet Cleveland, d. Sept. 8, 1796, aged 3 yrs. 3 mo. 12 d.
Betsey Cleveland, d. Oct. 7, 1796, aged 1 yr. 8 mo. 14 d.
(There is no record of their births.)

From Colbe C. Cleveland's family Bible I take the following:
Colbe C. Cleveland, b. Aug. 23, 1800.
Charles Cleveland, his son, b. Aug. 4, 1826.
Henry P. Cleveland, his son, b. Oct. 3, 1828.
George Cleveland, his son, b. July 16, 1831; d. Oct. 23, 1832.
Mary L. Cleveland, his daughter, b. May 19, 1833, m. Lafayette Spencer; d. Jan. 4, 1872.
Flora Jane Cleveland, his daughter, b. Nov. 6, 1835, m. L. Searls.
Catherine Cleveland, his daughter, b. Aug. 19, 1838, m. Jas. C. Palmer.
William B. Cleveland, his son, b. March 20, 1841.
Delia L. Cleveland, his daughter, b. Oct. 16, 1846, m. Aaron F. Walker.

WM. WOODBRIDGE, *Township Clerk*.

FROM THE TOWNSHIP RECORDS OF FREETOWN, MASS.

MARRIAGES.

Thankful Cleveland and Michael Chase, m. Feb. 1, 1738.
Dinah Cleveland and Joseph Davis, m. Nov. 28, 1745.
Benjamin Cleveland and Priscilla Paine, m. June 2, 1746.
Mary Cleveland and Jonathan Soule, m. Jan. 6, 1765.
William Cleveland and Rhoda Hathaway, m. July 17, 1786.
David Cleveland and Deborah Durfee, m. March 29, 1787.
Joseph Cleveland (2nd) and Content Read, m. April 5, 1787.
Elizabeth Cleveland and Hezekiah Hunter, of Rehoboth, m. March 9, 1797.
Sylvia Cleveland and Job Read, m. Oct. 26, 1797.
Eunice Cleveland and William Borden, m. March 26, 1802.

BIRTHS.

Ambrose Cleveland, father to ye following children, was m. Aug. ye 4th, 1753.

Ambrose, son of Ambrose and Keturah Cleveland, b. Aug. 14, 1755.
Tabitha, dau. of Ambrose and Keturah Cleveland, b. Nov. 25, 1757.
Elizabeth, dau. of Ambrose and Keturah Cleveland, b. May 31, 1760.
William, son of Ambrose and Keturah Cleveland, b. Feb. 11, 1763.
Jonathan, son of Ambrose and Keturah Cleveland, b. Jan. 27, 1766.
Hannah, dau. of Benjamin and Jerusha Cleveland, b. Aug. 28, 1750.
Benjamin, son of Benjamin and Jerusha Cleveland, b. April 10, 1755.
John, son of Benjamin and Jerusha Cleveland, b. Jan. 21, 1757.
Martha, dau. of Benjamin and Jerusha Cleveland, b. Jan. 21, 1759.
David, son of Benjamin and Bethiah Cleveland, b. Dec. 11, 1764.
Joseph, son of Benjamin and Bethiah Cleveland, b. Aug. 28, 1766.
Alpheus, son of Benjamin and Bethiah Cleveland, b. Sept. 18, 1768.

Enos, son of Benjamin and Bethiah Cleveland, b. Nov. 4, 1770.
Elizabeth, dau. of Benjamin and Bethiah Cleveland, b. June 2, 1773.

Cynthia, dau. of Jonathan and Abigail Cleveland, b. Dec. 29, 1792.
Elizabeth, dau. of Jonathan and Abigail Cleveland, b. Oct. 22, 1794.
Benjamin, son of Jonathan and Abigail Cleveland, b. April 1, 1798.
Annah, dau. of Jonathan and Abigail Cleveland, b. Oct. 12, 1800.

DEATHS.

I find no deaths on record until 1854, and learn from old residents, that the families moved from town many years ago.

From later information, I learn, that that part of the township set off and now called Fall River, contained all of the Clevelands.

"INTENTIONS" OF MARRIAGE RECORDED ARE AS FOLLOWS:

Oliver Chace and Elizabeth Cleveland, Dec. 19, 1734.
John Tompkins and Elizabeth Cleveland, Dec. 2, 1740.
William Hodge and Martha Cleveland, April 27, 1742.
Benjamin Cleveland and Jerusha Rouns, of Rehoboth, Oct. 20, 1750.
   (I think this is the Benjamin Cleveland who married Priscilla Paine in 1746, though there is no record of her death.)
Ambrose Cleveland and Katurah Briggs, of Berkeley, Nov. 27, 1755.
Benjamin Cleveland and Bethiah Whitney, Oct. 6, 1764.
   (Is not this the same Benjamin?)
David Butts and Content Cleveland, Feb. 20, 1790.
Nathan Clark and Rebecca Cleveland, of Berkeley, June 30, 1791.
Alpheus Cleveland and Olive Drake, of Dighton, Jan. 28, 1792.
Jonathan Cleveland and Abigail Bennett, April 27, 1792.
Ambrose Cleveland and Lavinia Hathaway, Aug. 8, 1803.

H. A. FRANCIS, Township Clerk.

Many other New England towns have records, more or less perfect, of persons bearing the family name.

The following copy of a letter to the Compiler from Ex-Gov. Chauncey Fitch Cleveland, of Hampton, Windham county, Conn., deserves the space it fills (if for no other reason) for the noble sentiments therein expressed in reference to honoring the name we bear:

"HAMPTON, CONN., Dec. 23, 1876.

"H. G. CLEVELAND, ESQ.:

"My Dear Sir — Your very interesting letter of Dec. 8th, is received, and by it I have learned more of the origin of the Clevelands than I knew before. You ask who my grandfather married, and the names of their children. He married a Hyde, of Canterbury. She belonged to a family distinguished for their love of money. Her Christian name I have forgotten. They had a family of five sons and four daughters: Solomon, Silas, Daniel, Isaac and Palmer; Irene, Clarissa, Elizabeth and Polly. Solomon married Hannah Sharp, of Pomfret. They had six children, all very talented: Palmer, Charles, Solomon; Hannah, Betsey and Lois. Of the sons, two were lawyers and one was a manufacturer. Of the three daughters, one was the grandmother of the authoress, Ellen Louise (Chandler) Moulton. These children are all dead, but all have descendants living, excepting Solomon, who never married. The names of these cousin's children I can not give you.

"Silas, Jr., my father, married Lois Sharp, of Pomfret, sister of Uncle Solomon's wife. They had three sons: Mason, John and Chauncey F., all born in Hampton.

"Mason married Eliza Perkins, and they have four sons. Mason died twenty years ago. The sons are: Perkins, unmarried, is clerk in the Comptroller's Office, New York; Edward S., a gentleman of leisure, married Caroline Bolles, of Hartford, Conn., has two sons living, and has buried one; Henry M., married Mary Welch, of Brooklyn, Conn., they have four children, two sons and two daughters; George Lee, unmarried, is in a banking house in Hartford. These my nephews are talented and prosperous.

"My brother John studied medicine, but died at the age of twenty-eight, unmarried.

"I married for my first wife, Diantha Hovey, of this town, and we raised two children: John J. and Delia D. My son graduated at Trinity College, Hartford, and my daughter also graduated in Hartford. John was a lawyer and clerk of the Federal Courts of this State; never married; died at the age of twenty-eight. My daughter married Alfred A. Burnham, of Windham, a lawyer; has been Speaker of House of Representatives, Lieut. Gov., and four years Member of Congress. Delia died at the age of twenty-eight. My children were very talented, and died universally loved and respected. My wife, Diantha, died Oct. 29, 1867, and I married her niece, Helen Litchfield, with whom I am now living.

"My Uncle Daniel died a bachelor. Palmer died early. Isaac married Abigail Brown, of Brooklyn. They had three children: two girls and one son. Nancy died early. Olive married Lester Burnett, and lives in San Francisco. They have two children. Harvey died three or four years ago and left one son, who is married and lives in Massachusetts. Polly never married. Irene, Elizabeth and Clarissa married, and their descendants are scattered about the world.

"Your questions regarding the Senior Edward I can not answer. Had I thought of it when young, my grandfather could have given me a history of the Cleveland family, from first to last. My ancestors, as far as I knew them, were talented, honorable men. But to be perfectly frank with you, my kinsman, I have been much more anxious to honor the name of Cleveland, than to be honored by it.

"I was pleased with the picture of your father, a fine looking old gentleman. I enclose my own to him, taken when I was seventy-five, most three years ago. The Clevelands are a long-lived race.

"With feelings of kinship I subscribe myself,
Your friend and servant,
C. F. CLEVELAND."

So many and urgent have been the inquiries of correspondents, during the compilation of this Genealogy, concerning the personal history of the Compiler, that he has concluded to insert the following biographical account, taken from Cleave's "Biographical Cyclopedia and Portrait Gallery of Distinguished Men of Ohio" (Cuyahoga County, page 94), the author of which, it appears, had the presumption to embrace him in that category. Making due allowances for the very flattering character of the sketch, it will no doubt fully answer the purpose of its insertion:

"CLEVELAND, HORACE GILLETTE, merchant, was born January 3d, 1832, at Winchester, Litchfield county, Connecticut, and was the youngest son of eleven children; living, April, 1875, at Cleveland, Ohio. His father, Oren Cleveland, being a man of good education and fine literary taste, devoted many years of his life to teaching, at the same time cultivating a farm. Moses Cleveland, from whom this branch of the Cleveland family descended, came over from Ipswich, England, about 1640, and settled in Woburn, Massachusetts; his son Samuel settled in Connecticut, in 1693. Oren Cleveland, the father of Horace, removed his family to Ohio in 1839, and settled in Geauga county. Horace lived at home, assisting in carrying on the farm, and attending the district school winters, until he was nineteen, when he entered the store of Kile, Wilkins & Co., at Huntsburgh, where he remained as general clerk for about a year. In 1852 he went to Cleveland and entered a mercantile college for the purpose of perfecting himself in book-keeping, and at the end of a few weeks he had so thoroughly mastered the science that he was offered the position of tutor in the college, but declined, wishing to connect himself more actively with the business of the city. Immediately on leaving the college he engaged as book-keeper, with Mr. A. M. Beebe, at that time doing a large and profitable business on Bank street. He remained with Mr. Beebe about a year, and then was employed in the Forest City Bank, organized under the free banking law of Ohio. At the end of about a year, he was prostrated by a severe and lingering illness, which necessitated his resignation, much to the regret of the officers of the institution, for his clerical abilities were of a high order, and joined to a uniformly courteous deportment, made him a general favorite. After his restoration to health he was employed for a short time by the Bank of Geauga, at Painesville, where his skill as an accountant was called into requisition in examining, writing up and balancing books and accounts that had been neglected for many years. This service done he returned to Cleveland, and in the spring of 1855, entered the well known wholesale store of George Worthington, then on the corner of Water and Superior streets, the present site of the Second National Bank building. He was the book-keeper and chief clerk of this enterprising and very successful business house for nearly ten years. These were years of close application, and taxed to the uttermost a constitution not naturally strong; yet the experience was of great advantage, for by it he was being educated for the more responsible duties the years were to bring to him. In the fall of 1864, he formed a copartnership with Joseph H. Brown, Richard Brown, Thomas Brown, and William Bonnell, of Youngstown, Ohio, under the name of Cleveland, Brown & Co., and opened a large hardware store, at Nos. 25 to 31 Merwin street, making heavy hardware a specialty. They imported largely of Swedish iron, English steel, etc. Their business operations reached an average of two millions per annum; their trade extended throughout Northern Ohio, Indiana, Michigan and the upper lakes, and in some lines of goods as far east as Boston. The reputation of the house for enterprise and honorable dealing was thoroughly established. There have been several changes of partners during the eleven years of its existence, and in 1875 the firm had seven partners, viz.: H. G. Cleveland, Joseph H. Brown, Richard Brown, J. O. Brown, William Bonnell, P. M. Hitchcock, and A. M. Wilcox. In 1870, he was elected president of the Painesville and Youngstown Railroad, a narrow gauge road running from Fairport, on the lake, to Youngstown, built for the special purpose of transporting iron ore from the lake to the extensive iron works at Youngstown, and coal from that region to the lake, and is under the control of parties engaged in these interests. After about a year he resigned, on account of the increasing demands of his regular business. Exemplary in all transactions whether of a public or private character; an active, earnest man, with a keen insight into the multiplied details of such a life, and rare judgment to meet them, he is the recognized head of one of Cleveland's most enterprising and substantial commercial houses. In politics he is a conservative Republican, thoroughly patriotic, and heartily supported the war, giving liberally to all those charitable enterprises that grew out of the struggle. He was two years in the city council, and rendered valuable services on the finance committee. He is a communicant in the Episcopal Church, uniting with the (Grace) Church about ten years ago, and engages actively in its Christian work, cheerfully giving his time and money to its advancement; indeed, all worthy charitable objects find in him a friend. He is warden of Grace Church, and one of the standing committee of the diocese. He was married to Miss Anna Maria Knapp, of Danbury, Connecticut, in 1853. They have three children, two sons and one daughter."

A BURLESQUE ON THE PRIDE OF FAMILY BLOOD,
WRITTEN BY
REV. AARON CLEVELAND,
After hearing a conversation on the subject.

Four kinds of blood flow in my veins,
And govern each, in turn, my brains;
From CLEVELAND, PORTER, SEWALL, WATERS,
I had my blood distinct in quarters.
My parents' parents' names I know,
But I no farther back can go.
Compound on compound from the flood,
Forms now my own ancestral blood,
But what my sires of old time were,
I neither wish to know nor care.
Some might be wise, and others fools;
Some might be tyrants, others tools;
Some might be rich, and others lack;
Some might be white, and others black:
No matter what in days of yore,
Since they are known and sung no more.
The name of CLEVELAND I must wear,
Which some poor foundling first might bear.
PORTER, I 'm told, from Scotland came,
A bonny bard of ancient fame;
SEWALL, an English derivation,
Perhaps some outcast from the nation;
WATERS, an Irishman, I ween,
Straight roundabout from Aberdeen—
Such is my heterogeneous "blood,"
A motley mixture, bad and good;
Each blood aspires to rule alone,
And each in turn ascends the throne,
And rules till others tear him down.
Each change must twist about my brains,
And move my tongue in different strains;
My mental powers are captive led,
And whim or wisdom rules the head.
My character, no one can know,
For none I have while things are so,
I 'm something, nothing, wise or fool,
As suits the blood which haps to rule.

When CLEVELAND reigns, I 'm thought a wit,
In making words the funny hit;
In social glee and humorous song,
I charm the fools that round me throng;
But soon, perhaps, this blood is down,
When PORTER next may wear the crown.
Now all is calm, discreet, and wise,
Whate'er I do, whate'er I advise,

What common sense and wisdom teach,
Direct my actions form my speech;
The wise and good now with me stay,
While laughing fools keep far away:
But soon, alas!—this happy reign
Must, for some other, change again.
SEWALL, perhaps, may next bear rule,
I 'm then a *philosophic fool!*
With Jefferson I correspond,
And soar with him the stars beyond,
While every fibre of the brain
To sense profound I nicely strain,
And then arise beyond the ken
Of common sense and common men.
Wise fools may soar themselves above,
And dream in rapturous spheres they move,
But airy castles must recoil,
And all their imagery despoil.
Thus great was I till SEWALL's crown
About my head came tumbling down.
But who comes next? alas! 't is WATERS
Rushing fearless to head-quarters.
He knows no manners, nor decorum,
But elbows headlong to the forum,
Uncouth and odd, abrupt and bold,
Untaught, unteachable, uncontrolled.
Devoid of wisdom, sense or wit,
Not one thing right he ever hit,
Unless by accident—not skill,
He blundered right, against his will—
Such am I now, no transmigration
Can sink me to a *lower* station.
Come, PORTER, come, depose this clown,
And once for all assume the crown.
If aught in SEWALL's blood you find
Will make your own still more refined,
If found in CLEVELAND's blood a trait
To aid you in the affairs of state,
Select such parts, but spurn the rest,
Never to rule my brains or breast;
Of WATERS' blood expel the whole,
Let not one drop pollute my soul.
Then rule my head, then rule my heart,
From folly, weakness, wit apart;
With all such qualities I 'll dispense,
And only give me *common sense.*

Appendix.   253

This brings to a conclusion the genealogical labors of the Compiler as relating to this volume. In glancing over the proof sheets some errors have been discovered, which are here briefly noted and corrected, with some additional matter received too late for insertion in the proper place, as follows:

Page 5. According to the Woburn (Mass.) records, if correctly transcribed, the first Joanna, daughter of Moses and Ann (Winn) Cleveland, d. March 12, 1667, instead of "July 2, 1667;" and Isaac, the ninth child, was b. Aug. 11, 1669, instead of "May 11, 1669." (see page 237).

Page 10. Letter from "Benjamin and Rachel Cleaveland" should conclude, "*This* from your loving Parents," the word "this" having been inadvertently omitted in copying.

Page 11. "Lucy," twelfth child of Abigail Cleveland, by husband Samuel Hovey, d. July 27, 1788.

Page 15. "Laura," eleventh child of Rufus Cleveland Hovey, d. Jan. 12, 1868. Also "James," sixth child of Rebecca Hovey, by husband James Sanderson, did not die as reported "March —, 1841," but is still living in Pilot Grove, Newton county, Ind.

Page 17. "Frances," second child, etc., d. Sept. —, 1836, instead of "Sept. —, 1830." Also "Charlotte," fifth child, d. Jan. —, 1858, instead of "Jan. —, 1856."

Page 18. "4. Nancy Seabury, b. Dec. 6, 1807," res. *Washington,* Vt., instead of "Williamstown, Vt.," (subsequently corrected, see page 140).

Page 19. "8. Emily Ann, b. Feb. 12, 1808," should read Feb. 12, 1818. Also for revised and corrected list of children of Abigail Hovey,[6] by husband Oliver Hibbard, see pages 142, 143.

Page 20. Full given names of ninth child of John F. Hovey,[6] "James *Monroe* Prouty."

Page 24. One correspondent gives the birth of Simeon Shepard,[7] "Oct. 14, 1805;" another has the date, "Jan. 4, 1806." (See page 167.) The Compiler has no means of deciding which is the correct date.

Page 28. "1. Mary, b. Nov. 9, 1809," d. in Montague, Mass., Aug. 29, 1869.

Page 30. For "Seth and Julia (Adams) Makepeace," read Seth and Lydia (Dean) Makepeace. Also for "William,[7]" third child of Ira Payne,[6] read *Willard,* (corrected subsequently, see page 182).

Page 38. For "Pembroke White,[7] youngest daughter," read youngest *son,* etc.

Page 72. For "Josephine,[7]" read *Josephus.*[7]

Page 91. Sixteenth line from bottom, after "Concord," add *or Chardon.*

Page 109. Rev. John L. Bradbury,[8] b. in Butler county, Ohio, Sept. 29, 1812, m. first, Oct. 21, 1838, Amelia J. Hess. Her parents' names not given, but she was b. Feb. 16, 1815; d. July 3, 1846. He m. second, June 27, 1847, Mrs. Cassandra (Gilmore) Wilson, widow of Thomas Wilson, and daughter of John and Magdalena Gilmore. She was b. in Rockbridge county, Va., July 13, 1808. He d. Oct. 8, 1866; was a Methodist preacher. Children, by wife Amelia: 1. Thomas Benton,[9] b. Oct. 12, 1839, m. Sarah Horner, dau. of George Horner; enlisted in the late war and d. in the service, Aug. 3, 1863. Child: Rhoda Alice,[10] living with her mother in Minnesota. 2. Isabel C.,[9] b. Jan. 16, 1841, m. Milton Barret. Res. near Knightstown, Henry county, Ind. 3. James M.,[9] b. Oct. 13, 1842; d. Nov. 17, 1864, a soldier in the army for the Union, unm. 4. Matilda H.,[9] b. April 29, 1844, m. Jason Trueblood the noted cattle dealer of Raysville, Henry county, Ind. Children, by wife Cassandra: 5. Mary Virginia,[9] b. April 16, 1848, m. Jan. 11, 1866, Joseph Henry Boxell, son of William and Catherine (Helpbringer) Boxell. He was b. Dec. 11, 1844. Res. Marion, Grant county, Ind. Children: 1. Charles,[10] b. Oct. 18, 1866. 2. Alden,[10] b. Jan. 26, 1868. 3. Minnie,[10] b. Aug. 7, 1870. 4. William,[10] b. Dec. 22, 1874. 6. Amanda,[9] b. Oct. 22, 1850; d. March 29, 1853.

Page 111. James N. Lord,[8] b. March 22, 1837, m. in Stevens county, W. T., 1876, Isabella Rinehart, dau. of Christopher and Lydia Ann (Taylor) Rinehart. She was b. in Angola, Steuben county, Ind., Oct. 3, 1858. Res. Dayton, Columbia county, W. T. Children: 1. Joseph Edwin,[9] b. in Umatilla county, Oregon, Sept. 30, 1877. 2. James William,[9] b. in Dayton, Columbia county, W. T., May 8, 1879.

Page 116. Col. Richard S. C. Lord,[8] m. Mary A. Wright, March 18, 1863, not "July 4, 1863."

Page 126. "Levina,[8]" m. Thomas Blake, Nov. 11, 1870. Eri W. Wilder is reported by his brother as not deceased, but still living somewhere in the State of Missouri.

Page 143. Edmund B. Clark,[8] had first wife, name not learned, who d. early after marriage. Oliver H. Clark,[8] had first wife, Mary Mack, from Canada; and second wife, Minerva Ayres, who d. in 1864. Anna Elizabeth Bare, wife of William L. H. Clark,[8] was b. near Lancaster, Pa., June 29, 1844.

Page 144. Second wife of Rev. Oliver D. Hibbard was b. in Sugar Grove, Warren county, Pa., instead of "near Belfast, Ireland."

Page 149. Eleventh line from top of page, for "Mary Kirth Wheatley," read Mary *Keith* Wheatley.

Page 173. Brigham Payne,[7] m. Julia Ann Chapman, Sept. 1, 1831. She was b. July 24, 1810, and d. Sept. 2, 1867. He d. March 11, 1877. Concerning their children it may be added, that "Marvin Henry," was b. July 22, 1832, and resides (1879) in St. Helena, Napa county, Cal.; "Julia Elizabeth," was b. May 14, 1834, m. Charles Pritchard, and resides in same place; "Edward *Warham*," (not "Wyman,") was b. June 15, 1836, and resides in Adabo, Madison county, Montana; "James Andrews," was b. Nov. 13, 1837, and resides in Littleton, Arapahoe county, Col.; "Albert Levant," was b. June 15, 1841; "Savilla Antoinette," was b. Sept. 13, 1846; and " Alice *Sophia*," (not "Alice May,") was b. June 17, 1850. The three last named reside in or near Garnett, Anderson county, Kan.

Page 180. Alexa *Ann* Martin,[7] m. Rev. John Marble, who was pastor of a Baptist church in Cherry Tree, Clearfield county, (?) Pa., and where she d. July 19, 1845. Their daughter "Ann Amelia,[8]" m. April 9, 1873, George W. Hockridge, a farmer, and son of John D. and Hester Ann (Rogers) Hockridge. He was b. in Morrisville, N. Y., Aug. 12, 1837. No children.

Page 204. The "Allen family" crest and coat of arms is thus described:

"ALLEN [ALLAN] — (Chelmsford, Essex, Eng.)
"*Coat of Arms.*—Shield, sable, a cross potent, or.
"*Crest.*—A demi-lion. azure, holding in the two paws a rudder, or, of a vessel.
"*Motto.*—Fortiter Gerit Crucem."

Before taking leave of the numerous correspondents and well wishers who have gratuitously rendered much assistance in the compilation of this volume, this opportunity is improved to heartily thank them, one and all, for their kindly interest and invaluable aid.

INDEX.

TABLE OF GENERAL CONTENTS.

Ancestry of Benjamin Cleveland, ... 5—8
Descendants of Benjamin Cleveland, 9—74, 96—156, 161—165, 166—183, 215—228
Descendants of Abigail (Cleveland) Hovey, ... 10—20, 96—156
Descendants of Zenas Cleveland, ... 20—23, 161—165
Descendants of Rachel (Cleveland) Hamblin, ... 23—26, 166—172
Descendants of Persis (Cleveland) Payne, ... 26—30, 173—183
Descendants of Rufus Cleveland, ... 30—68
Descendants of Phebe (Cleveland) Pearson, ... 68—72, 215—226
Descendants of Phebe (Cleveland) [Pearson] O'Brien, . 72—74, 226—228
Account of Edward Winn, etc., ... 77
Account of Moses Cleveland,[2] of Woburn, Mass., his family, etc., . . . 78—82
Fragmentary Records of other Children and Descendants of Moses Cleveland,[1] . . . . 82—94
Deed of Benjamin Cleveland, etc., ... 94, 95
Letter of Rev. C. P. Wing, D. D., and some account of Family of Zenas Cleveland, ... 157, 158
Account of the Burgess Family, ... 159—165
Account of Capt. James Chamberlain, his Ancestry and Descendants, 184—204
Account of Samuel Allen and some of his Descendants, ... 204—214
Account of Thomas Adams, of Colchester, Conn., etc., ... 208—214
Knapp — Barnum, ... 228—236
Extracts from Township Records of Woburn, Mass., ... 237
Extracts from Township Records of Chelmsford, Mass., ... 238
Extracts from Sudbury (Mass.) Records, ... 238
Extracts from Township Records of Canterbury, Conn., ... 238—245
Epitaphs, etc., from Old Cemetery, Canterbury, Conn., ... 246
Extracts from Township Records of Brooklyn, Conn., ... 247, 248
Extracts from Township Records of Freetown, Mass., ... 248, 249
Letter of Ex-Gov. Chauncey F. Cleveland, of Hampton, Conn., . . 249, 250
Biographical Notice of the Compiler, ... 250—252
"A Burlesque on the Pride of Family Blood," Poetry, by Rev. A. Cleveland, 252
Corrections and Additions, ... 253, 254

APPENDIX, ... { A, 77—90   D, 94—96   G, 159—165   J, 184—204
                     B, 90—92   E, 96—156   H, 166—172   K, 204—214
                     C, 92—94   F, 157, 158 I, 173—183   L, 215—228

INDEX, ... 255—260

☞ In the Index following, the Compiler has arranged the names, as will be seen, in family groups. In the Cleveland group, all bearing this name, whose names appear in the book, are given; but under all other groups appear only the heads or members of principal families.

ADAMS—
  Abigail, 214
  Henry, 208
  John, 208
  Lucy, 214
  Lydia, 212
  Mary, 43, 210
  Samuel, 208
  Sarah, 213
  Thomas, 208-210, 213

ALCOTT—
  Almon, 57, 58
  Clarissa, 57
  John B., 57
  Lucien P., 59
  Rufus C., 59
  Sidney W., 59

ALLEN—
  Abigail, 207
  Anson, 208, 211
  Azariah, 207
  David, 214
  Ebenezer, 207
  Elizabeth, 207
  Esther, 43, 44, 208, 212
  Ethan, 206
  Eunice, 207
  Frank N., 213
  George, 208, 211
  Hannah, 206
  Isaiah, 208, 211
  Israel, 207
  Jemima, 207, 208, 211
  John, 206, 207
  Jonathan, 213, 214
  Joseph, 205
  Luther, 208, 212
  Martha, 207
  Mary, 206-208
  Moses, 43, 207-211
  Nehemiah, 206
  Obadiah, 206, 214
  Patience, 207
  Rebecca, 206, 207
  Ruble, 208, 212
  Sabra, 208, 212
  Sally, 214
  Samuel, 204-206
  Solomon, 206
  Submit, 207
  Thomas, 205
  Willard S., 208

AYRES—
  Dana, 65
  Delia, 65, 66

AYRES—
  Jason, 65
  Minerva, 254

BABCOCK—
  Amos, 199
  Anna W., 196-198
  Elijah, 196, 199
  Stephen, 199

BARNUM—
  Albacinda, 235
  Caleb, 235
  Azor, 234, 235
  Daniel, 235
  Elizabeth, 234
  Hannah, 235
  Joshua, 234
  Phineas T., 236
  Rebecca, 234
  Thomas, 234
  William H., 236

BEAN—
  Abigail H., 26, 170
  Elvira, 26, 170
  Folsom, 25
  Frank G., 26, 171
  Joel H., 26, 170
  John, 25
  Lovina H., 26, 171
  Lovisa, 26, 170
  Susan C., 26, 171

BLAKE—
  Allen, 61
  Celia E., 61
  Charles H., 52
  Charles L., 61
  Hervey V., 61
  James C., 52
  Jonathan, 52
  Lorenzo M., 52
  Thomas, 126, 254

BONESTEL—
  George, 53
  George B., 53

BRADBURY—
  Josiah, 109
  David, 109
  John L., 109, 253

BURGESS—
  Caleb, 22
  Ebenezer, 160
  Eleanor, 22, 23, 163

BURGESS—
  Eunice, 22, 23, 162
  Hannah, 22, 23, 163
  Jacob, 159
  James, 22, 23, 161
  Samuel, 22, 23, 160, 161
  Thomas, 159
  William C., 22, 23, 164

CHAMBERLAIN—
  Abigail, 196
  Elizabeth, 196, 198
  Harriet, 196, 198
  James, 30, 32, 184, 186, 187, 204
  James, Jr., 187, 196
  Joseph, 184
  Mary, 30, 187
  Naomi, 187, 200
  Sally, 187
  Thomas, 185
  William, 185, 197

CLARK—
  Edmund, 143
  Edmund B., 143, 254
  Oliver H., 140, 254
  William C., 143
  William L. H., 140, 254

CLEVELAND—
  Aaron, 5, 83-85, 87, 252
  Abby K., 46, 47
  Abiel, 87
  Abigail, 6, 7, 9, 10, 12-16, 18-20, 26, 79, 83, 86, 87, 92, 93, 96, 101, 146, 155, 253
  Abijah, 88
  Ada B., 40
  Ada F., 47
  Alexander, 31, 38, 39, 60, 65
  Alexander H., 42
  Alexander P., 38, 41, 42
  Alice, 31, 65-67, 73, 91
  Amy, 91, 93
  Ann, 83
  Anna, 21, 78, 79, 84
  Anna C., 40
  Anna K., 41
  Anne, 88, 91
  Arunah, 93
  Asa, 93
  Asenath, 93
  Azubah, 91
  Barber A., 53, 55

CLEVELAND—
Bela, 89
Belinda, 60
Benjamin, 5, 7-10, 20, 26, 30, 60, 68, 79, 83, 84, 94-96, 160, 187, 253
Benjamin, N., 79
Betsey, 21, 31, 57, 86, 93, 157
Bolivar, 60
Bradford, 91
Bridget, 88
Caroline E., 39, 40
Catharine, 82
Catherine C., 40
Celia, 60, 61
Charles C. W., 31, 59-65, 73
Charles D., 40
Charles H., 60
Charles L., 50, 233, 236
Charles Marvin, 48
Charles Miller, 51, 52
Chauncey F., 86, 249, 250
Chester, 31, 38, 93
Chester D., 39, 40
Chloe, 84
Clara B., 55
Clarissa, 31-38
Clarissa B., 53, 54
Curtice, 88
Curtis, 86
Cyrus, 92
Daniel, 93
Daniel B., 39
David, 90, 91
Deborah, 86, 88
Deliverance, 86, 87
Dorcas, 83, 84
Dorothy, 7-9, 92, 93, 95
Ebenezer, 87
Ebenezer T., 82
Edward, 5, 6, 85, 86
Edward Hooker, 43, 49
Edward Horace, 50, 233, 236
Edwin F., 39
Eleanor, 21, 22, 160-165
Eleazer, 90, 91
Elijah, 7, 92
Elisha, 87
Elizabeth, 6, 60, 62, 63, 66, 86, 89, 91
Elkanah, 92
Ellen, 66
Ellen Annette, 39
Ellen Aurelia, 42
Ellen M., 48, 49
Emma, 66, 67
Emma J., 55

CLEVELAND—
Emma M., 50
Enoch, 5, 89
Ephraim, 6, 7, 92
Esther, 84, 91
Esther Allen, 43, 44
Esther Ann, 50
Esther M., 50, 233, 236
Eunice, 21
Experience, 86
Ezra, 7, 8, 93
Flora, 158
Florence B., 55
Frances, 66
Frances A., 48
Franklin, 92
Freddie B., 40
George A., 50
George B., 39
George H., 47
George L., 82
George M., 82
Gideon, 88
Grace L., 40
Gracie, 42
Grant T., 48
Hannah, 5, 82, 83, 88, 90
Hannah C., 53, 54
Henry, 87, 88
Henry C., 82
Henry E., 41, 42
Hopestill, 90
Horace, 31, 52-55
Horace B., 53, 55
Horace E., 50
Horace G., 43, 50, 99, 157, 233, 236, 249, 250
Ichabod, 79
Ida M., 40
Isaac, 5, 6, 85, 86, 88, 253
Isabel, 83
Jabez, 88
Jacob, 7, 92
James, 21, 86, 89
James B., 74, 86, 90
James C., 31, 43, 46, 47, 51, 52
James E., 46
Jane, 51
Jane E., 40
Jedediah, 93
Jemima M., 43, 45
Jeptha, 92
Jerusha, 93
Jesse, 88
Joanna, 5, 86, 88, 89, 253
John, 7, 83, 87, 88, 91, 93
John D., 82
John K., 31, 66-68, 73
John R. McD., 46

CLEVELAND—
John T., 82
Johnson, 86
Jonas, 88
Jonathan, 7, 87-89
Joseph, 6-9, 78-80, 82, 87, 88, 93, 94
Joseph B., 82
Joseph H., 93
Joseph P., 60, 64
Josiah, 5, 6, 83, 87
Julius A., 60, 65
Katie L., 40
Keziah, 87, 88
Lazarus, 79
Lemuel, 86
Lois, 87
Lucinda, 93
Lucretia, 92
Lucy, 88, 253
Lucy C., 46
Lydia, 87, 89, 92
Lydia M., 46, 47
Margaret, 6, 92
Martha, 60
Mary, 6, 7, 9, 31, 32, 58, 60, 63, 66, 69, 79, 83, 86-88, 91-93, 96
Mary A. T., 82
Mary C., 43, 47
Mary Eliza, 48, 49
Mary Ellen, 40
Mary L., 50
Mary Z., 82
Mehetabel, 79, 90, 91
Mercy, 86
Miriam, 5, 83-85, 88
Moses, 5, 77, 78, 80, 82-84, 87, 89, 253
Moses A., 43, 48, 49
Moses C., 80, 82
Nancy, 31, 55
Nathaniel H., 81
Nehemiah, 88
Newcomb, 93
Obadiah, 84
Oliver, 90
Oren, 31, 42-50, 73, 208, 212, 233, 236
Oren A., 43
Oren H., 48
Oren L., 43, 47
Paine, 86
Palmer, 85, 86
Parnel, 80, 82
Parnel C., 82
Patience, 91
Perez, 91
Persis, 6, 7, 9, 26-30, 89, 90, 96, 195

CLEVELAND—
  Phebe, 9, 68-74, 96
  Phebe A., 60, 64
  Phineas, 86
  Polly, 91
  Rachel, 9, 10, 23-25
    60, 64, 87, 88, 171, 172
  Rebecca, 84, 86, 91
  Rebekah, 7
  Reuben, 88
  Richard, J., 85
  Rufus, 9, 10, 30-32, 38-
    40, 42, 51, 52, 55, 57-
    59, 65, 66, 96, 187, 208,
    212
  Rufus B., 39, 40
  Rufus G., 40
  Samuel, 5-9, 83, 85, 86,
    90-94
  Sarah, 7, 41, 42, 83, 89,
    91, 93
  Sarah A., 48
  Sarah H., 82
  Sarah R., 42
  Silas, 86
  Solomon, 86
  Sophronia, 79
  Squier, 91
  Stephen, 85
  Sumner A., 48
  Susan, 94
  Susannah, 91
  Sybil, 88
  Sylvester, 93
  Thomas, 93
  Timothy, 6, 92
  Tracy, 91
  Tyxhall, 93
  Waitstill, 93
  Weltha, 91
  William, 88, 91
  William C., 43, 48
  William D., 93
  William H., 80-82
  Willie, 42
  Zebina S., 41, 42
  Zenas, 9, 10, 20, 21, 95,
    96, 157, 158, 160
  Zeruiah, 93
  Zipporah, 92

CLIFFORD—
  Elijah M., 24, 168
  Lorena, 25, 169
  Oliver H., 24, 168
  Polly, 24
  Samuel, 24
  Samuel, Jr., 25
  Sophronia, 25
  William P., 25, 169

COE—
  Anna H., 63
  Daniel, 63
  James R., 63

EATON—
  D'Estaing, 71, 221-223
  James, 71, 221
  John, 71, 223
  Joseph, 71, 223
  Nancy, 71, 222
  Nathan, 71, 222
  Susan, 94

HALLETT—
  Miriam, 165
  Sarah J., 165
  Solomon, 22, 165
  William, 22

HAMBLIN—
  Betsey, 23, 24, 168, 169
  Ellen, 25, 169
  James, 23, 25
  James M., 25, 169
  Joel, 23, 25
  Nancy, 23, 25, 170, 171
  Oliver, 23-25
  Orilla, 25, 169
  Polly, 23, 24, 166-168
  Theodotia, 23, 73

HIBBARD—
  Almira, 19, 145
  Amanda, 19, 143
  Elizabeth P., 19, 149
  Fanny B., 19, 149
  Gurdon, 19, 146-149
  Gurdon P., 19, 147
  John, 93
  Martha, 93
  Mary, 19, 146
  Oliver, 19, 143-145, 253
  Oliver D., 19, 144, 254
  Polly, 19, 143
  Ruth H., 19, 148
  Sarah D., 19, 148
  Sarah M., 19, 145
  William L., 19, 144

HILDRETH—
  Joseph, 90
  Persis, 6, 90
  Richard, 6, 90

HILLIARD—
  Barnes, 200
  Gennett, 200, 203
  James M., 200, 202

HILLIARD—
  Joseph, 200
  Miner, 200
  Oren, 200, 202

HOVEY—
  Abiel, 11, 16, 136-139
  Abigail, 11-13, 19, 97,
    103, 142-146, 253
  Abigail E., 20, 151
  Abner, 11, 13, 103-108
  Althea L., 16, 136
  Alvan, 11, 16, 18, 134,
    140-142
  Alvan S., 18, 20, 153
  Alvin P., 17, 139
  Amanda, 17, 137
  Amy, 15, 120
  Amy P., 16, 136
  Asahel K., 15, 122
  Beulah, 12
  Charles, 17, 138
  Charlotte, 17, 137, 253
  Daniel, 11-13, 96-102
  Daniel, Jr., 12, 96
  Daniel H., 20, 154
  Dudley, 13, 104
  Eliza, 17, 136
  Elizabeth, 11, 19, 146-151
  Elizabeth P., 13, 100
  Emily A., 19, 141, 253
  Esther, 13, 106
  Frances, 17, 136, 253
  George L., 13, 99
  Harriet A., 18, 141
  Horace N., 15, 123
  James H., 16, 135
  James M. P., 20, 154,
    253
  John F., 11, 19, 151-154,
    253
  John K., 20, 152
  Josiah F., 13
  Laura, 15, 123, 253
  Lois, 13, 107
  Lucretia K., 18, 141
  Lucy, 11, 20, 154, 155
  Lydia, 13
  Mary, 11-13, 109-117
  Minerva, 17, 138
  Nancy B., 13, 108
  Nancy S., 18, 140, 253
  Orange, 15, 120
  Pernelia, 16, 135
  Philemon H., 20, 153
  Rachel, 13, 107
  Rebecca, 11, 15, 125, 253
  Rhoda, 15, 121
  Rhoda L., 13, 98
  Rufus B., 15, 118

Index.

HOVEY—
  Rufus C., 11, 14, 16, 20, 118-124, 136, 253
  Ruth, 15
  Samuel, 9, 13, 103, 253
  Samuel, Jr., 11, 16, 134-136
  Samuel B., 20, 152
  Samuel S., 13
  Samuel W., 16, 134
  Sarah, 13, 98
  Silas, 15, 121
  Simeon S., 15, 122

HOWES—
  Abigail R., 20, 154
  Caroline M., 20, 154
  Lucius, 20, 154, 155
  Lucius E., 20, 155
  Nancy A., 20, 155
  Zachariah, 20

KNAPP—
  Amelia, 232
  Anna M., 50, 233, 236
  Betsey, 231
  Caleb, 229
  Chloe, 229, 233
  David, 231
  Eliza, 232
  Elizabeth, 229
  Ezra R., 232
  Hiram, 232
  Jehu, 229, 230
  John, 229-231
  Joshua, 229
  Levi, 229, 232, 233
  Lucinda A., 233, 236
  Lucy, 232
  Lydia, 233
  Moses, 229
  Nathan, 232
  Nicholas, 228
  Polly, 232
  Reuben B., 233, 236
  Ruth, 229, 230, 232
  Samuel, 229
  Sarah, 229
  Susannah, 232
  Timothy, 228

LEWIS—
  Elizabeth F., 63
  Ella C., 62
  John W., 62, 63
  Joseph, 62
  Julius W., 62
  Mary A., 62

LITTLEFIELD—
  Don C., 58
  Theodore B., 58
  Nellie A., 58
  Alice C., 58

LORD—
  Abiel H., 14, 115
  Abigail, 14, 117
  Alice, 14, 112
  David, 14
  James N., 111, 254
  John, 13
  John P., 14, 111
  Jonathan, 14, 114
  Joseph, 13, 109-117
  Joseph T., 14, 110
  Lucinda, 14, 109
  Mary, 14, 109
  Pamelia, 14, 109
  Rebecca, 14, 117
  Richard S. C., 14, 116, 254
  Ruth, 14, 113

MARTIN—
  Adaline, 29, 179
  Alexa A., 29, 180, 254
  Eluna, 28, 29, 178
  Hibbard, 29, 179
  John, 28
  Melona, 29, 178
  Savilla, 29
  Susan, 29, 179

O'BRIEN—
  Almira J., 73, 226
  Drusilla, 69, 73, 227
  James A. C., 73, 226
  Joseph, 69, 72
  Sarah, 69, 74, 228
  Timothy, 69, 72, 226

PAINE—
  Abigail, 187, 190
  Charles, 187
  Deborah, 187, 189
  Edward, 187, 195
  Harriet, 187, 193
  Henry, 187, 191
  Joseph C., 187, 195
  Roswell, 187, 191
  Sally, 187, 188

PALMER—
  Abigail, 186
  Hannah, 185
  John, 185
  Mehitabel, 186

PAYNE—
  Alvin, 26, 28
  Brigham, 27, 178, 254
  Calvin, 30, 182
  Charles H., 29, 180
  Edward, 26, 27, 177, 178
  Emeline, 30, 183
  Hannah, 27, 173
  Henrietta, 27, 176
  Henry N., 30, 181
  Ira, 26, 30, 181-183, 253
  James, 26, 27, 173-176
  John, 26, 29
  John A., 30, 183
  John F., 28, 178, 180, 181
  Julia A., 30, 183
  Lebbeus, 26, 28
  Lois, 26
  Lucinda, 27, 174
  Lyman, 27, 176
  Mary, 28, 177, 253
  Mary L., 29
  Miranda, 30, 181
  Nathan C., 28, 177
  Oren, 26, 29
  Persis, 26-28, 175, 178-180
  Samuel S., 27, 175
  Sarah S., 29, 180
  Selina, 27, 176
  Seril, 26
  Sophia, 27, 174
  Susan, 30, 183
  Willard, 30, 182, 253
  William H. H., 29, 180

PEARSON—
  Adaline, 72, 224
  Anna, 69, 70, 215-218
  Elias F., 72, 225
  Elizabeth B., 72, 224
  Ephraim, 68-71
  Ephraim J., 72, 225
  Eunice, 69, 71, 221-223
  Henry, 72
  Jacob, 69, 71, 224, 225
  Josephus, 72, 253
  Josiah M., 72, 224
  Mary, 69, 70, 219-221
  Phebe C., 72, 224

REESE—
  Haskell G. C., 73, 227
  Jacob, 73
  Jacob G., 73, 227
  Martha A., 73
  Rachel E. C., 73, 227
  Sarah C. M., 73, 227
  Simeon DeW. C., 73, 227
  Simeon G., 73

SANDERSON—
  Asenath, 15, 130
  Benjamin, 15, 132
  Electa, 15, 127
  James, 15, 130, 253
  Joel, 15, 133
  Lola, 15, 125
  Melissa, 15, 127
  Minerva, 15, 129
  Rebecca, 15, 127
  Sarah, 15

SHEPARD—
  Betsey H., 24, 166
  Hiram, 24, 167
  Joel H., 24, 168
  Roswell, 24, 166
  Simeon, 24, 167, 253

SPENCER—
  Alanson, 55
  Fred. A., 55, 56
  George C., 55, 56
  Seth, 55

STETSON—
  Adelia D., 74, 228
  Alvin C., 74
  Benjamin, 74
  Egbert J., 74, 228

STETSON—
  Ezra, 74
  Phebe L., 74, 228

SUTHERLAND—
  Albert, 71, 221
  Alonzo W., 71, 221
  Ammi, 70, 216
  Anna, 70
  Benjamin, 70, 218, 219
  Charles, 71, 220
  Delia, 70, 215
  Edgar, 70, 217
  Elon G., 70, 217
  Emeline, 70
  Giles, 71, 220
  Harriet, 70
  Jonah, 70, 217
  Julia, 70, 215
  Marcius, 70, 215
  Mark, 71, 220
  Mary P., 70, 216
  Noyes P., 71
  Samuel, 70, 217
  Seth, 70
  Walter, 70, 219
  William, 70, 218

TRAVIS—
  Melinda W., 53, 54
  Miles W., 53

WELSHEIMER—
  Clara M., 54
  James, 54
  Phillip H., 54

WHEATLEY—
  Jesse C., 149
  Mary K., 149, 254

WHITE—
  Daniel, 32
  George, 32
  Emily, 32, 33
  Harriet, 33, 35
  Horace C., 33, 35
  Lavinia, 32, 34
  Mary C., 32, 34
  Pembroke, 33, 38, 253
  Philenda M., 33, 37
  Urania C., 33, 36

WINN—
  Ann, 5, 77, 253
  Edward, 5, 77
  Elizabeth, 77
  Increase, 78
  Joseph, 77

www.ingramcontent.com/pod-product-compliance
Lightning Source LLC
Chambersburg PA
CBHW031347230426
43670CB00006B/462